"Dr. Howard's approach in research and writing is unique. It represents a rare blend of rigor and application--grounded, evidence-based findings that you can actually apply. Read this book but more importantly, use it! It really can change your life."

William L. Sparks, Ph.D.
Associate Dean, McColl School of Business, Queens University of Charlotte

"*The Owner's Manual for Happiness* is an inspirational model for increasing the quality of your life. Pierce Howard's captivating style combined with a wealth of research reels you in to a world of insights and application, teaching you how to work with your own unique qualities—regardless of your location on the happiness continuum—to create your optimal life. Comprehensive, user-friendly, and fascinating—a veritable interactive encyclopedia on happiness!"

Vicki Halsey Ph.D.
Vice President of Applied Learning for The Ken Blanchard Companies
Author: *Brilliance by Design*
San Diego, California

"Congratulations on the book. I have never seen such a deep dive into the subject of happiness. The book is like a series of cameras taking snap shots of the subject from different angles and directions. The subject remains the subject but is seen from different perspectives."

George T. K. Quek
Director, Distinctions Asia Pte. Ltd.
Singapore

"I enjoyed the book very much and have found very interesting information as well as practical advice."

Martha Königs
Managing Partner, IIAD (Instituto Interamericano de Alto Desempeño)
Santa Fe, Mexico

"I have a friend who likes to say to whiners and complainers, "Go get happy!" After reading Pierce Howard's new book, I will suggest she say, 'Go get in gear!' I was so inspired by Howard's research on this fascinating topic and felt a great sense of relief by knowing it's okay that I'm not a Happer, but I can be completely at peace and fulfilled by my life as a Mapper. Howard is a brilliant scholar and researcher, and I promise you'll learn something and experience some chuckles as his humor and wit shine through."

> Tamara D. Burrell, Former Student and Appreciative Colleague, Queens University of Charlotte
> Charlotte, North Carolina

"Life should not just be about endurance but also about meaningfulness, growth and contentment. Framed in an enjoyable and inviting writing style, *The Owner's Manual for Happiness* provides a friendly, accessible reading that not only enlivens and builds upon a foundation of extensive research, but *most importantly* encourages the reader to consciously explore the happiness concept. Intuitively organized to engage, The *Owner's Manual* is peppered with applicable and interesting information about happiness (integrated, thorough research; narratives; a variety of perspectives and comparisons; quotes; and insights) that not only informs the reader but guides the reader to a better understanding of one's happiness set. This personalized journey is supported by the inclusion of related, interactive activities: surveys, self-reflection, journaling, and guiding questions. Use of this reader-centered approach, as opposed to primarily an information based focus, entices readers to apply a variety of research based and/ or evidence based techniques that enhance the opportunities to increase one's 'happiness set' or to improve one's ability to 'get into gear!'"

> Carleen Osher, Executive Director of the Partnership for Dynamic Learning, Inc and the Senior Project Center
> Medford, Oregon

"This is a breathtaking piece of work! It boldly covers a vast variety of topics from different points of view, and then integrates them into key principles and practical tools. This book is not only about happiness, but about good life in general. Pierce Howard has created a masterpiece! "

> Jarkko Rantanen, M.Sc. (Psych)
> CEO, Human Advisor, Academy of Emotions
> Espoo, Finland

The Owner's Manual for
Happiness

Essential Elements of a Meaningful Life

Pierce J. Howard, Ph.D.

CENTER FOR
APPLIED COGNITIVE STUDIES

CentACS--Charlotte

The Owner's Manual for Happiness--
   Essential Elements of a Meaningful Life

Printed in the United States of America

CentACS Press
4701 Hedgemore Drive, Suite 210
Charlotte NC 28209-2200
Phone +1.704.331.0926   Fax +1.704.331.9408
www.centacs.com

Library of Congress Preassigned Control Number

Howard, Pierce J.
The owner's manual for happiness: Essential Elements of a Meaningful Life / Pierce J.
   Howard
Library of Congress Control Number: 2013905026

ISBN 978-0-578-12079-9 (pbk)

The author may be contacted through
        CentACS—Center for Applied Cognitive Studies
        4701 Hedgemore Drive, Suite 210
        Charlotte NC 28209-2200
        704-331-0926 phone
        704-331-9408 fax
        info@centacs.com or www.centacs.com

A CentACS Book
   Design: The Author
   Editing and Indexing: Steve Carrell
   Cover and Chapter Map:
      Wendy Accetta of W. Accetta Design
   Art: Jeanne P. Barefoot
   Printing: Lightning Source
   Font: Calibri

First Printed: June 2013

Preface

In the Fall of 2002, the program chair of our local organization development professional association called me two weeks before an upcoming meeting with news and a request: The speaker had backed out, and would I step in? I asked if I had free choice of topic. Desperate for a fill-in, she agreed. As I had been reading the happiness literature for several years, I decided that this was a good time to pull my notes together and organize my thoughts. Over the next 10 years I conducted workshops on the subject and collected assessment data. This book is the result.

Some comments on style...

1. We have resolved the thorny issue of referring to singular males and females by eschewing the awkward s/he and his/her constructions. We prefer the "singular their" as recommended by the Manhattan Institute's John McWhorter in his 2008 book, *Our Magnificent Bastard Tongue.* Hence, "One should mind *their* p's and q's."

2. For ease of reading, we have chosen to use the simple "scientific" footnote style, whereby, when citing a source, we list the author's last name and the year their work was published, e.g., Howard (2013). To fully identify the source, refer to the Resources.

3. This book's punctuation comes mainly from the *Publication Manual of the American Psychological Association.* However, readers of this book will range from academics who mainly use Chicago style to a general audience that commonly reads AP style. Therefore, this book uses a mixed collection of punctuation rules, chosen for their ability to communicate and not distract readers from the narrative.

Thanks to Taylor Ey for her early reading of the manuscript and ensuing suggestions, to my later readers and endorsers—Will Sparks, George Quek, Vicki Halsey, Martha Königs, Tamara Burrell , and Carleen Osher, and the CentACS team for making it possible for me to take time to write.

I dedicate this book to Jane Ellen Mitchell Howard, my wife and business partner. Jane, you inspire, support, critique, and leave me alone!

About the Author

Pierce J. Howard grew up in Kinston, North Carolina, the youngest of seven, attending public schools before studying at Davidson College (B.A.), East Carolina University (M.A.), and the University of North Carolina at Chapel Hill (Ph.D.). While studying at Chapel Hill, he taught English at Chapel Hill High School and later at North Carolina State University in Raleigh. Following his studies at Chapel Hill, he took a position as head of School Services at the North Carolina Advancement School in Winston-Salem—a special program for research and dissemination regarding underachievement among teenagers. He moved to Charlotte, NC, to teach and administer in a school-within-a school at West Charlotte High School. Since that time, Pierce has worked as an organization development consultant in a variety of settings around the world, while continuing to teach undergraduate and graduate students at Queens University (Charlotte), University of North Carolina at Charlotte, and Pfeiffer University at Charlotte. He has lived his life in an incubator of happiness comprised of wife Jane, daughters Hilary and Allegra, acquired sons Jy and Will, and grandchildren Liam, Stella, Rowan, and A.J. He is author of *The Owner's Manual for the Brain* (3rd edition, with 4th on the way thanks to William Morrow/ HarperCollins), *The Owner's Manual for Personality at Work* (2nd edition; with his wife, Jane), and *The Owner's Manual for Personality from 12 to 22* (also with Jane).

He devotes most of his time now at the Center for Applied Cognitive Studies as the Managing Director of Research and Development, where he is involved in research, writing, and product development, mostly focused on the Five-Factor Model of personality. He rounds out his professional life with model railroading (n-scale), chamber music, model building with grandchildren (next is a 19th century schooner), choral singing (at Providence United Methodist Church), walking the incomparable streets of his Dilworth neighborhood, reading classics and lighter fare, indulging his gustatory senses through cooking and dining his way through the world's cuisines, traveling with Jane and their family to the great national parks of the U.S. and to bucket list destinations around the world—from Petra to the terracotta army of Xi'an, teaching graduate students at McColl School of Business (of Queens University of Charlotte), attending professional meetings, attending family and school reunions, camping in the Appalachians, and, in general, staying young, or, as we will describe it later, staying in gear.

About the
Center for Applied Cognitive Studies (CentACS)

The vision of CentACS, the Center for Applied Cognitive Studies, is to optimize people through a global professional network. The company is the primary location of Pierce and Jane Howard's work and research with the Big Five. It is an information-based e-commerce company, developing and publishing materials, training and certifying consultants to use the Big Five, and conducting research to support the Five-Factor Model of personality and other brain-related research designed to help people learn, work, and grow more effectively.

Established in Charlotte, North Carolina, in July 1986 by Jane Mitchell Howard, M.B.A., managing director, and Pierce J. Howard, Ph.D., director of research, the company is currently located near downtown Charlotte. At this writing, CentACS has twelve full-time employees, several part-time employees, and a growing network of over four thousand certified and qualified Big Five consultants around the world, trained by the Howards and other CentACS Master Trainers. In 2008, they welcomed Caryn Clause Lee as their business partner, and she has directed the day-to-day operation of the company since that time.

The mission of CentACS is to establish personality assessment and brain research standards for the twenty-first century by building a global network of internal and external consultants and international affiliate companies who use the Five-Factor Model of personality, the Human Resource Optimization Model, and related brain research in their work. Through in-class and online certification and advanced training programs, learning conferences, valid and respected test instruments, on-line e-services, a scoring services bureau, consulting and selection projects for clients, and other resources, CentACS provides cutting-edge information, high-quality products, and support services.

CENTER FOR
APPLIED COGNITIVE STUDIES

Primarily, the company operates within the United States with certified consultants located from California to New York, from Florida to Wisconsin. Many Fortune 500 companies, medium-to-small companies, government agencies, university MBA and undergraduate programs, public and private high schools, and large and small consulting companies are customers of CentACS. Outside the United States,

CentACS has master trainers in Europe, China, Singapore, India, Mexico, and Brazil, who work with the Big Five in their respective geographic areas.

For further information about how you may use the Big Five and other CentACS assessments (values, multi-rater feedback) in your school, organization, or in your work, or to contact CentACS or its affiliate companies, or inquire how your organization may become an affiliate, please refer to the following information:

United States and all other countries not listed below:
The Center for Applied Cognitive Studies
4701 Hedgemore Drive, Suite 210, Charlotte, NC 28209-2200, USA

Contact: Caryn Lee, Managing Director, Marketing and Operations

Telephone: +1.704.331.0926
Toll Free in the US: +1.800.BIG.5555. Fax: +1.704.331.9408

E-mail: info@centacs.com
Website: www.centacs.com

WorkPlace Big Five Profile, SchoolPlace Big Five Profile, the Values Profile, and the Workplace Performance 360° project set-up form and related products and materials on-line: www.centacs.com

Additional copies of this book available through Amazon.com or through CentACS. Available through iTunes as an e-book.

International Contacts and Master Trainers:
Brazil: Fernando Cardoso
China: Vivian Kan
Europe: David Hudnut
Finland: Mia-Riitta Kivinen
India: Jayant and Chatura Damle
Japan: Nori Furuya
Mexico: Roberto Königs
Singapore and Hong Kong: George Quek

Table of Contents

The Owner's Manual for Happiness-- Essential Elements of a Meaningful Life
by Pierce J. Howard, Ph.D.

Preface 5

About the Author 6

About CentACS 7

Introduction 11

Part One: Happiness—Why All the Fuss?

1. What Is It?--18 Definitions of Happiness 17
2. What Affects It?—Boosters, Downers, and Myths 31
3. How Happy Are You?--Estimating Your Set Point 81

Part Two: Alternatives to Happiness—Defining the Right State for Staying In Gear

4. Happiness Isn't for Everyone—The Five Modes for Staying "In Gear" 109
5. Flow—The Absence of Emotions 125
6. Fit—Building on Your Strengths 143
7. Goals—Maintaining a Clear Sense of Progress 173
8. Community—Staying Connected to Your Lifeline 207
9. Altruism—Generativity and Your Legacy 231
10. Putting It All Together—A Template for Your Statement of Personal Priorities (SPP) 249

Part Three: Ongoing Maintenance--Tools for Staying In Gear

11. 119 Minor Adjustments that Make a Big Difference 259
12. Common Techniques for Keeping Focused 299
13. Staying Right 315

Appendices:

A. Thesaurus of Happiness 323
B. Three Millenia of Quotes About Happiness 327
C. Using Other Personality Tests to Obtain N and E Scores 351
D. Action Items 353
E. Worksheet for Evaluating Balance of Goals 357
F. Composing Your Life Story—A Process 359

Definitions 365

Resources 367

Index 377

Introduction

Why another book about happiness?

> "Happiness is like a butterfly—chase it and it evades you, but engage yourself in another way and it likely will light upon you."
> --common 19th century U.S. maxim (e.g., appears in Emerson, Thoreau, and Hawthorne)
>
> "The search for happiness is one of the chief sources of unhappiness."
> --Eric Hoffer, 20th century longshoreman and philosopher

A core characteristic of the American temperament is the emphasis on hard work. From the Puritan work ethic to the long hours of the 21st century entrepreneur, the call to earn one's way by the sweat of one's brow dominates our consciousness. No landed gentry we. No resting on one's laurels. No standing still. No couch potato-ing. "Action may not always entail happiness, but there is no happiness without action" is attributed both to the U.S. psychologist William James and U.K. statesman Benjamin Disraeli. Regardless of who said it first, both underscore the association between activity and right feeling. Our British kin agreed with the notion of action, work, sweat. In fact, if we probe the mind of the English, we discover Shakespeare had Macbeth declaim that "the labor we delight in physics (relieves) pain."

Wait a minute! Did you notice that Shakespeare limited the value of work to that effort we *delight* in? Ah, must we always return to Shakespeare to get it right? It is not just any ol' hard work and busy activity that is associated with happiness, but work and activity that, for whatever reason, we enjoy at some level. This insight leads to the justification I make for writing yet another book on happiness: Other writers focus on happiness as a goal—I don't. Other writers emphasize how to be happier—I emphasize how to find something better than happiness. For I maintain that, in fact, happiness is a false god. A better object of adoration, of longing, is being in a state of engagement, of being "in gear," of sensing that one is on a path making progress towards one or more goals. Goals that benefit others and that employ our natural qualities and whose pursuit leaves us at the end of the day feeling energized and eager for the morrow. Not "am I happy?" but "am I in gear?"

I propose that Emerson, Thoreau, and Hawthorne were all pointing to this mental state in their "happiness is like a butterfly" maxim. Look for butterflies and they evade your eye—weed your garden and the butterflies alight on your bonnet. Look for happiness and it eludes you—build a cradle for your soon-to-be grandbaby and you forget about happiness, but you feel positive, you flourish, you feel a kind of well-being that is satisfying, such that you'd like to feel this way more and more of the time. You haven't found happiness thereby, but you've found something equal or better—the non-emotional ecstasy of productive engagement with a purpose. Aristotle would call it *eudaimonia,* expressing your genius, like the acorn becoming the tree, like the doodler becoming the artist (King & Hicks, 2007). Not in the sense of predestination, but in the sense of one being allowed to, and wanting to, and finding satisfaction in, developing their strong points.

I further propose that Eric Hoffer was saying the same thing as his 19th century forebears but in a different way. Chase happiness—by trying to make a second million, by cosmetic surgery, by moving to a milder climate—and you soon find that the initial euphoria you felt after seeing your fattened bank account, your unwrinkled brow, or your cool afternoon breeze, has given way to your accustomed feelings of emptiness, boredom, frustration, loneliness, or low self-esteem. You just can't shake boredom with money—you must shake it with your mind. In the 1987 Danish film *Babette's Feast* that was based on a story by Isak Dinesen, the lead character, Babette, is a French chef forced out of her homeland by war. Two elder sisters take her in, and Babette cooks for them. Each year, she buys a ticket for the French national lottery. When she wins the lottery, Babette is left penniless after spending all her winnings to honor her rescuers with a "slow food" style feast. The sisters lament that she will now be bored. Babette retorts, "An artist is never bored."

This book serves as a guide to finding that sense of engagement, of being in gear, that Babette reveals. Part One sets the stage, Part Two presents the five modes of positive being, and Part Three invites you to apply these modes to your own life.

Part One defines happiness, explains why one out of nine people are naturally happy and the others aren't, lists factors that can raise and lower happiness, and helps you determine whether you are one of those rare, naturally happy people, and, if not, what you can do about it to feel right in your own way.

Part Two identifies five alternatives to happiness—flow, fit, goals, community, and altruism—that, when they are coordinated in an individual, can lead one to the state of being in gear in a way that is more satisfying than happiness. People in gear are absorbed in their tasks, those tasks call upon their strengths and not their weaknesses, they direct their activity towards goals and make steady progress thereto, they maintain a variety of relationships, and they serve the needs of society in some meaningful way. Research has demonstrated that these five modes of being—each of which is within the control of an individual—are intrinsically satisfying. They don't make us happy, necessarily, but they make us something even better—so engaged that we stop thinking, wishing, desiring for happiness.

Part Three offers examples of how individuals have used these five modes of being to compose their lives in a way that leaves them in gear. Part Three also helps you form your own personal plan for maximum engagement.

This emphasis on personal meaning is something of a Western value, as Eastern cultures have more commonly emphasized the group (family, clan, organization) more than the individual. Joseph Campbell (1991) writes:

> This, I believe, is the great Western truth: that each of us is a completely unique creature and that, if we are ever to give any gift to the world, it will have to come out of our own experience and fulfillment of our own potentialities, not someone else's. In the traditional Orient, on the other hand, and generally in all traditionally grounded societies, the individual is cookie-molded. His duties are put upon him in exact and precise terms, and there's no way of breaking out from them. When you go to a guru to be guided on the spiritual way, he knows just where you are… just where you have to go next…. That wouldn't be a proper Western pedagogical way of guidance. We have to give our students guidance in developing their own pictures of themselves. What each must seek in his life never was, on land or sea. It is to be something out of his own unique potentiality for experience, something that never has been and never could have been experienced by anyone else…. Hamlet's problem was that he wasn't [up to his imposed destiny]. He was given a destiny too big for him to handle, and it blew him to pieces. (pp. 186-187)

Perhaps Campbell exaggerates. I trust that the individual in the Orient can find a way to follow their bliss while honoring their family or group. On the other hand, in the West many individuals find it difficult to try their own wings, instead accepting goals and roles that their families have prescribed. Campbell himself fell under the spell of papa's expectations: "I did go into business with Dad for a couple of months, and then I thought, 'Geez, I can't do this.' And he let me go. There is that testing time in your life when you have got to test yourself out to your own flight." (1991, p. 193) Sinclair Lewis narrates a similar action in his novel *Babbitt*. Here the father, who never took the opportunity to do what he wanted to do, but instead deferred to his father's wishes, encourages his son to correct this unhealthy pattern. In the passage that follows, father is talking to the son and cheering him on:

> "I've never done a single thing I've wanted to in my whole life! I don't knows I've accomplished anything except just get along…. But I do get a kind of sneaking pleasure out of the fact that you knew what you wanted to do and did it. Well, those folks in there will try to bully you, and tame you down. Tell 'em to go to the devil! I'll back you. Take your factory job, if you want to. Don't be scared of the family. No, nor all of Zenith. Nor of yourself, the way I've been. Go ahead, old man! The world is yours!"

Louise Erdrich describes these times—when one is open to challenging one's past choices—as "rare moments when people are wide open and the lightest touch can wither or heal. A moment too late and we can never reach them any more in this world." (2010, p. 149; quoting from F. Scott Fitzgerald's "The Freshest Boy," in *Babylon Revisited*)

Campbell, Lewis, Erdrich, and Fitzgerald are all talking about readiness to change, or openness to change—a window of time during which one takes a deep breath and makes some bold decisions to act on their dreams. The forces against such actions can be crippling. Campbell writes that "It's quite possible to be so influenced by the ideals and commands of your neighborhood that you don't know what you really want and could be. I think that anyone brought up in an extremely strict, authoritative social situation is unlikely ever to come to the knowledge of himself." (1991, p. 176) This book is for people who want to take their personal knowledge of themselves and use it to compose the next chapter(s) of their lives. You may not be happier at the end, but you should be well on your way to what Campbell calls "the rapture of being alive" (1991, p. 5) and what I call being "in gear." I am going to give you the tools to stop chasing happiness so that you can find something even better. Enjoy the process.

Note: The page preceding each new chapter contains a map of my model for happiness. The particulars of the model will become clear as you progress through the book. Here is what you will be seeing:

Part One

Happiness—
Why All the Fuss?

STATEMENT OF
PERSONAL PRIORITIES

FLOW | FIT | GOALS | COMMUNITY | ALTRUISM

Happiness Boosters   **Happiness Downers**
(Choice)   *(Choice)*

119 Minor Adjustors

(more within personal control)

(more outside personal control)

HAPPINESS SET POINT

Happiness Boosters   **Happiness Downers**
(Circumstance)   *(Circumstance)*

Continuum of Trait Happiness

Perennially Happy (N- E+) .... Occasionally Happy (N + E-)

What is it?

1

18 Definitions of Happiness

> "Most people are about as happy as they make up their minds to be."
>
> --Abraham Lincoln, 16th president of the U.S.

Guide to this chapter:
- An Operational Definition of Happiness
- Traits Versus States
- "Allelonyms" for Happiness
- Natural Versus Acquired Happiness
- The Case Against Happiness
- How Happiness is Distributed

I like Honest Abe's comment on happiness because it succinctly describes the assumption of this book—a minority of the population, approximately one in nine, are born happy, while a majority of the population are somewhere between moderately happy and miserable. Hence, when he says "most people," he is describing those who are not born happy, but those who, like myself, lack the natural temperament to be happy 24-7-365¼. The remainder of this book will address Abe's quip about how people might "make up their minds to be" happy.

An Operational Definition of Happiness

But first, what is happiness? The word comes from the Old Norse *happ* for "good luck, chance, or fortune." It made its way into Middle English as "hap," again meaning good luck or fortune. This places the word in the western philosophical tradition of Lady (or Dame) Fortune and the Wheel of Fortune. The literature of the Middle Ages is peppered with references to fortune's wheel. According to medieval writers, life inexorably entailed changes in fortune, like a wheel turning, such that one may be at the top of the wheel experiencing good fortune, while later

the wheel turns and they experience the crushing effect of being under the wheel with bad fortune. This was likely the allusion intended in the title of the 54-year running soap opera *As the World Turns*. Characters would move from bliss and being on top of things to misery and being a victim. On a more realistic note, the Wheel of Fortune, 21st century style, takes center stage in *Waiting for Superman*, the 2010 documentary on the state of education in the U.S. Like someone literally waiting for the fictional Superman to swoop down and rescue them from Dame Fortune's crushing ill fortune, parents and their children cast their lot in various school lotteries in hopes of educational good luck—acceptance at a higher quality program than the one they're in. Happiness, then, or good luck, is associated with events and circumstances that lead to an abundance of the positive emotions such as joy, ecstasy, bliss, pleasure, and so forth, plus a minimum, or even absence, of the negative emotions such as fear, anger, and sorrow. Good luck, or "happ"-iness, has traditionally meant the absence of a punishing stress that beats you down.

Today, happiness means experiencing the positive emotions throughout one's lifetime, while only occasionally experiencing the negative emotions. As it turns out, happiness is not just a matter of luck. Current research leaves no doubt that some of us are born happy. The positive and negative emotions have not only a biological basis but a genetic basis. Specific genes, neurological pathways, and bodily chemicals are associated with the tendency to experience positive versus negative emotions (see Nettle [2005] for an excellent and very readable explanation of the biology of happiness). What this means is that a portion of the world's population is born with the natural temperament that is prone to exuberance day in and day out while seldom experiencing fear, anger, or sorrow: mostly "up," seldom "down." For them, it doesn't matter whether they are lucky—they remain upbeat in spite of misfortune.

This "lots of good stuff" and a "minimum of bad stuff" definition of happiness perhaps was most starkly defined by the English utilitarian philosopher Jeremy Bentham in his *An Introduction to the Principles of Morals and Legislation* (1789). This Age of Reason thinker reduced morality to the prevalence of pleasure over pain. He evaluated a given act by the strength, duration, certainty, immediacy, and contagion of its pleasure or pain. By awarding points to an act's scores on these dimensions, he would assign it a numerical value. This process was dubbed the "felicific calculus" (also the hedonic, hedonistic, or utility calculus). In Chapter 3 of this book, our discussion of the set point will arrive at a similar "calculus" based on more current thinking. We have broadened Bentham's thinking to include more than morality and more than pleasure and pain.

Three characters aptly illustrate the state of felicity. First is Maria (played by Julie Andrews) in the film *The Sound of Music* (1965). She is so full of positive emotion, and absent of negative, that shortly after entering a convent her fellow nuns evidence their discomfort by declaiming in song "Oh how do you solve a problem like Maria? How do you hold a moonbeam in your hand?" She is too exuberant for her surroundings. Then there is Guido (played by Roberto Benigni) in *La vita é bella* (*Life is Beautiful*) (1997), who loses his wife, find himself and his son in a Nazi concentration camp, and yet creates pranks aimed at the guards. No moping and whining for him. Finally there is Evelyn Ryan (played by Julianne Moore) in *The Prize Winner of Defiance, Ohio* (2005). Her character is married to an alcoholic husband who drinks up every paycheck. In order to support her large family, she enters jingle contests and wins prizes both small and large. Just can't keep her down. All three of these characters have a naturally happy disposition that even in stressful circumstances remains resilient and cheerful.

Although they experience bad luck and are pinned down by the Wheel of Fortune, their luck of birth serves to maintain positive mood.

The most widely accepted language to describe personality traits today is the Big Five model (see Howard & Howard, 2010, 2011; Nettle, 2005). Briefly, this model describes five broad "super-traits"[1] that account for much of the individual differences in everyday behavior:

- **N**eed for Stability (N): how we respond to stress,

- **E**xtraversion (E): how we respond to social stimulation,

- **O**riginality (O): how we respond to novelty,

- **A**ccommodation (A): how we respond to power, and

- **C**onsolidation (C): how we respond to distractions.

Psychologists today would generally agree with Paul T. Costa, Jr., and R. R. "Jeff" McCrae, Big Five scholars associated with the National Institute on Aging, that "happiness" describes the natural disposition of persons who score in the top third of Extraversion (E) and also score in the bottom third of Need for Stability (N). The combination of these two trait levels is associated with naturally happy people—those who experience mostly positive emotions (high levels of E) and little negative emotion (low levels of N). A convincing way to test the viability of this definition would be to measure the levels of N and E along with levels of happiness in a representative set of countries from around the world. Researchers for years have asserted that national trait profiles (e.g., Japan is lower on E than the U.S., and higher on N) were unrelated to levels of happiness in those nations. But Piers Steel and Deniz Ones (2002) had a hunch that the question had not been adequately addressed and set out to remedy the situation. Their study comprised 41,000 Five Factor Model scores and over 2,000,000 happiness scores (using Veenhoven's data) from 48 countries. They concluded that N and E were in fact strongly correlated with happiness scores, and that O, A, and C were not. In other words, the lower the aggregated N score for a nation, and the higher the aggregated E score for that same nation, then the higher the happiness score would be. This global trend is further support for abundance of positive emotion and absence of negative emotion as the core of what we call happiness.

On average, one person out of nine will fit this pattern. We get that by multiplying $1/3 \times 1/3 = 1/9$. Or, one person out of three scores high on E and one person out of three scores low on N. The chance of a person scoring *both* high on E *and* low on N is $1/3 \times 1/3$, or $1/9$, or one in nine. These people, by the "luck" of their birth, are destined to be happy (in this sense that we have defined) for the whole of their lives, barring traumatic injury that changes their brain structure and/or body chemistry. While the rest of us (I am NOT one of those 1-in-9-ers!) are happy from time to time, it is not our natural state. For example, I was happy last night at choir practice while singing a composition by Giovanni Gabrielli for double choir, but I turned irritable when subsequently having to sing a piece by a lesser

---

[1] For convenience, these supertraits are referred to by their initial letters: N for Need for Stability (also called Neuroticism), E for Extraversion, O for Originality (also called Openness), A for Accommodation (also called Agreeableness), and C for Consolidation (also called Conscientiousness).

contemporary composer that lacked melodic charm, harmonic complexity, rhythmic unpredictability, and compelling text. The 1-in-9-ers are happy independent of context or circumstance. Not I.

Traits Versus States

The 1-in-9-ers (let's call them the "Happers") have the luck (some would say the curse) of always having an even dispositional keel that leaves them positive and calm. The rest of us are that way from time to time, and some of us more than others. But even within the Happers, variety abounds. Some Happers could score very high on E but only moderately low on N: They would be extremely excitable most of the time, like a prototypical cheerleader throughout a game, but would experience somewhat more negative emotion than other Happers who score lower on N. Some Happers score moderately high on E and extremely low on N: They would often be "up" and have nerves of steel, like a test pilot who just can't get enough daring action. Then there are the (perhaps tiresome) Happers who are extremely high on E AND extremely low on N: They are like the Energizer Bunny, like a salesperson who blithely sails from call to call throughout the day and then hits the hotel bar at night for more action, never feeling a tad of worry, anger, or sadness.

In fact, if one were to randomly pick 900 people from a community, then to assemble the 100 Happers from this group of 900 (i.e., 100 = 1/9 of 900), and then place these 100 in a dance club after a hard day's work of selling, managing, building, or whatever, all 100 would go until late in the evening, and then start dropping out (i.e., going home or to their rooms) based on how extreme they scored on N and E. Those who scored moderately high on E and moderately low on N would be the first to call it quits—finally had enough stimulation. The stragglers who stayed until the wee hours of the morning would be the extreme scorers—extremely high on E and extremely low on N. So, not only do people in general fall on a continuum from very low on the happiness scale to very high on the happiness scale—the people in the high group also fall on a continuum. Current research has given us a name for where an individual falls in the happiness continuum—their "set point."

The set point defines a person's normal disposition with respect to happiness. Using percentages, if a person's set point was 67%, they would be "happier" than 66% of the population—they would experience relatively more positive emotion and relatively less negative emotion than 2/3 of the population. That puts them in the Happer group. However, they are at the bottom boundary of that group, with almost 1/3 of the Happers experiencing relatively more positive emotion and relatively less negative emotion most of the time. So even the Happers are not equally happy. But, as a group, they stand alone in the sense that these are not the people who chase after being happier. These are not the people who chase after the 19th century writers' butterfly. They don't need to. They already have their butterfly. They are already happy. The roll of the genetic dice comprised their luck.

We call this set point an example of a "trait." A personality trait is a predictable pattern of behavior that makes us recognizable. Each of the Big Five defined above (N, E, O, A, and C) is a trait. The trait Happiness is a combination of two traits (N and E). Happers—those with the trait of Happiness (high E plus low N) are predictably happy. Always up. Rarely down. When a Happer experiences the absence of positive emotions and the presence of negative emotions, as during a period of grief, it is not for very long. This exception to their norm of being upbeat is called a "state." Traits are one's normal level of functioning for a specific behavior, and states are exceptions to that normal level. Traits are permanent, while states are temporary.

The differences in traits and states are illustrated in Figure 1.0. In the first example (a. Moderate Sociability), imagine a teacher who is moderately sociable—one who enjoys being around other people about half the time, but who then likes solitude for the remainder. After a day of teaching, they look forward to reading, taking a long, restorative walk, grading papers, and so forth. Let us say that

Figure 1.0   Examples of Traits and Their Various States

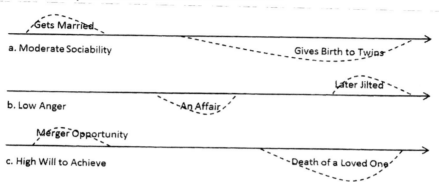

this teacher marries. Both before and after marriage there is an increase in their sociability, what with showers and other outings—especially time with the beloved. But this upward blip in gregariousness, represented by the dotted line at the left of the chart, is temporary. In relatively short order, this teacher will attempt to re-establish normal routine, while integrating the new partner in a way that does not destroy time for solitude. Then, a couple of years later, this teacher adds twins to the household, with an accompanying downward blip in sociability. With hands full of childcare, they schedule fewer social outings, fewer after school meetings, and the like. Over time, as things ease into a routine, earlier patterns may resume, unless some activities get replaced by time spent with kids. For example, the teacher's activity in a religious or civic group may be replaced by childcare. One scoring higher on sociability would be more likely to have the attitude of "Keep pouring it on—the more people the merrier."

For the second example in Figure 1.0 (b. Low Anger), imagine someone who normally felt and expressed little anger, someone typically calm and at ease, with a fairly slow trigger, temper-wise. Then, they experience a romantic affair, and the slow trigger becomes even slower, a period during which it seems that nothing can go wrong, nothing can get their goat. On cloud nine, as it were. Again, this "state" is temporary. They return to normal levels of occasional irritability. Then, say after a year or so, they are jilted by their romantic partner. This unexpected rejection results in an upward blip of anger during which even little things are unable to escape their displeasure. But again, this is temporary, with the quicker trigger becoming slow again.

The final example (c. High Will to Achieve) is about ambition. Imagine a company president who normally spends large amounts of time and energy devoted to being number one. Time with family is scarce, and personal time for exercise and hobbies is catch-as-catch-can. Then comes an opportunity to merge with a competitor to form a larger entity with staggering opportunities for growth. For a few weeks, an upward blip in ambition finds the executive with no time for family or self, with all available resources going into doing due diligence, along with wining and dining the new potential partners. Soon after the merger either fails or succeeds, things return to normal. A few years later, they unexpectedly lose a loved one. Their will to achieve evidences a downward blip as they spend more time with family. After a period of grieving, things return to normal.

When Carol Graham (2010) writes that "psychologists find that there is a remarkable degree of consistency in people's level of well-being over time," (loc. 847) she is referring to what I am calling a trait with its set point. While the genetic component of a trait is essentially unchangeable, other influences, such as choices one makes and the circumstances of one's lifestyle, are more changeable. In Chapter 2 we will discuss these non-genetic influences on one's level of happiness. And in Chapter 3, we will focus on how to determine your current level of happiness—whether you are a Happer or one of the rest of us. Then, beginning in Chapter 4, we will explore alternatives to happiness. These alternatives will focus on what Aristotle called *eudaimonia,* translated commonly as "flourishing." One may flourish yet experience few of the positive emotions and more than one's share of the negative ones. But for now, we will focus on the overall meaning of the term "happiness."

Allelonyms for Happiness

In researching for this book, I searched for a word other than "happiness" to express a state that could include both happiness and the larger sense of flourishing. I rejected "flourishing" because it sounded too strong, too positive. To say someone is flourishing is almost to paint them with a smile. However, a young violinist or baseballer who daily spends six hours practicing is not happy—emotions are probably inappropriate terms to describe their typical mental state during extended, committed, voluntary practice. They don't feel an emotion so much as they feel totally absorbed in the moment— what Mihalyi Csikszentmihalyi calls "flow" and which we will explore in depth in Chapter 5. People in flow are unconscious of emotions. When they are out of flow, they may or may not report feeling "happy." One does not need to be happy in order to be in flow, to flourish. So I wanted a bigger word that included both happiness and its complement.

So I decided to check my thesauri, beginning with Roget and continuing with every synonym finder I could muster from my shelves and from the Internet. The result was 235 words and brief phrases! Well, if the number of synonyms is any indication of how important a concept is to people, this certainly puts happiness front and center in contemporary consciousness. Over a period of several weeks, I tried sorting (with the assistance of several colleagues) this collection into groups, each of which had a slightly different meaning from the other groups. While all words/phrases were considered synonyms of "happiness," many of these terms clearly did not match the definition we have posited: abundance of positive emotions and scarcity of negative emotions. My analysis yielded 18 different clusters. (Appendix A provides a listing of all the synonyms within each group.) The number of synonyms within each cluster is parenthesized:

Group 1: Positive Emotions (29)
Group 2: High Energy (29)
Group 3: Calmness (20)
Group 4: Competence (6)

Group 5: Health (3)

Group 6: Engagement (15)

Group 7: Cheerful Disposition (29)

Group 8: Jollity (33)

Group 9: Passion (5)

Group 10: Cared About (5)

Group 11: Caring About Others (9)

Group 12: Mature Relationship (3)

Group 13: Pride (2)

Group 14: Optimism (6)

Group 15: Feeling Other Worldly (11)

Group 16: Material Comfort (17)

Group 17: Titillation of the Senses (8)

Group 18: Generally Positive Mood (5)

These 18 groups I will call allelonyms (from the Greek *allelo*, "alternative, or other" plus *onyma*, "name"), as opposed to synonyms (which means "the same name"). Allelonyms are like alleles—different versions of the same basic gene. Each of the 18 allelonyms contains its own set of synonyms, ranging from a high of 33 synonyms for "jollity" to only two for "pride." As we will see in Part 2 of this book, each of these allelonyms relates to one or more of the five modes of positive being that I propose as alternatives to happiness modes, or they relate to happiness itself. For example, Positive Emotions and Jollity clearly relate to the standard definition of Happiness, while Caring About Others and Pride do not. However, Caring About Others relates to a happiness alternative called Altruism, which I will discuss in Chapter 9. Pride relates to Goals, which will fill the pages of Chapter 7. The point here is that even synonyms for happiness do not all point to the same construct. If there is any meaning that they share, I propose that it is the sense of being engaged in a right path, of being on a course of that feels right and that is intrinsically motivating and energizing. As I have suggested earlier, I like to call this quality, this state of mind, the feeling of being "in gear." To not experience one of more of the 18 allelonyms of happiness is to feel "out of gear," disengaged, out of sorts.

Natural Versus Acquired Happiness

Just to be clear: I propose three kinds of happiness, or being In Gear:

1. **Natural Happiness**—the kind one is born with; one's genetic makeup; the "Happers"—characterized by abundant positive emotion and minimal negative emotion.
2. **Acquired Happiness**—the kind one creates for oneself by making certain decisions and altering one's circumstances (to be discussed in the next chapter), in order to increase levels of positive emotions and decrease levels of negative emotion; the increases/decreases are temporary, but renewable; the "Batters"—characterized by stepping up the plate and trying to improve one's average.

3. **Alternatives to Happiness**—the cumulative effect of the five modes of positive being that I discuss in Part 2; feeling not so much positive and negative emotions as feeling that one is in gear, that life has meaning, and that one is headed in a direction that is acceptable; the "Mappers"—characterized by mapping out or composing a satisfactory approach to life.

4. **Don't Care 'Bout Happiness**—those who are not naturally happy, do not wish to increase their happiness, and do not wish to live their lives any differently than they ever have; the "Nappers"—characterized by complete acceptance of their status quo. Yes, I know I said three kinds of happiness earlier, but I just couldn't resist adding this fourth category.

What we have been discussing up to this point is #1—Natural Happiness, or the abundance of positive emotions and the absence of negative emotions. The second kind is acquired, in the sense that one can be constitutionally made up as a Happer, yet not feel as happy as the typical Happer. Certain decisions and circumstances can cause this, and they will be identified in the next chapter. Living in a malevolent dictatorship is an example of the kind of circumstance that can decrease happiness, such that a person born with a natural disposition to be happy, according to our definition, while they would be happier than others under that dictatorship, they would be happier if they were to live without that malevolent dictatorship. This could happen either by a successful revolution or by leaving the country.

The Case Against Happiness

In a sense, the Happers are cheerleaders who urge the rest of us to make the world work. Happers are natural leaders. But leaders are a small part of the equation. Yes, without presidents, generals, coaches, and conductors, life would be cacophonous, discordant, warring, inefficient. However, without teachers, foot soldiers, players, and singers, the leaders would be like windmills without wind—poised to do great work, but lacking workers. In a sense, leaders emerge when the workers falter. In many situations, individuals spread throughout a group can severally provide leadership at different times, with no one single individual providing leadership all the time. There is no such thing as "leaderless groups," only groups that have no single leader. For in order to accomplish its mission, a group needs acts of leadership from time to time. Bertolt Brecht hints at the

> "Chase away the demons, and they will take the angels with them."
> --Joni Mitchell

idyllic leaderless group when he has Andrea say in his play *Life of Galileo* (1938), "Pity the land that has no hero." Galileo retorts, "No, Andrea: Pity the land that needs a hero." I remember speaking those lines as an undergraduate thespian, and they have resonated for me over a lifetime. To me, they mean: "Don't let the absence of a designated leader keep me from doing what needs doing."

What does it mean to be somber and solitary, to be absent of positive emotions and bordering on anxiety, furor, and depression? It means writing poetry, designing bridges, digging ditches, landscaping grounds, practicing unceasingly, rehearsing until perfect, tinkering with it until it works, experimenting to the point of discovery and then more, writing the great (American, Russian, Nigerian, Brazilian) novel, editing my manuscript (!).... Well, you get the idea. Solitary discontent is the engine of progress, or creation. Or, as the poet Emily Dickinson says, great works of art are the "gift of screws."

(Wilson, 2008, p. 104) In his provocative book *Against Happiness*, Wake Forest University English Department's Eric G. Wilson (2008) writes:

> The surest way to suffer what Thoreau calls 'quiet desperation' is to try to lead the perfectly happy American life. Attempting this, you will always be dissatisfied, for you are repressing that rich darkness of the soul. Allowing this creative gloom into the light, you inexorably move away from the silent worry to Thoreau's most cherished state, wildness. (p. 146)

Wilson makes the case that happiness breeds content and unhappiness breeds innovation. Faultfinding leads to creation. To rest in the corral of the Happers is to stagnate. You snooze, you lose.

Wilson and I both recognize that happiness has its place, but it is not the only place. Or, as Elizabeth Kolbert wrote March 22, 2010 in *The New Yorker*: "Happiness is a good thing; it's just not the only thing." (p. 74) Literature is replete with characters who eschew happiness in favor of perhaps a more satisfying mode of being. In the recent novel *The Executor* (G. P. Putnam's Sons, 2010), Jesse Kellerman narrates the relationship between a graduate student and an elderly woman with a mysterious past. She hires him to show up periodically and engage her in stimulating, intellectual, multi-disciplinary dialog. A friend at one point asks the student, "In your opinion, is she happy?"

> I wanted to blurt out yes, of course she was happy, of course. She had me, after all. But could I honestly make that claim? I felt ashamed to realize that in all the time I'd known Alma, I'd never thought to ask myself that question. How does one measure happiness? Can one assign it a quantity? The utilitarian attempt to do just that is now considered risible. Enumerate the soft signs, then: she still smiled when we talked (although, these days, how often did we talk?): still ate her chocolate (although how often did she feel hungry?). Did these behaviors mean anything? Were they artifacts? Where did the real proof lie? I thought back to our very first conversation, which had begun with the question of whether it is better to be happy or intelligent. At the time, setting those two concepts up in opposition had seemed eminently reasonable. Now, as I sat listening to the quiet fury on the stereo and the waitress telling the bartender to kiss her sweet ass and the men snorting into their beers, I wondered if the happiness I thought I'd given Alma was merely a wan projection of that which she gave me.
>
> "I don't know," I said.
> "If you don't know," he said, "the answer's no."

Not happy, but engaged. Not happy, but stimulated.

In another literary example, Ken Follett writes in his *World Without End* (Dutton, 2007) a conversation between two lady friends:

> Mattie: "Are you happy?"
> Caris: "I wasn't born to be happy. But I help people, I make a living, and I'm free."

Caris baldly declares that she is not a Happer, not one of the one-in-nine, when she says "I wasn't born to be happy." Then she goes on to say that she has embraced one (Altruism, discussed in Chapter 9) of our five modes for being In Gear ("I help people."), and that there are two circumstances of her existence that elevate her from unhappiness: adequate income and personal liberty (both discussed in the next chapter).

Kenji Yoshino (2006) in his autobiographical treatise *Covering* wrote of his struggle to keep his homosexuality secret by "covering." He eventually shed his cover and became Chief Justice Earl Warren Professor of Constitutional Law at New York University School of Law, as well as a human rights activist. In summing up his fate, he wrote, "I was meant for some great work… not for happiness but joy." He is not one of the Happers, but one of us other eight who, by dint of effort, experiences the occasional joy of achievement, of being of value to society.

Ray Bradbury (1950) in his biting satire *Fahrenheit 451* (named for the temperature at which books burn) elevates the role of firefighters to that of book burners in order to keep the citizenry "happy." The thesis that knowledge kills happiness underlies this passage:

> You must understand that our civilization is so vast that we can't have our minorities upset and stirred. Ask yourself, What do we want in this country above all? People want to be happy, isn't that right? Haven't you heard it all your life? I want to be happy, people say. Well, aren't they? Don't we keep them moving, don't we give them fun? That's all we live for, isn't it? For pleasure, for titillation? And you must admit our culture provides plenty of these…. Colored people don't like *Little Black Sambo.* Burn it. White people don't feel good about *Uncle Tom's Cabin.* Burn it. Someone's written a book on tobacco and cancer of the lungs? The cigarette people are weeping. Burn the book. Serenity. Montag, Peace, Montag." [punctuation changed] (p. 59)

Wilson (2008), as though echoing Bradbury, writes in a similar vein:

> I for one am afraid that our American culture's overemphasis on happiness at the expense of sadness might be dangerous, a wanton forgetting of an essential part of a full life. I further am wary in the face of this possibility: to desire only happiness in a world undoubtedly tragic is to become inauthentic, to settle for unrealistic abstractions that ignore concrete situations. I am finally fearful over our society's efforts to expunge melancholia from the system. Without the agitations of the soul, would all of our magnificently yearning towers topple? Would our heart-torn symphonies cease? (p. 6)

There is some evidence (cf. Hall, 2010) that one's degree of education is inversely related to one's level of happiness. It is said that the more one knows, the more one tends to find fault, to see flaws. Surely you've heard someone say to a learned musician being critical after a performance: "I don't envy you your musical knowledge, for I seem to be able to simply enjoy the concert far more than you, who anguishes over proper interpretation, resents inappropriate tempos, and is saddened by the orchestra's low budget and its consequence: too few in the string section. I can hear it for what it is and be pleased." Spoken like a Happer!

But such a critical stance is core to the human condition. Derek Bok (2010) puts it this way: "Apparently, individuals who reach the very highest level of happiness do not possess the nagging sense of unfulfilled ambition that drives others to work exceptionally hard for worldly success." (loc. 881) Fat and happy and comfy with the status quo. The British philosopher John Stuart Mill wrote: "It is better to be a human being dissatisfied than a pig satisfied; better to be Socrates dissatisfied than a fool satisfied." (1863, in *Utilitarianism*) In Chapter 4 we will see how a dissatisfied human being may channel their discontent in a way that they feel, not necessarily happy, but in gear. On track. Making progress. Contributing.

How Happiness Is Distributed

Opal Pickles—Gramma in the comic strip *Pickles*—is chopping (in the April 13, 2010, strip) in preparation for a meal when her grandson queries:

Nelson: "Gramma, can we go to Six Flags?"
Opal: "No."
N: "How come we never get to do anything fun?"
O: "We don't need to have fun."
N: "Why not?"
O: "Because we're happy. Happy people don't need to have fun."

Opal could have said: "We're Happers: We don't need Pierce Howard's book!" But Opal makes an important point: Happiness is forever, while fun is ephemeral. Happiness is like a well-running car that provides a satisfying journey throughout, while fun is like stopping at a beach on the way and taking a 30-minute swim/ dog run/Frisbee break. Dennis Prager (1998) writes: "To understand why fun doesn't create happiness and can even conflict with it, we must understand the major difference between fun and happiness: *fun is temporary; happiness is ongoing.* Or to put it another way, fun is during, happiness is during and after." (p. 47) The effects of "fun" are hygienic, like tooth brushing—the effect wears off and needs repeating. Natural happiness doesn't wear off.

This thing called happiness has become a new way of describing national, institutional, local, and individual health and wealth. Ruut Veenhoven of Erasmus University in Rotterdam, Netherlands, is director of the World Database of Happiness and also editor of the *Journal of Happiness Studies*. His research centers on asking persons around the world: "All things considered, how happy would you say you are these days?" (Weiner, 2008, p. 12) Veenhoven maintains data on 175 countries, ranking them on a 10-point scale. In May of 2011, the top five were Costa Rica, Denmark, Iceland, Switzerland, and Finland, each coming in at 8 or better out of 10 points. The bottom five, hovering around 3 on a 10-point scale, were Benin, Zimbabwe, Burundi, Tanzania, and Togo. The five in the middle, each close to 6 on a 10-point scale, were Jordan, Philippines, Slovakia, Syria, and Tunisia. The U.S. came in at 21st with a score of 7.4.[2] What should we make of this information? Eric Weiner (2008) takes a stab at answering that question in his *The Geography of Bliss.* His is an enjoyable read and an important issue, but my book is not really concerned about the happiness of nations. We are concerned about individuals. We do not advocate moving to a top-ranked country—we advocate finding a way to modify our current personal context. Maybe you'd like to visit one of the top-ranked countries just to see if it rubs off.

Another effort to quantify the levels of happiness (as well as about 5,000 other feelings) throughout the globe is the University of Vermont's Hedonometer. The Hedonometer (see http://wefeelfine.org/) runs a search engine that scans a large number of blogs throughout the Internet

---

[2] For a complete listing of the 175 nations in rank order, as well as Veenhoven's other data, how it is collected, and a variety of conclusions, visit his website at: http://worlddatabaseofhappiness.eur.nl/

every 10 minutes. A "hit" occurs when the engine finds the phrase "I feel…" or "I am feeling …. ." During each 10-minute span, between 15,000 and 20,000 feeling words are caught. The database may be queried at any time. If you want to know what Egyptian males over 60 years of age were feeling at the moment Hosni Mubarak's overthrow was announced, if you want to know what teenage girls in Biloxi felt during the 24 hours following Michael Jackson's death announcement, if you want to find the happiest moment of 2011, just visit the university's web site. A complete description of their methodology is available on the site. Interesting information, and a valuable resource for journalists. But not much help for our task. This is also something of a biased sample—that of bloggers!

In addition to global measures of happiness, or mood, local ones are popping up. At Massachusetts Institute of Technology, for example, you may check out the mood levels at four campus locations by reviewing their "MoodMeter" at http://moodmeter.media.mit.edu . Or, on a lower tech level, you might catch the result of the most recent citizen survey in Somerville, Massachusetts, where, with assistance from Harvard's Dan Gilbert, the mood of its citizens is checked on occasion.

For measurement of happiness levels throughout the U.S., the University of Chicago's National Opinion Research Center (NORC) periodically provides summary data. In 2006 they released a comparison of happiness levels across a 30-year span. The numbers appear in Table 1.0. From 1977 to 2006.

Table 1.0   Levels of Self-Reported Happiness in 1977 and 2006

Self Ratings:	1977	2006
"Very Happy"	35.7%	32.4%
"Pretty Happy"	53.2%	55.9%
"Not Too Happy"	11%	11.7%

Life expectancy and personal wealth increased significantly. However, happiness levels did not rise. The statistics trigger two questions: Why did happiness not rise along with longevity and income, and why is the "Very Happy" level so high?

First, happiness levels should not be expected to rise, all things being equal. If happiness levels are largely genetic, then more money and longer life should not elevate happiness any more than it should elevate intelligence or height. "All things being equal" presupposes, for example, that no major cultural stressors or boons, such as the Great Depression or the Second Coming, occurred around either the beginning or the end of the span. That is the case here. In fact, the same survey was administered in 2010 after two years of serious financial collapse and major unemployment, with the expected major decline in "Very Happy" levels to around 27%, a decline which is roughly equivalent to how much unemployment increased since 2006. So, in the absence of major stressors (famine, military invasion, epidemics, and so forth) or major boons (disappearance of crime, elimination of poverty, the end of war), we do not expect happiness levels to change very much. Why is increase in wealth not a major boon? Because, as most observers agree, income is a never-ending spiral in which individuals just can't get enough. The grass is always greener, and life will be better if I can just earn another $100,000.

Second, if I say one in nine is happy, why is one in three reported as happy here? This one is a bit easier. For a variety of reasons, people tend to inflate their levels of happiness. The NORC percentages for "Very Happy" will include a substantial number of people who, because their pride or self-image or reputation requires it, report that they indeed experience a very high level of positive emotions, but they do not mention that along with these positive feelings they also experience substantial negative emotions. The NORC survey, as do many others, fail to ask along with "Are you happy?" the parallel question "How frequently do you experience worry, anger, and sadness?" To truly qualify as a Happer according to my definition, both must be true: lots of joy and little sorrow. The important thing here is not whether the proportion of Happers in any given population is exactly 11% or 20% or 33%. What is important is to understand that there are Happers in the world who genuinely experience position emotions on a regular basis, and seldom experience negative emotions. And it is unrealistic for the rest of us to set a life goal of being like the Happers. To aspire to be a Happer is to worship a false god, to pursue an unattainable goal.

In the next chapter, we will review the various environmental influences on levels of happiness. We'll explore some myths, identify some downers, and celebrate some boosters.

STATEMENT OF PERSONAL PRIORITIES

FLOW | FIT | GOALS | COMMUNITY | ALTRUISM

| **Happiness Boosters** | **Happiness Downers** |
| *(Choice)* | *(Choice)* |

119 Minor Adjustors

(more within personal control)

(more outside personal control)

HAPPINESS SET POINT

| Happiness Boosters | Happiness Downers |
| *(Circumstance)* | *(Circumstance)* |

Continuum of Trait Happiness

Perennially Happy (N- E+) .... Occasionally Happy (N + E-)

2

What Affects It?

Myths, Boosters, and Downers

> "Just get over it."
>
> --Frustrated Psychiatrist to Resistant Patient

Guide to this chapter:
- The Myths of Happiness—What is Thought to Affect It But has No (or Brief) Impact
- Happiness Boosters—What is Known to Increase Happiness
- Happiness Downers—What is Known to Decrease Happiness

This chapter must be understood in the following manner: One's natural set point for happiness, whether higher or lower, cannot be permanently affected by any of the factors mentioned herein. One can increase one's experienced happiness by adding a "booster" activity, just like one can increase one's height by wearing elevator shoes. But discontinue the activity (or remove the shoes) and the effect is gone. In other words, the degree to which one feels happy is a combination of one's set point plus one's circumstances and one's choices. You can sometimes change the circumstances (like being born in Lower Slobovia—e.g., you can move to Upper Slobovia) and you can change most of your choices (oops, wrong church for me—think I'll find another), but you can't change your set point (without surgery and/or a lifetime of neuropharmaceuticals). So one's task, as I see it, is to know who you are (defined in Chapter 3) and to arrange your circumstances and make your choices in a way that is compatible with who you are.

The effect on mood of activities, choices, and circumstances listed in this chapter will be pretty much true regardless of who you are. For example, having quality relationships is good for you regardless of your personality or set point, and being isolated is bad for you regardless of the levels of your personality traits or your set point. Towards the end of this book, in Chapter 11 to be precise, I will present several dozen "adjustors" (actually 119!) that can make your life more or less satisfying. These adjustors depend more on your particular personality as to whether or not they might affect your quality of life. For example, I will suggest that you might consider the balance in your life between the two extremes of being a Participant versus being an Observer, as in watching sports, drama, or television cooking shows versus playing a sport, acting in a drama, or cooking from scratch. For instance, a person with a high activity level (what we call the trait E3) might realize sedentary activities have become too predominant; so the person changes to more active pursuits such as coaching or playing in a sports league. Or the active side of life might have crowded out time for necessary, and even satisfying, sedentary pursuits such as writing or reading. On the other hand, a person with a low activity level might feel overcommitted to active pursuits and would benefit from "weeding the garden"—eliminating one or more activities that require being up and about. Or, feeling too sedentary, the person might re-balance life by adding a moderately active pursuit, such as executing some new food preparation.

So, in the three sections that follow, we present:

- **Myths**—choices or circumstances that people have assumed to affect happiness levels but that in fact don't, at least not more than briefly;

- **Boosters**—choices or circumstances that will elevate your mood, but that are not permanent. However, unlike myths, it is not that their effect is short-lived, but their effect needs renewal. Helping your neighbor makes you feel better, but you need to keep up the helping in order to continue the benefit;

- **Downers**—choices or circumstances that will lower your mood, but that are not permanent. The most significant depressive effect of living in a malevolent dictatorship lasts only so long as one lives under the malevolent dictator, with the possibility, and hope, that things will change for the better eventually.

The positive or negative effect of any of the boosters or downers could in fact become permanent if one could find a way to make the booster continue without ceasing, or to make the downer disappear without returning.

The Myths of Happiness—What is Thought to Affect It But has No (or Brief) Impact

Much of the research that has exposed these beliefs as myths is based on the concept of the "hedonic treadmill." Imagine a treadmill: You begin walking on it with no elevation. Just as you become adjusted to it, the elevation increases more and more until you reach a point of maximum exertion (220 beats per minute minus your age). Then you step off of the treadmill and your heartbeat returns to its former level of around 72. Psychologists have used this process as a metaphor for what happens with the effects that some events have on one's happiness level. This is true, for example, with income: One gets a raise and feels a boost in happiness, only for the boost to evaporate, such that another raise becomes necessary to feel the boost again, and so on and on. Derek Bok (2010, loc. 176), says it this way: "As incomes rise, people soon grow used to their higher standard of living and feel they need even more money to lead a good life." Excitements continually return to their resting rate.

What is happening here is a series of events that we call "accommodating to a stimulus." At first, hearing the low hum of a room air conditioner may interfere with your attention, as in making it difficult to read or go to sleep. However, before too long, you accommodate to the low hum, such that you no longer hear it, and your mind slips into focusing its attention on reading or sleep. The hedonic treadmill is a series of these accommodations: normal day → good news → elation → back to normal day. In Figure 2.0, the set point for an individual is moderate, perhaps based on mid-range levels of both positive and negative emotions. Let us say that this individual begins life in poverty, such that an extremely low level of income is accompanied by a level of happiness that is somewhat lower than the set point. Not extremely low, but low enough to be under what might be normal. And, this depression

Figure 2.0   The Hedonic Treadmill (over time, increases in income lead to a bump in happiness only to return to previous levels)

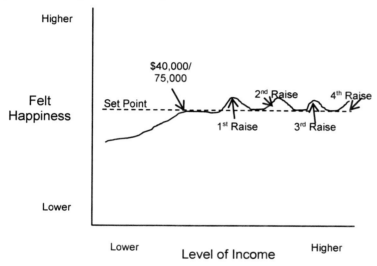

of mood is temporary, able to be lifted upon rising from poverty. According to research at Princeton University's Center for Health and Wellness, when a person achieves a household income of $75,000 (or $45,000 for a single earner; in 2011 U.S. dollars), lack of income no longer affects happiness. Of course, this exact income level will vary from region to region, country to country, based on local conditions. Subsequent increases in income, represented by a series of pay raises, cause a slight increase above one's happiness set point, only to evaporate. Each successive pay raise is accompanied by a brief rise and quick fall in happiness. Below this $75,000 (or $45,000), the set point is adversely, and continually, affected, until $75,000 (or $45,000) is reached. Increases after that are accompanied by positive blips that just don't stick. Carol Graham (2010, loc. 1408) cites research that pegs these blips from salary increase as lasting one year at the most, as compared to status increases, the positive effects of which last up to five years. (See discussion at Boosters/Status.)

Many of the myths that researchers have identified exhibit this pattern. The 15 myths most commonly referred to are, in alphabetical order[1]:

---

[1] More information on many of the myths, as well as many of the boosters, is available in Myers (1992).

- Crippling accidents
- Eating out
- Education level
- Income
- Insight

- Kids
- Lotteries
- Movies
- Moving
- New whatsit

- Positive thinking
- Spectator whatsit
- Television
- Vacation home
- Variety

I will briefly explain each myth. First, I want to be clear on one thing: These 15 "myths" are myths in the sense that they are thought by many to have a more permanent effect on mood, while in fact they don't. On the other hand, they *do* have a temporary, and in some cases fleeting, effect.

University of California, Riverside psychology professor Sonya Lyubomirsky (2008) has written about what she dubs the 40% solution (in reference, perhaps to Sherlock Holmes' seven percent solution (cocaine). She estimates that 50% of one's happiness quotient is determined by genes, 10% by one's circumstances, and the remaining 40% determined by one's choices. That is a rather precise conclusion, but for the moment we'll interpret it with some liberality. I propose we paraphrase her formula this way: Genes play the primary role in establishing our natural-born levels of positive and negative emotions (more about this in Chapter 3), and the circumstances of our birth and subsequent life history play a small role. But the decisions we make, both small (whether to buy a new item) and large (whether to build a vacation home), have a strong role in affecting our happiness levels. The difference, however, is that we basically can't change genetics very much, and we can't change our circumstances typically without significant cost, effort, or inconvenience. However, our choices—and I would add that one of our choices is to try and change our circumstances—are up for renewal, for the most part, on a daily basis. Because only one of the myths involves a circumstance (crippling accidents), I do not divide the 15 myths into the two categories of choice and circumstance. However, when we get to boosters and downers, so many are listed that I felt it would help to sort them into the two decks of choice and circumstance.

Crippling accidents. As with events that have a moderately positive yet brief impact on mood, such as eating out or seeing a movie, unpleasant events, even major events like a crippling accident, have only a temporary negative effect on mood. Persons disabled by accidents tend to return to their prior levels of happiness in relatively short order, with the exact required amount of time being different according to the individual and the circumstances.

Eating out. The pleasure of eating out is short-lived. Unless, that is, you make an experience of it. Take friends, grandchildren, and others with whom you wish to develop quality relationships, and the imprinted subject of the interaction will be more memorable than the vanishing taste of the food. We recently went to eat Thai cuisine with our grandchildren and their parents, and my grandson Liam's recitation of the 44 presidents of the U.S. glows in our proud memory while I have no idea what we ordered nor how it tasted. I'm sure it was good, but Liam was better! One theme that will emerge from this book is that, as a general rule, active experiences provide more, and longer lasting, mood elevation than passive events, e.g., getting together with friends to read through a play together, with each friend reading one or more parts, rather than getting together to watch a movie (or sporting event).

Education level. Obtaining years of education is not a matter of "the more the better" with respect to happiness. Research does indeed indicate that having an undergraduate degree is a boost to well-being. Having an undergraduate degree is a giant step towards more personal choice with respect to career, marriage, and other major life choices. However, to complete years or degrees beyond the undergraduate level provides no added boost in mood. In fact, the more educated one is beyond the undergraduate level, the more one is likely to become a critical thinker who sees flaws where the less educated see perfection. To be highly educated in this sense is to become keenly aware of life's flaws and shortcomings.

Income. As described earlier, increases in household income elevate mood until $75,000 is reached (or, $40,000 for single earners). Increases beyond this level do not affect day-to-day mood, but they do cause one to feel that one's quality of life is better. One feels more successful with further increases in income, but not happier. Earning below this $75,000 (or $45,000) threshold adversely affects one's set point, but earning above it does not positively affect it. It has no more effect, that is, than the momentary "Yes!" with accompanying raised fist or high five that soon gives way to one's accustomed mood level. Excellent analyses of the effect of income are available in Bok (2010), Csikszentmihalyi (1999), and Graham (2010). Over time, increases in income on the national level have the same effect. While nations such as the U.S. have shown dramatic increases in personal wealth, the number of citizens declaring themselves "very happy," "pretty happy," or "not too happy" has remained stable over the half century in which data have been collected. (Bok, 2010, loc. 166)

In his watershed study, University of Southern California economist Richard Easterlin (1974) uncovered an apparent contradiction that has come to be known as the Easterlin paradox. According to his, and others', results, even though more well-to-do people in a specific country are happier on average than their lesser off citizens, when comparing average levels of income and happiness between different countries one finds no relationship between national increases in mean income and mean happiness levels. Perhaps the recent finding that there is a point beyond which increases in income are not accompanied by increases in happiness finally explains Easterlin's "paradox."

While the fact that mood improvement stops at a certain income level may explain the Easterlin paradox, it does not explain the cap on mood improvement itself. Graham, Diener, Bok, and others explain the cap by reference to the hedonic treadmill. Namely, removal of an income deficit improves mood, but aspiring to more than "enough" is a never-ending feeding frenzy. While attaining more than one "needs" doesn't improve mood, it does improve one's standard or quality of living. Ed Diener and others call this subjective well-being (happiness, or smiling) versus objective well-being (satisfaction with life in general, or material comfort, or feeling successful).

Note: It should be said that knowing that the acquisition of more income won't increase happiness should not necessarily put a damper on pursuing more income. Without the advances made by those thirsty for growth, whether material, intellectual, or otherwise, we would be without vacuum cleaners and airplanes. Discontent breeds invention. We just need to realize that the goal of increased income should not be based on expected increase in our personal happiness. For some, knowing how much is enough is a reason to stop going after increases in income and pursuing other goals that may be more satisfying, while for others, knowing how much is enough may be an unsought-after damper on financial achievement. See discussion at Boosters/Status.

Insight. Insight-oriented therapies are based on the assumption that understanding the cause of one's anxiety, depression, or other uncomfortable feelings will lead to a more comfortable state. Research says the opposite. Psychiatrist Richard Friedman reported in the January 18, 2011, *The New York Times Digest* on his review of over 100 studies that attempted to tease out whether either traditional insight-oriented therapy or the more current cognitive-behavioral therapy had an advantage over the other. Insight therapy attempts to identify the cause of one's depression or other discomfort, while cognitive therapy attempts to correct or reframe self-defeating scripts and thought processes. In assessing two possible criteria for success in therapy—feeling happier and/or feeling less pain—he found that both therapies made patients feel better, but that insight therapy can on occasion increase one's suffering, as in intensifying a depressive patient's already strong tendency to recall unpleasant memories more easily than pleasant memories—a selection bias, as it were. Friedman identified the common element in both therapeutic approaches as the positive, nurturing bond that patient and therapist establish. Friedman comes down on the side that insight-oriented therapy too often adds to misery, with the sole advantage of alleviating the sufferer's wondering why they are miserable. Certainly, that knowledge is valuable, but it is not intrinsically associated with being happy. Hence, the focus of this book on alternatives to happiness.

Social psychologists Timothy Wilson (University of Virginia) and Jonathan Schooler (University of California—Santa Barbara) report (1991) that having depressed patients recall and dwell on unpleasant early memories tends to strengthen their neural networks, thus exacerbating their already excessive tendency to ruminate. Distracting such patients served to reduce their gloom and improve their problem-solving ability, while asking them to ruminate on unpleasant memories tended to increase gloom and thwart their problem-solving.

Kids. Derek Bok (2010) summarizes the research on the effect of children in a marriage by concluding that having kids is normally accompanied by higher levels of stress, tension, and depression than is reported by those who decide not to have children. Research shows that the typical awake baby requires some kind of adult assistance three times a minute, that their mothers suffer on average 700 hours of sleep deprivation during the first year of the baby's life, that the level of satisfaction with one's marriage drops on average 70% during that time, and that the mother's risk for depression doubles (Brooks, 2011). The mood dip begins after the first childbirth, with parents normally returning to pre-childbirth levels once the children leave home. As is the case with many human activities, stress, tension, and difficulties are not a reason to forswear the endeavor. Without our willingness to accept struggles along the way, there would be little progress, let alone survival. But I think it is important to mention this finding in order to keep in mind that raising kids is not a stroll in the park. Parents who opt to have kids as a way of improving their relationship are apt to be in for a disappointment.

> "Happiness is having a large, loving, caring, close-knit family in another city."
>
> --George Burns, U.S. humorist (1896-1996)

I have not seen whether or not parents who live with more of a support network experience any less stress—living in a commune or kibbutz, having in-house grandparents or other live-in helpers, or having close friends and family living nearby who can help at a moment's notice.

Lotteries. To put it simply, winning lotteries is like brushing your teeth, but on a larger scale. Even though many people dream of winning the lottery in hopes of a life of happiness, what they actually win is a pile of money that provides a temporary euphoria that only subsides to the way things were before the winning. Brush your teeth and you feel all sparkly for a while, but soon you need to brush again to avoid being where you were, mouth-wise. Similar to crippling accidents, lottery winners experience a temporary upward blip in mood that within a few months returns to one's set point. (Brickman, Coates, & Janoff-Bulman, 1978)

Movies. Movies are like television in their ephemeral impact (see entry below on Television). The more movies, the merrier—not! But just as with TV, if one watches the movie as part of a larger experience, such as a film discussion group or an evening with a friend where the movie is discussed over dinner, an effect is more likely. To watch a movie alone with no before, with, or after is not a mood-elevating event, at least not for long. But if it is part of a discussion, it becomes educational, which is satisfying if not titillating. And, if it involves seeing and discussing with a good friend, it becomes a relationship-building tool. I've only watched one movie multiple times—*The Sound of Music*. Each time it has been with one or both of our daughters. When they were in elementary and high school, we must have seen it a dozen times. Now, when we're together for the holidays, viewing Maria, Captain, and company is part of the tradition. Its characters, songs, lines, and issues also have peppered our conversations over the years.

Measures of mood elevation for movies and television are similar to those for dining at a restaurant or observing a sporting event. They consistently fail to compare favorably with the mood elevation achieved by gardening, exercising or playing sports. (Bok, 2010, loc. 347) Part of the ephemeral effect of the first four, it seems to me, is their essential passivity. As will be seen in Chapter 11, the balance of active versus passive activities in one's life can affect one's sense of well-being. It is like the difference between making and buying, between throwing a pot or playing a piano versus buying a ready-made pot or .mp3 file.

Moving. Bok (2010) reports that happiness research finds no measurable, lasting improvement in well-being as the result of moving to a more temperate climate. Again, a short-lived improvement in mood may accompany a move from, say, the frozen tundra of Fargo to the balmy surf of Malibu. "Isn't this bliss?" one may exult to one's partner while gazing into the Pacific from the new balcony. But one's set point reasserts itself in the den while paying bills or vacuuming. Clearly exceptions occur. But it is unlikely that the move, in-and-of-itself, will cause lasting mood improvement. Other factors come into play: commute time, congestion, neighbors, government quality, employment conditions, and the like. Unless one is able to control a long list of mood influencers, the move alone is unlikely to entail lasting bliss. I am reminded of my wife's father. His mood improved after moving from the deep South to Charlotte, NC, only to vanish when he learned that his lifelong religious group had no convenient places of worship nearby. Quality of life is a system, and change in one part of the system often entails changes in other parts of the system. These unintended changes may be welcome or unwelcome.

New whatsit. Materialism, or the accumulation of things, especially at the expense of the accumulation and cultivation of ideas, experiences, friends, and family, produces an effect on happiness much like the accumulation of wealth. Once a new possession comes on board, the urge for a next comes on deck. Three attitudes towards material things can soften this pattern: first, savor each unpossessed item for quite some time before acquiring it (e.g., study it, do research, comparison shop, and so forth), second, acquire it only for its own sake (i.e., not for the purpose of "keeping up with the Joneses"), and third prefer things that enable experiences (e.g., a tackle kit for fishing with a grandchild, or a book to discuss with friends). Bok (2010) comments that people "tend to focus too much on their initial response to changes in their daily lives and overlook how soon the pleasure of a new car or a pay raise or a move to warmer climes will disappear and leave them no happier than before." (loc. 3419)
The least materialistic person I've known was a fellow undergraduate—Knox Abernethy, a religion/philosophy major. The study area in Knox's dormitory room at Davidson College had two bookshelves. One was bare, the other containing only 16 books. Of these, six were required textbooks for current courses. The other ten were a reflection of his self-discipline, of his ardent desire to resist the unnecessary accumulation of material possessions. He explained: "I love books and reading them, and I could easily surround myself with thousands of volumes. However, I have committed to a lifetime ownership of only ten books. These are the ten that I most treasure at any given time—the ones that I want to be able to pick up and read at the moment. If I develop a strong urge to add another volume to my set of ten, first I must choose one to be replaced and give it away." Knox is now Fr. (Father) Ioannikios, hieromonk at the Holy Monastery of Sts. Cyprian and Justina. I understand from a colleague that Knox's room no longer has the ten volumes, just bare walls. Personal austerity. But then, there's always the library
Joe Cherepon, a friend and colleague, wrote me once about an anecdote about Joseph Heller, the late author famous for one novel, *Catch 22*. Joe wrote:

> According to the story, Heller was at a glitzy Long Island party, and one of the guests, a wealthy Wall Street executive, boasted to him that "I probably make more money in a week than you've made with all the books you've written." Heller is said to have responded, "That may be true, but I have something that you'll never have…. I have enough."

Eric Wilson (2008) has identified the particularly American desire to accumulate possessions as having roots in the English philosopher John Locke's *Second Treatise of Civil Government* (1690). Locke wrote that each person has the right to "life, liberty, and property." Thus, the U.S. Constitution's core declaration of the right to life, liberty, and happiness. This helps to define what the founding fathers meant by the right to happiness. Or, Ben Franklin put it: The true road to earthly joy is through the accumulation of stuff." (p. 13) Perhaps we should rewrite the constitution: life, liberty, and stuff! See a related discussion on Spending on Experiences under Boosters/Choice.

Positive thinking. Finding value in misery has achieved something like cult status. However, Barbara Ehrenreich (2009) has exposed this highly touted approach as empty at best and malicious at worst in her volume *Bright-Sided: How the Relentless Promotion of Positive Thinking Has Undermined America*. And other countries as well, I might add. The source of the positive thinking movement was David Spiegel, a Stanford University psychiatry professor who proposed that cancer patients join support groups and dwell on the benefits of life-threatening illness as a way of curing their cancers. Ehrenreich writes:

In the nineties, studies began to roll in refuting Spiegel's 1989 work on the curative value of support groups. The amazing survival rates or women in Spiegel's first study turned out to be a fluke. Then, in the May 2007 issue of *Psychological Bulletin*, James Coyne and two coauthors published the results of a systematic review of all the literature on the supposed effects of psychotherapy on cancer. The idea was that psychotherapy, like a support group, should help the patient improve her mood and decrease her level of stress. But Coyne and his coauthors found the existing literature full of "endemic problems." In fact, there seemed to be no positive effect of therapy at all. A few months later, a team led by David Spiegel himself reported in the journal *Cancer* that support groups conferred no survival advantage after all, effectively contradicting his earlier finding. Psychotherapy and support groups might improve one's mood, but they did nothing to overcome cancer. (p. 97) Part of the problem with Spiegel's approach is that support groups don't necessarily contain meaningful relationships, just other random people.

Ehrenreich takes on much more than breast cancer support groups, citing many studies that identify the stressful effects of forcing oneself to submerge negative feelings and only expressing positive ones. Essentially, such radical positive thinking has the effect of embracing the status quo. Everything is ok, nothing is wrong, this is the best of all possible worlds. Dr. Pangloss in the 21st century. Voltaire would likely have a violent reaction to some of the questions and affirmations that are used in "happiness" questionnaires and evaluations:

In most ways my life is close to my ideal.
The conditions of my life are excellent.
I am satisfied with my life.
So far I have gotten the important things I want in life.
If I could live my life over, I would change almost nothing.

Ehrenreich, rightly in my opinion, observes that affirming these questionnaire items is tantamount to being either ignorant of or indifferent towards threats to one's welfare: climate change, dramatic income inequalities, ideologues attempting to control our options, organizations dear to us that are on the verge of financial collapse, coal ash in our water supply, poor air quality threatening the viability of our respiratory systems, loved ones in need of support (dare I mention an NFL team with a losing streak?).

No, I am not satisfied with my life, it is far from my ideal, I would change much on my second go 'round, and many important things I want from life are still out of my reach (at the moment). I am not a grouse, nor am I am Pollyanna. I want more. I want language fluency, and I am willing to work for it. I want to master the Vivaldi piccolo concerto that profoundly deaf Evelyn Glennie shamed me with during her recent performance. I want to read, digest, and share so many books that my eyes ache at the prospect. I want to extirpate the prostate cancer that threatens to cut life short.

When the positive thinkers create websites that urge folks to "Get rid of the negative people in your life," they are asking us to get rid of people with consciences, people with ideas, people with noble discontent. Without pessimists, bridges would be weaker. With only optimists, details would be lost. We need the creative tension of positive and negative. Certainly excessive negativity, like excessive positivity, is toxic. Like William Butler Yeats' phrase (from the poem "Sailing to Byzantium") we must "perne in a gyre," must balance forces as a gyroscope spinning on a string, careful not to get too close to either extreme lest we fall.

Spectator you-name-it. Watching a game, play, concert, event, demonstration, ballet, jousting contest, and other "spectator sports" is just not the same as performing in them. That is not to say that spectating is not worthy—just that the enjoyment felt in spectating is short-lived. Performers need spectators, to be sure. But in fact you don't have to have an audience to perform. I've spent hours of my life playing various musical instruments, singing madrigals and motets, improvising with Jane (I play recorder, she sings) on the patio on Lake Sequoia, but I don't need an audience for the music-making to be satisfying. In fact, once Jane and I were improvising close to dusk on the patio by the lake, and several canoes made their way to a spot under a shady oak and just rested there, paddles up, listening, politely clapping, then on their way. Yes, audiences are not necessary, but are nice on occasion. Now for professionals, that is another matter! I am not suggesting here that one curtail one's spectating, only that one considers balancing time spent spectating with time spent "performing." Doing trumps watching doers.

Television. The number of hours spent watching television essentially has zero effect on mood levels. Worriers will not worry less as the result of TV watching. Sadness will not be lifted by watching the tube (oops, the LCD! Or, according to the *Urban Dictionary*, electronic valium). Smiles will not last much beyond an episode of *The Office*. Such viewings are no different from downing a candy bar or a beer. Brief titillations. Why watch, then? Just as savoring food or drink will increase its pleasure, so savoring TV will enhance its mood boost. For example, to the degree that television is watched with a friend or family member, and to the degree that you (and they) are students of the programs' contents, and to the degree that you and your friend/family have frequent dialog around the issues treated, then the TV watching in fact becomes a relationship building experience and not a thing in itself. For example, when Jane and I watch a drama on television, we frequently pause the action and look up background information via Google or our home library. This makes the viewing more of an interactive experience.

Much of the research on television watching involves dramas, reality shows, and the like. Little research focuses on education via television. Remaining knowledgeable of current events and issues is intrinsically satisfying, if not felicitous. To be able to converse about environmental threats in one's hometown is the obligation of a citizen, and to be caught unawares can be somewhat depressing. So whether through television, radio, print media, or lunchtime exchange, acquisition of knowledge is satisfying, if not gleeful.

Vacation home. Persons with vacation homes tend to report no higher levels of happiness than those without. This is one of those hedonic treadmill phenomena where the boost in mood is short-lived. Having a vacation home introduces a new set of potential worries, in addition to its pleasures. In fact, those who vacation on a pay-as-you-go basis (trips, hotels, resorts, rental cottages, and the like) get most of the benefits with few of the concerns. My wife and I dreamed for many years of a vacation home in the mountains, only to be eventually dissuaded by the realities of knowing that we would have to deal with the maintenance and other details. We decided to keep it simple.

Variety. Behavioral economists have taken great delight in uncovering the dark side of variety. Give a person no choice and they're displeased. Give a person moderate choices, and they are pleased. Give a person a plethora of choices, and they are stressed. Clearly, some persons are less stressed by a large number of choices. On average, however, abundance of choice entails no happiness advantage. The truth be known, I've come to distrust restaurants that offer longer menus—how could they possibly make that many dishes that well? Let's prefer less choice, higher quality, whether from greater practice, higher concentration, or more time spent in preparation.

Happiness Boosters—What is Known to Increase Happiness

Each of the 63 boosters identified in this section has a measurable effect on mood. The positive effect may last for days or for years, but the effect is real. Some are more complicated than others. For example, exercise has both a momentary and a cumulative effect: You feel a boost in mood immediately after exercising soon wears off, but the cumulative effect of regular exercise also has a positive effect that is longer lasting.

That said, there is a disturbing problem with interpreting happiness research. I know that you have read elsewhere that "correlation is not the same as causation." This phrase serves as a warning that, just because two things tend to occur together, that does not *necessarily* mean that one causes the other. They could in fact be unrelated, or either could cause the other. For example, just because shark attacks and ice cream consumption at the beach are correlated, that does not mean that the two have a causal relationship. There could be, and is, a third factor that relates to both and in fact causes both—hot weather. Hot weather increases the number of swimmers (hence the number of shark attacks) and also causes a stronger desire for ice cream (and other cold, wet treats).

Similarly, the fact that happiness levels and income levels are correlated does not identify the direction in which the cause might occur. Happier people may have higher income levels because happy people are by nature more ambitious and more successful at revenue generation. On the other hand, success at revenue generation might make people happier. These are classic chicken-and-egg questions: Which of the two correlated states precedes the other? With happiness and marriage correlated, is that because happier people are more likely to get married, or because marriage makes them happier? With happiness and an active sex life correlated, is that because happier people are more likely to embark on an active sex life, or because a more active sex life makes one happier? Derek Bok (2010, loc. 246) reports on a piece of research that compared first-year college students' self-reported happiness of and their incomes 20 years later. The happier students were making on average 30% more than the less happy. In this case, the correlation of happiness and income does clarify that happiness preceded income.

In the relationships reported in this chapter, not all have data as clear as this to back them up. So, exercise caution in interpretation. In the case of the college study just cited, clearly other factors are at work. For example, many happy people are also optimistic, and optimistic people, as a rule, are more likely to be interested in managerial and sales roles, both of which are associated with higher income levels. I should note that the first-year students' socioeconomic standing was not reported; so it is possible that the happier frosh were also from more prosperous families. There, I've muddied the water again!

I have divided the list of happiness boosters into two sections: those that are more a matter of choice and those that are more circumstantial. For example, gardening appears in the "choice" group, but certainly one's circumstances could affect it (e.g., living in a high rise). And, government responsiveness is in the "circumstantial" group, but certainly one could become engaged in trying to change the level of government's responsiveness. Consider Tarek al-Tayyib Muhammad ibn Bouazizi, the Tunisian street vendor whose stock was confiscated by the Tunisian government. On December 1, 2010, he protested with the ultimate act of self-immolation. This is seen by many as the spark that began the successful regime change in his country and spread to what we now refer to as the Arab Spring.

> "Happiness is in your choices."
> --Starbucks slogan

Fortunately, choices for happiness (45) outnumber circumstances (20). Again, the division between choices and circumstances are not black-white. With most circumstances, there is a degree of choice, and with most choices there is a degree of circumstantial constraint.

Choice:

- Affairs
- Alcohol moderation
- Anticipating purchases
- Anticipation of good stuff
- Attendance of club or other group meetings
- Being busy
- Being Republican
- Buying for the thing itself
- Charitable acts
- Child care
- College/undergrad degree
- Conversation
- Eating
- Exercising
- Experiences
- Extrinsic rewards for algorithmic tasks
- Gardening
- Generativity
- Gratitude
- Health (perceived)
- Meditating/praying
- Music listening
- Optimism
- Pets
- Playing with children
- Political involvement
- Pro-market attitude
- Reading
- Recreational sports
- Relationships
- Religion/Faith
- Self-employment
- Sex
- Shopping
- Socializing
- Spending for experiences
- Spending on equipment for experiences
- Spending on others
- Taking a walk
- Touch

- Intrinsic motives
- Marriage
- Meals with family/friends

- Transcranial magnetic stimulation (TMS)
- Volunteering

 Circumstance:

- Aging (approaching seniority)
- Beauty
- Democracy
- Employment
- Environmental conditions
- Feeling safe
- Financial freedom
- Government efficiency
- Government responsiveness
- Government trustworthiness

- Law-abiding/Law enforcement
- Minimal corruption/violence
- Personal freedom
- Retirement
- Status increase
- Temperate climate
- Tolerance of minorities
- Trust
- Trust in management
- Trust in public officials

 Choice:

Affairs. I apologize for leading out with this one. In this case, it is all about alphabetization! Extramarital (or extra-relationship) affairs are a boost in mood for the ones having the affair. They represent novelty, affirmation, adventure, escape, and perhaps even a means to an end. This there is no denying. However, that does not overcome the moral, legal, and spiritual morass that affairs incur.

Alcohol moderation. Abstention from drinking alcohol (teetotaling) and excessive drinking are both associated with lower levels of happiness than is moderate alcohol consumption. The most common explanation of moderate drinking's effects (cf. Graham, 2010, loc. 1035) is that people are known to drink more when with others than when alone. Hence, it is not necessarily the drinking itself that is making folks happier, but the social life, the relationships. Alcohol has often been called a social "lubricant," a relaxing chemical that tends to make conversation more free-flowing. It is also interesting to note that married people tend to drink more than unmarried, a fact that supports the drinking/socializing association. (Excessive drinking can be a social lubricant in groups that require heavy drinking. But overall, the physical and psychological damage from excessive drinking outweighs any perceived benefits.)

Anticipating purchases. One may prolong the positive impact of a purchase by engaging in a long prelude. Wait to make the purchase until you just can't stand it any longer, and then wait a while longer. By protracting the wait before making the purchase, three things could happen: You benefit from the anticipation, you appreciate the purchase all the more from having waited so long, and you even decide that you can live without it!

Anticipation of good stuff. Similar to anticipating purchases, one experiences a boost in mood while anticipating an event that is sure to be joyful. Examples are a long marital engagement, the return of a loved one after a prolonged absence, or a trip to the big city (or beach, mountains) planned for some time in the future. In one sense, this is like having a "bucket list," a popular trend since Rob Reiner's 2007 film had Jack Nicholson and Morgan Freeman playing two old men escaped from a cancer ward and dead-set on having some experiences they had been hoping to have before they died. Hence, the bucket list, or things you/I would like to do before we kick the bucket. This is anticipation of good stuff at its best. Some items on my bucket list: camping at Puget Sound, mastering Vivaldi's Concerto in C for Flauto Dolce, building a screened-in patio porch with overhead fan in my backyard, writing a novel based on my consulting experiences, cooking a successful cassoulet (the cheese topping is never hard enough), and so forth. What's on yours? Remember: emphasize experiences, not possessions (though possessions can facilitate some experiences).

Attendance of club or other group meetings. Derek Bok (2010, loc. 397) comments that going to monthly meetings of a club or other organization, or volunteering one time every month, provides a boost in reported happiness equivalent to doubling one's income. What is nice about this is that, it is highly unlikely that one can double one's income monthly, one can certainly attend or volunteer once monthly. Bok concedes that it may be that Happers are the ones going to the meetings. However, he concludes that causality in this case runs both ways: Happy people are more likely to volunteer and attend meetings, but the acts of volunteering and attending are also likely to boost one's mood.

Being busy. This one is tricky. Clearly idleness is the devil's workshop, in that time on one's hands is an invitation to both mischief and depression. But being busy has many different faces. To some, it looks like flitting from one appointment to another, from the neighborhood walking/jogging group at 6:30 a.m. to the family conference call at 10:00 p.m., with soccer practices, business lunches, and so forth in between. The more events, the merrier. However, to some of us, being busy can be waking up to a good book and going to bed still reading the same good book. What both have in common is the fact that one is meaningfully engaged throughout one's waking hours, regardless of the number and duration of the engagements. Hans Selye, the McGill University psychologist who made stress famous, captured these contrasting modes with his parable of the racehorse and the turtle. The racehorse is like the day full of many activities, and the turtle is like the long, slow book reading. Both are legitimate styles, both happiness producing. However, a racehorse trying to act like a turtle would be miserable. And conversely, if a turtle were to act like a racehorse, the turtle would not be a happy camper. This happens all too often, with spouses, bosses, children, friends, and the like demanding or just wanting us to be someone we are not. Happiness is in large part being able to be yourself.

Being Republican. Being contented with the way things are is one way to define conservatism. Accordingly, we could say "happy" with the way things are or the way things used to be. So, there you have it! Want to be happy, register yourself as a conservative. The liberal is discontent and wants and needs change. I always have said there were drawbacks to happiness—such as lack of progress. And, drawbacks to progress—such as lack of happiness.

Buying for the thing itself. The kind of purchasing that is least satisfying is the kind of thing that you buy in order to keep up with your "competition." My friend buys a Dolmetsch grenadillo soprano recorder with ivory bushings and mouthpiece, so I have to buy either the same thing in order to keep "up" with him, or I have to buy one with a little extra, something beyond his expenditure. Perhaps a brass finger rest and a silver tone projector. Or maybe some gold inserts to indicate proper shank alignments. For the moment, I can bask in the glory of having made the superior purchase. But as I discuss towards the end of this chapter, this process of "social comparison" is a vicious cycle. No sooner do I compare myself favorably to him than he goes out and buys a new satinwood soprano with etc. etc. etc., and I now compare myself unfavorably and must make another purchase to feel better. This is not a path to happiness, but it may be a fun competition. For one in pursuit of a more sustainably pleasant expenditure, emphasize making purchases for the thing in and of itself, with no intention of comparing whether one's purchase is inferior or superior to that of others. The question here is: Did I get exactly what I wanted? Was I patient and careful in knowing the details of my requirements? Am I proud of what I ended up with, regardless of what others close to me may have that is similar but different in some way? Can I allow myself to remain satisfied that my purchase reflects my values and needs, and not those of other people?

Charitable acts. As we will see in Chapter 9 on altruism, charity is a significant boost to well-being. So much so that it deserves a chapter unto itself. Suffice it to say at this point that small and varied acts of charity are mood boosters. There is some evidence that doing the same act repeatedly, while satisfying, is not as satisfying as introducing some variation. It feels good always to return a frail, elderly neighbor's garbage can to its weeklong resting place before she risks breaking a bone retrieving it. But an act of charity that feels even better is noting that one morning her newspaper was thrown into an awkward place to retrieve it so you lob it to safety closer to her front door. Be open to variety in the ways that you serve others.

Childcare. There are at least three issues around children: having them, caring for them, and playing with them. Having children is hard work, stressful, and generally not a mood booster, as we saw earlier in Myths/Kids. However, having children and caring for/playing with them is like the difference between carpentry as a vocation and carpentry as an avocation. When my wife and I choose to care for our grandchildren, that is not generally stressful—oh, sure, at times, yeah! And even better, when we have the opportunity to choose to play with children, to abandon adult inhibition and play blind man's bluff or Go Fishin', and to really focus on being fully with them in the moment, much like savoring a piece of chocolate or a cup of fresh-roasted coffee—that is mood-boosting. Reminds me of our friend Judy Kiser, who came to choir practice one Thursday night with a tee-shirt that read, "If I'd known that grandkids were so great, I'd of had them first!"

College/undergrad degree. Robert Putnam (2000) points out that persons who have completed an undergraduate degree tend to be much more trusting of others than are those without a college education. Perhaps the dynamic here is that education tends to remove barriers to trust, such as stereotyping of various groups or types and caution around the unknown and different. In addition, college-educated folks are more likely to feel more in control of their life choices, and less subject to the circumstances of their birth. (Brooks, 2011, loc. 5775) College graduates also feel more inclined to take action in pursuit of major career goals, as though the college education were intrinsically supportive of achievement.

It is noteworthy that mental challenges such as those required for learning new material and skills are associated with living longer. (Brooks, 2011, loc. 6209) For example, college-educated nuns outlive their degreeless sisters, in spite of equivalent life styles. Also, adolescents with bigger vocabularies are at significantly lower risk for developing dementia in their graying years. And, seniors active in arts activities (they are more likely to participate in arts activities if they are college-educated) see the doctor less, take fewer meds, and on total have superior health in comparison to those who do not participate in arts activities. Of course, arts activities typically involve interaction with others, so which is the dominant influence on well-being—arts activities or relation development? Probably relationship development.

Conversation. Conversation is intrinsically pleasing. Brain scans reveal that pleasure centers of the brain typically light up when an individual is conversing. Again, however, we must ask the question: Is it the conversation itself that is pleasing or rather is it the relationship that is being developed while conversing? Surely, it is difficult to have one without the other. However, relationship-wise, conversation is a maintenance activity. It is possible for two or more people in a relationship of some kind to go for long stretches without verbal interaction, as in silence or a monolog. But relationships require the kind of periodic exploratory diagnostic comments such as "How's it going?", "Need some help?", "Anything I can get for you while I'm up?", "How was work today?", or "What's on your agenda for this evening/weekend?"

Clearly the kind and amount of conversation will vary among individuals. Some abhor small talk and cherish philosophical inquiry or political debate. Some are stressed by too much talk, some stressed by not enough. I recall Marilyn Whirlwind of the CBS drama *Northern Exposure*, who, while attempting to understand and console her male companion, a mime who voluntarily chose not to talk to anyone, knowingly consoled him with: "Words are heavy things...they weigh you down. If birds talked, they couldn't fly."

Eating. Ever heard the phrase, "Some eat to live, others live to eat."? There are two aspects of eating that affect mood: the eating itself, and the company with whom you eat. We'll discuss the latter when we get to Meals with family/friends, in a couple of pages. For now, let's look at the eating itself. I am aware of five eating styles: eating enough for energy, engorgement, eating for taste, eating for health, and eating as gratitude. Each has its own kind of pleasure, but the last three are the most satisfying. One who simply eats enough to get through the next several hours is unlikely to receive a boost in well-being—just grab a sandwich, a jar of yogurt, and get back to work. Eating for engorgement is stuffing yourself—taking large portions, and seconds and thirds, and loosening the belt, stretching, yawning, napping. The immediate effect can be moderately titillating, but the long-term effect is depressing. For maximum benefit to mood, emphasize 1) eating good food well prepared for maximum flavor—chewing slowly, savoring the various tastes, making it a sensory experience, 2) eating a balanced diet—the new "food plate," (www.choosemyplate.gov) with a balance of modest portions of protein, grains, vegetables, fruits, and dairy, and/or 3) eating as a spiritual act, in which one eats whatever is available with a sense of appreciation, humility, and thankfulness.

Exercising. Both aerobic (e.g., jogging) and anaerobic (e.g., weight lifting) exercise improve mood, but aerobic has the greater positive effect. Here's how. Stressful episodes cause the spread of cortisol throughout one's system, thus eliciting the "fight-or-flight" response, whereby the body becomes fully prepared to defend against attack. The cortisol will stay in your system for up to 2 ½ days, *unless* you actually burn it up by exercising feverishly. That's the whole idea: Under threat, we get pumped up by cortisol, and we have to follow through by figuratively running away or fighting the tiger (i.e., aerobic exercise) in order to burn away the cortisol. Without the exercise, the cortisol remains and causes problems with mood, learning, and health. As a general rule, one should engage in 15-30 minutes of aerobic exercise as soon as possible after a highly stressful experience. If you have a stress-free life, then have aerobic exercise five times per week at a time of day convenient for you.

Martin Seligman (2011) makes a case for regular exercise being more important that weight control. After examining the literature, he concludes that

> These data show the risk for death in normal-weight versus obese people who are fit or unfit. In the unfit groups, normal and obese people both have a high risk for death, and it does not seem to matter if you are fat or thin. In the fit groups, both fat and thin people have a much lower risk of death than their counterparts in the unfit groups, with fat but fit people at only slightly more risk than thin fit people. But what I now emphasize is that fat people who are fit have a low risk of death. Steve concludes that a major part of the obesity epidemic is really a couch potato epidemic. Fatness contributes to mortality, but so does lack of exercise. There are not enough data to say which contributes more, but they are compelling enough to require that all future studies of obesity and death adjust carefully for exercise. (loc. 3863)

Seligman concludes, and I concur, that the guideline for achieving fitness is the 2008 surgeon general's report that identifies 10,000 steps a day (or its equivalent) as the optimal level, with severe warnings (because of significantly increased death risk) of falling below 5,000 steps daily. As a matter of interest, on average 2,000 steps equals one mile, as do ten city blocks. For a simple indicator of physical fitness, I have seen "able to briskly climb a set of ten stairs without getting winded."

Experiences. Experiences don't have to cost dollars. Elsewhere we emphasize spending on experiences rather than spending on possessions. Here we are saying something of the same thing, but with a different emphasis. Have experiences, especially experiences with others, that you can relate to others over a coffee, over a meal, with a drink. Relating your experiences to others is more satisfying both to you and others, than is relating how you feel about your most recently acquired material possession. Consider: "Last night we walked the neighborhood in search of fireflies. I've never seen so many. When I was a kid, it seemed like we were lucky to see a dozen all evening. Last night, we saw several dozen in 30 minutes." Versus: "Last night I pulled out my ten-gauge, cradled it, just enjoying its balance, and put it back on the rack. A real beaut." Of course, while the latter is not much of experience, a friend with a common interest could make it so, with maybe a "How do you go about cleaning your weapon?"

Extrinsic rewards for algorithmic tasks. A natural motivation killer is extrinsic reward (i.e., when someone other than you rewards you for doing an activity; see more below at "Intrinsic rewards"). The exception is when the external reward is offered for completion of a series of steps that entail constraining guidelines. An example would be a scholarship competition, an artistic contest, a summer reading competition, and the like, in which everyone must follow the same steps and guidelines or rules. Read more about this in Pink (2009).

Gardening. Preparing soil, planting, weeding, nurturing, harvesting, and then giving away, selling, cooking, or canning provides a sense of satisfaction that beats going to the farmer's market, much less the grocery store. Normally a solitary activity, if two or more can garden together, all the better. The enjoyment comes from feeling in control and independent, plus several other sources (freshness, being outdoors, better taste, visual splendor).

Generativity. This is a big one. What will you leave for the next generation? Your children, your grandchildren, your employees, your friends. What will there be for them to remember you by once you are gone? In middle age, one's mind tends to turn towards one's legacy. Whether one leaves money, works of art, books, scrapbooks, a handmade cradle for future babies, a hand-sewn christening gown for future infants, handmade ornaments, crafts—the knowledge that one is leaving something to be remembered by is a sustaining source of personal satisfaction. If you have nothing in the pipeline, now is the time to consider your options! If nothing else, write your own autobiography, complete with pictures!

Gratitude. This subject is a part of the larger topic that occupies the whole of Chapter 9: Altruism. Here's a summary of the research. First, gratitude completes an act of service. Service must be given as well as received. When it is freely given, the giver does not expect a receipt, a thank-you, or even some form of reciprocity. However, as is so important in many eastern cultures, reciprocity is often expected. One good turn deserves another. Bring me a hot meal when I'm ill, and I'll remember when you're incapacitated. Maybe I'll bring you a meal, or maybe I'll go chop some firewood for you, or shovel the snow from your driveway. Gratitude is the proper response to a generous gesture, the second half of an act of service.

Second, to receive a generous act from someone else is a boost in well-being inasmuch as it makes us feel valued, accepted, and perhaps even loved. To return the favor in some way makes the other person feel valued, accepted, perhaps even loved. To return the favor boosts one's own well-being because it makes us feel responsible, that we've done our duty, that we pull our share of the weight. When we fail to reciprocate, to show gratitude, we run the risk of feeling guilt, or even shame. Reciprocating generosity in some appropriate way prevents that dark cloud of remorse from adversely affecting our mood. The Chinese have an expression for this "reciprocity in relationships,"—*ren qing*.

Health (perceived). The way one evaluates one's own health is more important, happiness-wise, than what one's physicians think. I can personally attest. My three brothers aged into their gray years with enlarged prostates but no cancer. Five years ago when my urologist spotted cancer cells in my bi-opsy, they said the march towards full-blown prostate cancer had begun. They were more worried than I, as I was confident that my genes would prevail. I was wrong, as the cancer has now grown to the point of needing treatment. Still, I'm upbeat, knowing it hasn't taken anyone in my family. Yet. Bok (2010) states that a person's self-reported drop of 20% in perceived health is connected to a 6-point drop in happiness (on a 100-point scale). Doctors' ratings of their patients' health are moderately correlated with patients' self-ratings of health, but only weakly correlated with patients' reported happiness levels.

> "Happiness is nothing more than good health and a bad memory."
> --Albert Schweitzer, Alsatian physician and philosopher (1875-1965)

Not only is one's perception of one's health more im-portant than others' perceptions, including physicians'—it also boasts one of the strongest correlations with reported happi-ness, and, on some questionnaires, the strongest correlation of all the factors. (Graham, 2010, loc. 1103) Clearly this relates to a person's degree of optimism. Optimistic people are more likely to evaluate their personal health more robust than are more pessimistic folks. Also evaluating their health more positively are people who en-gage in health maintenance activities—Mediterranean diet, aerobic exercise (such as the 10,000 steps a day), fresh air and sunshine, moderate alcohol and caffeine, good night's sleep, stress minimization, adequate rest, and quality relationships. Eduardo Punset (2007, pp. 134-135) explains that, from an evolutionary perspective, we were designed to live for only 30 years. Our extra 40 years of life are not accompanied by the physical support necessary to sustain life. This ups the priority on "maintenance" type activities, whether personal maintenance or maintenance of our planet/environment.

Intrinsic motives. Daniel Pink (2009) has summarized the research on what motivates people. He calls the finding that tangible rewards discourage intrinsic motivation "one of the most robust findings in social science and also one of the most ignored.... When institutions—families, schools, teams—fo-cus on the short term and opt for controlling people's behavior, they do considerable long term damage." (loc. 562) In short, it discourages individually initiated activity if a person receives a concrete reward for it. Why? Because the individual learns to expect the reward and so fails to originate activity.

Scenario: Child does homework in the time allotted. Parent says, "That's great! Here's an extra 25 cents for this week's allowance." Tomorrow, before the child begins homework, "How much tonight?" Thus, extrinsic motivation, i.e., an unexpected external reward (external in the sense that someone else offered it), has replaced intrinsic motivation (the child has been supplying personal internal, or intrinsic, reward for timely completion of homework, such as being able to text with friends).Research concludes that intrinsic motives—doing it because you want to do it, not because someone else wants you to—is ultimately more satisfying and is a stronger motive than is doing it in hopes of external reward. See more above at "Extrinsic rewards."

Some situations would benefit from using extrinsic rewards initially, and then gradually over time transitioning to intrinsic rewards. For example, the so-called "Tiger mom" approach clearly entails ex-trinsic motivation, but often the child is able to internalize the discipline, be it practicing a musical instrument or studying history, and begins to prefer the activity that had been drudgery heretofore. When that happens, Tiger mom needs to back off and just be supportive.

Marriage. Here is another one that invites the chicken-egg paradox, as in which came first. While studies consistently show marrieds reporting higher happiness levels than singles, separated, divorced, and unwed cohabiters, not all studies satisfactorily address the question about whether happier people are more likely to get married, or whether the state of marriage itself elevates mood. The tricky part here is the quality of the marriage. Regardless of the quality of the marriage experience, there is a measurable boost in happiness during the period of engagement (i.e., the anticipatory period) as well

> "Find a good partner and you'll be happy—otherwise you'll become a philosopher."
> --Paraphrase of Socrates

as a continuation up to two or three years after nuptials, with most persons then returning to pre-nup levels. (Lucas, Clark, Georgellis, & Diener, 2003) This finding was based on a German study that surveyed yearly 25,000 individuals over 15 years (cited in Lyubomirsky, 2008). However, there do exist those close, high-quality marriage relationships that continue for a lifetime. Research suggests that such relationships provide a "buffer against adversity and helps the immune system protect against illness." (Bok, 2010, loc. 353) This would explain why married individuals on average report fewer health problems, less depression, and less frequently commit suicide. An added boost: Marriage tacks on an average of seven years to men's lives, two years to women's. Those are better life extenders than many medical treatments! (Christakis & Fowler, 2009, p. 86)

Clearly more cheerful, optimistic people are more likely to marry, and good marriages contribute to one's cheerful disposition and outlook. The issue here is not really whether to marry or not in order to boost mood, but rather to identify relationships that have long-term potential to be satisfying and nurture them. I will address this in some detail in Chapter 8. We will also look at specific behaviors and practices—such as date nights and nonjudgmental feedback—that help in nurturing good marriages over their lifetime.

Meals with family/friends. In addition to the pleasure derived from sweet, salty, sour, bitter, and complex tastes, eating *together* provides even greater pleasure than eating alone. Research has shown that families who dine together all show higher levels of oxytocin, the "cuddle" chemical. Teens who eat the evening meal with their family show reduced signs of stressed behavior. The more oxytocin, the more bonding occurs. This is the same chemical released in mother and child during breast-feeding. The same would apply to the workplace: Coworkers who eat alone at their desk miss out on the opportunity to increase their sense of well-being at work by eating together and conversing in a common area.

Meditating/praying. Two systems of the brain tend to toggle for dominance during our waking hours. One orients us in time and space, giving us a sense of where we are in the universe. This system enabled hunter-gatherers to detect prey and sniff out berries, and today enables salespeople to detect prospects. The other system essentially draws the curtains on time and space and enables us to focus entirely on the task at hand. This system enabled hunter-gatherers to work for hours on end chiseling arrowheads and nursing their young. It is this system that separates us from time, temperature, and space that is associated with meditation, prayer, and any other activity that entails focused attention without distraction. Chapter 5 (Flow) explores this state of mind in some detail. While being in this mental state is not a form of happiness (it is actually emotion-free), people who are able to spend time in this state report higher levels of well-being. In fact, taking a nap—not the kind where you actually go to sleep but the kind, as I take every day, where you simply close your eyes and "shut down" your system, as though you were going to fall asleep, but don't—has the same degree of boost in well-being as meditation and praying. People who nap/pray/meditate report less absenteeism, higher morale, and fewer sick days than persons who don't take this time out on a daily basis to regroup. Scientifically speaking, achieving the nap/meditative state—especially between 2 and 4 p.m., when the body's temperature is at a low point, attention dips, and the largest number of home, industrial, and highway accidents occur—allows a kind of reset for our bodies that magically dissipates the typical afternoon doldrums.

Music listening. Music is another form of language (see the work of University of California at San Diego psychologist Diana Deutsch). As we discussed under Conversation, the pleasure pathways of the brain activate during conversation and, surprise, surprise, during music listening. Research suggests that there are no universally pleasing composers—Mozart comes close, however. So, this effect is limited to the kinds of music we have grown to prefer. There is little as soothing to me as listening to Bach's Brandenburg Concertos, and little so irritating to me as having to listen to a kind of music (that will remain unlabeled so I don't alienate any dear readers) which I have come to find grating, cacophonous, vapid, repetitive, and/or amplified. Oh, did I say repetitive? To listen to one's musical favorites is eternally satisfying. I believe it was Robert Frost who once described a great work of art as similar to a good friend, both having the characteristic that, each time they were revisited, we learned or felt something new or unexpected or different. I recall one day in high school when my friend Charles Peery had been jilted by a girl of his dreams. We sat in his room after school listening to one Beethoven symphony after another (Toscanini was our favorite conductor back then). All of a sudden, Charles looked up from his reverie and commented, "Pierce, music is one love that will never let you down!"

If listening to music is satisfying, making music with others is more so. Just as making conversation with a friend is more satisfying then just listening to them talk, making music with friends intensifies the pleasure. Not only is the music you are making pleasing in and of itself, but you are getting the added pleasure of developing one or more relationships. Also, while making music you are typically in flow—that meditative state that frees one of all distractions. It is also an "experience" of the kind we have talked about earlier. So making music with others packs a quadruple dose of mood boosting: music, relationships, flow, and experience.

Optimism. Martin Seligman (1991; see extended discussion of optimism in Chapter 7) approaches "explanatory style" as a learnable cognitive skill. In brief, he says that optimists tend to see positive outcomes as personally achieved, long lasting, and pervasive, while they see negative outcomes as bad luck, temporary, and isolated. Pessimists see the reverse: positive outcomes are just good luck that won't last beyond today, while negative outcomes are the result of personal failure and set the stage for continuing ill fortune. Seligman has taught this model to a variety of audiences, from sales people who need to be more resilient in the face of daily rejection to depressive patients who need to find rays of hope. In one controlled study, salespeople trained in his method of positive explanatory style, or optimism, outperformed the untrained by some 30%. In another study with a student population, training in his model reduced levels of depression by half over three years. Put another way, those not trained in his optimism model were twice as likely to report depressive symptoms over the next three years.

Critics of optimism call looking at the world with rose-tinted glasses a big lie. This is another of those areas that, while making us happy, blinds us to real world realities. Some interesting research on self-deception and lying has shown that the prefrontal cortex of compulsive liars has proportionately more white matter than normal. This has been interpreted to mean that they can bring more mental resources to bear when they need to lie/think on the fly. The less white matter in the prefrontal cortex, we either have to tell the truth or lie and get caught. Other research on self-deception, as measured by denying questions about thoughts that everyone supposedly has (e.g., "Have you ever doubted your sexual adequacy?", "Have you ever enjoyed a bowel movement?", "Have you ever wanted to rape or be raped by somebody?", "Have you ever thought of committing suicide in order to get back at someone?"), suggest that those who engage in self-deception tend to be higher achievers—in sports, in business, in arenas where competition is important. Conclusion: It helps to have a certain amount of self-deception, or optimism, for otherwise a realistic assessment of the odds might lead to backing out of the fray. (Sackeim & Gur, 1979)

In summary, both optimism and self-deception are associated with higher levels of happiness, realism/pessimism and honesty with lower levels.

Pets. My first thought was to locate "pets" under "Touch." However, recent research by McConnell, Brown, Shoda, Stayton, and Martin (2011) has shown that pets are far more than something to touch. Pets provide a boost in well-being above and beyond all other factors. Their constant loyalty, playfulness, and affection provide a protection against the effects of social rejection. Pet owners also get more exercise (especially those with dogs) and have higher activity levels (as the result of caring for—feeding, cleaning, grooming, etc.—the pets).

Playing with children. Having children, caring for children, and playing with children are three different matters. (See Myths/Kids and Boosters/Child care.) Playing with children, in and of itself, is a mood booster. This assumes that you can draw a distinction between playing with them and the more long-term states of having kids and providing ongoing care. One reason that playing with children boosts mood is that, if we allow ourselves to, we get into a childlike frame of mind ourselves and loosen our inhibitions by being silly, creative, spontaneous, and active. And, we are also developing relationships—there it is again!

Political involvement. Swiss economists Bruno Frey (University of Zurich) and Alois Stutzer (University of Basel) analyzed the degree of "direct democracy" practiced by Swiss citizens in the various cantons across the country. Counting the number of events for citizen involvement—elections, initiatives, meetings, rallies, referenda, hearings—canton by canton, they found that the quantity of opportunities for political involvement varied precisely as levels of reported well-being varied. (Bok, 2010, loc. 1050) The more opportunities for political involvement in a given canton, the happier its citizens. This relationship is only for citizens—foreigners living in a given canton did not show variation in well-being based on the number of opportunities for political involvement. In reviewing this research, Derek Bok concludes that it is not the results brought about by political action that are associated with happiness, but the opportunity to get involved. Similar to research on stress, which points to the stress-reducing effects of feeling that one has some control over stressors, these citizens are buoyed more by the sense of control than by the results of their efforts at control.

Pro-market attitude. Graham (2010) reported on studies that show that individuals who espouse a pro-market attitude recorded higher average happiness levels that those who favored more central controls on market prices and policies. This could indicate an underlying optimism on the part of pro-market individuals and a more pessimistic attitude of these favoring controls. It is also characteristic of "being Republican"!

Reading. Reading provides an entry into flow, such that we lose all sense of time, space, and place. This assumes that the book or other material is not too easy for us (lest we become bored) or too difficult for us (lest we become frustrated). Reading is a state like prayer, meditation, napping, music-making, and flow, characterized by pulling the curtains on the outside world and enabling us to focus on the world created by the author, whether it is fiction, poetry, biography, or technical. Many has been the time that I was so absorbed in my reading that I would

> "Thank you for sending me a copy of your book; I'll waste no time reading it."
> --Moses Hadas (1900-1986), American literary critic

"wake up" startled and unsure of time and place. Being in such a "zone" is intrinsically satisfying, but not really "happy," as when you're in the zone you don't feel emotions. Sure, the occasional fear or joy or anger arises at the behavior of a character, but those are not really personal feelings that are sustained over time. Reading does *not* develop relationships, as a rule. However, it could. When I lived in Winston-Salem, North Carolina, we had a "readers' theatre" get together every couple of months, in which we would assemble a dozen friends and have a covered-dish dinner and drinks. This informal dinner theatre would proceed with a handful of folks reading their parts from a classic or popular play while others provided the live audience.

Recreational sports. Here is another activity that merges multiple mood boosters into one: developing relationships, exercise, moderate alcohol, being busy, experiences, attendance at meetings, conversation, eating, health, optimism, playing with children, socializing, and spending for experiences.

Relationships. As Derek Bok (2010, loc. 391) puts it, "Both shy introverts and bounding extroverts report feeling happier when they are with other people than when they are alone; and, several researchers have concluded that human relationships and connections of all kinds contribute more to happiness than anything else. Close friends certainly matter, especially one's closest friend (though seldom to the same extent as a spouse in a successful marriage)." More on this in Chapter 8. I should add here that quality and quantity of relationships into one's gray years is also associated with minimizing risk for dementia.

Religion/Faith. Mark Ardis, a retired psychiatrist and personal friend and fellow bass in the choir, once commented to me that something is religion if it has "hope, ethics, explanations for the unexplained, and myth." It is clear that all four of these components work towards elevating mood. Each in effect removes something from uncertain to certain. For some individuals, uncertainty, ambiguity, paradox, and the unknown are scary, intimidating, even depressing. Religion, as Mark defines it, provides an option to uncertainty. Certainly hope is more of a mood booster than cynicism or despair, even if the hope is "blind." If one is unable to live without hope, then embrace it. Ethics, at least ethics in the sense of a moral code, makes right behavior less of an internal struggle and more of an easy rule to follow. For some individuals, unexplained phenomena are disturbing, so having a ready explanation eases the burden and permits happiness. Why do bad things happen to good people? For me, it is usually a matter of chance. For others, chance is disturbing, so they look to religion for resolution. Finally, myth. Jesus, Mohammad, Buddha, Mother Teresa, and Martin Luther King, Jr., were all people with their respective lives comprised of facts. Over time, people have elevated the lives of these five to include more than fact. When facts fade and give way to the accentuated aspects of a popular character, that character has become mythical. In its extreme form, myth refers to characters such as Zeus or the Hindu monkey god Hanuman. Whether or not these characters ever existed is unimportant—it is their qualities that we embrace. The myths that are core to a religion are another reason that religion is associated with happiness—they emphasize eternal verities and not facts like needing a bath or stealing a melon. Embracing myth is another move from uncertainty to certainty, and rounds out the four elements of religion that help explain why people of faith tend to be happier, even if not always wise or intelligent.

Graham (2010) and Bok (2010) both describe the co-occurrence of higher levels of religious activity and higher levels of happiness. Not only do countries with greater degrees of participation in religion (as in attendance at services and other events) report higher happiness levels, but the happiness levels of non-religious persons in those same countries appear to be higher as well. Whether one measures "religion" as practice (e.g., attendance) or as belief (e.g., degree of expressed faith, independent of attendance), the relationship holds. Graham (2010, loc. 1736) notes that, while Protestants and Catholics each are happier when they live in an area where their religion is dominant, Protestants are happier when in the minority, than Catholics are when they are in the minority. Could this be explained by the doctrine of original sin and the practice of confession, such that being in the majority boosts happiness because of the "misery loves company" phenomenon, while being in the minority provides the conscientious Catholic with fewer to commiserate on the human condition from their point of view, hence less camaraderie, which we have seen is an important influence on happiness levels?

Graham (2010, loc. 1732) cites a study by Andrew Clark and Orsolya Lelkes (2009) that surveyed 90,000 persons from 26 countries in Europe. They attempted to differentiate between the effects of belonging to a religion/religiosity on the one hand and having social networks on the other. They found a separate effect for religiosity, with degree of religiosity in a region positively affecting happiness levels, even for the nonreligious. Moreover, they found that where the proportion of atheists in a region increased, the happiness levels decreased accordingly, even for the religious.

One needs to be cautious in interpreting these findings: Are Happers the ones who tend to be more religious? If so, then measuring happiness of the religious is a biased sample. I have seen no data that indicates whether people who describe themselves as more religious have a trait profile that is different from the populace at large. One possible explanation of the higher happiness levels reported among the religious is that the religious are typically encouraged to trust, have faith, and have hope, rather than to think deeply for more rational explanations of disturbing phenomena. "God works in mysterious ways" is a preventive palliative for the souls disturbed by events. To accept on faith and discontinue asking why can certainly be a mood booster. The individual must pay and accept the price of discontinued questioning.

A recent study has clarified some of the mysterious relationship between religiosity and well-being. (Diener, Tay, and Myers, 2011) Using U.S. and world Gallup data for hundreds of thousands of people, they formed three conclusions:

- Nations with adverse living conditions (poverty, famine, short life span, war) tend to exhibit more religiosity, and within those nations, persons practicing religion exhibited greater well-being than non-religious persons. The authors attributed this to greater social support under adverse conditions.
- Nations with favorable living conditions tend to exhibit less religiosity, and within those nations, persons who are more religious show similar levels of well-being in comparison to persons who are less religious. The authors interpret this to mean than favorable living conditions offer greater support for all individuals.
- Persons who report themselves to be more religious tend to have greater well-being in more religious countries than do less religious persons in those countries, but self-proclaimed religious persons in less religious countries show levels of well-being that are no different than levels for non-religious persons. The authors interpret call this a person-culture fit issue, whereby living in a culture whose values match your own provides a boost in well-being.

Self-employment. Persons who start and continue their own business have plenty of stress and disappointment, but the overall effect of being self-employed is mood boosting. One reason is that stress occurs when one feels unable to control something that is getting in their way. This is more likely to occur when one is employed by others than when one is employed by oneself. The feeling of having some control over a situation, of having options to deal with what life throws your way, is the best preventive for stress. When you know that you have options if things get too bad, then things just don't bother you as much. See discussion below on Downers/Circumstance/Stress.

Sex. An active sex life is an unarguable boon. Of course, what is active for one person may be overactive for another, or underactive for yet another. Hopefully, one's partner's needs are similar to one's own. Otherwise, stress. If I am more active than my partner, then I must take things in hand, lest I become resentful. If I am less active than my partner, then I must negotiate lest I become resentful.

Shopping. Yes, shopping is a mood-booster. For some. Never has been for me. It is a chore. I remember being floored when I asked a group of adult students how often they went shopping. Over half the group said they went shopping at least once a day, and often several times a day! Imagine that. Recall that spending for others and for experiences boosts mood more than spending for self. An unnecessary pair of shoes will bring less joy over time than an item bought for a family member or for a family/friends experience—maybe a new camping gadget.

Socializing. Kahneman (2006) found that socializing with friends after work is associated with higher levels of well-being. For maximum effect, this socializing would not include passive activities such as watching television or a sports event, but something active that in fact serves to build relationships, whether playing a sport together or conversing while dining out and/or going for a walk.

Spending for experiences. Achor (2010) points out that spending money on experiences is better than spending money on stuff (see earlier discussion of "New whatsit" under Myths). Research shows that people's boosts in mood as the result of positive experiences are both more intense and longer lasting than their mood boosts from acquiring new stuff. Some examples would include:

Experiences:	Stuff Alone:
picnic	new chair
family vacation	new car
bowling league	new suit of clothes
going camping	pay someone to build a new patio
dinner party	new entertainment center
building a Habitat for Humanity home	new dining room table
singing in a choral group	new wind chimes for the yard

Research on this kind of "calculated buying" involving experiences is being conducted by psychology professor Elizabeth Dunn of the University of British Columbia. She lamented when interviewed for an article in *The New York Times* (August 8, 2010) that too much research is done on income levels and happiness, and not enough on the way people spend their income. She summarizes her research by quipping, "It's better to go on a vacation than buy a new couch is basically the idea." A recent publication by Daniel T. Gilbert (Harvard University) and Timothy D. Wilson (University of Virginia) had the thoughtful title "If Money Doesn't Make You Happy Then You Probably Aren't Spending It Right." (available online at http://dunn.psych.ubc.ca/files/2011/04/Journal-of-consumer-psychology.pdf)

The University of Colorado at Boulder's Leaf Van Boven (2005) offers three reasons for the superiority of spending on experiences versus spending on things:

- **Experiences age better than possessions.** An early childhood school experience, a memory of a poignant moment with grandparents, a camping adventure, a summer camp caper, a vacation at the Grand Canyon, a family reunion in the mountains—all these memories wear well, embellished here, deleted there, becoming the lore that we love to retell time and again. The sofa just sits there in need of dusting. Hmmm, there's a way to make an experience out of a possession in disrepair—involve the family or friends in reupholstering the sofa!
- **Experiences stand on their own uniqueness and are thus difficult to compare.** At the end of this chapter, we discuss the tendency of people to engage in *social comparison*, in which, for example, one compares what one owns to what others have. If others have more than we do, that is a downer, and we want more. If others have less, we are more comforted. Solnick and Hemenway (1998) found that people generally would prefer making $50,000 when other acquaintances are making $25,000, than make twice as much (e.g., $100,000) when their acquaintances are making twice again as much as them ($200,000). Experiences tend to resist such comparison. While one

might say dejectedly that "you did more with your vacation time than I did—I squandered it," it is also possible, and easier to say, and feel good about it, that "you got more reading done on your vacation, and I got more time getting to know my grandkids—both sound good; maybe we'll swap emphases next time!" In other words, it is easier and more natural to get competitive about material things than about experiences

- **Experiences build more social capital.** By their very nature, experiences build relationships (unless you have them alone!). In addition, to talk of one's experiences is usually less off-putting than to talk of one's possessions.

Research professors Thomas DeLeire of the University of Wisconsin in Madison and Ariel Kalil of the University of Chicago have analyzed nine categories of consumer spending to determine which categories relate to happiness levels. Their data came from the National Institute of Aging's U.S. Health and Retirement Study, a 20-year longitudinal project that followed some 20,000 Americans over the age of 50. The final cross-sectional sample comprised 937 individuals, as not everyone in the larger sample completed the supplementary questionnaires. These are the nine spending categories:

- Leisure—trips, vacations (including "staycations"), exercise, spectator events, hobbies, equipment for leisure;
- Durables—appliances, vehicles;
- Charity and Gifts;
- Personal Care and Clothing—plus housekeeping, yard maintenance, laundry;
- Health Care—health insurance, medications, supplies, visits;
- Food In—purchased to prepare and consume at home (including alcohol);
- Food Out—purchased at a restaurant/bar, including takeout;
- Utilities and Housing—plus house furnishings, home repair home insurance;
- Vehicles—vehicle insurance, maintenance, payments.

Only two of the nine showed a significant association with happiness: leisure and vehicles. The researchers point out that both are related to experiences and to social connectedness, while the others are related more to one's material possessions. In fact, they estimated that spending $20,000 for leisure is associated with the same happiness increase as that associated with getting married.

Gene Cohen, founder of the Center on Aging of the National Institute of Mental Health, concludes (cited in Brooks, 2011, loc. 6170) that the length of time committed to an experience is a major determinant of the experience's impact on happiness. And it is not just length, but the way the experience develops over time. For example, to play with one rock band this weekend, another the following weekend, and so on playing for a different rock band every weekend, Cohen would propose that playing with the same rock band every weekend over the same time frame would be more satisfying. So it is duration of the experience *plus* developing relationship during the experience that elevates mood. Fewer one-night stands, more affairs of the heart, mind, body, or soul.

But what about Charity and Gifts? If other research shows that altruism is positively related to happiness, why is that not reflected here? The answer would be that you have to give more than money to others in order to get the happiness benefit. You can't buy your happiness by just giving money: You have to give time and energy—what we often call "sweat equity." Chapter 9 has more details on charity.

Spending on equipment for experiences. The exception to the rule for the preceding booster is that stuff bought and actually used in experiences provides more of a boost than stuff that does not become part of experiences. So, in the list above, if the new patio is actively used for experiences with family and/or friends, then the patio has more mood value than one that is built and seldom used. In addition to stuff that is used for experiences, if those experiences are with others and amount to developing and enriching relationships, then all the better.

Spending on others. Bok (2010) mentions an experiment in which subjects were given the option of spending money on themselves or giving it away to others. A few days after the experiment, happiness levels were higher for those who gave their money to others.

Taking a walk. Brisk walking for periods of 20-30 minutes raises endorphin levels and oxygenates the blood (especially if you walk outdoors). Both effects heighten alertness and mood. If you walk with someone else, you develop a relationship. If you walk with an iPod or Walkman, you can "read" or listen to music. I walk with either my wife or my iPod or (if it's news time) my radio. I eagerly await the next alone walk so I can listen to WNYC's Radiolab. I eagerly await the next walk with Jane so I can develop the relationship. Outside.

Touch. Dacher Keltner (2009) writes convincingly of the power of touch to heighten positive mood in both toucher and touchee. Physiologically, touch lowers activity in the amygdala (seat of negative emotions), increases activity in the orbitofrontal cortex (associated with empathy, emotional recognition, social understanding, and inhibition of impulsive responses), reduction of the stress response (measured by decreased cortisol production), and increased levels of oxytocin (associated with heightened trust), serotonin (relaxation), and endorphins (pleasure). (loc. 3078) The reward circuitry activated by touch is equal to that activated by chocolate or "the scent of Mother to an infant." (loc. 3075) The satisfaction associated with touching extends to being touched by pleasing nonhuman textures, such as velvet, silk, fine sand, and the like.

Whether a passing touch or a prolonged massage, touching boosts the mood of both parties. Seniors touching infants or pets report improved mood. Students casually touched by librarians report a more positive attitude toward their library. Students receiving casual pats on the back by their teachers volunteer comments in class at twice the rate of the untouched. Patients touched in a friendly manner by their physician feel that their visit was twice as long as it actually was. Patients receiving fMRI scans while their romantic partner was touching their arm showed no brain activation in response to the stressful burst of noise, while unaccompanied, untouched patients did. Keltner quips that "touch turned off the threat switch in the brain." Premature babies receiving massages average 47% greater weight gain than unmassaged preemies. Infants held by their mothers during painful medical procedures such as lancing cry 82% less, grimace 65 % less and record slower heartbeats than infants simply lying in an examination bed. Touch boosts the mood of depressed teen moms, as well as autistic, asthmatic, and diabetic children, and as well as the infirm in general. Keltner calls each of these acts of touching "the original contact high." (locs. 3112, 3136, 3348)

All of this is based on wanted touching, not on the kind of touching associated with sexual abuse. How does one define the threshold for acceptable and unacceptable touching? This question concerned Dudley Flood, a representative of the North Carolina State Department of Public Instruction staffer who travelled the state back in the 1960s in order to conduct human relations workshops for faculty and students during the stressful times of racial integration. Flood, knowing that touch is necessary for relationship building, addressed the issue humorously but accurately by saying that it is acceptable to touch the "hard" places above the waist, such as elbow, shoulder, and top of the head. Stray from there and, unless you're with a romantic partner, you're in unwanted touch territory. Certainly some societies encourage touching more than others. Keltner describes a study by the University of Florida's Sidney Jourard in which pairs conversing and sipping coffee in cafés around the world were observed for incidents of touching: London, zero; Florida, two; Paris, 110; San Juan, Puerto Rico, 180! (loc. 3337)

Transcranial magnetic stimulation (TMS). A new tool in the therapist's toolbox is manufactured by Neuronetics in Philadelphia. TMS is a refinement of what used to be known as electroshock, or electroconvulsive therapy. With 30 sessions over a month and a half, patients report substantial mood improvement without the side effects of pharmaceuticals or older electroshock methods. The patient remains fully alert during the 40 minutes of stimulation, and may read, watch TV, and so forth. Approved in 2008 by the FDA, the cost is approximately $8,000. With increased demand and good results, perhaps insurance companies will soon cover it.

Volunteering. Chapter 9 will develop the larger theme of altruism more fully. Suffice it to say here that volunteering is a major source of heightened well-being. So much so, that secondary schools, colleges, and universities around the country have developed "service learning" curricula (see more at the National Service Learning Clearinghouse: http://www.servicelearning.org/). Whether helping an elementary school teacher by reading to young learners or helping a crew build a Habitat for Humanity house, volunteering boosts mood. But it needs to repeated. The effect wears off and must be renewed. That is a good thing, right? Also, research (Lyubomirsky, 2008) suggests that you vary the way in which you volunteer in order to get the maximum boost. Volunteering is similar to charitable acts. Charity suggests activity for those in need (as in Big Brothers). Volunteering suggests working without pay (as in a political campaign). Either is satisfying, and both are to be encouraged.

 **Circumstance:**

Aging (approaching seniority). A major study by Andrew Oswald of Warwick University, England, and David Blanchflower of Dartmouth College, U.S., has identified a U-shaped curve that describes the effect of aging on reported levels of happiness. After scanning data on more than two million subjects from 80 countries, they found that happiness decreased into middle age and increased into seniority.

Globally, the reported low point is 48 years of age, with individual countries ranging from 36 in England, 53 in the U.S., and 65 in Portugal. Exceptions to this rule were a half dozen or so developing countries, where graying was not mood lifting. Also, the pattern held true regardless of sex, marital status, income level, or number of children (including zero). Several explanations have been offered:

- the natural tendency to be self-critical during midlife;
- peaks in the complexity of one's life with gradual simplifying;
- the reduction of one's options with its accompanying sense of relief;
- the sense of running out of time in middle age, combined with coming to peace with accomplishments in later decades;
- as we age we do not hold onto our regrets so long as we did earlier
- downward comparisons—beginning to see others dying off and appreciating one's relative health;
- developing a sense of one's legacy to the next generation.

> "How pleasant is the day when we give up striving to be young—or slender."
> --William James

In a related study, the University of Chicago sociologist Yang found that folks in their 80s were twice as likely to engage in a weekly social activity as those in their 50s. This underscores the importance of forming and maintaining high-quality relationships. Moreover, brain scans conducted by MIT's John Gabrielli reveal that seniors' amygdalas fire freely when exposed to positive pictures but shut down when viewing negative ones—apparently we learn to turn a cold shoulder to misery as we age. Not necessarily denial, rather a choice to not let it disturb us for the most part. (Brooks, 2011, loc. 5964)

Beauty. Called by many the "dean of beauty," University of Texas at Austin's Daniel Hamermesh has defined the relationship between beauty, income, and happiness. (Hamermesh & Abrevaya, 2011) Studying 25,000 citizens in the U.S., Canada, Germany, and the U.K. over 40 years, Hamermesh concluded that the top 15% as rated by beauty were 10% happier than individuals rated in the bottom 10%. At least half of this effect can be accounted for by the added earning potential of the beautiful. The effect is true for both sexes, but stronger for women than for men. Beauty gets you more money, a more beautiful mate (who also greater earning potential), and more happiness. Beauty is defined mostly by facial symmetry, with clothing, cosmetics, and hair treatments having minimal impact.

Democracy. This is a complex one: People who express a preference for democracy tend to be happier than people who express a preference for non-democratic forms of government. In addition, as seen elsewhere in this chapter, the quality of one's democracy makes a difference. So, wanting a democracy, having one, having an efficient one, having a responsive one, having a trusted one, and having a respected one relatively free of corruption and moral turpitude—each aspect of democracy contributes to one's positive mood. (Graham, 2010) Derek Bok (2010) points out that most of the countries who rank highest in happiness levels have had effective democracies for over eight decades.
In a recent nationwide experiment in changing from an undemocratic form of government to a democratic form, the percentage of residents of former East Germany who reported the lowest level of happiness dropped from 28 to 15, while the percentage of those reporting in as happy increased from 38 to 54.19. (Bok, 2010, loc. 908)

Employment. Most surveys show that the majority of employed persons would change jobs if they could. We think that is largely a matter of a poor fit between the characteristics of the worker and the demands of the work. An example of poor fit would be a creative person doing repetitive work, or a sedentary person doing door-to-door sales. This issue is probed in depth in Chapter 6. Meanwhile, being employed is in-and-of-itself satisfying. Better to have a job than the alternative. But employment's boost to well-being is amplified when other factors play their part: trust in management, meaningful work, agreeable coworkers, sense of status, sufficient personal freedom, capable and fair supervisors, and environmental conditions.

Environmental conditions. Brooks (2011) writes correctly that "researchers have found, not surprisingly, that sunlight and natural scenes can have a profound effect on mind and mood." (loc. 6396) Let's get specific: sunlight and fresh air. Being deprived of natural sunlight is depressing. Residents of extreme latitudes suffer a higher incidence of depression during winter months than is typical of other zones. Same goes for persons who reside on the western edge of their time zone, as they experience proportionately less sunlight during their day than do their eastern edge counterparts. Jimmy lives in Atlantic City and sees the sun at 7:00 a.m., while cousin Fran in Indianapolis, also in the Eastern time zone, doesn't see the sun until almost 8:00 a.m., thus experiencing almost one hour of darkness more while trying to shake off the doldrums and get alert for work. However, Ling Ling in Chicago, just over the border into the Central zone, gets the same extra hour that Jimmy gets in Atlantic City, as the clock jumps back to 7:00 a.m. in Illinois just as Indiana hits 8:00 a.m. Same goes for night shift workers who struggle to keep alert when getting no sunlight.

What's it with sunlight? The presence of natural sunlight, whether one is blind or sighted, tells the pineal gland to stop producing melatonin, the sleep neurotransmitter, and allow a person to become awake, alert, chipper. In the absence of sunlight, as in night shift, or in working days in an office building with no external windows nearby, one may use indoor lamps with a CRI (color rendering index) rating of 90 or higher and get the same melatonin shutdown available in natural sunlight. Lamps with a CRI less than 90 will be missing at least the blue area of the spectrum and will not shut down melatonin production. Not a believer yet? How's this: A study in Milan found that patients suffering from bipolar depression who were in hospital beds with eastern exposures on average left the hospital 3½ days earlier than those with western exposures, which received less sunlight!

How about air? Alertness is the handmaiden of positive mood, and drowsiness the harbinger of negative. Alertness is partially dependent on the availability of natural sunlight, or its equivalent, and also dependent on the presence of abundant negative ions in the atmosphere. Why? The brain needs oxygen in the bloodstream in order to burn glucose for energy. The less oxygenated your blood, the less alert and the poorer your mood. Negative ions have the quality of attaching themselves to particulates in the air around you and escorting these particulates to the ground/floor. This purifies the air you breathe, with the result that you take in proportionately more oxygen with each breath.

So what's the problem here? Air conditioning. It depletes the air of negative ions. Hence, one is likely to have less oxygenated blood when living or working in air conditioning for long periods. Three remedies are available: either pop outdoors from time to time for a hit of fresh air, open your windows, or purchase an ion generator either for your room or for your building's air handling system. Do not

61

confuse ion generators with ozone generators, which may produce harmful levels of ozone. The fact that people who live close to nature (as opposed to in the city) perform higher on assessments of focus and memory (Brooks, 2011, loc. 6408) should close the book on this case!

Feeling safe. Safety comes in different modes: feeling psychologically safe (i.e., free from verbal abuse), feeling physically safe (i.e., free from physical abuse and aggression), and behaviorally safe (i.e., free to make appropriate errors). When others condemn you at the slightest error, when they ridicule you for being who you are, and when they use you as a punching bag, it would be understandable if you were to withdraw into a cocoon-like ball and seldom venture out into society. In the absence of feeling safe, one would feel constrained to always "play it safe." Such a way of life is the opposite of well-being. One must feel safe in all three ways in order to embrace goals and pursue them.

Financial freedom. Wealthy, highly developed countries tend to value a different kind of freedom from poorer, less developed countries. (Bok, 2010) The former value personal freedom while the latter value economic freedom. Where jobs are scarce and income inadequate, greater value is placed on the freedom to be entrepreneurial than on governmental constraints on social behaviors such as abortion, euthanasia, and terrorism. I am reminded of the euphoria in Russia when the hated ban on entrepreneurial activity was lifted during *perestroika*, with the people taking to the streets with anything of value to bring in cash—clothing, eggs, jewelry, books, furniture. Scenes of this new financial freedom are particularly poignant in volume two of the economic documentary film *Commanding Heights* (2002). Today in Mexico, cash is scarce for many, and thousands of street vendors offer colorful allure to get your attention (and pesos).

Government efficiency. Regularity of payments, dependability of schedules, quality of services, and speed of delivery are associated with citizens' happiness levels, as government does its part in making life less stressful. Bok (2010) writes that "how government functions and how citizens think it functions have significant effects on their well-being."

Government responsiveness. When citizens perceive that government officials turn a deaf ear to their requests for assistance, whether for needs pertaining to safety, health, education, transportation, documentation, or other areas, then its citizens veer towards hopelessness or anger. On the other hand, when government attempts to respond promptly to appropriate requests from individuals, the people's fears are allayed, their anger calmed, their despair abated, and sighs of relief abound. The Arab Spring, the tidal wave of social unrest in 2011, showed what happens when, over time, government fails to respond to citizens' needs. Promises, promises, say the people, as they topple first one, then two, then several arrogant tyrants from power for their history of disregard for the needs of the people. While tyrants topple, nearby kingdoms scurry for ways to improve their image by providing long awaited concessions, lest they topple too.

Government trustworthiness. Trust is bimodal—to be trusted one must be both good and reliable. You may trust me to do the right thing, but you may distrust me to do it in a timely manner. You may trust me to do what I say in a timely manner, but you may not trust me to say the right things. This dual aspect of trust is reflected in the New Testament lament of Paul: "The good I would I do not, and the ill I would not I do." A trusted government does the right things in a dependable manner. Fairness and reliability. Do the right thing, and do it now. Bok (2010) mentions that the peoples' trust of police is more impactful on well-being than their trust of the remainder of government, but both are important.

Law-abiding/Law enforcement. Whether or not a society supports the rule of law is a specific instance of government trustworthiness, efficiency, and responsiveness. Knowledge that adequate laws are in place, coupled with adequate enforcement of these laws, constitutes the rule of law. The certainty that, when new laws are needed, government will be sufficiently responsive to enact them, completes the rule of law. Sounds simple. However, not all citizens want the same laws. While most people abhor rape, torture, theft, and murder, people are more divided on euthanasia and abortion. Some feel that Kevorkian and Planned Parenthood violate the rule of law, and some feel that they represent attempts to expand the law. Laws reflect culture, and not all aspects of culture are consistent within that culture. The tension between the degree to which one is protected by law and the degree to which one needs greater protection will never go away. But the knowledge that one can be heard, that one can debate, provides some comfort.

Minimal corruption/violence. Happy campers lose their buzz when mugged, robbed, or expected to pay bribes. Universally. However, the effect is greater when the prevalence of corruption and violence is not consistently spread throughout a culture. Bok (2010) observes that happiness levels are less affected by violence and corruption if the two are widely prevalent. However, happiness levels are more severely decreased in cultures violence and corruption are more random. It is as though people adapt to violence and corruption when it is widespread and unavoidable. Also, when everyone is a victim, there is no loss of face. When muggings abound, victims have less shame. Misery has company. As Carol Graham (2010) puts it, "victimization will affect you less both because of lower stigma and because you have already adapted to the increased likelihood that you will be a crime victim." (loc. 1856) Graham calls this the "adaptation hypothesis." People get used to widespread crime and, for quite some time, make their peace with it. She thinks this explains much of what has happened in Afghanistan and explains the difficulty encountered in nation building there. In such countries where the people have adapted to higher crime levels, their happiness levels are not affected. However, the well-being of the country as a whole is clearly at risk. In time, as witnessed with the Arab Spring of 2011, adaptation gives way to aspirations for a higher quality of life.

Personal freedom. Wealthy, highly developed countries tend to value a different kind of freedom from poorer, less developed countries. (Bok, 2010) The former value personal freedom while the latter value economic freedom. Where jobs are relatively plentiful and one is free to start a business if one likes, personal freedom rises in importance, with economic freedom assumed. Hence, in the U.S. people get more worked up over abortion rights, voting rights, health care reform, euthanasia, and censorship than over job creation and opportunity, income inequality, and taxation. In a meta-analysis of well-being studies across 63 nations, Ronald Fischer and Diana Boer (2011) of Victoria University of Wellington report that individual freedom is much more closely linked to happiness than income level, but that income is a way of acquiring personal freedom. The principle value of increased income, they maintain, is that it enables greater personal freedom and expression of individualism.

Nonetheless, when considering freedom in its broadest sense, citizens' happiness rise as their perceived freedom of their homeland rises. (Helliwell & Barrington-Leigh, 2010) Again, whether talking about personal or financial freedom, Graham (2010, loc. 1750) points out that freedom seems to matter more to the happiness of those who have come to expect it than to those who do not. I suppose this is why child psychologists say that it is easier to back away from discipline than to increase it—it is easier to go easy than to get tough, for as people get used to their freedom they don't like it encroached on.

It should be noted that personal freedom includes the freedom to submit oneself to a circumstance in which freedom is mostly surrendered. Joining the Marines or taking holy orders come to mind. However, the virtue of personal freedom is that even though one might voluntarily give up one's freedom, one is also able to reclaim one's freedom in the future. Throughout Ibsen's play *A Doll's House,* Nora submits to the will of her husband Torvald, only to walk to her freedom at the end.

Retirement. For most people, assuming that financial security exists for them, retirement is welcome and emotionally satisfying. Apart from the need to be free of financial worry, the well-being experienced during retirement is enhanced by spending time with friends and family, by deeds of altruism and service, and by having experiences. Also, if one wishes, one can continue one's life work but on their own terms. Research has shown that people who continue to take on new challenges in retirement tend to be happier and to maintain better emotional and mental acuity.

Status increase. The boosts provided by elevations in status are not just for well-being: Higher status individuals live longer! Derek Bok (2010) reports on a study of Oscar nominees (best actor/actress, and so forth) in which winners outlived the merely nominated an average of four years, "a curious fact that cannot be explained by differences in income." (loc. 1438) Bok mentions another status study, this one conducted by Michael Marmot on British public officials. Higher-level managers outlived lower level managers by a wide margin. However, all the officials had plenty of income and the benefit of the British health care system.

Studies cited by Carol Graham (2010, loc. 1408) have shown that the emotional boost from the typical status increase lasts five years, which is five times longer than the boost from the typical salary increase. Status increases would include, but be limited to, promotions, awards, new titles, and completion of degrees, certificates, and licenses. Some joke that, with a Ph.D., one can present it at Starbucks and get a latte for $5 (or whatever the regular price is). While status increases do not always entail monetary increases, they almost always increase one's self-esteem. That is not the same thing as happiness, but is a close cousin.

Note: I have placed "Status" here in the "Circumstance" section, as status-boosting outcomes are more often within the control of others, not of oneself. However, I do certainly acknowledge that one's effort and talent certainly influence others' decisions to reward us with status-boosting acts. Ultimately, most status decisions are controlled by others. I am aware of several exceptions, such as purchasing a "paper" diploma (last time I looked, a Ph.D. from one paper diploma mill cost $1,000 with no requirements other than a check that doesn't bounce). Another exception is giving oneself a new and better sounding title (say, from sales rep to vice-president for sales—I know someone who did that!). These false-status pranks perhaps work OK until someone starts probing. I questioned a guy once who introduced himself as vice-president of sales for XYZ, Inc. In a friendly but curious manner, I asked how many reps he had working for him. He looked down and mumbled, "Just me. But we plan to grow the department." The company only had three people: president, vice-president, and operator. It lasted less than a year. In such cases, less insult to self-esteem might come from introducing oneself as "in sales," handing out the card at some point, but not vocally calling oneself "vice-president." If it is ever questioned, one can just say that's the way the company printed it, or some such.

I once extended a job offer to someone with a Ph.D. Before welcoming him onboard, I decided to check the authenticity of his diploma, only to find that it was "granted" by a diploma mill in the UK. The British government had shut it down and was requesting all diplomas pointing to it be reported so that the mill owner could be deported and prosecuted. Needless to say, I had to withdraw the job offer.

Temperate climate. What's there to complain about if it's never too hot and never too cold and never too rainy and never too arid? But where is such a place? And is there room for everyone there? The technology of winemaking is such that there is little excuse these days for not making an excellent bottle of wine. The same goes for climate. The technology of climate control is such that there is little excuse these days for not having an agreeable climate. I suspect that much of the impact of climate on mood is related to what one grew up with and has become accustomed to. I grew up in the muggy heat of eastern North Carolina and muggy heat doesn't bother me—I feel right at home in it. That is not to say, however, that my optimal climate is not temperate—ah, the bliss of a cool breeze in the shade of the big oak tree!

Tolerance of minorities. Bok (2010, loc. 451) notes that a World Values study identified tolerance of minorities as a boon to happiness levels, both for the minorities within a country as well as the remainder of the citizenry. This relationship holds regardless of how "minority" is defined—ethnicity, faith, sex, sexual orientation, age, language, and so forth.

Trust. Trust is both a learned and an inherited characteristic. One can be born with higher or lower levels of trust. We are finding that levels of chemicals such as oxytocin and vasopressin are associated with the natural tendency to trust. When families dine together, oxytocin levels rise. When one touches another in appropriate ways, oxytocin rises. When two people "do lunch," oxytocin levels rise. When parents ignore their infants through inadequate touch and caressing, oxytocin levels fall. To a small degree, lost trust can be regained by progressive acts of intimacy, contrition, and right behavior.

But trust in others is not the only form of trust that is associated with higher happiness. Graham (2010, loc. 1754) points out that happiness is positively affected by the rising degree one trusts both the government of one's country and political organizations such as the European Union, the United Nations, and the International Monetary Fund (I write this as its head has been charged with raping a hotel employee).

In Chapter 8, I will address the issue of trust in relationships.

Trust in management. Bok (2010) relates that research by John Helliwell, Haifang Huang, and Robert Putnam has identified trust in one's managers as the feature of work that has the strongest effect on one's reported happiness, much more so than one's pay level. Perhaps this is because if one trusts one's manager, one trusts that appropriate pay will be forthcoming.

Trust in public officials. Bok (2010) found that U.S. citizens report significantly less trust in their politicos than do countries that score higher on happiness scales—countries such as Switzerland, the Netherlands, and Denmark. He further speculates that Americans' distrust in political leaders likely accounts for much of the country's lower happiness scores, especially in light of it being one of the most well-to-do.

Happiness Downers—What is Known to Decrease Happiness

The 29 downers are also divided into two groups: more a matter of circumstance and more a matter of personal choice. Ten are matters of choice, while 19 are matters of circumstance. For some of these, their category is arbitrary, as they are both circumstantial and subject to personal choice. An example is alcohol excess: Genetic factors can predispose one towards alcoholism, but one can also exercise choice over what to do about it. The same is true for hormone fluctuation—certainly a circumstance, but one over which one does have some choices, such as medication, exercise, diet, and psychotherapy.

 Choice:

- Alcohol abstinence
- Alcohol excess
- Commuting
- Deep thinking
- Envy
- Graduate educational level
- Holding onto lost goals
- Isolation
- Mind-wandering
- Personal grooming

 Circumstance:

- Aging (approaching middle age)
- Anticipation of bad stuff
- Being Female
- Betrayal of trust
- Chronic Pain
- Disaster
- Divorce/Separation
- Extrinsic rewards for non-algorithmic tasks
- Hormone fluctuation
- Job loss
- Lack of control
- Loss of a loved one
- Mental illness
- Neurotoxins
- Noise
- Poverty
- Sleep disorders
- Stressors
- Working

Choice:

Alcohol abstinence. (See "Alcohol moderation" above under Boosters/Choice.) Persons who say that they abstain from consuming alcohol report lower levels of happiness than those who say they consume moderate amounts. (Graham, 2010, loc. 1035) Three primary classes of folks abstain: those who have never developed a taste for alcohol or its effects, those who refrain for religious or other values-based reasons, and those who are alcoholic and must refrain or suffer a relapse. In all three groups, abstinence could serve as a constraint on making new and meaningful relationships, as well as a constraint on developing existing relationships. I remember I once experimented with vegetarianism, alcohol abstinence, and caffeine abstinence as the result of reading a biography of Leo Tolstoy (who submitted to that regimen in midlife). During this phase, I went to a party comprised mostly of fellow educators. An assistant superintendent nudged me and said, looking at my glass of ice and amber liquid, "Whatcha drinkin'?" Me: "Iced tea." Well, this guy I had known for some years, and he knew that I enjoyed a toddy or three. He challenged me with "Why? Taking antibiotics or something?" I uncomfortably explained that I was experimenting with Tolstoy's way of life, so abstaining. He snorted, "Hmpf! You think you're better than the rest of us, huh?" Even though he smiled as he said it, I felt somewhat caught, even shamed. I said, "Nah," and immediately moseyed over to the bar and replaced one amber with another amber of a different molecular structure. The rest is history. Social history. ;-) On the flip side, abstinence could enhance developing a relationship with a 12-step or other values-based group or individual who value abstinence.

Alcohol excess. Excessive alcohol consumption is not the best relationship builder, nor is it the best builder of self-esteem. I recall a professor from my graduate school days who was an alcoholic. He had a harpsichord and played it well. He and I joined a cellist and a violinist once every other week to play 18th century chamber music. The evening went like this: For about an hour and a half, we played while the harpsichordist drank bourbon (there's that amber again) nonstop, taking a sip at the end of every line, as it were. The rest of us took sips at the end of every movement. After this first 90 minutes, the harpsichordist passed out. The three remaining played music that did not require keyboard, and allowed the dozing ivorist to be a silent audience. Had he not passed out, alcoholic or not, his behavior would have become aberrant in a way not conducive to relationship development and, hence, happiness: slurred speech, impaired memory, uninhibited language and gestures, domineering conversation (or its opposite, withdrawal), and such. Nor is this intoxicated state conducive to thinking well of oneself. Feelings of remorse, shame, guilt, regret, and embarrassment are not associated with happiness or well-being or whatever we name it. Not everyone suffers who over-imbibes, but more do than don't, enough to make their mean happiness level lower than that of others.

Commuting. Swiss economists Bruno Frey and Alois Stutzer (2008), who also conducted research mentioned earlier on political involvement, examined levels of happiness associated with commuting. They set out to examine what they called the "balance" hypothesis, whereby the supposed advantages of higher pay and more desirable residential areas offset the negative effects of commuting. However, this was not the case. Commuting, even when done so for strong advantages, was consistently associated with lower levels of well-being. One pays an emotional price for commuting for whatever the reason. Certainly one can offset some of these negative effects by one or more of various means: finding carpool companions who are stimulating conversationalists or even friends, listening to music or recorded books, and the like.

Deep thinking. To engage in deep thinking is to attempt to understand the world as accurately as possible. There is simply no way to think deeply without dwelling on both the pleasing and the disturbing. To think deeply is to understand the joys of romance as well as the seeming hopelessness of eradicating terrorism, madness, greed, and their cousins. Deep thinking is inimical to optimism. In order to maintain optimism, one must think shallowly and narrowly, ignoring the details that do not please. To be self-deceived is to ignore one's limitations and to take on the world. That is why people who pursue university training beyond the bachelor's level are less happy than those who stop with their four-year degree. Advanced education requires deep thinking: surveys of the literature, identifying weaknesses or limitations of one's own research, submitting to the rigors of scientific method, adhering to the findings of researchers before us, and so on. To conduct a research project and to have to write it up, closing with a section called "Limitations of This Study" is not happiness-inducing. To be a graduate student is to embrace self-criticism, not self-deception. To be a career scholar is to live the life of the critic, finding fault (as well as credit, of course) with students' work, with colleagues' work, and with one's own work. Kruger & Dunning (1995) reported that the most gifted in their field—surgeons, athletes, writers, business leaders—have an acute sense of their errors and inadequacies, and they are plagued by playing Monday-morning quarterback to most everything that they do. They have a nagging sense that they could always have done better. Meanwhile, people who perform one level lower than these most gifted, in other words, people who are merely very good, tend to be clueless as to their inadequacies and are characterized by supreme satisfaction with how things are going. It is the difference in noble discontent and conceited content, of Brett Favre and Terrell Owens.

Envy. Not included as one of the seven deadly sins for nothing! In the 1496 engraving by Frenchman Nicholas le Rouge, the envious suffer in hell by submersing their heated jealous passion in freezing waters. I wrote earlier about spending money for an item for its own sake, which is associated with higher well-being, versus spending money for an item in order to have something equal to or better than what one's neighbor (or other acquaintance) has. To want what others have is envy. One can never have what others have: their spouse, their yard, their car, their reputation. So to be envious is a losing battle. Want what you have, and you have what you want. The ability to feel gratitude for what one is and has is the core skill for fighting envy. More in Chapter 9 on altruism.

Graduate educational level. See Downers/Choice/Thinking deeply. The bottom line: The more education one has beyond an undergraduate degree, the more sees the faults in self, others, and the world. This takes a significant toll on happiness levels.

Holding onto lost goals. Laura King and Joshua Hicks of the University of Missouri—Columbia (2007) write that the mature personality—not necessarily the *happy* personality mind you—is able to let go of lost opportunities, of missed goals. Cut bait, close up shop, call it quits, cut your losses, and move on. Those who continue to pursue, or to grieve over, lost causes are doomed to a continuing assault on one's level of well-being. Psychologists call this "escalation of commitment," or throwing good resources after bad. The difference in escalation of commitment and "grit" is, according to my friend Joe Cherepon, the evidence of progress towards one's goal—some degree of reward for one's continuing devotion or effort. Grit is continuing in the face of difficulty, but not blindly so, rather allowing glimmers of tangible evidence of progress to fuel one's continuation. In the absence of evidence of progress, it is time to move on, to embrace new goals, and to detach oneself from the albatross of regret. More on this in Chapter 7 on goals.

Isolation. No person is an island. Two of the best predictors for Alzheimer's disease are isolation and mental inactivity. Relationships boost mood. This is different from introversion and solitary activity. More introverted persons typically prefer quieter settings with less sensory bombardment. One can still maintain satisfying relationships without living in a three-ring circus. Solitude is not isolation. I like my solitude and am comfortable being apart from other people. However, I yearn for companionship just as I yearn for solitude. To be isolated is to intentionally cut oneself off from companions. The story of Ted Kaczynski (the Unabomber) comes to mind. Even the monks of Mt. Athos, who isolate themselves from mainstream society, do not isolate themselves from one another. More in Chapter 8 on Community. Lack of human interaction, both verbal and physical, is stressful and does damage to the central nervous system over time.

Mind-wandering. Some interesting recent research (Killingsworth & Gilbert, 2010) finds that the ability to focus without distraction is mood boosting, while the tendency to allow one's mind to wander is associated with mood lowering. After reflecting on the content of Chapter 5, you will likely reach the same conclusion I did. Mainly, when one is in flow, one's mind doesn't wander. When one is in flow, one is at peace with the world, neither happy nor sad, but rather in gear, engaged. When one's mind wanders, one is either frustrated because the task is too demanding, bored because the task is too easy, or unengaged in a task. To be frustrated, bored, or idle is to have a lowered sense of well-being.

Personal grooming. I suspect that the relationship of happiness to personal grooming is highly dependent on the groomer's 1) intelligence and 2) reason for grooming. Personally, I believe that grooming is a boring activity in need of the quickest possible completion—20 minutes maximum, for shower, shave, deodorant, brush, and pull-ons. So fast it is hard to be bored, as I am focused on balancing myself so as not to fall. To not be bored by personal grooming is to either 1) lack sufficient intelligence to wish to be engaged in something else more challenging or 2) to be preparing for an encounter that requires extraordinary atten-

> "Dressing up is a bore. At a certain age, you decorate yourself to attract the opposite sex, and at a certain age, I did that. But I'm past that age."
> --Katharine Hepburn

tion to grooming. If I take more than 20 minutes to groom myself as I prepare to be father-of-the-bride at my two daughters' weddings, that is because I am desirous of pleasing my daughters by not committing such solecisms as mismatched socks, navy instead of black, splotches on my shoe, or hairs and dandruff (horrors) on the back of my coat. It is a sign that I care for them and their feelings. I don't care for the values of what I see as excessive grooming, but that is another matter.

My wife once had long, Godiva-like, golden tresses. It took an inordinate amount of time for her to wash, untangle, dry, and shape her locks. But the results were stunningly simple and lovely. However, when she (and I) started our own business, something had to give. Taking such time to groom meant getting up too early or beginning work too late. She cut her hair. Still lovely and stunningly simple, but oh so much quicker. Where there is a full, active life, let us celebrate minimizing time on personal grooming, and thus maximizing our happiness.

 **Circumstance:**

Aging (approaching middle age). See the explanation of aging (approaching seniority) under Boosters/Circumstances above. To recap briefly, as we approach middle age, we experience gradual decreases in mood that are associated with increasing complexity, child-rearing, marital stress, and career developments, culminating in the nadir of a U-shaved curve that is associated with the legendary midlife crisis. Clearly these are averages, as some who maintain relatively simple lives and high quality relationships may avoid the decline typical of most. Along this line of thinking, consider the conversation that Eric Weiner (2008) had with Karma Ura, who coordinates a think tank in Bhutan, a country that scores high on happiness levels and that tracks its Gross National Happiness rather than its Gross National Product. Ura has the reputation of being the country's national philosopher of happiness. Asked his secret, he replies to Weiner, "I have achieved happiness because I don't have unrealistic expectations." (p. 63) When Weiner conducted interviews in high-scoring Denmark, a similar theme emerged. Lesson: To prevent the downward happiness spiral towards middle age, surrender high expectations for career and all else and learn to be "happy with what is." This may be attractive to some, but others clearly embrace the excitement of creation and discovery, preferring it to the calmer waters of happiness. I am reminded of the Princeton Nobel Laureate John Forbes Nash (of the book and film *A Beautiful Mind),* who resisted medication for schizophrenia because it robbed him of his mental powers. He struggled to live with his demons alongside his mathematics rather than clear away the demons and along with them his passion. As it were, the medications would have drained the baby along with the bath water.

Anticipation of bad stuff. Dread is dreadful. Just as the anticipation of good stuff ("I can't wait 'til our beach vacation!") provides a boost in mood throughout the waiting period, so does dread of future unpleasant events cast a dark cloud over the waiting period ("I dread the proofreading job I'm going to have to do on this manuscript.") Even though future unpleasant events can't always be changed to lift the dark cloud of dread, one can change how one frames or manages them. For example, a dreaded event might be followed by a reward for having survived the dreaded event, as in having a gelati after the proofreading is complete (or, if it is really bad, maybe a gelati after proofreading each chapter!).

Being female. Researchers Betsey Stevenson and Justin Wolfers of The Wharton School of the University of Pennsylvania report (2009) that the last four decades have witnessed a decline in women's level of happiness, in spite of being better off materially. While women c. 1970 reported higher levels of happiness in comparison to men, more recent studies show a sizable gap in which not only do women report lower levels of happiness than they did in the 70s—they also report lower levels of happiness than men (Exception: African American females are happier now than they used to be, but less so than African American males). Much of the explanation entails the changing role of women in U.S. society. Women have taken on more new roles without typically relinquishing any of their former ones. As Maureen Dowd quipped in a recent op ed column in *The New York Times*, "If they once judged themselves on looks, kids, hubbies, gardens and dinner parties, now they judge themselves on looks, kids, hubbies, gardens, dinner parties—and grad school, work and meshing a two-career marriage." Clearly there's a solution here, and it is a combination of choice and circumstance: If a woman is married to a traditional male who declines to take on kids, gardens, and dinner parties (I'm assuming the distaff sex must still do their looks and accept their mate), then either you ditch him for a more egalitarian male. Or, you ditch gardens and dinner parties (hire them out). So, when you take on new responsibilities, you have to let go of old ones. Basic law of physics.

Marcus Buckingham expands on the decline on women's happiness (2009) by identifying what happier women do to reverse the decline:

- Embrace who they are and let go of wishing they were who they aren't. This will be discussed in some detail in Chapter 6, where we define the typical personal characteristics that make us who we are, and how we are similar and different.
- Prioritize—weed the garden, as it were. Say goodbye to energy and resource drains that are less important to them.
- Focus on activities that make them feel good, strong, worthy, needed, and don't worry about maintaining some arbitrary sense of "balance" in your life. i.e., don't keep something on your plate just because others say you should.
- Know, affirm, and ask for what gives you a sense of vitality.

Betrayal of trust. When you have an understanding with a person, and that person violates that understanding, you tend to feel betrayed. When we make promises, whether marital, business, interracial, or casual, and either of us breaks that promise, both feel a decrease of well-being. If you break our promise, then I feel angry, sad, maybe even shamed. If I break our promise, then I feel guilty, anxious, maybe even shamed. The path to rebuilding trust is more difficult than the path to betraying it. All too often, betrayals of trust abrogate the relationship, as both parties feel that the only way to rebuild trust is to start over again with someone else, someone with whom we have no history, no garbage. However, betrayal of trust does not have to mean the dissolution of a contract. It does mean that the contract may need to be renegotiated. Based on the number of books on the subject, many are ready with advice.

Chronic pain. Chronic physical pain and chronic psychological pain can occur separately or together. People with chronic physical pain often benefit from consulting a pain specialist, who also can help handle psychological distress. Such a physician has many ways to help patients, including correctly prescribing potentially addictive medications (most pain patients do not become addicted to pain meds). Unfortunately, other physicians often prescribe only medication for physical or psychological pain. Especially with psychological pain, changes in behavior also are necessary. The meds are intended to permit the behavioral changes. Prescribing a med for a malady without assisting the patient in understanding the personal decisions, circumstances, and behaviors that lead to the malady is irresponsible, ineffective, and, with some drugs, encourages addiction. To prescribe without training for behavior change is like giving a job searcher unlimited free room and board and clothing and entertainment with no expectation of having to set up job interviews and actually trying to land a new job—they become addicted to the easy life without working and give short shrift to trying to find a new job. With proper supervision, pharmaceuticals can alleviate pain as the sufferer learns new skills to minimize or even eliminate the pain. Bok (2010) reports that only about 15% of seriously depressed individuals get adequate treatment, which usually involves drug and behavioral treatment.

Disaster. When disaster—flood, fire, tornado, gang violence, hate crimes, war, epidemic, drive-by killing, tsunami—strikes, everyone affected feels a drop in well-being. Yet, if there is one thing that disaster can chalk up to the good, it is calling forth the character of a community. The trite version of this is that when life gives us lemons, make lemonade. The closest I have ever come to being part of a disaster was Hurricane Hugo in 1989. I was more inconvenienced than pained. However, I have fond memories of neighbors pooling resources. One night we had a dozen people at our home, each bringing makings for spaghetti, as we combined thawing meat and perishing salad makings (and aging wines!) to prepare a feast for friends, with several who had no heat in their homes staying with us overnight.

Disaster is also a time for government to reestablish citizens' trust, and for us to discover the degree of efficiency in government. After the New Orleans disaster with Hurricane Katrina in 2005, many government agencies found themselves in the position of having to reestablish trust with the people. Subsequent disasters have provided ample opportunity for government to strut its stuff, with overall satisfactory results.

Divorce/Separation. Bok (2010) relates that the victims of divorce experience on average a decrease of five points in happiness (on a 100-point scale), and a maritally separated person's happiness decreases an average of eight points, with both effects lasting up to a decade. This protracted depressive effect is unusual, as most people tend to rebound from other downers more quickly than that. Bok (loc. 371) says normally several months are sufficient to recover from other reversals of fortune.

Extrinsic rewards for non-algorithmic tasks. Put simply, virtue should be its own reward. We risk turning spontaneous good behavior into conditional good behavior when we use animal training techniques to encourage good behavior. When a pigeon approaches the desired target, we reward them with a food pellet. When a dog heels, we offer a pat and a bone. When a human child does their homework... No! Stop right there. Do not pass Go. Do not give money. Do not give ice cream. Perhaps a smile or an attaboy/girl. Kids are not pets. If we treat kids like pets, we are risking the probability that they will arrive at a point where they only perform for the promise of a tangible reward: money, sweets, and so forth. (Pink, 2009)

Extrinsic rewards are associated with extrinsic goals. Goals that others (teachers, bosses, parents, partners) impose upon you are extrinsic. Goals that you set for yourself, that originate from within your personal wants and needs, are intrinsic goals. Goals that you set for yourself, but only to please someone else, are in fact extrinsic goals.

Hormone fluctuation. In both men and women, hormones vary by time of day, time of month, time of year, and placement in one's hierarchy. Many resources are available for understanding these issues and what one's options are for minimizing their effect. For example, the classic PMS for women can be minimized by taking moderate snacks through the appropriate days involved so as to even out levels of blood sugar. This technique was developed by London's Katharina Dalton, a physician who also treats PMS with progesterone, diet, and/or exercise. Men, on the other hand, experience VMT (Violent Male Testosterone), which can be treated behaviorally and/or pharmaceutically with testosterone suppressors. Competitive exercise increases testosterone levels when one wins, and lowers it when one loses. So, for a man to do his best to minimize VMS prior to an important activity, he might 1) engage in a competitive sport against someone he is sure to lose to (unless losing makes him angry), or 2) engage in noncompetitive, aerobic exercise (such as running), which has a calming effect.

Job loss. Bok (2010) points out that the involuntary loss of one's job—through firing, reduction in force, position elimination, business failure, market downturn, or some other unforeseen reason—is a universally acknowledged mood bandit. In fact, job loss creates greater drops in reported happiness levels than either marital divorce or separation. This assumes, of course, that job loss was involuntary and a partner was rejected by their spouse. Clearly, divorce or separation can be a mood lifter for some who found the marriage itself depressive.

A seldom-understood fact is that if someone loses a job, even if a job paying the same quickly replaces it, the person may not achieve the same level of happiness they had before they were let go. It is not just the absence of income—that can be addressed by unemployment insurance—it is the shock, embarrassment, and shame at being assessed as unwanted, unneeded, incompetent, or some such. Bok observes that the U.S. does far less than other nations with respect to easing the pain of job loss. The circumstance of job loss should be a target of government as well as private intervention and support. Unemployment insurance and educational assistance are two forms of such support.

Lack of control. In his highly readable *The Geography of Bliss,* Eric Weiner (2008) describes the cultures of several countries rated higher and lower on Veenhoven's list of nations' happiness. Near the bottom, Moldova is a fragmented country in which citizens do not trust government and feel little personal control over their lives. The current term for this condition is disempowerment. Empowered people feel capable of solving their problems. Disempowered people do not. Stress—a major cause of unhappiness—is nothing but the inability to remove an obstacle from one's way. Stressors are what keep you from accomplishing what you need to accomplish. When you feel you have no control over a stressor, you feel helpless. When this feeling pervades all areas of your life, you are unhappy. The problem here is that often persons perceive that they have no control over aspects of their lives when in fact they do. In order to find some control, some of us require assistance. All too often, the decision to exercise control is simply a matter of personality traits, with some people being more naturally optimistic than others. Some spouses of alcoholics capitulate, while others like Evelyn Ryan enter jingle contests and prevail. This is to say that while lack of control is often a "circumstance" apparently beyond one's control, occasionally there are opportunities for control that need only to be revealed.

Another form on control that is circumstantial is autonomy at work—a situation in which one can choose what one does, at one extreme, versus being told what to do. Starting in 1967, Michael Marmot of University College London began the Whitehall Studies, which collected-health data from 10,000 government employees at various salary levels. He found that higher salaried jobs were more stressful but were associated with greater health and longevity, while lower salaried jobs were associated with increased probability of earlier death from coronary heart disease. The explanation for this effect was that the imposed, repetitive tasks associated with low salary jobs were more stressful than the pressure associated with high salary jobs. Having little or no choice over what kind of tasks one engaged in was associated with more sick days, more mental illness, and more back ailments. (Iyengar, 2010)

Loss of a loved one. Economist Paul Fritjers of Australia's University of Queensland has studied the relative impact of major life events on happiness levels and determined that the death of a partner or child has two profound effects. First, you can take the positive effect of a good marriage and double the negative strength of how death of a loved one sends happiness plummeting. Both in intensity and duration, the grief of loss by death is twice that of the joy of gaining a relationship. Moreover, the effect on men is more than twice the effect on women, with men apparently more emotionally dependent on their wives' support than wives are on their husbands. This makes sense with respect to the woman typically being more attuned to relationship needs and having more empathy towards those around her than do men. Men would typically have fewer emotional resources outside the marriage than would the woman, and women as a rule would find it easier to develop whatever resources would be needed after such a loss.

Mental illness. Bok (2010) urges the health care industry, with or without government assistance, to find a way to a) properly identify all persons with mental illness, b) get them properly diagnosed, and c) hook them up with appropriate treatments. But someone with distress that's mental (emotional, psychological, whatever you wish to call it), should not wait for outside help to find them. If a troubled person seeks qualified help, that's already progress.

Neurotoxins. Pollutants in air, water, paint, plastics, and other environmental media not only play a role in damaging health—they also have an adverse effect on mood. Leonard Sax (2007) has identified phthalates in plastic bottles and food storage containers as leaching into the containers' contents when heated, as in warming food or beverage in plastic containers in a microwave, or sitting in the sun for some time. These phthalates apparently mimic estrogen with devastating effects on boys—namely, endocrine imbalances and anomalies that lead to anomie/lack of motivation. See more about Sax's work in Appendix D of Howard & Howard (2011).

Noise. The OSHA threshold for noise levels that damage hearing is 89 decibels. The typical hair dryer is 90 decibels. Oops! On the basis of that information, persons who use hair dryers should use earplugs. A hockey-game crowd registers 120 decibels on average. Daily use of hair dryers and regular attendance at hockey games will damage one's hearing, unless precautions are taken. Check the Internet for OSHA decibel levels of noisy activities that you must endure, and then use earplugs that will significantly decrease those noise levels. My wife and I have a pet peeve: movie theatres that turn the volume so high that it hurts to hear it. We are convinced that the operators are hearing-damaged from ear buds pumping pulsating punk to a middle ear that was made for birds and waves.

Various studies show that chronic noise, such as overhead airplanes taking off and landing, is associated with residents, especially children, showing increased blood pressure, heart attacks, impaired physical and cognitive development, lower educational achievement, lower overall health, and, among children, lower reading levels and poorer language skills. (Stewart, 2011) One study by Arlene Bronzaft (in Stewart, 2011) showed problems among sixth grade students whose classrooms in New York City were on the side of the building adjacent to the elevated subway trains that passed by every 4.5 minutes. They tested a full grade level lower than their peers on the other side of the building away from the incessant noise. Not only did the noise cause emotional strain, but instructors lost over 10% of instructional time because of having to stop for the trains. Interestingly, when this effect was revealed, authorities built noise reduction structures and, voila, the reading achievement differences disappeared! Similar improvements in reading and memory accompanied Munich's (Germany) airport's move from a residential to a remote area. Apparently students undergo a stress response that tunes out not only the unrelenting and unwanted noises but also tunes out the speech of their teachers. Noise in hospitals also impacts patients' health and recovery speed, with levels having grown from an average of 57 decibels (from sirens, machinery, monitoring equipment, and so forth) in the 1960s to an average of 72 in 2011. The recommended limit of noise around patients, especially in neonatal units, is 35 decibels. Another new and growing source of noise is power-generating wind turbines. No evidence has shown damage to date, but studies are underway. Look for results. There is reason to believe that studies will show sleep interruption, headaches, and elevated stress in residential areas near the so-called "wind farms." (Pierpont, 2009; Novotney, 2011)

Noise is stressful, especially when modulating it is out of our control. Irregular noise is even more stressful than regular noise. A leaky faucet that goes drip…drip…drip…drip…drip…drip is less stressful than one that goes drip…drip-drip……drip..drip…drip………..drip-drip. The first series of drips occurs with steady regularity so you can "habituate" to, or get accustomed to it. The second series, by its very irregularity, resists habituation. I can read with a regular noise in the background. An irregular noise prevents my getting used to it and ignoring it. One remedy for such attention-grabbing noises is the use of "white noise." At the office, I have a little machine that is a white noise generator. I can choose rain forest, ocean waves, a low hum, or a gentle rain, and the noise plays indefinitely in a regular pattern. It masks other, more irregular noises, so that concentration is easier.

Poverty. British epidemiologists Richard Wilkinson and Kate Pickett (2009) in their data-rich *The Spirit Level: Why Greater Equality Makes Societies Stronger* make the case that income inequality is a major determinant of many of the downers I have listed. When the best-off 1% of the populace have greater total net worth than all of the lowest 90%--and that is true in the U.S. today, income is said to be unequally distributed. If all of the individuals in the lower 90% brought in the $75,000 per household that I have identified earlier as the base requirement for happiness, then there would be no problem. But that is not the case. Societies with greater income inequality, according to these two researchers, have more prisoners, drug abuse, violent crime, gangs, and widespread distrust. They also have poorer health overall, plus more suicide, other mental illness, obesity, infant mortality, pregnant children, and school dropouts...

Sleep disorders. A major source of misery is inadequate sleep due to the body's failure to sleep when needed. A study by Daniel Kahneman (2006) found that the negative effect of inadequate sleep on mood was greater than the effect of any other factor in the study, including job quality, education level, and income. (I am not including here sleep deprivation caused by an individual's refusal to get a good night's sleep—those ambitious, aggressive night owls who'd rather chug Red Bull and espresso than be seen as a wimp who gets a good night's sleep. Such night owls have their own mental troubles.) Here, we are dealing only with those individuals who wish to get a good night's sleep but who just can't get to sleep and stay asleep long enough to feel refreshed afterwards. Allan Pack, neuroscientist at the University of Pennsylvania School of Medicine, has explained the effect of sleep deprivation with the "unfolded protein response." New proteins in one's cells must "fold" properly in order to achieve the proper three-dimensional structure. Sleep deprivation prevents proper folding and leads to aggregated clusters of malformed proteins that interfere with normal alertness and cause fatigue and disorientation. A good night's sleep will eliminate unfolded proteins and replace them with the right stuff. In a podcast on Pack's work ("Sleep," May 24, 2007), WNYC's Radiolab hosts quipped that "sleep is the best housemaid you've ever had in the hotel of you."

Sleep clinic studies are expensive and not always covered by one's insurance. An adequate health care system would make a good night's sleep a universal right. But everyone does not need a costly sleep study to find out what their body's doing wrong. It could be that they are not victims of a sleep disorder, but that they are victims of their own choices. Education by family doctors, counselors, teachers, and the media can help individuals learn how certain choices interfere with sleep: excessive caffeine, consuming caffeine to close to sleep onset, exercising too close to sleep onset, eating too close to sleep onset, and the like. Information on good choices for good sleep abound. One of America's biggest problems—obesity—aggravates sleep quality. A friend who had sleep apnea and slept nightly with a breathing machine (C-PAP) lost 100 pounds and the apnea as well. The body is a system, and disruptions in one part of it can affect performance in other parts.

To give sleeping pills or C-PAP machines to help someone sleep without first determining whether they are engaging in sleep-disturbing behaviors is irresponsible. Taking a sleeping pill after consuming too much caffeine, for example, is like giving Ritalin to a teenager who eats donuts for breakfast and drinks Red Bull throughout the day.

Stressors. A stressor is anything that obstructs you from making progress towards a goal. Stressors are not intrinsically good or bad. If I am trying to get to work on time, and my partner wants to play, then her wanting to play—intrinsically a good thing—becomes a stressor because it interferes with my goal attainment. If I have to drop out of school in order to care for a dependent family member, then that caregiving is a stressor. Things become stressors when we feel that we have no control over them. So, if my car has a flat tire, and I have the proper tools and a fresh tire to use, the flat is not so stressful. I have some control over the situation. However, if my car has a flat on the way to an important meeting, and my cell phone has no towers, and there is no traffic on the road I'm on, and I have no spare tire, then I am out of options, and the flat tire becomes a serious stressor. On the other hand, if my car has a flat on the way to an important meeting, and my cell phone has towers, and I know someone who is also going to the meeting, and I can call them and ask for a lift, and I can also call AAA to come fix the flat, then what was a stressor in one situation is no longer so intense a stressor.

So, the key to stressors is our degree of personal control over them. When a stressor interferes with one of our short or long-term goals, we need to assess how important the goal is and how potent the stressor is. If the goal is unimportant, or if we can somehow modify the goal, then the stressor is less bothersome. The key to offsetting the decrease of well-being caused by stressors is to exert our control by either a) modifying the goal or b) disempowering the stressor. In short, we need to either change our goal or figure out a way to accomplish it.

Working. For too many people, work is for survival. One recent survey reported that 70% of Americans would change jobs if one were available. In no surveys I have seen is work correlated positively with happiness, well-being, or whatever. Again, this is not an absolute. Some of the population finds their work satisfying, meaningful, perhaps even happiness-inducing. For most, however, it is a necessary drudgery. Bok (2010) reports that the typical retiree reports greater pleasure in retirement than when working.

These sobering conditions lead me to two suggestions. First, we need to help people learn to find work that enables them to experience the five modes of positive being (explained in Part Two). Second, we need to train people in skills for leisure, not just skills for work, so that they may begin now to enrich their lives before retirement and then continue with these skills after retirement.

In closing this discussion of uppers and downers, I want to mention a prevalent principle that affects many of the individual factors I have presented. This is the principle of social comparison: upward comparison and downward comparison. (Christakis & Fowler, 2009) According to this phenomenon, people have a tendency to compare themselves to others who are higher on a significant factor, and also compare themselves to persons who are lower. People tend to feel better/happier when they have more than their neighbors, or coworkers, or friends, or even family, have, and worse when they have less. For example, a beautiful woman feels better about herself when her "competition" (office mates, teammates, and so forth) is less beautiful. However, the same beautiful woman would be less satisfied when her competition is more beautiful. In the former case, she would be more likely to rest on her current level of beauty. In the latter case, she would be more likely to pursue strategies that, in her mind, would make her more beautiful, which could include anything from using a different cosmetic to plastic surgery and anything in between (e.g., wardrobe). Or, if a man makes more than his "competition," he feels better than if, even at the same income level, he were making less than they. In effect, with most of these boosters and downers, a person's felt well-being would be enhanced if they felt they possessed boosters to a greater degree than their comparison groups, and/or they felt downers to a lesser degree.

And, one last "last" comment: One of the great downers not mentioned above is "the insistence on not accepting that happiness is ephemeral." (Punset, 2007) One option to the rat race of constantly chasing boosters and eliminating downers and avoiding myths is to find options to happiness that are just as satisfying as happiness itself. And you will get a cornucopia of suggestions along this line in Part Two of this book. Be patient!

STATEMENT OF PERSONAL PRIORITIES

FLOW | FIT | GOALS | COMMUNITY | ALTRUISM

Happiness Boosters
(Choice)

Happiness Downers
(Choice)

119 Minor Adjustors

(more within personal control)

(more outside personal control)

HAPPINESS SET POINT

Happiness Boosters
(Circumstance)

Happiness Downers
(Circumstance)

Continuum of Trait Happiness

Perennially Happy (N- E+) .... Occasionally Happy (N + E-)

3

How Happy Are You?

Estimating Your Set Point

> "My life has no purpose, no direction, no aim, no meaning, and yet I'm happy. I can't figure it out. What am I doing right?"
>
> -- Charles Schulz, creator of the Peanuts cartoon
>
> "Being happy is something you have to learn. I often surprise myself by saying "Wow, this is it. I guess I'm happy. I got a home I love. A career that I love. I'm even feeling more and more at peace with myself." If there's something else to happiness, let me know. I'm ambitious for that, too."
>
> -- Harrison Ford, U.S. actor
>
> "It is a great mitzvah to be happy always."
>
> -- Rebbe Nachman of Breslov (1772-1810), founder of the Breslov Hasidic movement

Guide to this chapter:
- The Happiness Set Point Survey
- Scoring the Survey
- The Biology of Happiness
- The Happiness Quotient
- If You Want to Change Your Set Point

Charles Schulz' comment epitomizes what we have been saying about the Happers—those who have the set point for being naturally happy. They are born with an abundance of positive emotion and a minimum of negative emotion. In this chapter we will determine whether you are like Charles Schulz, or perhaps more like Harrison Ford or me. Mr. Ford's comments suggest that his life has been characterized by more negative emotion than the typical Happer would experience, but that he (almost 70 years old at the time of this writing) has come to accept meaningful work and family in lieu of natural happiness. This would suggest that he is what we have called a Mapper, one who has carved out a way of life that is satisfying. Rebbe Nachman of Breslov exhorts his followers to always be happy, as though he believed that all the world were completely in control of their disposition. A mitzvah is a commandment, and shame on you if you do not always express positive emotions and suppress negative ones! For Rebbe Nachman, the world should only contain Happers and Batters, with us Mappers being second-class citizens. Well, we'll see. I'm not sure that the Rebbe of Breslov would accept the five modes of being in gear that we explore in Part Two, but we'll see. So, which are you?

The Happiness Set Point Survey

Before we discuss any further, take the survey in Table 3.0 on the facing page. Your survey results will be compared to a representative sample of the U.S. workforce. This norm group of 1,200 full-time working adults was selected from a larger sample of some 60,000 individuals. The size of the norm group was reduced so drastically to insure that the final norms were as representative of the U.S. workforce as possible. The group of 1,200 was balanced in terms of age, sex, ethnicity, occupation, and industry. No subgroup was over- or under-represented.

The survey has 20 statements. For each statement, determine whether it describes you accurately, or not at all, or somewhere in between. If the statement does not describe you at all, then circle the "1" on the scale to the right. If the statement describes you perfectly, then circle the "5." If you circle the "3," then that would mean that the statement is true of you for part of the time in some situations, but not true of you at other times in other situations. A "4" would mean that the statement is more often true of you than not true, but not always true in every situation. A "2" would mean that the statement is seldom true of you, but is true on a few occasions.

Work quickly. Typically, a person's first response is the most accurate. The statements are taken from the WorkPlace Big Five Profile, a 107-item assessment of the Big Five personality traits for full-time working people. Two questions contain the term "associates." If that is not meaningful for you, perhaps because you are a student, work at home, or work alone in some other context, then simply substitute the word "acquaintances." You will get the most value from this survey if you answer each question as honestly, as candidly, as possible.

> **Complete the survey now, and do not continue reading until you've finished it!!!**

Scoring the Survey

Now that you've completed the survey, let's calculate your set point score. After we've completed the calculations, I'll explain what it means.

1. Add your responses to items 2, 5, and 15: _____
2. Add you responses to items 7, 9, 11, 13, and 18: _____
3. Subtract line 2 sum from 30: _____
4. Add the sums for lines 1 and 3: N = _____
5. Add your responses to items 1, 4, 6, 8, 10, 12, 16, 17, and 20: _____
6. Add your responses to items 3, 14, and 19: _____
7. Subtract line 6 sum from 18: _____
8. Add the sums for lines 5 and 7: E = _____

Table 3.0 **The Happiness Set Point Survey** (Make a copy or two for other family members or close friends to take, if you like. But do not mass produce without permission!)

		1 Not Like Me At All	2	3	4	5 Very Much Like Me
1.	Shares a lot of information with work associates.					
2.	Gets tense awaiting outcomes.					
3.	Shows little emotion.					
4.	Works to develop relations with many associates.					
5.	Takes criticism personally.					
6.	Initiates get-togethers.					
7.	Is calm in the middle of conflict.					
8.	Makes the first move for face-to-face contact.					
9.	Recovers promptly after setbacks.					
10.	Thrives on working with people.					
11.	Maintains composure under personal attack.					
12.	Has energy to spare.					
13.	Exhibits no self-doubt.					
14.	Resists taking the leadership role.					
15.	Takes rejection personally.					
16.	Facilitates discussion effectively.					
17.	Inspires others to action.					
18.	Bounces back quickly from disappointment.					
19.	Dislikes leadership roles.					
20.	States opinions freely.					

© CentACS/Center for Applied Cognitive Studies, 2001, 2011

I want to make sure that you score your responses accurately. Plus, you should know how I score! So, I am going to use my responses as an example of how to calculate your scores:

1. For items 2, 5, and 15, I responded <u>4, 4, and 4</u>:   <u>**12**</u>
2. For items 7, 9, 11, 13, and 18, I put <u>2, 4, 4, 3, and 4</u>:   <u>**17**</u>
3. Subtract line 2 sum from 30 (i.e., <u>30 minus 17</u>):   <u>**13**</u>
4. Add the sums for lines 1 and 3 (<u>12 + 13</u>):   N = <u>**25**</u>
5. For items 1, 4, 6, 8, 10, 12, 16, 17, and 20,
     I put <u>5, 4, 4, 3, 3, 2, 4, 3, and 5</u>:   <u>**33**</u>
6. For items 3, 14, and 19, I put <u>3, 5, and 5</u>:   <u>**13**</u>
7. Subtract line 6 sum from 18 (i.e., <u>18 minus 13</u>):   <u>**5**</u>
8. Add the sums for lines 5 and 7 (33 + 5):   E = <u>**38**</u>

So, what does it mean that I got 25 for N (Need for Stability) and 40 for E (Extraversion)? Table 3.1 below provides an interpretive label and explanation for the high, medium, and low levels for each of these two personality traits. Your two levels—one for each trait—determines your set point for happiness. Table 3.2 reinterprets your unique combination of two scores with respect to your set point.

Table 3.1   Explanation of Scores for Need for Stability and Extraversion

Ranges for N: (Need for Stability)	Interpretive Label:	Explanation:
8 to 21	More Resilient (Low N)	Roughly 1/3 of the population scores this low—these folks seldom experience the negative emotions of anxiety, anger, and sadness, and they tend to get over setbacks rather quickly. The lower their score, the more stress-free they are. As their score approaches 21, they will experience some negative emotions on occasion, but not as much as those scoring above 21.
22 to 25	Responsive (Mid N)	Roughly 1/3 of the population scores in this range. There are two ways to interpret these midrange scores. First, if most of the scores on lines 1 and 2 of the Scoring Instructions above are 3's, then they get moderately stressed in many different situations, but not majorly stressed in any one kind of situation. Second, the more varied their scores in lines 1 and 2, then their stress is contextual—it depends on the situation. They may get highly stressed in some situations, but in other situations that might stress some people they don't get stressed hardly at all. In both conditions, becoming stressed means feeling negative emotions such as anxiety, anger, and sadness.
26 to 40	More Reactive (High N)	Roughly 1/3 of the population scores in this range. These folks have a relatively "quick trigger" with respect to stress, as they are likely to experience anxiety, anger, and/or sadness more quickly and intensely than most, and take longer to recover from setbacks. They are the conscience of any group.

Table 3.1, cont.

Ranges for E: (Extraversion)	Interpretive Label:	Explanation:
12 to 40	More Introverted (Low E)	The 1/3 of the population scoring in this range tend to prefer being away from sensory stimulation. They like it generally quiet and are comfortable being alone for long stretches (e.g., working in a library all day).
41 to 46	Ambiverted (Mid E)	The 1/3 of the population scoring in this midrange could be described in one of two ways: Either they like moderate amounts of sensory stimulation most of the time (e.g., days full of scheduled meetings), but never too much or too little, or they like lots of sensory stimulation in some situations and little or no sensory stimulation in other situations (e.g., alternating between press conferences and reading).
47 to 60	More Extroverted (High E)	The 1/3 scoring in the high range typically is comfortable being around a substantial amount of sensory stimulation for most of the day (e.g. elementary school teachers and manufacturing supervisors).

you will refer to Table 3.2, you will find which of the nine combinations best describes you. For each of the nine levels, we have offered a catchy label and an explanation. Before you embrace the level that best describes you, you might want to modify your actual score. For example, notice that I score close to the border on both N and E. My N score is 25, which puts me at the top of the midrange of N. With only one more point, I would have been in the high range of N. So, because of the "error of measurement," I should read the explanation of the mid and high levels of N carefully, and in my heart of hearts embrace the one that sounds most like me most of the time. I have done this already, and I accept that I am in the midrange for N.

Also, my E score is 40, which puts me at the top of the low range for Extraversion. Only one more point and I would have scored Ambiverted. So, I should again read the two descriptions carefully and determine which one better describes me most of the time—More Introverted or Ambiverted. In this case, I think Ambivert better describes me. With only one point keeping me from that level, I feel OK about nudging my score up. I would be fine calling myself an introvert. I really do prefer quietness. Noisy situations make me nervous. I detest amplified music and typically leave venues that offer amped up music. On the other hand, I enjoy teaching, working with committees, dinner parties, and am frequently sociable, joke telling, and the like. I even take on a little leadership from time to time, but I really don't like it. Also, when I take longer tests, which are more accurate and valid than short tests such as the one in Table 3.0, I usually score in the low range of Ambiverted. So, I'll call myself that. Midrange on both N and E.

So, where does this leave me with respect to happiness? For that, let's turn to Table 3.2. For a quick overview, understand that the Happers are in the first row, and all the rest of us are progressively less endowed with the capacity for natural happiness as we move down from row two to row nine. The first three rows all experience lots of positive emotions, but rows two and three experience progressively more negative emotion. The middle three rows all experience moderate amounts of positive emotion, with progressively greater amounts of negative emotion thrown in as you progress from row four to row six. The bottom three rows seldom experience the positive emotions, and their experience of negative emotion increases as they move from row seven to row nine. My "row" is number five—right smack in the middle. Where is yours?

Table 3.2   The Nine Levels of the Set Point for Natural Happiness

Combination of N and E Score:	Label:	Explanation:
1. Low N + High E (Resilient and Extraverted)	"Happer"	Characterized by being calm and outgoing, the Happer experiences an abundance of positive emotion and seldom experiences negative emotion. Stress doesn't affect their sense of happiness.
2. Mid N + High E (Responsive and Extraverted)	"Happer's Cousin"	The Happer's Cousin enjoys all of the positive emotion of the Happer but experiences somewhat higher levels of the negative emotions of anxiety, anger, and sadness. Is happiest in moderate to low stress situations.
3. High N + High E (Reactive and Extraverted)	"Wired"	The Wired person experiences a rich emotional life: lots of positive and negative emotion. It is as though they were wired—connected to every "outlet" around them, and experiencing every opportunity for both positive and negative emotional expression. Is happiest in low stress situations.
4. Low N + Mid E (Resilient and Ambiverted)	"Tentative"	The Tentative is typically calm but on occasion will experience joy, ecstasy, amusement, or other positive emotions. You can't stress them very easily, but you can please them. Stress doesn't particularly affect their sense of happiness.
5. Mid N + Mid E (Responsive and Ambiverted)	"Moderate"	The Moderate is somewhat unpredictable emotionally. This is where I score. Often it is very clear what I am feeling, but at other times people say to me, "Hey, Pierce, are you there?" Is happiest in moderate to low stress situations.
6. High N + Mid (Reactive and Ambiverted)	"Edgy"	The Edgy has a very active emotional life like the Wired, but this combination experiences somewhat more negative emotion than positive. Is happiest in low stress situations.
7. Low N + Low E (Resilient and Introverted)	"Vulcan"	The Vulcan rarely expresses either positive or negative emotion and tends to be calm, steady, and predictable in most situations. Their happiness levels are relatively unaffected by stress.
8. Mid N + Low E (Responsive and Introverted)	"Sensitive"	The Sensitive is characterized by rare expressions of positive emotion, while they tend to react when things go wrong. Is happiest in moderate to low stress situations.
9. High N + Low E (Reactive and Introverted)	"Barometer"	The Barometer is like a conscience for what is going on, with scant experience of positive emotion and frequent reactions of fear, anger, and sadness. Is happiest in low stress situations.

The Biology of Happiness

How do we come to be made the way we are? In other words, since we fall under one of these nine "set points," what causes them to become "set" in the first place? The simple answer is that our set point is the result of the interaction between our biological inheritance and our life experience, with inheritance holding the upper hand. My best estimate is that inheritance contributes around 60%. Life experience contributes the remainder, which comes from two sources. These are the choices we make and the circumstances into which we are born or otherwise find ourselves situated, as described in Chapter 2. Choices contribute more than circumstances, say around 30%, with circumstances contributing around 10%. Researchers vary somewhat on these estimates, but the relative degree of contribution to the set point is rather consistent among researchers: genes contribute the most, choices next, and then circumstances. So, Happiness Set Point = genes + choices + circumstances. Or, in plain English: We are born with a core set of dispositions, and our choices and circumstances shape them. We adapt to circumstances, while choices are generally easier to change, should we wish to. The answers to the behavioral questions in Table 3.0 give us our best estimate of the results of this interaction between genetics and environment, as reflected in our scores on Need for Stability (N) and Extraversion (E).

The Need for Stability trait has to do with how we react to stressful situations, such that some of us are "wired" to react at the slightest slight (i.e., we have a quick "trigger"), and others are wired to ignore such slights (i.e., they are practically "unwired," or not plugged into their environment). In fact, everyone falls somewhere on a continuum, from highly reactive to not reactive at all. Your score on the N scale, as described in Table 3.1, could range anywhere from 8 to 40, depending on how you answered the eight items that measure N. Most people score towards the middle, with fewer people getting the more extreme scores. However, the biological and chemical composition that influences our scores is so complex that no two people are exactly alike, with all of us having subtle, or not so subtle, differences from one another.

These subtle differences include many that are not evident or observable. I score higher on the N scale than my wife, Jane. I am more plugged in than she is. More things happen that get a reaction out of me. But you can't always see them. Our delightful marriage of 25+ years was presented with an "aha" a few months back during an innocent conversation. I happened to mention that when I take my morning cold cereal, hot tea, and newspaper perched precariously underarms and in hands from kitchen to eating area, that I worry the entire trip about the possibility that the delicate handle to the handcrafted ceramic cereal bowl would detach and the milk would spill into the rug. Then I'd have to stop everything and scrub and wash intensely to prevent sour milk odors disturbing future days. To prevent such a catastrophe, I avoid picking up the bowl by its handle. Instead I place my palm under the bottom of the bowl. I don't worry so much about the handle of the hot tea breaking off, as the mess would be less, with no consequence of lingering odors. Jane was astonished to hear this report of my daily interior, unobservable voice that considers all manner of catastrophes (but I also fantasize about felicitous occurrences in other situations!). She said that she never had such films playing in her head. We worriers just don't get no sympathy or understanding!

OK, back to the biology. The N and E traits are related to two different brain systems. One is associated with stress and the negative emotions. The other is associated with rewards and the positive emotions. Let's take a brief look at the two systems. Together, the brain and nervous system have two principle divisions: the central nervous system and the peripheral nervous system.

The central system includes the spine and part of the brain.

The peripheral system includes the parts of the brain and nerves that comprise two systems, the autonomic (or internal) system and the somatic (or external system).

The autonomic system is associated with Need for Stability. The autonomic system has two phases: the sympathetic and parasympathetic states of arousal. Under sympathetic arousal, the body becomes vigilant in the presence of threats. This is what we know of as the stress response, or "fight or flight," or the General Adaptation Syndrome. When we return to our normal state after the threat fades, the parasympathetic state dominates.

The degree to which we experience the negative emotions is determined by three things:

- the chemical bath in which our autonomic nervous system lives,
- our genes and which ones are "expressed," and
- the decisions we make in the presence of threats.

The chemical bath comprises a variety of neurotransmitters, proteins, and hormones, including but not limited to serotonin, norepinephrine, acetylcholine, cortisol, stathmin, oxytocin, prolactin, glutamates, corticotropin-releasing hormone, monoamine oxidase, vasopressin, cyclic guanosine monophosphate, and endorphins. Each has its own way of affecting our reaction to stress—a discussion of which is beyond the scope of this book. Suffice it to say that, should you desire to have a therapist help you increase or decrease your level of N, then it would likely involve modifying your levels of one or more of these chemicals by taking pharmaceuticals, undergoing surgery, modifying your diet, changing your environment, modifying your behavior, or changing your exercise routine.

University of Minnesota researchers David Lykken and Auke Tellegen estimate that upwards of 80% of happiness is inherited. They based this on studies of identical twins reared apart. Their findings are consistent with other studies. Whether happiness is only 50% genetic or as much as 80%, that still leaves a lot of wiggle room (my estimate of 60% is on the conservative side). Even though geneticists make stark comments such as "trying to be happier is as futile as trying to be taller" (Lykken & Tellegen, 1996), there is nothing wrong with knowing what is "given" in life. Like a problem in geometry in which one starts with "Givens," we start life with a set point that is mostly genetic but that can be shaped by parental nurture among other factors. As with intelligence, that 20-40% left to choice and circumstance leaves a lot of room for what Yale University psychologist Robert Sternberg would call mental self-management, and what I would call managing our circumstances and choices. Those born with the highest levels of happiness, or very high Extraversion and very low Need for Stability, have less need to focus on managing their choices and circumstances in order to be happy, for such are merely icing on the cake. They will be happy regardless.

Just because we inherit something does not mean it is impervious to change. Even grandma's antique four-poster bed can undergo transmogrification! Some aspects of our inheritance are more resistant to change than others. For example, depression is mostly inherited, but it can be treated both with pharmaceuticals and with psychotherapy. And, certain genes do not express themselves unless circumstances are conducive. Take, for example, the long and short alleles (i.e., forms or versions) of the 5-HTTLPR gene. Research shows that persons with the short form tend to depression, as the short form reduces levels of serotonin. But depression only occurs if circumstances lead there. The short allele doesn't mandate depression. (Lyubomirsky, 2008, p. 59)

The decisions that affect our level of N are threefold: deciding what is and is not a threat, whether we have resources to address the threat, and deciding when the threat is over. If I decide that an impending deadline is a threat, and hence a stressor, then I will feel stressed as the deadline approaches. My sympathetic nervous system will go into action, pumping more blood, adding digestive juices to my stomach, dilating my eyes, and all of the other features that prime us for peak performance in the face of attack. This behavior helped us survive attacks from Bengal tigers in the jungle, and they remain with us today as we face other kinds of threats.

Now, if you face the same deadline as I do, you may make a different decision than I did, saying to yourself, "That deadline is not important. I'll keep on working, but I'm not going to lose any sleep over whether I make it or not." Consequently, your body would not exhibit the fight-or-flight response, all because of your decision. However, it should be understood that the difference in your and my genetic and chemical composition could also affect our tendency to make that decision. Chemistry does affect decision-making. Just as too much coffee could lead a jittery driver to overcompensate in a curve and have an accident, so could a suboptimal level of serotonin cause one to make the decision that a deadline was a threat.

Our memory is an important influence on how we decide what is and is not a threat, whether we have resources to address the threat, and when it is over. Deep in the brain, the hippocampus stores our life history in a database of events. The hippocampus is like a library, while a neighboring area, the amygdala, is the seat of the emotions. The neural networks that connect the hippocampus and amygdala are extensive, such that each memory is connected to one or more emotional associations. If I got violently sick from eating oysters in my past, then it is likely that when the subject of oysters comes up, I have an immediate sense of disgust and discomfort. The overall balance of pleasant versus unpleasant emotional associations with a particular kind of event, such as deadlines, deep sea fishing trips, or trips to big cities, will influence whether we see a situation as appealing or unappealing, stress-free or stressful. That is why no event is seen as a threat or stressor by everyone, because we all have different experiences with a given kind of event. Two country bumpkins might feel either attracted to visiting the big city or repelled by the idea if one bumpkin had been mugged there and one hadn't.

And let us not ignore the role of the environment in shaping our trait levels. For example, second-hand smoke levels have been linked to anxiety, depression, and attention-deficit disorder. Exposure to second-hand smoke appears to affect one's inhibitory processes, or those neural pathways that are associated with self-control. Early childhood abuse, another kind of environmental toxin, tends to be more associated with adult depression when a particular gene is present. An environmental boost comes from music. For example, listening to music in a minor key ("sad" music; e.g., Samuel Barber's *Adagio for Strings*) tends to be associated with a rush of the neurotransmitter prolactin, the same chemical released during lactation. Persons unable to produce the prolactin rush while listening to sad music do not get the same mood boost benefit. The interaction between genes, chemistry, and environment is complex and just now beginning to be understood. (Gray, 1982; Rothbart, Ahadi, and Evans, 2001; DeYoung et al., 2010; Ridley, 2003; Hamer and Copeland, 1998; Stix, 2011)

Now that I have made the case for a biological basis of the negative emotion side of happiness, I'll turn things around and suggest that training alone may also be able to influence levels of negative emotions. Martin Seligman (2011 and earlier) has had immense success with the Penn Resiliency Program, where he has trained children to reframe their experience as a way to prevent and reduce depression and anxiety. The U.S. Army is currently engaging in a huge intervention that will train noncommissioned officers in Seligman's optimism model. The Army's program targets 1 million solders, who will be trained by other soldiers, who in turn will have been trained by Seligman's staff. The program costs $125 million over 5 years. Critics include George Bonanno (Teachers College Columbia) and William P. Nash (a physician working with stress among Marines), who feel that the vast majority of folks do not need resilience training since they are naturally resilient. Fewer than 5% need it, they say. And, they fear that the training hurts rather than helps. Hmmm. Say most people get over trauma fine. The ones who don't would be the bottom 5% on our Need for Stability scale.

So, what about the biological basis for Extraversion? The negative emotions and the Need for Stability are primarily involved with the autonomic/internal component of the peripheral nervous system along with the hippocampus and amygdala. Extraversion and the positive emotions are primarily involved with the somatic/external component along with the "pleasure pathway" of the brain—the medial forebrain bundle and the lateral hypothalamus. The somatic division of the peripheral nervous system is called the "external" component because it contains the sensors that connect to the outside world—the afferent and efferent nerves that control sense perception and motor reaction. The afferent nerve endings detect smells, sights, tastes, textures, and sounds, and the efferent nerves control our body's reaction to the perceptions through movements: eating, embracing, approaching, avoiding, and the like. Jeffrey Gray (1982) calls it the Behavioral Activation System (BAS). Just as with the negative emotions, our degree of positive emotions is influenced by three factors: the chemical bath in which our somatic nervous system lives, our genes and which ones are "expressed," and the decisions we make in the presence of threats. The chemicals comprising the bath that caresses the BAS include dopamine, norepinephrine, gamma-aminobutyric acid (GABA), oxytocin, endorphins, androgens, and estrogens, among others. In the event that someone might consult a therapist in order to adjust their level of positive mood, a prescription would likely include a pharmaceutical that would increase one of more of these chemicals. One's overall mood is a function of minimizing activity in the autonomic system (i.e., staying in parasympathetic arousal and avoiding sympathetic arousal) and maximizing activity in the somatic system (i.e., activating the reward system, also known as the pleasure pathway).

As with the negative emotions, each of us decides not only what is aversive but also what is pleasurable. We decide what we want to avoid and what we want to approach. And, like with the negative emotions, our past history is the major determinant of how we go about making these decisions. If I see someone who in the past has made my life miserable, the storage of those memories in my hippocampus is activated and sends signals to my amygdala that activate feelings of anger or one of its cousins (fear, sadness, disgust, shame, etc.). This instantaneous triggering of past memories and their allied feelings leads me to decide to approach or avoid this person. Similarly, if I see someone or something for whom I have memories that associate with pleasure or one of 18 allelonymns and hundreds of synonyms (see Appendix A), then I am likely to approach that person or situation.

One's levels of specific chemicals can affect the degree of pleasure we feel for specific situations as well as in general. For example, the dopamine-rich areas of the brain are not the same in everyone. Some of us have more dopamine receptors than others, and some of us manufacture more dopamine than others. Those of us who make lots of dopamine *and* have lots of dopamine receptors experience maximum pleasure. Two people who have the same capacity for making dopamine, but who have different densities of dopamine receptors, will not experience the same levels of pleasure. Having lots of dopamine does not make any impact if you don't have the receptors to respond to it, like having a big budget but no qualified people to do the work.

Oxytocin is another chemical that the body manufactures. During breastfeeding, both infant and mother (or wet nurse) generate lots of oxytocin with the effect of strengthening the bond between them. In fact, when adults eat meals together, their oxytocin levels increase with the typical effect that their friendship is strengthened. When a family with teenage children dines together in the evening on a regular basis, the oxytocin burst and resulting bond strengthening is rewarded with the teens showing improved mood, school performance, and health. Families that dine together (regularly), bind together. In fact, oxytocin is proving to be such an important influence on positive mood that Paul Zak (2008) of Claremont Graduate School calls it the "molecule of connection." Vero Labs in Boca Raton, Florida, produces Liquid Trust, an atomizer that contains a 2 month supply of oxytocin. Some physicians and therapists are now prescribing whiffs of Liquid Trust for patients with mood issues, including those with an autism spectrum disorder. This chemical trust therapy has been shown to increase charitable giving, number of friends, quality of romance, and quality of sex. Autistic individuals taking oxytocin have reported increases in trust and awareness of facial and social cues.

Much has been written recently about the "plasticity" of the human body—of its ability to re-shape neural pathways, chemical levels, muscular structures. These writer-researchers make the point that prodigious effort can lead to significant change. I laud efforts at self-improvement, and the plasticity "movement" certainly is at home in the self-improvement community. However, I am cautious, even skeptical, of some of the claims made. One of the more evangelical writers of recent days is David Shenk, whose *The Genius in All of Us* (2010) has caused quite a stir. Shenk writes that "Genes are constantly activated and deactivated by environmental stimuli, nutrition, hormones, nerve impulses, and other genes." (loc. 268) What he suggests is that the genome is like a symphony orchestra, subject to the demands of conductors, the requests of audiences, the acoustical properties of concert halls, and the atmospheric whims of Mother Nature. That is true, but that does not deny the core properties of the strings, brass, woodwinds, and percussion. Just as instruments can change according to the characteristics of their environment, so genes can change. But the changes are minimal, with their core qualities continued. I remember once waking up so I could play a rousing reveille to awaken my fellow scouts at Camp Croaten. However, when I put horn to lips, no sound emerged! The very low temperatures had clogged the pipes. I took the bugle back into my sleeping bag with me, warmed it up, then re-emerged and played a successful wake-up call, much to the groans of my fellow scouts. Once a bugle, always a bugle, with variations.

Shenk (loc. 514-517) points out that intelligence, long thought to be fixed permanently at birth, actually can be changed by a variety of sources. He cites Cornell University's Stephen Ceci as declaring that IQ "can change quite dramatically as a result of changes in family environment, work environment, historical environment, styles of parenting, and, most especially, shifts in level of schooling." Earlier studies that insisted on the permanence of IQ levels were based on middle class samples that were more stable, where the individuals being assessed were less subject to significant changes in their environment. Yet even the changes that Shenk and Ceci report do not deny the core genetic basis of mental ability. The fact that IQ scores can vary as much as 15-20% throughout one's lifetime is not an argument against inheritance, but rather an argument in support of making the most out of what one is born with. Some of us do more with our endowment than others. Just like the New Testaments parable of the talents, some of us simply guard what we have, while others take on new challenges, even though there is slim hope of mastering them. On a wing and a prayer, as it were.

In a delightful description of the biological and environmental sources of athleticism, Shenk illustrates the complex process of genes interacting with environment:

> As the search for athletic genes continues, therefore, the overwhelming evidence suggests that researchers will instead locate genes prone to certain types of interactions: gene variant A in combination with gene variant B, provoked into expression by X amount of training + Y altitude + Z will to win + a hundred other life variables (coaching, injury rate, etc.), will produce some specific result R. What this means, of course, is that we need to dispense rhetorically with the thick firewall between biology (nature) and training (nurture). The reality of GxE [gene-environment interaction] assures that each person's genes interact with his climate, altitude, culture, meals, language, customs, and spirituality—everything—to produce unique life trajectories. Genes play a critical role, but as dynamic instruments, not a fixed blueprint. A seven- or fourteen- or twenty-eight-year-old outfitted with a certain height, shape, muscle-fiber proportion, and so on is not that way merely because of genetic instruction. (loc. 1,462-1,469) . . . Rather than passing on quickness genes, he passes on crucial external ingredients, such as the knowledge and means to attain maximal nutrition, inspiring stories, the most propitious attitude and habits, access to the best trainers, the most leisure time to pursue training, and so on. This nongenetic aspect of inheritance is often overlooked by genetic determinists: culture, knowledge, attitudes, and environments are also passed on in many different ways. (loc. 1,473-1,476)

Shenk invokes the specific example of Jamaica, which shows how a culture's values can shape individual talent:

> In Jamaica, track events are beloved. The annual high school Boys' and Girls' Athletic Championships is as important to Jamaicans as the Super Bowl is to Americans. "Think Notre Dame football," write Sports Illustrated's Tim Layden and David Epstein. "Names like Donald Quarrie and Merlene Ottey are holy on the island. In the United States, track and field is a marginal, niche sport that pops its head out of the sand every four years and occasionally produces a superstar. In Jamaica … it's a major sport. When Sports Illustrated [recently] visited the island … dozens of small children showed up for a Saturday morning youth track practice. That was impressive. That they were all wearing spikes was stunning." (loc. 1,487-1,494)

Shenk concludes the Jamaica story relating the coup de grâce of Dennis Johnson. A champion sprinter in the 1970s, Johnson took his learning from San Jose State University home to Jamaica and developed a world-class college track program at the University of Technology in Kingston. After a modest beginning, the Jamaican runners began consistently bringing medals home from international competitions. Johnson combined current running technology with cultural values to put distance between Jamaica and her competitors. Jamaica's genes for running do not differ from that of many other cultures. But informed, extensive practice trumps innate ability every time. You snooze, you lose, even with the right genes.

Genes are not destiny, but direction. As the 16th century educator Richard Mulcaster penned, "Nature makes the boy toward, nurture sees him forward." What are the limits of nurture, of plasticity? Just how much can a person change? My contention is that a person's core disposition cannot change, but we can change what we do with that disposition. We can't change being gregarious, but we can change whether we harness our gregariousness into being a door-to-door salesperson or an emergency room triage nurse. In a fascinating description of how early disposition endures and influences later life and behavior, Dacher Keltner (2009) measured the "Duchennes" smiles, aka the authentic smiles (i.e., not faked, or forced smiles) of 110 Mills College females in their 1960 college yearbook. The women with the warmest smiles (i.e., smiles which make crow's feet to the side of one's eyes and turn the ends of one's lips upward) 30 years later reported being more satisfied, having accomplished more of their goals, felt less anxiety day to day, and felt happier in their marriages. So, inheritance is not fate, but it is a powerful determinant.

For an excellent, and more extensive, discussion of the biological basis of happiness I suggest Chapter 5 of Daniel Nettle's *Happiness* (2005).

The Happiness Quotient

At this point, you may find it useful to calculate your "happiness quotient." This is a way to express your set point in combination with your current life situation. As you recall, there are a few activities related to happiness that are either illegal, immoral, or embarrassing, or all three. I will not include them in the list. There are clearly enough other factors for us not to need them! I have also not included "being Republican," so if you are, consider that a bonus point for you.

Here's how it works. I have made a personal checklist that is based on the boosters and downers enumerated in Chapter 2. I have taken each booster and downer and rephrased it so that it has become a personal statement. For example, the booster "Gardening" has become "I garden, either indoors or outdoors." As you read each of the statements in Table 3.3, indicate over to the right whether you think that statement is

> "Ever since happiness heard your name, it has been running through the streets trying to find you."
> --Hafiz of Persia

true of you or not true of you. If it is true, circle "Yes." If it is not true, circle "No." Be candid about yourself. For example, I garden once or maybe twice a year, so I should mark "No" for "I garden, either indoors or outdoors." My wife gardens several times a week, so she should mark "Yes." If the statement is truer of you than not true, mark "Yes." If it is more false about you than true, mark "No." Got it? Good. Now complete the checklist in Table 3.3. It comprises four sections: boosters that are choices, boosters that are circumstances, downers that are choices, and downers that are circumstances. You may want to make a copy of this four-page checklist so that a couple of family members or friends might complete it along with you. It might also be an interesting exercise for you and your partner or a close friend or associate to complete the checklist about each other, and then compare how you answered about yourself with how your partner or close friend answered about you. You could then discuss any discrepancies. You might say No to "I make enough time to socialize with friends," and your partner/friend might say Yes (about you). This could make for an interesting discussion!

Table 3.3   Personal Checklist of Happiness Boosters and Downers : Part A

Choices that Boost (40):	True for You?
I consume alcohol in moderation.	Yes----------No
I tend to put off non-urgent purchases and think about them for a while.	Yes----------No
I can think of at least one major event or experience in my future that I am anticipating with relish.	Yes----------No
I attend at least one club or other group meeting.	Yes----------No
I would describe myself as a busy person.	Yes----------No
I never spend money for the purpose of keeping up with what other people have—rather I buy things because I want them for what they are.	Yes----------No
I regularly engage in acts of charity, whether it involves giving money, time, or other resources.	Yes----------No
From time to time, I spend some time caring for children.	Yes----------No
I have an undergraduate college degree.	Yes----------No
I regularly engage in conversation with others.	Yes----------No
I daily eat two or more satisfying meals.	Yes----------No
I exercise on a regular basis.	Yes----------No
I frequently have experiences that I enjoy talking about afterwards with others.	Yes----------No
From time to time, I engage in some kind of organized competition in order to win something.	Yes----------No
I garden, either indoors or outdoors.	Yes----------No
I have worked on at least one thing that future generations, either in my own family or elsewhere, will remember me by.	Yes----------No
I show my gratitude to others whenever appropriate.	Yes----------No
I feel that I am generally in good health.	Yes----------No
There are many things that I do simply because I enjoy doing them—if there are other benefits, that is just icing on the cake.	Yes----------No

Table 3.3: Part A, cont.

![icon] Choices that Boost (40):	True for You?
I have what I regard as a high quality marriage.	Yes----------No
I regularly eat meals with family and/or friends.	Yes----------No
I regularly take time to shut down and be still, whether I call it meditating, resting, or praying.	Yes----------No
I regularly listen to music that I enjoy.	Yes----------No
I have an optimistic outlook on most things.	Yes----------No
From time to time, I have the opportunity to play with children.	Yes----------No
I am involved to some degree with political activities.	Yes----------No
On balance I think that market-based economies do more good for more people than tightly controlled economies.	Yes----------No
I would describe myself as a reader—of books, magazines, newspapers, journals, blogs, and the like.	Yes----------No
I engage in recreational sports from time to time.	Yes----------No
I have a satisfying number of high-quality relationships.	Yes----------No
I have at least one friend I can trust and confide in and discuss serious personal issues.	Yes----------No
I would describe myself as a person of religious faith.	Yes----------No
I am self-employed.	Yes----------No
I have a satisfying sex life.	Yes----------No
I enjoy going shopping from time to time.	Yes----------No
I make enough time to socialize with friends.	Yes----------No
I spend much more of my discretionary income on experiences (or things related to experiences) than I do on things in-and-of-themselves.	Yes----------No
I frequently spend money on things for other people.	Yes----------No
I take walks from time to time.	Yes----------No
I volunteer my time and/or talent on occasion at a school, hospital, or some other venue that needs such extra help.	Yes----------No

Table 3.3: Part B

Circumstances that Boost (21):	True for You?
I am middle-aged and approaching my senior/gray years.	Yes----------No
On a scale of beauty, I consider myself near the top.	Yes----------No
I live in a democracy.	Yes----------No
I have a job.	Yes----------No
The environment I live in is healthy and pleasant.	Yes----------No
I feel physically safe where I live and work.	Yes----------No
I have the freedom to work, spend, and invest as I choose, given my qualifications.	Yes----------No
The government agencies with which I have had dealings are efficient.	Yes----------No
The government agencies with which I have had dealings have been responsive to my concerns.	Yes----------No
I regard my government officials as trustworthy.	Yes----------No
The community in which I work and live is law-abiding	Yes----------No
I see a minimum of corruption and violence in my community.	Yes----------No
I have the personal freedom to move and be as I choose.	Yes----------No
I have retired from my principle career or job.	Yes----------No
Overall, I am satisfied with the quality of the democracy in which I live.	Yes----------No
I have experienced an increase in my personal or professional status or social standing in the recent past.	Yes----------No
I live in a temperate climate.	Yes----------No
I live and work in a community that regards minorities with dignity and respect.	Yes----------No
I trust most people with whom I associate.	Yes----------No
I trust the management where I work.	Yes----------No
I trust the public officials in my community.	Yes----------No

Table 3.3: Part C

Choices that are Downers (9):	True for You?
I drink alcoholic beverages to excess **OR** I do not drink any alcoholic beverages.	Yes----------No
I have what I think is a bad commute to work.	Yes----------No
I think deeply and seriously on a regular basis.	Yes----------No
I feel a sense of envy with regard to some of my associates.	Yes----------No

Table 3.3: Part C, cont.

Choices that are Downers (9):	True for You?
I have at least one goal or dream that I have lost or failed to attain that I have been unable to let go of.	Yes----------No
I have at least one year of graduate education beyond the undergraduate level.	Yes----------No
I am relatively isolated from other people for much of the time.	Yes----------No
My mind wanders frequently, either through daydreaming or other distractions.	Yes----------No
I spend an hour or more daily on personal grooming.	Yes----------No

Table 3.3: Part D

Circumstances that are Downers (19):	True for You?
I am not yet 45 years old.	Yes----------No
At this time of my life, there is at least one event or experience that I am anticipating with a sense of dread, fear, anger, or sadness.	Yes----------No
I am a female.	Yes----------No
I have recently experienced a betrayal of trust towards me.	Yes----------No
I experience pain daily, on a chronic basis.	Yes----------No
I have recently experienced and been personally affected by a disaster.	Yes----------No
I have recently experienced an unwanted separation or divorce from my partner.	Yes----------No
I tend to get rewards for things that I would normally do just because I like to do them.	Yes----------No
I experience noticeable hormone fluctuations.	Yes----------No
I have recently been involuntarily terminated from a job.	Yes----------No
I do not feel that I have very much control over my choices.	Yes----------No
I have recently experienced the loss of a loved one.	Yes----------No
I have a mental illness.	Yes----------No
I have some kind of toxins in my body that negatively affect my sense of well-being.	Yes----------No

Table 3.3: Part D, cont.

Circumstances that are Downers (19):	True for You?
I am frequently around loud noise.	Yes----------No
I do not earn as much as $40,000 (if you live alone) OR as much as $75,000 (if you are part of a household).	Yes----------No
I have a sleep disorder.	Yes----------No
I experience at least one serious stressor on a daily basis.	Yes----------No
I work hard daily.	Yes----------No

When you have completed the four parts of Table 3.3, add the number of Yes's for Part A and divide the sum of Yes's by the total number of statements in Part A. Repeat the process for Part B. Next, add the number of No's for Parts C and divide the total by the total number of statements in Part C. Repeat the process for Part D.

Here are four instructions that will lead you through the process:

Count the number of Yes's for Choices that are Boosters and divide by 40:   ___ / 40 = ___%

Count the number of Yes's for Circumstances that are Boosters and divide by 21:   ___ / 21 = ___%

Count the number of No's for Choices that are Downers and divide by 9:   ___ / 9 = ___%

Count the number of No's for Circumstances that are Downers and dived by 19:   ___ / 19 = ___%

To make sure you and I are thinking alike about this process, here is how I scored myself:

Count the number of Yes's for Choices that are Boosters and divide by 40:   __31_ / 40 = _78%_

Count the number of Yes's for Circumstances that are Boosters and divide by 21:   _19_ / 21 = _90%_

Count the number of No's for Choices that are Downers and divide by 9:   _7__ / 9 = _78%_

Count the number of No's for Circumstances that are Downers and dived by 19:   _17_ / 19 = _89%_

Let me explain my scores, and how I think about them. Then you can do the same for yourself. On Part A my checklist, I said "Yes" to 78% of the choices. That means that out of the 40 kinds of choices that research says are related to happiness, I marked just over three out of four in the "happy" direction. If I were a person who felt that I wanted to be happier (and I am not), then I could look at the choices I said "No" to and determine which of them I might begin approaching differently. For example, I said "No" to "I engage in recreational sports from time to time." So, if I were a person who felt that I wanted to be happier, then I might join a volleyball league, or sign up for the Jazzercise class that our younger daughter teaches, or find someone to play shuffleboard with regularly. In other words, for a person who wants to be happier, the No's checked in Part A of Table 3.3 are an excellent place to start thinking about some choices one could make. This is the best place to start, because research says these 40 items are "slam dunks" in the happiness game: Do them and you'll feel better. But, because of our different pasts, values, and tastes, not each of the 40 will be equally appealing to you and to me.

The next best place for a person who wants to be happier (and I am not) to find some insights is Part C—the Downers that are choices. These nine decisions have been shown to lower one's mood, and they are within our power to decide to do or not to do. I said "Yes" to only two of them: "I think deeply and seriously on a regular basis" and "I have at least one year of graduate education beyond the under-graduate level." So, if I were a person who wanted to be happier, then I could choose to think seriously and deeply less often, but unfortunately (fortunately?) I cannot undo taking four years of graduate edu-cation in pursuit of a Ph.D. Oh, but I teach graduate school! In fact, I am teaching four graduate classes over the next twelve months. Perhaps I would feel happier if I stopped teaching graduate students, es-pecially knowing that I am making them unhappy by acquiring more graduate education. But if I stopped teaching them, someone else would, and they'd still be miserable wretches! This little discus-sion highlights one of the difficulties with the positive psychology and happiness and well-being movement that I introduced in Chapter 1: Happiness is a good thing, but not the only thing. There are other modes of being in addition to happiness that are satisfying in their own way, as we shall see in the next section of this book. I would not trade my graduate education and my thinking seriously for a mouthful of belly laughs.

I must confess, however, that in early adulthood I decided that I might be too serious for my own good. I am a voracious reader: professional books, philosophy, biography, history, current events, poetry, classic novels (you know, the "serious" ones, like *Anna Karenina* or *War and Peace*—both of which I've reread recently). So I decided that one way to lighten up would be—not to read less (heaven forbid!)—but to read some light fiction. Accordingly, I have become a great fan of crime novels and spy thrillers—you know, Agatha Christie and Ken Follett and their ilk. In fact, now I look forward to retiring each evening to a novel in bed. About half are classic/serious, the other half are crime novels and spy thrillers. Tonight I'm looking forward to getting into Patricia Cornwell's latest, *Port Mortuary*. So I'm even serious about being light! Sorry.

Now the other two parts of Table 3.3 are a bit trickier. These are boosters and downers that are "circumstances" and by definition are less under our personal control. I'm in pretty good shape here. I said "Yes" to 90% of the 21 circumstance boosters. Only two were No's: I am not beautiful, and I am not retired. I can do nothing about retirement, but I don't want to do anything about retirement! I'd just as soon work until I draw my last breath. As Greg Mortenson's board member averred, "I want to be used up when I die." I love to work. Or rather, I love *my* work. Writing books for you guys, doing consulting, making presentations, doing research, planning all kinds of interesting stuff. What's not to like about work? I'm sure retired folks have a happiness advantage over me, but I'll take my interesting work in exchange for their happiness. Now, about the beauty. By circumstance of birth, I do not count myself among the upper ranks of physical beauty. However, I know that there are some choices I could make that might nudge me up the ladder a rung or two. I could tone my abs, trim or shear my beard, dye my hair, visit a tanning booth, use cologne, tailor my clothing, use light facial makeup, maybe a tat-too or three subtly placed, some jewelry, pay attention to my nails (all 20 of them), blow dry my hair….

Aw, heck, I'm sure you know more about this than I do. And maybe even care more about it! I don't really give much of a flip about my appearance. I do just fine with the way Lady Fortune made me. Interesting work, a loving and beautiful wife, children I'm proud of, and grandchildren about whom I can hardly contain myself. Why would I want to be more beautiful? If I were, they might leave me! When my wife or daughters or grandkids tease me about my appearance (dad, those dark socks with Bermuda shorts have got to go), I typically comply with their suggestions. Not to make me happy, but to humor them.

With respect to downers that are circumstances, I said "No" to 89% of them. Only two are true of me: "I work hard daily" and "I tend to get rewards for things that I would normally do just because I like to do them." Hard work may be a downer for some, but I thrive on it. (It is 11:58 p.m. on a Wednesday night as I review this first draft, and all is well.) Hans Selye, McGill University stress guru, calls it "eustress." Healthy stress. The kind that keeps you alert and alive. If you enjoy it, or at least if it is not punishing, it is not stressful, at least not in the bad sense. Remember, stress occurs when something keeps you from making progress towards a goal. My goal is to do interesting work, so how is hard work stressful for me? Hard work in the service of reaching a goal is intrinsically satisfying, if not always titillating. I'm not going to try to change the circumstance of working hard daily. As to getting rewards for things that I love, well, research says that is demotivating, that if folks reward me for doing something I love that I'll quit doing it for the love of it and start doing it only when I sense a reward awaits. I don't mind if I get rewards for doing things I want to do. But I'm not going to stop doing the things I love to do that don't get rewarded.

Now I invite you to go through a similar process:

1. Review the choice boosters (Part A) that you said No to and see if there are any that you would like to seriously consider changing to a Yes. If so, then I suggest you find a piece of paper and start a To Do list and use it as a bookmark. This can be what I call a "parking lot," a place to put things until you have time to deal with them. Or, you may use the space provided for this purpose at the end of this chapter. When we get to Chapter 10, you will have an opportunity to incorporate them into your Personal Mission Statement.
2. Next, review the choice downers (Part C) and see if there are any Yes items that you would like to change to a No. If so, add them to your To Do sheet (parking lot).
3. Third, review your circumstance boosters (Part B) and see if there are any No items that you would like to try to find a way to change to a Yes. Maybe with the help of friends, professional associations, civic clubs, religious organization, political party, or other entity you might find allies who are also interesting in effecting the kind of change you are interested in. If you find one or more such items, add them to your parking lot.
4. Finally, review your circumstance downers (Part D) and see if there are any Yes items that you would like to find a way to influence and possibly change to a No. Add them to your parking lot.

To determine your actual Happiness Quotient, you need to refer to your Natural Happiness level in Table 3.2. Remember there are nine levels: Level 1 is the Happers—those who are naturally happy. Level 9 is the least naturally happy—full of negative emotion and seldom experiencing positive emotions. My level is five, right in the middle.

Now, compute your average percentage for the four parts of the Boosters and Downers Checklist in Table 3.3. To do this, add the four percentages you calculated for parts A, B, C, and D and divide that sum by 4. My average across the four parts is 84%. By looking at Table 3.4, I see my 84% score gives me a booster/downer level of 2. Evaluate your total percentage of boosters and downers according to Table 3.4.

Table 3.4   Conversion of Boosters and Downers Percentage to the Nine Levels

If your average % is:	Then your booster/downer level is:
90 to 100	1
80 to 89	2
70 to 79	3
60 to 69	4
50 to 59	5
40 to 49	6
30 to 39	7
20 to 29	8
0 to 19	9

With my set point score of 5 (my Natural Happiness level from Table 3.2) and a booster/downer score of 2, my Happiness Quotient is the average of these two, i.e., 2 + 5 = 7 / 2 = 3.5. The highest happiness score would be an average of one. The lowest happiness score would be an average of nine. The farther your Happiness Quotient is away from one, the more you might want to consider changing some of your booster No's to Yes's, and some of your downer Yes's to No's, as we have discussed. On the other hand, you may be perfectly content with your level of happiness, whether your Happiness Quotient is a 3.2 or a 7.4. That certainly describes me. My 3.5 sounds fine to me. I don't want to be any happier.

But I do want to lead the most interesting life possible, and that is what we are going to learn how to manage in Part 2 of this book. We're almost there! But I want to share with you just a little more information about ways to be happier, in case you're the kind of person who wants to be happier. This has to do with actually changing your set point, not just moving around your boosters and downers.

If You Want to Change Your Set Point

Let me begin this by saying that I'm not in favor of folks trying to change their set point as a general rule, but I do recognize that in some cases changing the happiness set point is a necessary therapy rather than a convenient cosmetic. Eric Wilson underscores this point in his *Against Happiness* (2008):

> Given these virtues of melancholia, why are thousands of psychiatrists and psychologists attempting to 'cure' depression as if it were a terrible disease? Obviously, those suffering severe depression, suicidal and bordering on psychosis, require serious medications. But what of those millions of people who possess mild to moderate depression? Should these potential visionaries also be asked to eradicate their melancholia with

the help of a pill? Should these possible innovators relinquish what might well be their greatest muse, their demons giving birth to angels? (p. 149)

Wilson's quote reminds me of the case of John Forbes Nash, the "beautiful mind" mathematician who suffered from schizophrenia. Medication put him at peace but robbed him of his creative and analytical prowess. He had to learn to accept his demons as co-inhabitants with his angels. (Modern medications more likely could have controlled his illness while leaving his creativity undulled.)

That said, here's what the research suggests could modify one's set point on a permanent or temporary (but recurring) basis. The suggestions are of two kinds: how to decrease the negative emotions and how to increase the positive emotions. The negative emotions are of three major kinds: depression, anger, and anxiety. We will look at them in turn.

Psychoactive drugs such as selective serotonin reuptake inhibitors (SSRIs), serotonin-norepinephrine reuptake inhibitors (SNRIs), monoamine oxidase inhibitors (MAOIs), and tricyclic antidepressants (TCAs) have been used to reduce depression, and extreme pessimism. I want to re-emphasize that psychoactive drugs should NOT be taken/prescribed without also learning new behaviors with the aid of a therapist. The purpose of psychoactive drugs is not just to decrease a behavior but to permit learning of new behaviors. We need to stop being so depressed that we can't function; then we can learn new behaviors capable of warding off depressive states that are not biologically based—and even some that are.

The same goes for all of these families of drugs: Drugs exist to reduce anger levels to enable anger management, and anti-anxiety drugs can help enable fear management. Other than psychoactive prescription drugs, Vitamin B12 supplements and lean, protein-rich diets have been effective elevating mood. Also, listening to "sad" music tends to elevate levels of prolactin (for those with sufficient natural prolactin) and improve mood. And, Martin Seligman (2011) reports dramatic results in mood elevation from training all ages in his Penn Resiliency model that is based on training in explanatory style, expressions of gratitude, and other positive psychology strategies.

Anger is a twofold problem: getting angry too quickly, and then not letting go of it for some time. Duke University Psychiatrist Redford Williams (1989, & Williams, 1994) writes about unrelenting anger and hostility as the core of the Type A personality and is associated with coronary heart disease proneness. There are basically two ways to prevent the quick ramping up of the anger response: Train people to recognize the beginning of an angry outburst and how to redirect it, and/or take beta blockers. These psychoactive drugs prevent sympathetic arousal of the autonomic nervous system, thus protecting the heart. (Like most prescription medicines, beta blockers have potential side effects that the patient and physician must consider.)

At the other end of anger—how to let go of it, research has found a couple of chemicals associated with decreasing the effects of cortisol: DHEA (dehydroepiandrosterone) and neuropeptide Y (NPY). For example, soldiers undergoing the intense stress of mock interrogations do better when they have higher levels of neuropeptide Y. Also, combat veterans with higher levels of neuropeptide Y have lower risk for post-traumatic stress disorder (PTSD). (Stix, 2011) Nitric oxide has been found to increase blood flow and decrease blood pressure. Turmeric reputedly boosts mood. Competition affects testosterone levels, which affect anger. Higher testosterone exacerbates anger. Compete and win, and testosterone rises. Compete and lose, it falls. So, a cheap prescription (but with costs!) is to compete only or mostly with people you know will beat you! Before an event where anger control is important, perhaps that is the time to find someone to beat you straight sets in tennis (unless losing makes you angry).

For the control of anxiety, anxiolytic drugs are available. Also, levels of the protein stathmin are associated with levels of fear: higher levels of stathmin with more fear, lower levels with absence of fear. Watch for developments on how to modulate your stathmin levels. Breast-feeding is calming for mother and infant, with long-term benefits for both. Ongoing touch is calming—in lieu of humans at home and work, try pets. With respect to diet, caffeine exacerbates the fight-or-flight response, inasmuch as caffeine triggers the release of cortisol. To improve mood, limit yourself to one "dose" of caffeine every seven hours, or no more than 100 ml of caffeine per pound of body weight. That's about one cup of drip coffee (c. 150 ml) every seven hours for a 150-pounder. Check the Web for caffeine contents of various beverages and foods (e.g., chocolate). Avoid, just stay away from, secondhand smoke. Studies show that secondhand smoke increases coronary heart disease among non-smokers as well as increasing associated mood problems. Recently, a South Dakota town outlawed smoking in public places, thus virtually eliminating secondhand smoke. Coronary heart disease incidents treated by health providers plummeted. After a half year or so, the law was reversed, with the ensuing result that coronary heart disease returned to its former (higher) levels. A diet missing fat will affect mood—the critical neurotransmitter acetylcholine is only available from dietary fat; so fat-free diets will result in breakdown of neural membranes and associated problems with mood and memory will occur. Aerobic exercise calms and improves mood, as does anaerobic exercise to a lesser degree. Aerobic exercise flushes out cortisol (which accumulates in your system after, for example, a stressful episode)—anaerobic doesn't.

Now, for the positive emotions. A key difference in managing positive emotions is that one doesn't need to consider different kinds. For negative emotions, there are the big three: fear, anger, and sadness, each with somewhat different neurochemical bases. For position emotions, there is the one: positive emotions. They are one continuum, ranging from less intense positivity (e.g., amusement) to more intense positivity (e.g., ecstasy). All the positive emotions are happy emotions. Prescription uppers (i.e., amphetamines) have been a traditional mood booster. Non-prescription alternatives include caffeine (but only one dose per seven hours!), sugars, a protein-rich diet, hot chili peppers, chocolate, and, well, calories. Oh, and did I say chocolate? Access to fresh air and natural sunlight boost mood—both increase oxygen levels in the bloodstream, thus increasing alertness and boosting mood (oxygen in the blood is necessary for fueling the burning of glucose in the brain in order to have energy to be alert). Winning a competition boosts mood, so if you are the kind of person who wants to change their set point (and I am not), then you might pick your competition so that you always win. Doing lunch (or any meal) with a friend, family member, or colleague boosts mood and relationship bonding (as the result of elevating levels of oxytocin). Alcohol in moderation boosts mood. Try a whiff of Liquid Trust (atomized oxytocin) to promote positivity in relationships. Chemically, you might explore with your therapist how you might increase levels of dopamine (it promotes warmth and pleasure) and GABA (Gamma-aminobutyric acid; the more you have. the more inhibited you are, so find a way to lower your levels!).

Eduardo Punset (2007, p. 140) suggests that there are four prerequisites for changing one's level of happiness. In other words, before trying any of the boosters, eliminating any of the downers, or engaging in any other activity specifically intended to make you happier, you need to take care of four prerequisites, as though you were cleaning house before receiving guests:

- Unlearning what is counterproductive (e.g., bad habits, fears, etc.)
- "Filtering out unfounded social beliefs"
- "Allowing nature to take its self-organizing course"
- "Overcoming fear"

What Punset means is that the boosters are less likely to work if you don't eliminate the kinds of things that interfere with their effect, much like needing to lose weight before becoming a competitive long-distance runner. An overweight person may start running and benefit from it, but a lean runner wins races. The four items above, paraphrased, are:

- Think through, either with family, friends, or a therapist, whether you engage in any self-defeating behaviors that no amount of "boosters" will be able to overcome long term, such as smoking, alcoholism, or being hypercritical.
- Get over racial, gender, age, ethnic, or other stereotypes that will forever cast a dark cloud over any mood-boost initiatives
- Do not fight aging—go with it, and enjoy the benefits of not having to do any more the things that aging does not support.
- Desensitize yourself to your fears by gradually approaching them and making peace.

To allow bad habits, prejudice, denial, and phobias to continue while trying to boost your mood is like trying to diet on unrestricted amounts of mayonnaise and white bread.

There is a way of looking at the world that makes letting go of Punset's four obstacles easier—the Eastern sense of detachment. Eric Weiner (2008) describes it this way, referring to the Hindu belief that all is illusion, or *maya*:

> Once we see life as a game, no more consequential than a game of chess, then the world seems a lot lighter, a lot happier. Personal failure becomes "as small a cause for concern as playing the role of loser in a summer theater performance," writes Huston Smith in his book *The World's Religions*. If it's all theater, it doesn't matter which role you play, as long as you realize it's only a role. Or, as Alan Watts said: "A genuine person is one who knows he is a big act and does it with complete zip." (p. 306)

With respect to efforts at changing one's personality, one needs to be clear about one's goal: Is it changing a core disposition or changing a choice, circumstance, or other factor? I do not recommend trying to change a core disposition, of trying to raise or lower one's N and E scores. Through prodigious effort using multiple resources, small change may be possible, and small change may be enough. If one's motive to change is to fix a medical problem, that is another matter—surgery, psychoactive drugs, and other resources may be brought to bear in this case. I define a medical problem with respect to personality traits as a condition that prevents one from keeping a job and/or a relationship. Short of such a condition, I suggest NOT trying to change one's traits, but rather trying to change one's choices and circumstances. In Chapter 10, I will present a template for you to plan what you want to do in order to feel that you are thriving in this lifetime, and not merely surviving, that you are in gear, on the road with the journey that you are choosing to make, knowing that it is being on a right journey that will make meaning for your life, and not arriving at any given destination. As a preview, by the end of this book, you will have a plan that includes:

- A personal priorities statement that includes goals, fit, flow, community, and altruism;
- A first codicil to that priorities statement that includes choices and circumstances to change;
- A second codicil that identifies small adjustments to monitor daily for maximum personal satisfaction with life;
- A way to keep track of it all.

Composing Your Next Chapter

Review Table 3.3 for your No's to booster choices and circumstances and your Yes's to downer choices and circumstances. Then enter below new choices you'd like to make and new circumstances you'd like to work towards.

_____

_____

_____

_____

_____

_____

_____

Part Two

Alternatives to Happiness—
Defining the Right State for
Staying In Gear

STATEMENT OF PERSONAL PRIORITIES

FLOW | FIT | GOALS | COMMUNITY | ALTRUISM

Happiness Boosters
(Choice)

Happiness Downers
(Choice)

119 Minor Adjustors

(more within personal control)

(more outside personal control)

HAPPINESS SET POINT

Happiness Boosters
(Circumstance)

Happiness Downers
(Circumstance)

Continuum of Trait Happiness

Perennially Happy (N- E+) .... Occasionally Happy (N + E-)

4

Happiness Isn't for Everyone

The Five Modes for Staying In Gear

> "Every block of stone has a statue inside it and it is the task of the sculptor to discover it."
>
> "I saw the angel in the marble and carved until I set him free."
>
> --Michelangelo

Guide to this chapter:
- On the Problem of Definition of Terms
- How the Five Modes Evolved
- The Purpose that They Serve
- The Criteria for Selecting Them
- The Mind as Maker
- Brief Definitions

Last night I was reading on the porch of Blowing Rock Conference Center. Jane and I had been enjoying a long weekend writing retreat in North Carolina's High Country—cooler by far than this July 4th weekend back in Charlotte. But fresh air feeds the brain and fires the writing engine, and we had been living in open air without air conditioning for three days. An older man emerged from the lodge and plopped down in the rocking chair beside me, introducing himself as a retired minister. Actually appreciative of a conversational break from writing and reading all day, I searched for common ground. It was easy. We recapped the career of a mutual friend who had spent her early adult years struggling in a career that just didn't suit her—a Ph.D. in electrical engineering working in a manufacturing environment as a manager who was too sensitive, outgoing, creative, and kind to endure the role cut out for a more rational, solitary, down-to-earth, and tough nature. She took her sensitive, outgoing, creative, and kind qualities to seminary and was now herself an active minister. My companion commented, "She found her home." I remarked, "Yes, better late than never."

What happened in mid-career to this woman is what happened to Michelangelo's marble. Her natural disposition somehow got ignored in her first career pursuit, only for her to find the "angel" within and set herself free. In this chapter, as in this book, as in my life's work, I propose to outline the basis for finding the statue within us. I regard each of us as the composer of our own work, the sculptor of our own statue, the painter of our own portrait. I will describe for you the five modes of being that you may use in your composition, just as a painter would use the five basic colors or red, yellow, blue, white, and black, or the musician would use melody, harmony, timbre, and rhythm. My goal is for each of us to compose the next chapter (or more) of our lives.

The assumption of this approach is perhaps best described by Rabbi Hyman Schachtel (1954): "Happiness is not having what you want, but wanting what you have." In our pursuit of happiness, we have talked of Happers (those who are naturally happy), Batters (those who try to be happier), Mappers (those who sidestep happiness and plan with what is available to them), and Nappers (those who are content, but not necessarily happy). This section of the book is for the Mappers, the planners. Or, as I suggested earlier, the composers. Take the material we have and make something of it that has meaning. Jeff Larsen of Texas Tech University has investigated (Larsen & McKibban, 2008; Norris & Larsen, 2010) Rabbi Schachtel's dictum and found it both true and not true:

> He was right in that people who want what they have more than others do tend to be happier; he was wrong in that people who have more of what they want than others do also tend to be happier.... In contrast, simply wanting things was uncorrelated with happiness, and simply having things accounted for no [additional] happiness.... Thus, the effect of possessions on well-being depends on how people value those possessions, a finding that speaks to the subjectivity of well-being. (Larsen & McKibban, 2008, p. 375)

Permit me to paraphrase and extend their meaning personally, as I read it and as it applies to this book:

- These mental attitudes are associated with a higher sense of well-being:
  - I want what I have, e.g.:
    - I have a temperament that is uncomfortable around crowds and noises, and I have no desire to be any different—I don't want to learn to enjoy noisy crowds (i.e., I like/want my quiet).
    - I have a lower-priced sedan that is safe and durable, and that is fine—I don't dream about a more expensive car with more features.
    - I have a 3' x 6' N-scale model railroad to enjoy with my grandchildren (and any other children of all ages), and I have no need or desire for a larger layout.
  - I have what I want, e.g.:
    - I wanted both children and grandchildren, and I have them.
    - I wanted a collection of early musical instruments, and I have them.
    - I wanted a laptop computer that would enable me to work anywhere, and I have it.
- These mental attitudes add nothing to one's sense of well-being:
  - I want something that I don't have, e.g.:
    - I want a resort cabin in the mountains.
    - I want to have less of a temper, i.e., to have a slower trigger.
    - I want a child or grandchild with whom I can play duets.
  - I have something that I don't want, e.g.:
    - I have a pet cat towards whom I am indifferent.
    - I have a front yard and back yard that are more of a burden than a pleasure or source of pride.
    - I have a balalaika (3-stringed Russian musical instrument) that I have never learned to play nor have I maintained it properly (cleaning, and so forth).

According to Larsen and his associates' research, the first two sets of attitudes boost happiness. I am expanding his thought to include more than material possessions. For example, I have included at least two personality traits. To be comfortable with what one has—material possessions, traits, abilities, values, experiences, family, friends—is a boon to happiness. In Chapter 6, we will attempt to define the ingredients of the whole person. This will give each of us an opportunity to have a complete description of who we are, and to make up our minds to be comfortable with that—i.e., to want what we have, to embrace our individuality, and use it as building material as we compose the rest of our life.

> Mr. Pontifex never lacked anything he much cared about. True, he might have been happier than he was if he had cared about things which he did not care for, but the gist of this lies in the "if he had cared."
>
> --Samuel Butler.

As we saw in Chapter 2, looking forward to a blissful experience or event is a happiness booster. That is the same as wanting something that we don't have. So, this appears to contradict Larsen's research. Not really, and here's why. To want something that one does not have does not contribute to happiness, *unless* you are actively working to someday have that object of your dreams. Whether you are saving money, honing your skill, engaged in constructing the thing, laying the political groundwork, studying towards a degree or license, or some other form of preparation, then you are doing two things that are indeed satisfying: You are making progress towards a goal (a mode of positive mood described in Chapter 7), and you are anticipating a positive experience (a booster in Chapter 2).

True, to want something that you don't have and not to be working towards having it, is nothing but lustful materialism, like window-shopping with no commitment to someday making a purchase. It is the other side of the coin from having something that you don't want—you've acquired something that has no meaning for you, you don't maintain it properly if at all, you're not proud of it, perhaps you can't even figure out why you really ever acquired it in the first place. I have some books that are like that—books I bought but have never read, and likely never will. To want without pursuit is lust, greed, and/or envy, and to have without want is gluttony and/or sloth. Depressing, huh?

On the Problem of Definition of Terms

I continue to struggle with what to call the state of mind that the five modes of positive mood offer as an alternative to "happiness" or "well-being." "Well-being" tends to be used as an umbrella term that includes happiness, job satisfaction, quality of life, education level, health, and so forth. It is a combination of both subjective and objective indicators: smiles and dollars (smiles and piles?!).

On the other hand, "well-being" is often used as a synonym for "happiness." Some people use the phrase "well-being" in two senses: subjective well-being and objective well-being. "Subjective well-being" tends to be used as a synonym for "happiness." "Objective well-being" seems to be used as a synonym for quality-of-life indicators. This quagmire of definitional confusion makes communication difficult.

In this book, I am proposing an alternative to both. Imagine a person who is not prone to smile and laugh, who is seldom amused by events, who worries about the state of the world, who gets upset at an injustice, who is saddened by repeated tales of genocide, corruption, human trafficking, and so forth, who makes enough money so that food, shelter, clothing, and modest extras are of no concern, whose health and physical condition are average. This individual takes a happiness (or well-being) test. Two representative questions are: how happy are you most of the time, and how would you describe the overall quality of your life at this time? This first question asks about emotions, while the second asks about success factors.

In attempting to answer these questions, he gets angry at the test itself and writes in the margins:

"I am working long days to help poor people learn basic life skills. I am not around happy people very often, nor would I describe myself as happy. I do enjoy seeing appreciative smiles from time to time, and that helps me continue in my work. Happiness is a meaningless word for me and the people with whom I work. We are trying to move from mere survival to a somewhat better quality of life. No, I am not happy. I live somewhere in the vortex of disgust, anger, and despair. The quality of my life is acceptable. I am not rich, and I work hard, but my work has meaning. Every day I am eager to wake up and continue working with my associates to eradicate poverty in my region. I am using my strengths, I am never bored, I never run out of interesting people to work with and help, my mind is challenged by intransigent problems that resist traditional solutions. So, I cannot answer your stupid questionnaire. I am neither "very happy" nor "very unhappy" nor anywhere in between. I have neither a "very high quality of life" nor a "very low quality of life." It is more complex than that. I have goals to accomplish with my coworkers--goals that use my strengths, challenge my mind, and help my fellow humans. I feel a sense of vitality that I would trade neither for the millionaire's pad nor for the cheerleader's exultation. You tell me: Where do I fit on your happiness/well-being scale?"

Where, indeed? For the moment, let's not try to measure him. Rather, we will hold up our five modes of positive being and ask if he exhibits each of them: making progress towards a goal, check; good fit between personal qualities and environmental demands, check; absorbed in his work (flow), check; connected with others in the community, check; altruism, check. Forget happiness and well-being. This fellow is in gear, vital, engaged. Martin Seligman would say "flourishing," but I think that is too positive, too smiley. My wife, Jane, prefers to call it "thriving," as opposed to merely "surviving." A Mapper as opposed to a Napper.

I want a word or phrase that describes both his state of mind, as well as that of the Happers and Batters. It needs a neutral emotional ring to it. It needs to suggest a state of mind characterized by self-respect, motivation, competency, and progress. I really like the phrase "in gear," as it includes all four of those meanings, and it could describe Maria in *The Sound of Music*, in all of her ebullience, as well as Mother Teresa and the poverty fighter just described, in all of their anguish. If I were to use happiness or thriving or vitality or flourishing, it would likely sell more (books, lectures, work-

> "The opposite of depression is not happiness. It's vitality."

shops). But it would not be accurate. There are many Mappers in the world who are full of self-respect, motivation, competency, and who are making progress towards goals but who exhibit little positive emotional tone. They are serious, determined, and in pursuit of something. They are practicing, devoted, and working hard. They seldom smile or perhaps even touch. But though they do not giggle much, neither do they wallow in the depths of despair, much. It is these people who are In gear that in all likelihood are turned off by the happiness literature specifically and the positive psychology literature in general. They are my primary target, for they have been neglected. But all can benefit from the five modes. Now, let's move into the story of how I formulated them.

How the Five Modes Evolved

First, understand that I am a reader. Philosophy, social science, history, literature, why I even read the comic strips! I remember one morning in June 2006 sitting on the sofa in our daughter's Manhattan high-rise living room reading Darrin McMahon's *Happiness: A History* (2006). Our one-year old granddaughter, Stella, was asleep by our side, her parents on a jaunt to a friend's wedding in the UK. Page after page, this history of one aspect of philosophy invited associations with many areas that I had studied: ethics, positive psychology, flow, McAdams' life narrative, personality theory, social psychology, motivation, explanatory style, locus of control, the triarchic brain…. As I frequently paused to consider all these aspects of happiness, I stared reflectively out of their 12th floor view onto the East River and the United Nations Building. I thought of the Universal Declaration of Human Rights, the Dalai Lama, and veins of misery on this rich earth. I was hooked by the subject, and a new reading impetus had begun.

I read everything I could get my hands on. There was a modest literature on happiness at the time, but it has since mushroomed. In November of that year, an associate called two weeks before an upcoming professional meeting and asked if I would be willing to do the program—the planned-on speaker had cancelled. I quipped, "Speaker's choice?" And she quickly retorted, "Absolutely!" In my mind I considered my options. During my flurry of reading since that day in June, a model for "happiness" had slowly taken shape. This was an opportunity for me to collect all of my reading notes and make order out of them.

My model was empirically derived from upwards of 100 different beliefs, practices, habits, activities, traits, abilities, and other aspects of life that research had found to be associated with happiness, well-being, life satisfaction, and eudaimonia. There was, and is, no agreement in the literature about the taxonomy of happiness. In fact, Appendix A with its allelonyms and synonyms is the first attempt I know of to establish a semantic map of this domain of whatchamacallit. And it is only a beginning, in need of rigorous and extensive testing.

If there was no agreement about what to call it, there was even less agreement about how to organize the 100 or so factors contributing to it. Confounding the lack of conceptual organization was the perplexing issue of chicken-and-egg relationships, the question of correlation versus causation. If watching television is not correlated with happiness, is that because TV watching does not elicit happiness or because happy people do not watch TV? My first effort at organization centered on my core interest, which is the Big Five model of personality structure. Accordingly, I was interested in separating the factors into those that influenced a positive frame of mind among everyone, regardless of their personality traits, as opposed to those that influenced frame of mind depending on trait scores. For example, making progress towards a goal and doing a kind deed provide a lift for everyone, regardless of their trait scores. On the other hand, the number of activities one has scheduled in a day has differential effects depending on traits—people with more active natures (what I call E3: Activity Level) are boosted by busier calendars and a more out-and-about lifestyle, while those with less active natures prefer fewer activities and a more sedentary lifestyle.

So, I divided everything into two categories: modes and adjustors. The modes made everyone feel positive regardless of traits, while the adjustors were more idiosyncratic, more reflective of individual differences. My first stab had eight modes:

- Flow—being totally absorbed in a task, based on the work of Mihalyi Csikszentmihalyi (1990),
- Fit—incorporating one's strengths into tasks, based on the work of many industrial-organizational psychologists,

- Goals—having meaningful goals and making progress towards them, based on the work of Gary Latham (2007) and others,
- Community—having both quantity and quality of relationships at home and at large, based on the work of Robert Putnam (2000), John Gottman (Gottman & Silver, 1999), and others,
- Altruism—service in its many forms, based on the work of Lyubomirsky (2008) and others,
- Pleasure—based on research on savoring and mindfulness as reported by Seligman (2002) and others,
- Submission—degree of independence and autonomy, and
- Activities—having more activities of shorter duration versus fewer activities with either longer duration or more unscheduled time.

My feeling at the time (fall of 2006) is that these eight were sources of positive meaning for everyone, regardless of individuals' differences. To address the needs of individuals with different traits (extraverts and introverts, challengers and submitters, and so forth), different abilities (verbal, kinesthetic, and so forth), and values (intellectual, spiritual, entrepreneurial, and so forth), I collected a second list of "adjustors"—things that an individual might do more or less of, depending on their individual strengths and preferences—small adjustments to make in an otherwise operative engine. These adjustors will be discussed in full later in Chapter 11. Here are a few:

- Serious vs. Light,
- Optimism vs. Realism vs. Pessimism (explanatory style),
- Active vs. Passive,
- Meditation vs. Activity,
- Short Term vs. Long Term,
- Drug therapy vs. non-pharmaceutical therapy (exercise, diet, cognitive/behavioral therapy),
- Mental vs. Physical,
- Material vs. Spiritual,
- Academic vs. Everyday,
- Requires money vs. Is free, and
- Maintenance vs. Production.

What these all have in common, in contrast to the eight "modes," is that each represents a continuum from more of one thing to more of its opposite. Neither extreme is intrinsically pleasing. Instead they depend on the individual's traits, talents, and values as to which extreme (or somewhere closer to the middle) might be more satisfying.

After using this model for several years (I developed a workshop, an assessment, a report, and now this book), several things became clear:

- The last three modes---pleasure, submission, and activities—were not universal boosters. Their boosting power depended on differences among individuals. Not everyone takes pleasure in sensory experience, be it chocolate, brandy, béarnaise sauce, or sex. For them, talk of savoring and mindfulness versus gluttony was all gluttony. These folks were either ascetic or lived simple lives without appetites. They did not live to eat—they ate to live. Submission to a system—a convent, the military, a bureaucracy—again was not for everyone, nor was independence and autonomy. Clearly this was a continuum that belonged with the adjustors. And we have already discussed "activities"—it also is a continuum and dependent on individual traits.

- The "happiness" umbrella under which I had been working was breaking apart—the ribs, or spokes, were cracking and bending under the torrent of new research that showed clearly that happiness was not the be-all, end-all of positive psychology and the theory of optimal experience. I originated the notion that "Happers" occurred at a rate of 1 in 9 in the population. Happiness applied to them. The rest of us were faced with a decision of whether to try to be more like them (Batters), to stay just as we were (Nappers), or to look elsewhere for optimal quality of life (Mappers). This clarified for me that the "modes" were not meant for happiness per se, although being in one of the five modes did not preclude experiencing happiness. The five modes were rather to be addressed to the Mappers, those who wanted to compose the rest of their life without regard to happiness as such, but rather to living a life with meaning and self-respect.
- New research was adding a new way of categorizing happiness factors: choices and circumstances (Lyubomirsky, 2008; Seligman, 2011).

So, my map of this domain began to emerge:

- Happers don't need help.
- Batters need to embrace boosters and avoid downers through right choices and managing circumstances.
- Mappers need to wrestle with the five modes of optimal experiences, and then monitor their lives from time to time with the list of adjustors, much like adjusting the radio controls in a car throughout a long journey.
- Nappers may continue their march with our best wishes, knowing that they are welcome to join the ranks of the Batters or Mappers, either full-time or as needed.

In reviewing current writing about our subject, I found that my model is consistent with what others are writing, with a few unique twists of my own. For example, Martin Seligman came out with his *Flourish* (2011) just a month ago. I eagerly read it and was deflated to find his "PERMA" concept. I thought he had beat me to the publishing punch. But in carefully reading his five ingredients of well-being (PERMA), I realized that there were important differences in his five and my five. I summarize them in Table 4.0.

There are two major differences and three minor differences. The first major difference is that I do not include what he calls Positive Emotion in my Five Modes. Seligman is including positive emotions as an ingredient of well-being, and that is fine. But I have excluded positive emotion from my model because it intentionally excludes the Happers. While Happers may benefit from using my model, I am more interested in what it takes to live a life of meaning and self-respect for those who are not born happy, and for whom happiness is not a goal. I address Positive Emotion in Chapter 3 as the Happiness Quotient, and the ingredients thereof are identified.

The second major difference is PE-Fit (person-to-environment). In his latest book (2011), Seligman does not identify the match between individual attributes and environmental demands as a means to optimal experience. PE-Fit, you will recall, is about extraverts doing extraverted activities, solitary folks doing solitary activities, detail-oriented people doing detail work, and so forth. If he addressed this in a major way, I missed it. Perhaps this is because I focus on the world of work, and he does not—his focus is on life in general, and that is fine. However, in the workplace, using a person's strong points is a major source of job satisfaction, employee morale, and organizational effectiveness in general. (Howard, 2010; Buckingham and Coffman, 1999)

Table 4.0   **Comparison of Seligman's PERMA and the Five Modes of Optimal Experience**

Seligman's PERMA	Howard	Comment
Positive Emotion	(Happiness Quotient)	Not in Howard Model
Engagement	Flow	Same
Positive Relationships	Community	Similar
Meaning	Altruism	Similar
Accomplishment	Goals	Similar
	PE-Fit	Not in Seligman Model

Seligman's description of "Engagement" is essentially the same as my use of Csikszentmihalyi's Flow concept. However, minor differences exist with the three remaining elements in both models. Two are differences in scope and one is in emphasis.

Seligman's "Positive Relationships" is somewhat narrower than my "Community." I will include a good bit of information about what makes a quality relationship in Chapter 8, but I treat relationships as part of the larger construct of "social capital" (cf. Putnam, 2005) that includes involvement in community, regional, national, and world affairs.

Another difference in scope is between "Accomplishment" and "Goals"—Seligman's is loftier, while I include the mundane, with an emphasis on goal-setting of a very local and short-term nature on the one hand and of a very global and long-term on the other, and everything in between. Also, my emphasis is more on making progress towards goals, not all of which can necessarily be attained, whereas Seligman's emphasis is more on achievement, or completion, of goals.

One final difference is one of emphasis, or definition: His "Meaning" is directed at pursuing a lifestyle that is committed to something higher or greater than oneself. My "Altruism" does in fact include actions that could fall under that category, but also include charity for selfish motives. Altruism, as we will see in Chapter 9, is a complex landscape that includes everything from writing thank-you notes to doing pro-bono work on a large scale. I think we both are talking about the same domain, but with small differences of emphasis. In fact, I applaud Seligman for giving his time to the U. S. Army's resiliency program as a token of his gratitude for liberating the Nazi concentration camps that took his parents from him.

Bok (2010, loc. 351) reported that six factors tend to account for most of the variation in happiness beyond the genetic set point: marriage, social relationships, employment, perceived health, religion, and quality of government. Five of these are primarily choices, with one—quality of government—primarily circumstance. My model includes two of Bok's six under Community (marriage and social relationships), one under Altruism (religion), and I have broken his "employment" into three aspects—part of it is treated in P-E Fit, another dimension of it in Flow, and yet a third dimension of employment is treated under Goals. I have treated neither perceived health nor quality of government under one of my five major modes. That is not to deny their impact, but rather I have not included them because 1) perceived health is primarily a matter of temperament, with persons high in Need for Stability more likely to worry or be saddened about their actual or perceived health, and 2) quality of government is less a matter of individual choice and more a matter of collective action.

My five modes are also consistent with Deci and Ryan's self-determination theory (1985, described in Pink, 2001), which begins with the notion of universal human needs. They argue that all citizens of planet Earth have three needs:

- Competence (e.g., flow, goal progress),
- Autonomy (e.g., person-environment fit), and
- Relatedness (e.g., community, altruism).

As you can see in my parenthetical notes to the right of these three bulleted items, I think my five modes fit nicely into their three universal needs, with flow and goals driving competence, PE-Fit driving Autonomy, and Community and Altruism driving Relatedness. Deci and Ryan's work is described as a theory of motivation. Maybe that is the word I have been looking for!?

The Purpose that They Serve

The purpose of this book and the model on which it is based is to expand the domain of Positive Psychology so that it includes the miserable wretches of the world—along with everyone else—in such a way that we take them as they are, but with the invitation to make the most of what they are and have. While I do not object to people taking on the goal of becoming happier, I regard it as a risky adventure rife with the prospect of leading to guilt—"I've tried everything you suggested, and I'm no happier. Either it doesn't work or I'm a hopeless case." Instead, I invite readers to consider composing the remainder of their lives around the 5 modes and 119 adjustors.

Specifically, the purposes for immersing oneself in the modes and adjustors are fourfold:

1. I want to give everyone the opportunity to feel that they are making progress towards one or more meaningful goals.
2. I want everyone to experience total absorption in their work, both private and public, while feeling that they are building on their deepest sources of energy and not on their lesser energy sources.
3. I want everyone to enjoy a maximum sense of vitality, that they are thriving rather than merely surviving, even if they seldom experience positive emotions.
4. I want everyone to feel that they have quality relationships with family, associates, and friends.
5. I want everyone to feel as though they are grounded, that they have found their own voice, and are not merely following others' dicta, much in the spirit of the moving speech delivered by ex-Yale Professor William Deresiewicz to West Point freshers in October 2009, "Solitude and Leadership." (published in *American Scholar* Spring 2010) Here is a brief excerpt:

   I started by noting that solitude and leadership would seem to be contradictory things. But it seems to me that solitude is the very essence of leadership. The position of the leader is ultimately an intensely solitary, even intensely lonely one. However many people you may consult, you are the one who has to make the hard decisions. And at such moments, all you really have is yourself.

6. In sum, I want everyone to feel In gear, a metaphor which includes making progress, using one's strengths, having vitality, and being grounded and connected.

Eric Wilson (2008, p. 4) comments: "We are wantonly hankering to rid the world of numerous ideas and visions, multitudinous innovations and meditations. We are right at this moment annihilating melancholia. We wonder if the wide array of antidepressants will one day make sweet sorrow a thing of the past. We wonder if soon enough every single American will be happy. We wonder if we will become a society of self-satisfied smiles."

Short of prefrontal lobotomies and extensive sedation, not likely. We with Wilson celebrate melancholy as well as emotional neutrality in the spirit of promoting vitality of the unhappy kind. I am reminded of the beautiful Czechoslovakian film and novel (by Milan Kundera), translated as *The Unbearable Lightness of Being*. It treats the Prague Spring in 1968 in which residents were subjected to the Soviet tank invasion that changed their lives for the worse. One character is bothered by her partner's flip attitude, and she comments on it in such a way that gives the book/film its title. In essence, she asks how can her partner feel so high when everyone else is so low? Well, either he was a Happer or a jerk.

Notice that my reasons for adopting the modes and adjustors did not mention income level or standard of living. For the moment, we will assume the reader has at least a minimal income that is capable of sustaining a meaningful, satisfying life, at least when personal priorities and viewpoints are properly adjusted. There has been too much emphasis on wealth and materialism. We need to focus on individual character. The economist John Maynard Keynes seconds this notion:

> The time is not far off when the economic problem will take the back seat where it belongs, and the heart will be occupied . . . by the real problems—the problems of life and human relations, of creation and behavior and religion. [Then], man will be faced with his permanent problem—how to use his freedom from pressing economic cares, how to occupy the leisure, which science and compound interest will have won for him, to live wisely, and agreeably, and well. (in Bok, 2010, loc. 1,119)

At the risk of appearing to pile up evidence in support of my approach, here is a similar passage by Eric Weiner (2008):

> Sometimes people choose not to be happy, and that's okay. [Sigmund] Freud was dying of cancer...yet he refused morphine. He wanted to continue to work and didn't want to have his mind clouded. If you believe that pleasure, or at least the absence of pain, is man's highest ideal, then Freud's decision made no sense. Yet happiness...is more than simply an uninterrupted series of pleasurable moments, and that's a point...the positive-psychology movement misses. (p. 257)

Weiner goes on to quote Tim LeBon (2001), a specialist in happiness philosophy but not a radical adherent to it, as saying: "Part of positive psychology is about being positive, but sometimes laughter and clowns are not appropriate. Some people don't want to be happy, and that's okay. They want meaningful lives, and those are not always the same as happy lives." (Weiner, 2008, p. 257)

The Criteria for Selecting the Five Modes

I have attempted to keep several criteria in mind as I selected the five modes, the core processes for optimal experience:

1. **Cost-free**. Each of the modes must be capable of being pursued without spending any money. Time and energy would be mandatory, but money, no. Of course, one may always choose to use financial resources if one wishes, but for a core process to be available to all, it must be available to those without financial resources. All five fit this requirement.

118

2.   **Trait-free**. Each mode must feel natural to pursue, regardless of one's traits, abilities, and values. All five fit this requirement.

3.   **Credential-free**. Each mode must work with any level of education or experience, so that one may engage in it regardless of the person's starting point: high school dropouts as well as post-docs, those fresh out of home and school, as well as those with 40 years of experience. All five fit this requirement.

4.   **Stress-free**. Each mode must be intrinsically satisfying and not stress-inducing. While there will clearly be obstacles along the way, the processes do fit this requirement.

5.   **Synergistic**. Each mode must be capable of working in sync with the other modes. Each fits this requirement. For example, it is possible to have a service goal that involves others and builds on one's strengths at an appropriate level of challenge—that incorporates all five modes in one activity: altruism, goals, community, fit, and flow.

The Mind as Maker

We cannot wait for government, religious bodies, teachers, counselors, family, or friends to lead our lives to greater meaning. Nor can we do it all by ourselves. Some of us may select goals that change government policy, change the school system, change any of various social institutions in such a way that everyone would benefit. Those are great goals, and a listing of such possible social-action goals is provided in Appendix D. So, in our goal-setting, we can choose more local or more global objectives—to learn Sanskrit in order to read the Vedas in the original (more local, as it mostly affects only me) or to join a lobbying effort to enact stronger laws and enforcement with respect to sex trafficking of young children.

But regardless of the scope of our goals, we the individuals are the composer of our personal plan. Marcus Aurelius was an emperor of Rome in the 2nd century CE. He wrote the great reflective work *Meditations*, in which he stressed that the mind could make reality. The mind as maker. How we think about everyday events informs our reactions to them. Prejudices, fears, and assumptions based on appearances all shape our actions, and our mind is capable of changing those prejudices, fears, and assumptions. Here is a sample of the emperor's advice: "Because your own strength is unequal to the task, do not assume that it is beyond the powers of man; but if anything is within the powers and province of man, believe that it is within your own compass also."

Richard Lazarus was the first psychologist to use the term "reappraisal" (Ochsner, 2006) to refer to our capability of reevaluating stressors and other threats to our emotional life. Reappraisal, reframing, spin-doctoring—these all refer to the mind's ability to treat external reality as clay to our sculptor's hands, as a palette to our artist's eye, as building blocks to our architect's vision. The world is what we make of it. Wallace Stephens described the mind as maker in these verses from his "The Man with the Blue Guitar":

> They said, "You have a blue guitar,
> You do not play things as they are."
>
> The man replied, "Things as they are
> Are changed upon the blue guitar."
>
> And they said to him, "But play, you must,
> A tune beyond us, yet ourselves,A tune upon the blue guitar,
> Of things exactly as they are."

Here the guitarist represents the mind, the guitar the world, and the music that emanates is what the mind makes of the world.

In very much the same sense, Martin Seligman's explanatory style shows a way for the mind to change one's first impressions of why certain events happen. We will explain this in more detail in Chapter 7 in our discussion of goals. Seligman offers three cognitive procedures that enable us to explain the outcomes of everyday events as more optimistic or more pessimistic. Just as the hands can make, the mind can mold, whether through words (as in Seligman's explanatory style) or through visualization (as in the kind of visual rehearsal used in Olympic training).

Zebras don't get ulcers, and humans do. Why? Robert Sapolsky (2004) points out that zebras forget the Bengal tiger that they just escaped, and proceed with their day. Humans can't just turn off recent stressors, as we tend to replay them and remain agitated and cautious in anticipation of their return. In this little section on "The Mind as Maker," I want to make the point that we have choices. We can reappraise our stressors and decide they are not as potent as we once thought, or that we have more resources to deal with them than we thought. By applying our mind to our world, we are able to exert some control over it with the benefit of living life in a more optimal manner.

Eric Weiner (2008) writes, "When you get down to it, there are basically three, and only three, ways to make yourself happier. You can increase the amount of positive affect (good feelings). You can decrease the amount of negative affect (bad feelings). Or you can change the subject"—by which he means the Thai attitude of *mai pen lai*, or "never mind." In other words, don't worry about it, forget it, move on, get a life, and don't ruminate, rethink, Monday morning quarterback, and so forth. (p. 226) The five modes are an option for *mai pen lai*. Forget happiness: Pursue with others a service goal in a way that builds on your virtues.

Brief Definitions

Timothy Leary is famous for his self-experimenting with LSD, but he also was a Harvard professor who created the popular relationship model that evaluated an individual in a relationship with respect to the importance that individual placed on "Agency" and "Communion." Agency is associated with achievement and one's emphasis on attaining one's goals, while communion is associated with nurture and one's emphasis on maintaining high-quality relationships. It is interesting to note that the five modes of positive mood and optimal experience divide nicely between these two dimensions. Agency is driven by goals, fit, and flow, while Communion is driven by Community and Altruism. Let us now define what we mean by these five modes. In the ensuing five chapters, we will provide more in-depth explanations along with "how to" suggestions.

Flow

Mihalyi Csikszentmihalyi (1990) and a team of graduate students set out to interview professionals in a variety of fields who reportedly experienced a high level of satisfaction with their lives. The research question was to find out what all of these highly motivated and productive people had in common. The findings were presented in *Flow: The Psychology of Optimal Experience*. I like that subtitle— "optimal experience." I believe I've used that phrase several times already! Doesn't sound like giggles and smiles. Sounds optimal, like St. Anselm's definition of God: that than which nothing greater can be thought.

They found that people who experience life optimally all reported extended periods in which they lost all sense of time, temperature, hunger—in short, it was as though they had pulled a curtain on the rest of the world and were totally absorbed in the task at hand, be it reading, calculating, crafting, teaching, exercising, you name it.... In Chapter 5, I will present the two variables that an individual can learn to control in order to stay in the "flow" state.

Fit

Henry Ford is reputed to have commented, "Why is it that they send me a whole person when all I want is a pair of hands?" Ford is espousing the "warm body" view of human resources planning: All you need to get the job done is a warm body—forget the details. Well, it is clear that most anyone can hammer a nail, but if you want someone who can hammer a nail repeatedly, days on end, and be good at it, and never tire of it, then you need more than a warm body that's just a pair of hands. You need certain personality characteristics that provide the natural energy for performing work that is simple, repetitive, and mentally undemanding. In Chapter 6, we will explore in some detail the

> "If you are not happy you had better stop worrying about it and see what treasures you can pluck from your own brand of unhappiness."
> --Robertson Davies

ingredients that should be taken into considerations when looking for a person with the appropriate characteristics to fit the demands of a specific job. Eduardo Punset (2007, p. 88) puts it this way: "Happiness, rather, may be an unconscious recognition, felt physically and emotionally, indicating an organism's synchrony with itself and its environment, its living and nonliving surroundings." The "synchrony with itself and its environment" is precisely what we mean by matching one's traits, abilities, values, and experiences to the demands of a particular type of work.

Sonya Lyubomirsky (2008) suggests this approach: "One of the themes of this book is that in order to become happier, we must learn to imitate the habits of very happy people." (p. 138) Poppycock! Perhaps she could modify that dictum thusly: "In order to become happier, we must learn to imitate the habits of persons who are happy *and* who share our traits, values, abilities, memories, and physical characteristics."

Goals

Barbara Ehrenreich (2009) accuses the positive psychology movement of attending "solely to the changes a person can make internally by adjusting his or her own outlook." (p. 171) She is saying that positive psychologists advocate that people only form goals that are aimed at changing their personal behavior or attitude, rather than being aimed at changing institutions and other people. That clearly is not only an exaggeration—it is unfounded. Witness Martin Seligman's huge project to change the culture of the U.S. Army! How's that for an external goal?

In Chapter 7, we will examine goal-setting from a variety of perspectives: mastery goals versus performance goals, local versus global goals, internal versus external goals, the characteristics of goal formulations that are most likely to be achieved, and so forth. We will explore how to integrate all five modes (and even some adjustors) into our goal formulations. Not only do people who set goals accomplish more than people who do not, people who make steady progress towards goals report feelings of self-respect and self-confidence.

Community

Just as Extraversion and Accommodation (see definitions in Chapter 1) are the relationship traits, Community and Altruism are the relationship modes. The other three can be done in solitude, while Community and Altruism are essentially relational. Admittedly, Secret Santas can do their thing in solitude, but even altruistic acts done while alone will impact others.

Community involves what Robert Putnam (2001) defined as social capital, as opposed to personal capital (as in knowledge and experience) or material capital (cash and possessions). Social capital is relationships, pure and simple. Quantity and quality. The more relationships, the better. The higher quality relationships, the better. Relationships help us avoid isolation. Contact with other people raises serotonin levels, thus helping inoculate us against depression and reducing stress. And, having relationships with happy people, just incidentally, makes us happier. In one study (Christakis & Fowler, 2009), social network analysis revealed that "a person is about 15 percent more likely to be happy if a directly connected person (at one degree of separation) is happy. And the spread of happiness doesn't stop there. The happiness effect for people at two degrees of separation (the friend of a friend) is 10 percent, and for people at three degrees of separation (the friend of a friend of a friend), it is about 6 percent." (p. 51) The researchers point out that even though this effect seems small, it is greater than the effect of increased income on happiness. A corollary of this finding is that the number of friends that one has does not impact happiness so much as the number who are themselves happy. (Christakis & Fowler, 2009) More in Chapter 8.

Altruism

Altruism is perhaps the most complex of the five modes. What comprises an altruistic act, one that serves the interests and needs of others? Some of the forms of altruism that we will explore in Chapter 9 include volunteering, charity, prayer, positive thoughts and energy, visualization, gratefulness, donations, random acts of kindness, thank you's, itemized responses for constructive criticism, crediting, compassion, service, love, and friendship. The positive impact of altruistic acts on others has a boomerang effect by making us feel better about ourselves. Maya Angelou, Wake Forest University American Studies professor and well-loved poet, was suggesting this, I believe, when she wrote:

> People will forget what you said,
> People will forget what you did,
> But people will never forget how you made them feel.

Dennis Prager (1998), responding to a woman who said she wished her husband had accompanied her to Prager's lecture, told the woman and the audience that her husband should have attended the talk because "he had a moral obligation to his daily partner in life to be as happy as he could be." (p. 3) I agree with the moral obligation part, but certainly there are other ways to fulfil it than by attending Prager's lectures. Attend mine! Just kidding. I do not think that one has the moral obligation to be happy, but rather the moral obligation to be caring, supportive, loving, appreciative, or something like that.

As a final comment before getting into the specifics of the five modes, I think it would be instructive to see how the 18 happiness allelonyms sort among the traditional set point of happiness and our five modes of optimal experience:

Happiness:
- Positive Emotions
- Cheerful Disposition
- Jollity
- Generally Positive Mood

Flow:
- Calmness
- Engagement
- Feeling Other-Worldly
- Titillation of the Senses

Fit:
- High Energy
- Passion
- Health

Goals:
- Competence
- Pride
- Optimism
- Material Comfort

Community:
- Mature Relationship
- Cared About

Altruism:
- Caring About Others

Eric Weiner (2008) remarks on an ad for Dos Equis beer: "The text reads, 'Being boring is a choice. Those mild salsas and pleated khakis don't buy themselves.' And so it is with happiness. When the talk of genetics and communal bonds and relative income is stripped away, happiness is a choice. Not an easy choice, not always a desirable one, but a choice nonetheless." (p. 184) Substitute "being In gear" for happiness and we're talking the same language. Now, for the specifics of the five modes.

STATEMENT OF PERSONAL PRIORITIES

FLOW | FIT | GOALS | COMMUNITY | ALTRUISM

Happiness Boosters
(Choice)

Happiness Downers
(Choice)

119 Minor Adjustors

(more within personal control)

(more outside personal control)

HAPPINESS SET POINT

Happiness Boosters
(Circumstance)

Happiness Downers
(Circumstance)

Continuum of Trait Happiness

Perennially Happy (N- E+) .... Occasionally Happy (N + E-)

5

Flow

The Absence of Emotions

"I am sorry if I seem distracted," he said. "I'm always a bit slow to come out of the trance that I enter when I tune. It is another world. It's always a bit startling to be interrupted by . . . visitors. . . . It is hard to explain."

"Perhaps like being awakened from a dream."

"Perhaps. Perhaps. . . . But I am awake in a world of sounds. . . . " (pp. 272–273)

Daniel Mason, *The Piano Tuner*

Guide to this chapter:

- Csikszentmihalyi's Flow Concept
- The Flow Channel
- Staying in Flow
- The Neurological Basis of Flow and Similar States
- The Benefits and Harm of Being In or Out of Flow
- Examples from Literature and Other Case Studies

In the fictional world of Daniel Mason's *The Piano Tuner* (2002), Edgar Drake tuned pianos. Called by the British government to travel to Burma, Drake found himself committed to tune an instrument that was both seriously affected by jungle conditions and caught in the middle of a diplomatic crisis. In the passage at the head of this chapter, the piano tuner perfectly describes to his lady friend, Khin Myo, what it is like to be in "flow" and the disorienting aura that accompanies being called out of that state. [Look for a movie of the book to come out in 2013, directed by Werner Herzog.] In this chapter, we will identify the conditions for one's being in flow, the benefits of being in flow, and how one might manage to stay in that state.

Csikszentmihalyi's Flow Concept

Mihaly Csikszentmihalyi (pronounced "Mee-HIGH Chick-SENT-mee-high", meaning "St. Michael of Csik") was fascinated by people such as Edgar Drake—people who were absorbed in their work and reported great satisfaction with their lives. Determined to find their commonalities, he and his associates interviewed them until their secrets emerged. Let's take a look at what Csikszentmihalyi found.

In a sense, psychologist Csikszentmihalyi and his colleagues at the University of Chicago (he is now at Claremont Graduate School in California) had set out to find something like the fountain of youth--what makes some people feel more satisfied with their lives than others do? In search of the secret to eternal motivation, rather than to eternal youth. Through a series of interviews with persons who reported very high satisfaction with their lives, Csikszentmihalyi (1990) identified a state of mind that he calls "flow," in which a person experiences complete engagement in the task of the moment, losing all sense of time, place, and extraneous physical sensations. An interesting choice of words, in that the Old Norse origin (*floa*) means "flood." Hence, "flow" suggests being submerged or carried along by an overwhelming circumstance. In such a state, the individual is so absorbed in the event that nothing else intrudes into their awareness. He enumerates eight components of this flow state: (pp. 49 ff.)

- The individual feels they have a chance of successfully completing the event; this requires a sense of having sufficient energy, resources, and skill for the event.
- The individual is able to concentrate and become one with the activity.
- The individual's goals are clear.
- The individual receives immediate feedback (i.e., not necessarily from another person, but from the task itself, as in "I think I'm on top of this—it's going to work.")
- The individual engages in a deep, effortless involvement that pushes away everyday cares.
- The individual has a sense of control over their actions.
- The concern for self disappears, but the self feels stronger afterward.
- Time is altered: Minutes seem like hours, and hours seem like minutes.

In writing about the flow state a few years later (1993), he identified a set of external factors that shape the flow state, as well as a set of internal factors necessary for experiencing flow. The external factors describe the task, activity, event, or process itself:

Certain activities are more likely to produce flow than others because (1) they have concrete goals and manageable rules, (2) they make it possible to adjust opportunities for action to our capacities, (3) they provide clear information about how well we are doing, and (4) they screen out distractions and make concentration possible. Games, artistic performances, and religious rituals are good examples of such "flow activities." But one of the most important findings of our studies has been that any activity can produce the optimal flow experience, as long as it meets the above requirements. (p. xiv)

I have found the flow state to be so satisfying, addictive really, that I have taken Csikszentmihalyi at his word by testing the capability of every one of my actions to be characterized by flow. From folding clothes on a Saturday afternoon to writing this book, from walking for miles on end to practicing my recorder, I try to become totally absorbed.

But, as he cautions, not every task yields to the flow state naturally. For example, a flat tire has a concrete goal (replace flat with good tire), provides information about how well we are doing (is the jack lifting the car without slipping, etc.), but if we have never changed a tire before and we are on the shoulder of a busy highway, then conditions 2 and 4 are missing: there's no adjusting our abilities/experience to the task, and we can't screen out the distraction of trucks and other vehicular missiles whizzing by at an arm's length. Hence, we are unlikely to experience flow under those conditions.

The other conditions that permit flow are internal—qualities within us, the doers. These qualities include both inborn traits and abilities as well as momentary attitudes:

> Some people have an uncanny ability to match their skills to the opportunities around them. They set manageable goals for themselves even when there does not seem to be anything for them to do. They are good at reading feedback that others fail to notice. They can concentrate easily and do not get distracted. They are not afraid of losing their self, so their ego can slip easily out of awareness. Persons who have learned to control consciousness in these ways have a "flow personality.... Some of these persons were homeless drifters while others had suffered devastating tragedies like blindness or paralysis; yet all had been able to transform seemingly hopeless conditions into a serene, joyful existence. But I also remarked on the fact that it is difficult to build a happy life by the simple addition of a series of flow experiences. The whole in this case is definitely more than the sum of its parts. An artist may paint for decades and love every minute of it, yet become depressed and hopeless in middle age. A tennis pro who enjoyed most of his career could end up disillusioned and bitter. To transform the entirety of life into a unified flow experience, it helps to have faith in a system of meanings that gives purpose to one's being. (Csikszentmihalyi, 1993, pp. xiv-xv)

When he stipulates that one must "not be afraid of losing their self, so their ego can slip easily out of awareness," I am reminded of the work of Matthew B. Crawford. In his *Shopcraft as Soulcraft: An Inquiry into the Value of Work* (2009), we find this passage:

> Since the standards of craftsmanship issue from the logic of things rather than the art of persuasion, practiced submission to them perhaps gives the craftsman some psychic ground to stand on against fantastic hopes aroused by demagogues...." (p. 18)

I mentioned this to psychiatrist and friend Mark Ardis as a sample of submitting oneself to a system as a source of subjective well-being. He identified with the passage as a woodworker and added that a ritual was more satisfying than the submission itself. I suggested it was ritual plus more exacting standards, as rituals vary significantly on the level of quality associated. Now, as I cogitate on this maelstrom of Csikszentmihalyi, Crawford, Ardis, and self, I sense that what they all have in common is the capacity to put everything out of one's attention but the task at hand. This is not a happy place, perhaps, for the proud multitasker who finds joy in flitting from task to task yet lags woefully in both productivity and quality of results.

Towards the end of Csikszentmihalyi's passage above, he suggests that flow must be integrated with our long-term goals. In Chapter 7, we will discuss long and short-term goals. Or, life goals and goals now. The goal to be a good parent always versus the goal to give my daughter my full attention while she is talking to me later this evening. Flow is a characteristic of short-term goals, such as listening to someone. When in flow, it is neither satisfying nor dissatisfying—we are emotionless, like a monk meditating. When we feel an emotion, we have come out of the flow state. We may feel a strong positive sense of satisfaction, or pleasure, or joy, after breaking with flow, but back during the flow we were emotionless. For to feel an emotion is to make a judgment on an experience, and to judge it is to be outside of it. It is possible to slip in and out of flow with some frequency. I can be reading, and be in flow, and come upon a humorous passage. Sometimes I read quickly through the humorous passage, recognizing the humor but not reacting to it by laughing aloud. Other times, I stop reading and have a good laugh, and Jane says "What's so funny?" and I'll relate the episode to her, and then get right back into the flow of reading.

The point here is that the hundreds of flow episodes are more satisfying over time if they are connected in some way by one or more overarching, long-term goals. One kind of long-term goal is one's values. For example, I place strong value on "learning"—I want to learn as much as I can about the subjects that affect me over my lifetime. So, whenever my flow experience is an expression of that value, it has more meaning to me than a flow experience that is unrelated to a goal or value that is unimportant to me. So, while flow experiences are intrinsically satisfying, over time they are more satisfying if it is more than hundreds of unrelated absorbing activities. As Csikszentmihalyi writes, the whole is more than the sum of the parts.

When speaking of the meaning of one's life, one must consider Victor Frankl. This resilient man survived concentration camps to become a famous psychiatrist and founder of "logotherapy." In a nutshell, logotherapy expects one to create a purpose, or meaning, for their life, and to take responsibility for realizing that purpose by setting goals based on current realities. (Frankl, 1984; 2000) His approach is much like the "purpose driven life" of Rick Warren (2004), the Passion Test of the Attwoods (2006), the "follow your bliss" described by Joseph Campbell, and so on. Frankl writes that "logotherapy regards its assignment as that of assisting the patient to find meaning in his life." (1984, p. 108) Often referred to as "existential" therapy, it deals with one's current realities, or existence, rather than one's past. It is analytical of the present, not so much of the past. Frankl quotes his German neighbor, Friedrich Nietzsche: "He who has a *why* to live for can bear almost any *how*." (1984, p. 109) Or, as Frankl writes, "There is nothing in the world…that would so effectively help one to survive even the worst conditions as the knowledge that there is a meaning in one's life." (1984, p. 109)

The next section is about the flow "channel." Czikszentmihalyi writes about needing ever-increasing challenges to stay in the flow channel. Perhaps he knew this passage from Frankl:

> Mental health is based on a certain degree of tension, the tension between what one has already achieved and what one still ought to accomplish, or the gap between what one is and what one should become…. What man actually needs is not a tensionless state but rather the striving and struggling for a worthwhile goal, a freely chosen task. What he needs is not the discharge of tension at any cost but the call of a potential meaning waiting to be fulfilled by him…. So if therapists wish to foster their patients' mental health, they should not be afraid to create a sound amount of tension through a reorientation toward the meaning of one's life." (1984, p. 110)

The Flow Channel

Csikszentmihalyi discovered two variables that control whether one is in or out of flow:

- **Personal Resources**. What the individual brings to the task by way of skill, budget, time, en ergy, experience, knowledge, attitude, traits, and so forth.
- **Demands of the Task**. What the task demands of the individual. When a task demands more in the way of personal resources than is available to a person, it is said to be more difficult.

The chances of being in a flow state are optimum when one's personal resources match the demands of the task—or, put another way, when one's skills match the difficulty of the task. The flow state is uncommon when skill exceeds or falls below the level of difficulty. Excess skill leads to boredom; deficient skill leads to frustration. Csikszentmihalyi (1990, p. 52) describes the relationship this way: "Enjoyment [flow] appears at the boundary between boredom and anxiety, when the challenges are just balanced with the person's capacity to act." This relationship is illustrated in Figure 5.0.

Figure 5.0   The Flow Channel

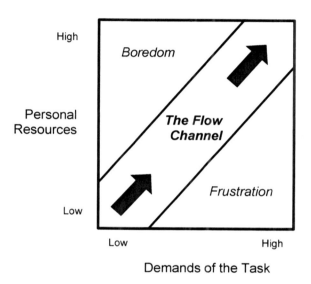

Demands of the Task

The flow channel is defined by the points at which person and task are matched. Low skill and low demand can experience flow, as well as high skill and high demand. In the Orff-Kodaly approach to music instruction, the xylophone is simplified by removing all of the keys but one. The beginning child-musician learns to hit that one key with accuracy. Sometimes they hit it hard, sometimes soft, sometimes in between. But always accurately. A beginning xylophonist can engage in this task and be in flow. Low skill and low difficulty—a match made in the classroom. But, as Csikszentmihalyi points out, once mastery is achieved, the novice gets bored. So, the child slips out of flow and into the area to the north of the channel called Boredom, where skill exceeds demands. The teacher perceives the boredom and recognizes the need to add a degree of challenge by placing a second key on the xylophone, but at some distance from the first key. This way, the child gets back into flow because the demands have increased, but not by too much. If the new key were placed adjacent to the first key, then the task would be too difficult, with the possibility of hitting the wrong key being very high.

Through this process of recognizing mastery and adding or reducing difficulty, the teacher manages to avoid allowing the learner to remain in either boredom or frustration for very long. I am reminded of the story about flat sales of cake mix sometime after the add-only-water products were introduced back in the 20th century. One explanation was that the cooks were bored or even insulted by the too-simple procedure. By adding an egg to the directions, both the quality of the cakes and the involvement of the cooks were increased.

129

To stay in the flow channel is to stay focused on the task at hand. To be distracted from the flow channel is unsatisfying. In fact, some recent research by Harvard's Matthew Killingsworth and Dan Gilbert (2010) used an iPhone app (trackyourhappiness) to determine what several thousand people were doing, feeling, and focusing on at various times during their day. Using more than a quarter million observations, the researchers found that being focused on the task at hand was a better predictor of happiness than the nature of the task itself. When people reported that their minds were wandering—regardless of the task—they reported lower levels of happiness. Headlines in the popular media reported in November 2010 that "Mind wandering leads to unhappiness." In fact, the researchers concluded that unhappiness led to greater distractibility, and that being distracted (i.e., allowing one's mind to wander) led to decreased happiness—a two-edged sword.

What was of interest to me was that, in spite of the widespread knowledge of Csikszentmihalyi's research in the positive psychology community, I saw no mention made of his "flow" concept as an explanation of the mind-wandering/happiness connection. They did not connect the two. Yet from our understanding of flow, we see that disruption of flow typically results in boredom (because the task is too easy) or frustration (because the task is too hard). The clear message here is that one needs to manage both one's resources and one's task difficulty in order to stay in flow and minimize the wanderings of one's mind. We will turn now to specific strategies for staying in flow.

Staying in Flow

Most of us are attracted to tasks or activities that engage us and are repelled by tasks or activities than bore or frustrate us. The bridge player who looks forward to an evening of bidding and strategy with other card players is looking forward to being engaged, to being in flow, not to being bored or being frustrated. Should the other three players at the table be less skilled, the player is likely to be bored. Should the other three be much more skilled, the player is likely to be frustrated. In order to be in flow, the player must feel that they have at least a 50% chance of success, but not too high a chance of success. If their chances are less than 50%, they are likely to be frustrated, while if their chances of success are more than 90%, they are likely to be bored. One needs just enough challenge so that one must pay close attention, lest one get outsmarted.

Four kinds of strategies are available for managing oneself so as to stay in flow. Each represents the four possible reasons for being out of flow:

- When I am bored, I could either
  - Increase task difficulty, or
  - Decrease my resources.
- When I am frustrated, I could either
  - Decrease task difficulty, or
  - Increase my resources.

Let us look at several illustrations for each of these conditions.

First, we will look at what to do when we are *bored*. Boredom is the result of bringing more to a task than the task requires. This could be characteristic of many different situations:

- A tennis pro plays a novice.
- A calculus teacher tutors someone in arithmetic.
- A successful creative writer must write a series of obituaries.
- An accomplished chef is cooking for someone who doesn't like any seasoning in their food.
- A skilled researcher is volunteering for a political campaign and is stuffing envelopes.

Each of these situations is a prelude to boredom. The two strategies to relieve boredom involve increasing the difficulty of the task or decreasing one's resources. "Difficulty" includes anything that the task throws at you, such as the complexity of the task, the "resources" of the other people who may be working with or against you, the amount of experience (i.e., the "learning curve") required to perform the task, the context in which the task occurs (i.e., distractions, climate) the

> An artist is never bored.
> - Babette, in *Babette's Feast*

amount of education required to succeed at the task—in short, anything about the task that might make it easier or more challenging for you. *Increasing difficulty* to minimize boredom could involve any of these kinds of strategies:

- Changing the task, to a more difficult one.
- Adding to the task, to make it more complex, hence more challenging.
- Adding tasks, as in multi-tasking.
- Changing the competition, so that you are up against others with more resources.

"Resources" include anything that you bring to the task, such as your skill level, knowledge, experience, budget, social or professional network, decision-making authority, intelligence, personality traits, values—in short, anything about you that makes it more natural for you to engage in the task and more likely that you will be successful at it. *Decreasing your resources* in order minimize boredom could involve any of these kinds of strategies:

- Self-handicapping, so that you cannot use all of your resources, or so that others may have more resources than you.
- Taking on one or more partners who have fewer resources than you, thus potentially obstructing your effectiveness.
- Changing the circumstances, so that your resources are not as effective as usual.
- Changing the criteria, so that your resources are less impactful.

For each of the five examples of boredom listed earlier, let's now examine some options to lessen the boredom and hopefully to allow the bored folks to ease into flow:

- A tennis pro plays a novice: *The pro uses the opportunity to work on a new technique (serve, footwork, backhand, grip, and so forth), or the pro works on very high-risk shots, many of which will go out.*
- A calculus teacher tutors someone in arithmetic: *The teacher uses the opportunity to learn how to use a new device or a new piece of software, or the teacher learns how to use Skype video with whiteboard features to tutor remotely.*

- A successful creative writer must write a series of obituaries: *The writer composes without certain options such as not using any linking verbs, not using the letter "s", attempts to include a story in each article, or attempts to imitate the style of a specific writer (Hemingway, for example).*
- An accomplished chef is cooking for someone who doesn't like any seasoning in their food: *The chef uses the opportunity to try or create new recipes, or the chef asks the diner to select the ingredients they'd like, then creates something out of just those ingredients.*
- A skilled researcher is volunteering for a political campaign and is stuffing envelopes: *The researcher attempts to redesign the process and evaluates various options for their efficiency* (I actually did this back in the 1990s when volunteering at a campaign headquarters!).

Next let's look at what we can do when we are *frustrated*. Frustration is the result of engaging in a task when one has inadequate resources, given the degree of difficulty of the task or the degree of expertise among others around you who are working either with or against (as in a competition) you. This could be characteristic of situations such as:

- An average tennis player takes on a friend they've never played before and who turns out to be substantially better.
- An algebra teacher tries to fill in for a calculus teacher.
- A technical writer is asked to write a poem to read at a wedding.
- A person of provincial background commits to hosting dinner for a world traveler with sophisticated taste.
- A secretary without the required skill is asked to write macros to automate a task.

Each of these situations is a prelude to frustration. The two strategies to relieve frustration involve decreasing the difficulty of the task or increasing one's resources. *Decreasing the difficulty* of a task in order to minimize frustration could involve any of these kinds of strategies:

- Handicapping the other persons involved, so that they cannot use all of their resources.
- Changing the task, to a less difficult one.
- Removing elements of the task, to make it simpler, hence less challenging.
- Changing the competition, so that you are up against others with fewer or lesser resources.

Increasing your resources in order to minimize frustration could involve any of these strategies:

- Practice, so that you increase your skill.
- Study, so that you increase your knowledge.
- Take a class, workshop, degree program, or other course of study.
- Join or create a support group, as a source of new ideas.
- Observe, so that you increase your experience factor.
- Obtain tutoring, coaching, or mentoring.
- Solicit feedback, so that you can discover opportunities to improve aspects of your performance.
- Obtain new equipment, materials, or facilities that might enhance your performance.

- Read biographies/autobiographies of persons who have mastered the task, so that you might learn their keys to development and success

For each of the five examples of frustration listed earlier, let's now examine some options to relieve the frustration and hopefully to allow the frustrated folks to ease into flow:

- An average tennis player takes on a friend they've never played before and who turns out to be substantially better: *Suggest the average player hit to the doubles court, and the superior player hits to the singles court, or the average player forgets trying to win and uses the opportunity to practice a particular part of their game (such as rushing the net, passing shots, lobs, and so forth).*
- An algebra teacher tries to fill in for a calculus teacher: *The algebra teacher uses the opportunity to have the students review earlier concepts; suggests that brighter students in the class teach modules.*
- A technical writer is asked to write a poem to read at a wedding: *The writer finds a classic poem they like and modifies the wording as a spoof; the writer asks everyone who knows the wedding couple to give the writer four lines of iambic pentameter, and the writer then puts them all together.*
- A person of provincial background commits to hosting dinner for a world traveler with sophisticated taste: *The host prepares a traditional family meal along with a fancy menu complete with historical and other notes; the host finds a partner to help plan and cook and uses it as an opportunity to learn some new dishes.*
- A secretary without the required skill is asked to write macros to automate a task: *The secretary asks to attend a class or retain a coach to learn how to write macros; the secretary asks a coworker who knows macros to assist, in exchange for, say, getting their office organized.*

Earlier we talked about having a flat tire, and about having the necessary experience and tools to change such a tire. In my lifetime, I have changed many tires on many different kinds of cars and trucks, from Fords to Fiats, from Mustangs to Mercedes Benzes. One recent evening I had to change the tire on my Honda. It was dark. Our choir had just sung a concert. We were to go out to dinner with friends afterwards. I was to go get the car and drive back to pick up Jane and friends. I arrived at the car only to notice the flat tire. While I had changed several tires on Hondas, I had never changed one of this car's tires. All things being equal, it should have been a flow experience—focus on the task at hand, gather my equipment, change the tire, and be off to join my friends for an after-concert dinner. So, that was what I did. I focused with the frame of mind of "let's make this short, sweet, and efficient." I opened the trunk to get the jack and spare tire. There was no jack and no spare. I checked every cranny of the trunk with no success. Frustration mounted. I called Jane to ask for patience. Aware of my growing frustration, mixed with anger and worry, and eager to assuage my after-concert hunger and thirst, I realized that I was badly out of flow. Problem: lack of skill and knowledge of this new car. Solution: Increase resources. Strategy: Find the manual. I immediately looked in the glove compartment, found the manual, took it to a nearby lamppost, and read the section on tire changing. Now I knew where to find the tire and jack! Back into flow, and for the next five minutes I was focused and effective. This was a classic example of recognizing frustration and identifying what to do about it—in this case, increasing resources.

Before we leave this section, I want to emphasize one point. In order to remain in the flow channel, one must continue to take on greater challenges. Let's use tennis as an example. Let's say I play an opponent and we have a close match: 6-4, 4-6, 6-4, with me winning the third set and match. I was in flow, and the score shows that I clearly had a 50-50 chance of winning, but that it was no cake-walk. I was neither bored from my competition being too slight, nor frustrated from it being too overwhelming. Let us say that I continue to play this same opponent and that, over time, I gain the upper hand. After 20 or so matches, I am now regularly winning with scores like 6-2, 6-1. For whatever reason, I am now bringing more resources/skill to the matches than my opponent. Maybe I have been taking lessons or reading *The Inner Game of Tennis*. Whatever the reason, I am winning hands down. I have reached a winning probability in excess of 80%. Boredom is setting in, and tennis no longer is a flow experience. In order to return to flow, I must do something different. A sure way to win a lot of tennis matches is continue with the same goal of beating this competitor, but it will be empty of meaning. As we will see in Chapter 7, Carol Dweck (2006) writes about mastery goals and performance goals, the former being goals that require

> The happiness that is genuinely satisfying is accompanied by the fullest exercise of our faculties and the fullest realization of the world in which we live.
> - Bertrand Russell

one to take on a goal that has an element of difficulty that does not guarantee success, while performance goals are "slam dunks," goals that one is sure to succeed at, to look good, to show off. Not only do we not grow by preferring performance goals, we also do not experience the satisfaction of full engagement. By playing it safe and doing only what we know we can do well, we invite boredom. Csikszentmihalyi warns that in order to continue to experience flow in any given area of our life, then we must continue to take on greater challenges. Once we have reached a certain level of performance, we must find new aspects to master. This is what Anders Ericsson (Ericcson and Charness, 1994) calls "deliberate practice." Ericcson's now famous 10,000 hour rule requires not that one practice four hours every weekday for ten years in order to become expert, but that one engage in deliberate practice that continually changes. You don't do the same thing over and over again—you introduce variations that require new and unaccustomed effort. This prevents boredom and maintains practice in the flow channel. David Shenk (2010) writes about the same phenomenon when he says that "In any competitive arena, the single best way to inspire better performance is to be surrounded by the fiercest possible competitors and a culture of extreme excellence." (loc. 1,438-1,439) And later, "The great success stories in our world come about when parents and their children learn to turn straight into the wind and gain satisfaction from marching against its ever-increasing force." (loc. 1,926-1,928)

Robert Bjork (1994) calls this process "introducing difficulties." Rather than a child repeatedly practicing a ring toss at a distance of three feet, with no variation of distance, Bjork found that if the child varies the distance—now at two feet, now at four feet, and so forth—then that child will be more accurate at the ring toss from three feet than if they had practiced only at three feet. The same principle applies to every endeavor—if you always do it the same way, you won't improve as much as you would if you do it different ways. Deliberate practice, mastery goals, introducing difficulties, increasing one's resources, increasing the difficulty of the task—each of these insights is aimed at staying in flow through continually raising the bar. In order to stay in the flow channel, we need to keep moving upward in the channel. That is what the poet Adrienne Rich means when she writes about "the experience of repetition as Death." (cited in Yoshino, 2006, p. 81) Life without change is death. Vitality means continual experimentation. This does not mean that one cannot polish and perfect the same task over a lifetime, whether it is a culinary, athletic, aesthetic, or business task. But we must try new variations on it. There is little in life that cannot be improved on.

The Neurological Basis of Flow and Similar States

Gerald Edelman (1992) writes about the two most common forms of waking consciousness—basic (core, or primary) consciousness and higher (secondary) consciousness. Hamer (2004) elaborates (pp. 92 ff.) that consciousness is selective, continuous, and personal. Core consciousness enables the perception of the present, so that we perceive meaningful images and not just lines, curves, dots, etc. Higher consciousness links this current perception both to our stored past experience and our antici-pated future. The assumed difference between animals and humans is that animals lack higher consciousness. A cat thinks a tin of tuna is just a tasty treat; for us, it engenders memories of past cats, past cat foods, the need to clean the bowl, tomorrow's dinner menu, and a myriad of other associa-tions. Because animals are totally focused on the present, with no sense of self, they can be said to be in a permanent flow state, never experiencing boredom or frustration.

These two systems are described in Table 5.0. As the will focuses, the self recedes, and vice versa, like a toggle switch. Hamer describes research documenting this relationship among Tibetan monks, whose meditation exercises the will and entails a subsiding of the self. He identifies this process as *deafferentation* (p. 125), the switching off of the afferent and efferent nerves that keep our senses going. This is the same state that Csikszentmihalyi calls *flow*. In short, the going back and forth between self and will is very much like listening to a lecture as your mind wanders from time to time. You can't wander *and* listen! Listening is will, and wandering is self. Or, as often happens with me, I'll

Table 5.0 **Defining the Difference Between Flow and Normal Consciousness**

	Flow	Normal Consciousness
Biological Location:	Thalamocortical loop, comprising the cin-gulate gyrus, dorsolateral prefrontal cortices, inferior and orbital prefrontal cor-tices, sensorimotor cortex, and dorsomedial cortex pathway.	Posterior Superior Parietal Lobes
Features:	• Also called Core, or Primary, Conscious-ness (Edelman) • Seat of the Will • Orients us to the Present • Where our attention focuses through study, meditation, and so forth • Damage here makes it difficult to make decisions and make connections among sets of information • We share this feature with animals	• Also called Secondary Consciousness (Edelman) • Seat of the Self • Orients us to our Past and Future • Where our sense perception orients us to our immediate environment as we locate ourselves in space and time • Damage here makes it difficult to know who we are—to connect the present to our past or future • Thought to be unique to humans

be listening to others talk in a meeting, and from time to time my mind will drift to a concern other than the one being discussed, and I'll lose the drift of the conversation and have to ask for a recap. My will to listen to the present alternates on center stage with my self's connections to past and future. The relationship of these two processes is precisely the same as being in and out of Czikszentmihalyi's flow state, which he describes as the state of total absorption in the activity of the moment (= will), so much so that one loses one's sense of time and space (= self).

The Benefits and Harm of Being In or Out of Flow

Csikszentmihalyi once conducted an experiment in which he removed flow from subjects' lives through a series of benign distractions. The results were almost immediate. At end of the first day, participants noticed increased sluggishness about their behavior. After two days of deprivation, the general deterioration of mood became so advanced that he discontinued the experiment. Two days without flow plunged people into a state eerily similar to a serious psychiatric disorder. Flow is needed to survive. It is the oxygen of the soul.

Daniel Pink (2009) describes a condition known as generalized anxiety disorder. The symptoms include:

- restlessness or feeling keyed up or on edge,
- being easily fatigued,
- difficulty concentrating or mind going blank,
- irritability,
- muscle tension, and
- sleep disturbance.

The way to get rid of it is to increase the amount of flow in your life. Again, flow is essential to vitality. Being in flow is evidence that one is engaged in a task that is appropriate for one's skill, knowledge, experience, values, and abilities. In short, being in flow means you are using your personal resources appropriately. Being bored or frustrated means that you are not using your resources appropriately. Later, once we have completely described the five modes of positive being that enable one to be fully In Gear, we will take some time to identify the areas of our life that would benefit from increased flow.

Examples from Literature and Other Case Studies

Literature is peppered with examples of people in and out of flow. At the beginning of this chapter, we introduced Daniel Mason's piano tuner, Edgar Drake. Drake, like any piano tuner, would easily become bored if every piano maintenance task were the same. It is the different contexts that the tuner runs into—water damage, fire, sun exposure, knife marks, food and drink deposits, different kinds of tuning specifications, unusual acoustical environments—that provide new challenges and chase away boredom to bring on flow, or what Mason describes as being awake in a dream. The experienced piano tuner needs new challenges in order to stay in flow. Otherwise, they risk boredom. However, for the novice, such variety would be frustrating, until such time as their personal resources or skills grow to be second nature. Staying in flow is like the Marxian or Piagetian dialectic: thesis, antithesis, and synthesis. Or, mastery, challenge, and new mastery. Comfort with one's current degree of complexity is disturbed by new, complex challenges. Eventually, one gains comfort with this greater complexity. And so on, forever, whether you are piano tuner, mathematician, carpenter, poet, or manager. In fact, some recent research shows that managers who throughout their career continue to take on more difficult challenges (rather than staying with the familiar) prove to be more resistant to Alzheimer's disease and other forms of dementia. Use it, or lose it!

In Ken Follett's *World Without End* (Dutton, 2007), we exist in the medieval world of the cathedral master builder. In the following scene, the young apprentice Merthin Fitzgerald is described in the flow of applying his craft:

> He must have heard her [Caris] footsteps on the stone staircase, but he was too absorbed in his work to glance up. She regarded him for a second, anger competing with love in her heart. He had the look of total concentration that she knew so well: his slight body bent over his work, his strong hands and dexterous fingers making fine adjustments, his face immobile, his gaze unwavering. He had the perfect grace of a young deer bending its head to drink from a stream. This was what a man looked like, she thought, when he was doing what he was born to do. He was in a state like happiness, but more profound. He was fulfilling his destiny. (p. 179)

In Leo Tolstoy's short novel *Family Happiness,* his narrator reveals being out of flow as the result of what Adrienne Rich would call the repetition that is death: "I suffered most from the feeling that custom was daily petrifying our lives into one fixed shape, that our minds were losing their freedom and becoming enslaved to the steady passionless course of time." (loc. 883-885) Later, she reprises this theme: "I have no complaint to make of you... I am merely bored and want not to be bored. But you say that it can't be helped, and, as always, you are right." (loc. 946-948) And yet again she lets us know her unchallenged mental state: "I love my child, but to sit beside him all day long would bore me; and nothing will make me pretend what I do not really feel." (loc. 1,210-1,211)

Robert Pirsig narrated (1974) the cross-country motorcycle trip of father and son in his *Zen and the Art of Motorcycle Maintenance: An Inquiry into Values.* In this philosophical novel Pirsig launches many so-called Chatauquas on a variety of epistemological, ethical, and scientific topics. One of the most memorable scenes for me was an occasion when they needed to take the cycle in for repair. Upon hearing rock-and-roll music from inside the garage, he decided this shop was not for them and their bike. Who could trust a mechanic who would listen to music while attempting to diagnose and repair the bike? Here are some of his musings:

> ...A radio was going full blast and they were clowning around and talking and seemed not to notice me. When one of them finally came over he barely listened to the piston slap before saying, 'Oh yeah. Tappets."
> Tappets? I should have known then what was coming.
> ...When I brought it back they accused me of not breaking it in properly, but after much argument agreed to look into it....They took it out themselves for a high-speed road test.
> It seized on *them* this time.
> After the third overhaul...[it] did not start. I found the plugs were disconnected.... The kid came with an open-end adjustable wrench, set wrong, and swiftly rounded both of the sheet-aluminum tappet covers, ruing both of them.
> On the next blow he missed the chisel completely and struck the head with the hammer, breaking off a portion of two of the cooling fans.

"Just stop," I said politely, feeling this was a bad dream.

I got out of there as fast as possible….At the curb I discovered two of the four engine-mounting bolts were missing and a nut was missing from the third. The whole engine was hanging on by only one bolt.

The question *why* comes back again and again and has become a major reason for wanting to deliver this Chautauqua. Why did they butcher it so?…They sat down to do a job and they performed it like chimpanzees. Nothing personal in it.

The radio was a clue. You can't really think hard about what you're doing and listen to the radio at the same time. Maybe they didn't see their job as having anything to do with hard thought, just wrench twiddling. If you can twiddle wrenches while listening to the radio that's more enjoyable….

But the biggest clue seemed to be their expressions. They were like spectators. You had the feeling they had just wandered in there themselves and somebody had handed them a wrench. There was no identification with the job. No saying, "I am a mechanic."…Their own selves were outside of it, detached, removed. They were involved in it but not in such a way as to care. (pp. 33-34)

What the narrator meant was that he wanted his mechanic to be in flow with no distractions, lest a bolt not get tightened due to a momentary lapse of attention by a mechanic with divided attention, a distracted mind. I wonder if Csikszentmihalyi has read this passage? It offers a classic example of someone who does not *want* to be in flow, but who could perhaps have done a better job if they eliminated the distractions (i.e., the radio) that made flow, or deep engagement in the task, less likely.

Stephen Sondheim used James Lapine's book to write *Sunday in the Park with George.* We get to know the painter Georges Seurat and his mistress Dot, played on stage and in the film version by Mandy Patinkin and Bernadette Peters. In the second act, scene 22, Seurat's great-grandson has an imaginary dialog with Dot, who herself imagines him to be her lover Georges. It goes like this:

Dot: "You gave me so much!"
Georges: "What did I give you?"
Dot: "Oh…many things. You taught me about concentration. At first I thought that meant just being still, but I was to understand it meant much more. You meant to tell me to be where I was, not some place in the past or the future. I worried too much about tomorrow…."

Who better to teach one about being in flow than an innovative painter absorbed in the process of placing his points of paint on canvas like pixels on a monitor, but with no computer other than his brain to manage the placements?

Allow me three personal examples of finding myself out of flow, and what I did to return to that most satisfying of states. The first occurred on a Saturday some years ago when I was spending a day in the stacks of Atkins Library at the University of North Carolina at Charlotte. I had been in flow while reading a series of journal articles, so much so that I suddenly realized that it was 2:30 p.m.; I was ravenous. I'd forgotten to eat lunch. I remedied that with a quick trip to the cafeteria for a sandwich. I resumed my reading with a new article. After 15 minutes or so, I found myself stumbling, rereading the same paragraph five or six times, just not able to understand what I was reading. All of a sudden, I realized that I was frustrated—out of flow. The cause of the frustration was a statistical procedure with which I was unfamiliar, but whose understanding was crucial for continuing to read the article. To return to flow, I had one of two choices: decrease the difficulty or increase my resources. In this case, there was no way to make the article any simpler, but I could increase my resources. I found a statistics text that had a suitable explanation of the statistical procedure in question, and I studied the flow-disrupting formulas for a half-hour or so before returning to the article I'd had trouble with. Resuming at the point of frustration, I found myself back in flow and continued my afternoon of reading, delightfully unaware of the rest of the world.

Some years before that library episode, I was playing tennis on the neighborhood courts with our younger daughter, Allegra. At the time, she was 13 and had been playing tennis for a couple of years. While she had some nice ground strokes, even my very average game was too much for her. She was frustrated at not winning more points, and I was bored at not having enough of a challenge. I tried to figure out a way to limit my resources through handicapping. It occurred to me that I could limit myself to hitting to her singles court while permitting her to hit to my doubles court. That extra margin proved just the tonic to cure what ailed us. We finished the session which a much more satisfying level of competition with each other. That became, for a while, our new arrangement on the tennis court.

Finally, I offered to drive a friend's son to Atlanta one weekend. This surly youth and I had little in common. Faced with a boring four-hour drive, I searched my repertoire of conversation topics for something that would be mutually engaging. Being a fan of the "Values Clarification" material, I decided that I would attempt to conduct the 7-step values interview with him (see example in Howard & Howard, 2011, pp. 89-90). I began by asking if he would share with me something that was very important to him at that period in his life. He eagerly shared his passion of the moment, and I eagerly began the interview process. Four hours later, we entered Atlanta, having lost all sense of time, hunger, and temperature, having had a lovely interaction that gave me excellent practice with the values interview and him a deeper understanding of his passion!

Some boredom and frustration is inevitable, even necessary. Without boredom, we'd lack the impetus to make changes. Eric Wilson (2008) says it this way:

> Indeed, the world is much of the time boring, controlled as it is by staid habits. It seems overly familiar, tired, repetitious. Then along comes what Keats calls the melancholy fit, and suddenly the planet again turns interesting. The veil of familiarity falls away. There before us flare bracing possibilities. We are called to forge untested links to our environments. We are summoned to be creative. (p. 149)

The ultimate satisfaction of the flow process is not to stay at one level but to work upward, becoming more skilled and taking on greater challenges. Should skill or challenge level become fixed, one risks boredom and, hence, loss of flow. But don't mistake flow for fun. Martin Seligman (2002, p. 117) points out that studies of high-flow and low-flow adolescents show superior scores for the high-flow kids on all the self-esteem variables but one: They would like to be hanging out at the mall with the low-flow kids because they are having more fun. However, there is a long-term payoff of early high-flow experience. As we age and develop our strengths and virtues, simply hanging out becomes boring and unfun, and our longing for total engagement grows. But even though flow is not smiley-faced fun, it is healthy, productive, and nonfattening! The natural companion of flow is fit. In the next chapter we will explore fit in some depth, and we will show how a good fit between a person and their environment is a prerequisite for flow.

Composing Your Next Chapter

Review your highlights and notes from this chapter on flow and list activities that either bore or frustrate you. Then think up ways you could make the boring activities more challenging, and the frustrating activities more engaging. Ask associates to help with these suggestions.

_____

_____

_____

_____

_____

_____

_____

_____

_____

_____

_____

STATEMENT OF
PERSONAL PRIORITIES

FLOW | FIT | GOALS | COMMUNITY | ALTRUISM

Happiness Boosters
(Choice)

Happiness Downers
(Choice)

119 Minor Adjustors

(more within personal control)

(more outside personal control)

HAPPINESS SET POINT

Happiness Boosters
(Circumstance)

Happiness Downers
(Circumstance)

Continuum of Trait Happiness

Perennially Happy (N- E+) .... Occasionally Happy (N + E-)

6

Fit

Building on Your Strengths

> "Be who God meant you to be and you will set the world on fire."
>
> --Catherine of Siena, 14th century
>
> "Who you are is who you are, not what you do."
>
> --Chris Gardner, *The Pursuit of Happyness* (2006)

Guide to this chapter:
- The Wisdom of the Ages on Person-Environment Fit
- The Interaction of Nature and Nurture to Form the Person
- Howardian Man—Traits, Abilities, Physical Characteristics, Values, and Memories
- Obstacles to Good Person-Environment Fit

From the medieval mantra of Saint Catherine to the Wall Street wisdom of Chris Gardner, we can hear the voices of the ages urging us to pay attention to the content of this chapter! By the end, you will have a palette for composing your self-portrait, a set of terms for identifying many of the characteristics that make you you. While contemporary research has confirmed the wisdom of the ages (cf. Pervin, 1968; Fletcher, 1993; Buckingham & Coffman, 1999), wise voices have been strong and insistent for centuries on the necessity of fitting the person to the job. In its most recent expression, the Bishop of London preached to the royal couple Prince William and Catherine Middleton on April 29, 2011 with Catherine of Siena's exhortation to be true to oneself.

The Wisdom of the Ages on Person-Environment Fit

Perhaps the most famous of all exhortations to practice good person-environment fit is Shakespeare's, surely due to its brevity—"Know thyself." There it is, just, know thyself. How am I similar to and different from other people, and how can I build on my strengths and avoid unnecessary reliance on my weaknesses? To know oneself, and to be true to that self, is to know one's strengths, one's natural sources of energy—energy so natural that it is virtually impossible to deplete. "I could have danced all night" is the lilting line of someone who is identifying a strength, a source of natural energy bordering on limitless.

There is a good and a bad, a productive and a destructive, aspect to the exploratory years of youth. We try all manner of activities in order to find the ones we like and are good at, the ones that build on our natural energy. In my youth, I had art lessons in school, and I soon came to see that the struggle between learning to draw and my lack of drawing talent would be won by my lack of talent. Then I tried football and basketball, only to find my lack of kinesthetic ability winning out over my desire to star in sports. And I also tried the thrills of thespian theatrics, only to become discouraged because my memorization ability made line learning a chore. I experimented widely and explored many different kinds of activities in order to find my fit. And I found them: music, math, words, and taxonomic organization and construction. Nathan Brody, Columbia University emeritus psychology professor, commented at a professional meeting in Baltimore that "Growing up is the process of becoming more like who we are." We try on many costumes in our youth, gradually returning most of them to the wardrobe closets of schools, recreation departments, religious organizations, and family traditions, while keeping the few costumes that fit, that match our natural strengths. The process of becoming "more like who we are" means we let go of interests that, over time, just don't feel comfortable. I used to accept leadership positions in high school clubs, but I've learned that leadership is not "me." I do not have the natural energy for taking charge and leading. So in my 20s when I gave up all interest in being a manager, principle, coach, conductor, or any other kind of leader of people, I was exhibiting Brody's process of becoming more like who I am—in this case, an independent—not a follower, not a leader, but an independent.

Youthful exploration is both productive and destructive because sometimes we fail to let go of explorations that don't fit us. It is destructive when we try on a new costume and keep it in our repertoire far longer than we should. Such was the case of a childhood friend who yielded to his parents to go to medical school when he really didn't want to go. He had explored science at his father's insistence. Upon finishing medical school, he gave his diploma to his father, then turned and applied to law school. To this day he practices law gleefully, having eschewed the unnatural and embraced the natural. In the Introduction to this book, we referred to Joseph Campbell's comment that he tried working with his father for a while only to learn "Geez, I can't do this!" We also referred to Sinclair Lewis's *Babbitt* in which father Babbitt laments that "I've never done a single thing I've wanted to in my whole life!" and finds some vicarious pleasure in son Babbitt's breaking from family expectations in order to do what he finds more natural:

> "But I do get a kind of sneaking pleasure out of the fact that you knew what you wanted to do and did it. Well, those folks in there will try to bully you, and tame you down. Tell 'em to go to the devil! I'll back you. Take your factory job, if you want to. Don't be scared of the family. No, nor all of Zenith. Nor of yourself, the way I've been. Go ahead, old man! The world is yours!"

Campbell (1991) calls this following your bliss: "If you follow your bliss, you put yourself on a kind of track that has been there all the while, waiting for you, and the life that you ought to be living is the one you are living. Wherever you are—if you are following your bliss, you are enjoying that refreshment, that life within you, all the time." (p. 113) This notion of putting yourself on a kind of track that has been there all the while is much like Michelangelo's "statue within," the process of eschewing false costumes much like removing pieces of marble until the core design, the core self, remains.

Joseph Campbell and Bill Moyers in their interview-cum-book (1991) mention a scene in the film *Star Wars* in which Ben Kenobi and Luke Skywalker talk about person-environment fit in their own way. Their reference to the "Force" is the same as what we are calling one's true self, one's natural sources of energy, roles that arise from within and not imposed on us by others:

Moyers: The voice of Ben Kenobi says to Skywalker in the climactic moment of the last fight, "Turn off your computer, turn off your machine and do it yourself, follow your feelings, trust your feelings." And when he did, he achieved success, and the audience broke out into applause.

Campbell: When Ben Kenobi says, "May the Force be with you," he's speaking of the power and energy of life, not of programmed political intentions.

Moyers: I was intrigued by the definition of the Force. Ben Kenobi says, "The Force is an energy field created by all living things. It surrounds us, it penetrates us, it binds the galaxy together."

Campbell: Consciousness thinks it's running the shop. But it's a secondary organ of a total human being, and it must not put itself in control. It must submit and serve the humanity of the body. When it does put itself in control, you get a man like Darth Vader in *Star Wars,* the man who goes over to the consciously intentional side.... If the person insists on a certain program, and doesn't listen to the demands of his own heart, he's going to risk a schizophrenic crackup. Such a person has put himself off center. He has aligned himself with a program for life, and it's not the one the body's interested in at all. The world is full of people who have stopped listening to themselves or have listened only to their neighbors to learn what they ought to do, how they ought to behave, and what the values are that they should be living for." (pp. 178-179, 181)

I could go on like this for many more pages, as the literature of the ages is full of such testimonials to the virtues of good person-environment fit (PE fit). Rather than overstaying my welcome on this aspect of the process, let me simply list here some representative statements from some wise folks:

By embracing the diversity of human beings, we will find our way to true happiness.
--Malcolm Gladwell, in his February 2004 TED presentation on "Tomato Sauce"

Success is liking yourself, liking what you do, and liking how you do it.
--Maya Angelou, author and poet

I love him who does not hold back one drop of spirit for himself, but wants to be entirely the spirit of his virtue: thus he strides over the bridge as spirit. I love him who makes his virtue his addiction and his catastrophe: for his virtue's sake he wants to live on and to live no longer.
--Friedrich Nietzsche, *Thus Spoke Zarathustra*

Love wol nat been constreyned by maistrye   [*Love will not be tied down by a tyrant.*]
Whan maistrie comth, the God of Love anon,   [*With such a controlling partner, one's soul*]
Beteth his wynges, and farewell, he is gon.   [*Beats his wings, and, farewell, he is gone.*]
   --Geoffrey Chaucer, "The Franklin's Tale," 14th century

If you bring forth what is within you, what you bring forth will save you. If you do not bring forth what is within you, what you do not bring forth will destroy you.
    --Jesus, in the Gospel of Thomas

Our Lord! Lay not on us a burden greater than we have strength to bear.
    --Qur'an, 2:286, trans. Yusuf Ali

Every man's work, whether it be literature or music or pictures or architecture or anything else, is always a portrait of himself, and the more he tries to conceal himself the more clearly will his character appear in spite of him.
    --Samuel Butler, *The Way of All Flesh* (1903)

Poor fellow! He has done his best, but what does a fish's best come to when the fish is out of water?
    --Samuel Butler, *The Way of All Flesh* (1903)

We must all be alike. Not everyone is born free and equal, as the Constitution says, but everyone *made* equal. Each man the image of every other; then all are happy for there are no mountains to make them cower to judge themselves against. So! A book is a loaded gun in the house next door. Burn it. Take the shot from the weapon. Breach man's mind. Who knows who might be the target of the well-read man? Me? I won't stomach them for a minute. And so when houses were finally fireproofed completely all over the world...there was no longer need of firemen for the old purposes. They were given the new job, as custodi-ans of our peace of mind, the focus of our understandable and rightful dread of being inferior: official censors judges and executors."
    --Ray Bradbury, *Fahrenheit 451* (1950)

"Yes, I know; I am a delightful child who must be humored and kept quiet," I said in a voice that astonished him, so that he looked up as if this was a new experience; "but I don't want to be quiet and calm; that is more in your line, and too much in your line," I added.
    --Leo Tolstoy, *Family Happiness* (1859)

I was drawn to my work by doing what came naturally. My work seemed the consequence of being who I was, where I was, when I was. I went, in James Baldwin's essential phrase, the way my blood beat.
    --Kenji Yoshino *Covering* (2006)

Later that night, I [Amir] was passing by my father's study when I overheard him speaking to Rahim Khan [friend of the family]. I pressed my ear to the closed door.

"—grateful that he's healthy," Rahim Khan was saying.

"I know, I know. But he's always buried in those books or shuffling around the house like he's lost in some dream."

"And?"

"I wasn't like that." Baba sounded frustrated, almost angry.

Rahim Khan laughed. "Children aren't coloring books. You don't get to fill them with your favorite colors."

    --Khaled Hosseini, *The Kite Runner*, Riverhead Books/Penguin, 2003. p. 21

The Interaction of Nature and Nurture to Form the Person

Before we look at the palette of who we are—the set of abilities, traits, physical characteristics, values, and memories that make up the raw materials of our self, let us be mindful of how these elements of our self originate. In Chapter 3, we had a brief review of the genetics and biology of individual differences, but I want to make sure that we are all of a mind before proceeding.

Until the 1980s, most scholars considered personality traits and abilities as characteristics that were formed by parents, peers, and other members of one's community upbringing throughout childhood and into young adulthood. Nature (or genetics or inheritance) was dismissed as having minimal influence. This extreme position on Nurture as dictator of personality is best summed up by this statement from John Watson (1925):

> "Nature is often hidden, sometimes overcome, seldom extinguished."
> --Sir Francis Bacon

Give me a dozen healthy infants, well-formed, and my own specified world to bring them up in and I'll guarantee to take any one at random and train him [or her!] to become any type of specialist I might select—doctor, lawyer, artist, merchant-chief, and yes, even beggar-man and thief, regardless of his [or her] talents, penchants, tendencies, and abilities, vocations, and race of his [or her] ancestors.

When Hitler espoused his eugenics policies of breeding a master race through mating persons only with superior qualities, Watson's creed-like statement became all the more entrenched worldwide in the halls of psychology and science. Watson was writing well before Hitler set out to destroy his "inferiors," which highlights dramatically what it was that Hitler was trying to refute. If you believe Watson completely, then there can be no such thing as an intrinsically superior group of people, for the only thing keeping one person from being a perfect copy of another is proper training, in his opinion. People who believed in a genetic basis of personality in the aftermath of Hitler were considered racists, the bad guys, while those advocating for environmental nurture were the good guys. I remember encountering Watson's creed many times during my graduate studies in the 1960s.

However, there has been a strong undercurrent of belief in a role for genetics in the formation of personality. The first instance of the terms "nature" and "nurture" was around 1600 by English schoolmaster Richard Mulcaster, who wrote that "Nature makes the boy toward, and nurture sees him forward," and also somewhat later, "By nature emplanted, for nurture to enlarge." Mulcaster's pre-scientific intuition served him well, as his voice prefigures the discoveries of the 1980s. Research studies with identical twins in Minnesota, the United Kingdom, Scandinavia, and Australia were the first to announce that, in fact, individual differences have a substantial genetic basis. We do inherit from our ancestors—we are not *tabula rasa*, blank slates for parents, peers, educators, and religious leaders to program.

Current estimates place the genetic contribution to behavior around 60%. Just as we get Grampa's extreme height, so we also get Mom's gift for words, and Great Grandma's near-obsessive preoccupation with keeping organized. But as Mulcaster says, nature makes one lean toward certain behavioral tendencies such as loquaciousness and tidiness, but it is nurture that determines what we do with that "leaning." The tidiness may make us susceptible to becoming a librarian, while the loquaciousness would make us lean toward a more sociable role within the library, say, reference librarian or children's collection. Or, we could have taken those same two "leanings" and, because of the various

147

influences during our growing up, become a (loquacious) nurse in a (tidy) hospital, or become a (loquacious) car salesperson in an (tidy) urban showroom.

The interaction of genes and environment is complex. Even though genes form the raw material of personality, that raw material can change over time, much like exposure to the sun can modify the structure of various chemicals. As we read in Chapter 3, David Shenk writes knowingly about these multifaceted interactions whose complexity and inscrutability are difficult to appreciate. Even though he argues vehemently for an interactionist approach to the relation between genes and environment and tends to emphasize the plasticity, or malleability, of genes and neurons, Shenk reveals his understanding that genes are really the raw materials that determine the dispositional underpinnings of who we are. At one point he writes (2010) that "The problem isn't our inadequate genetic assets, but our inability, so far, to tap into what we already have." (loc. 149-150) Said another way, use it or lose it. We are born with innate abilities and dispositions, but being born with them doesn't necessarily mean that we apply ourselves in developing and perfecting them. In support of this view, he cites the early American psychologist (1842-1910) William James, who wrote:

> Compared with what we ought to be, we are only half awake. We are making use of only a small part of our physical and mental resources. Stating the thing broadly, the human individual thus lives far within his limits. He possesses powers of various sorts, which he habitually fails to use. (loc. 7-9)

You will hear many times from both me and others the finding of Anders Ericsson that 10,000 hours of deliberate practice over 10 years leads to expert performance. This sounds as though genes don't matter—only practice matters. However, Shank poses this question to himself and answers it (2010) thusly:

> What about those who practice regularly and strenuously, pursuing their pursuits seriously, but who do not improve significantly? Are they just missing that magic genetic spark? Not as far as Ericsson and his team can tell. "A careful review of the published evidence on the heritability of acquisition of elite sports achievement," he writes, "failed to reveal reproducible evidence for any genetic constraints for attaining elite levels by healthy individuals (excluding, of course, the evidence on body size)." Rather, nonachievers seem to be missing something in their process—one or more aspects of style or intensity of practice, or technique, or mindset, or response to failure. (loc. 911-917)

I would interpret this to mean that genes do not limit your development into a concert violinist or an Olympic athlete, but your behavioral traits, values, memories, abilities, and physical characteristics—all of which are the product of genes and environment interacting—certainly do. At is simplest level, for example, the trait of perfectionism could certainly contribute substantially to the quality of one's practice efforts, regardless of the task being practiced.

With this preamble, let us now look at Howardian Person, my try at creating a palette of characteristics for you to define you. Just keep in mind that, by the time of adulthood, most of these characteristics will have become hardwired in you as the result of years of genes and environment interacting, and that they are highly unlikely to change. Hence, wisdom suggests that we build our lives around them, that we make our jobs, hobbies, and relationships harness our natural energy. If some of the terms in Figure 6.0 are a bit unclear, keep reading. I'll explain all of them.

Howardian Person—Traits, Abilities, Physical Characteristics, Values, and Memories

Marcus Vitruvius Pollio was a Roman architect who wrote appealingly about the relation of the human body to sound architectural principles. He de

Figure 6.0   Howardian Person: The Palette of Who We Are (Adapted from Howard & Howard, 2011)

Mental Tools:

Semantic STM	Presentation
Procedural STM	Imagination
Semantic LTM	Fluency
Procedural LTM	Elaboration
Organizing	Learn from Context
Planning	Judgment
Evaluating	Processing Speed
Critical Thinking	Time to Mastery
Composition	Time Span

Mental Talents:

Language	Kinesthetic
Numbers	Interpersonal
Visual	Intrapersonal
Hearing	Taxonomies

Physical Characteristics:

Height	Sensitivity of skin to sunlight
Skin quality	Sensitivity of eyes to light/dark
Nails	
Weight	Sensitivity to noise
Speed	Muscular/skeletal
Tics	Sensitivity of touch
Figure	Sensitivity to odors
Date of puberty	Taste preferences
Visual acuity	Ease of falling asleep
Strength	Predispositions for diseases
Dexterity	
Balance	Sensitivity of digestive system
Teeth Endurance	
Allergies	Sleep requirements
Flexibility	Hand-eye coordination
Reaction time	
Handedness	Hair
Tendency to motion sickness	Eyes

Behavioral Traits:

N- Resilient	N= Responsive	N+ Reactive
E- Introvert	E= Ambivert	E+ Extravert
O- Preserver	O= Moderate	O+ Explorer
A- Challenger	A= Negotiator	A+ Adapter
C- Flexible	C= Balanced	C+ Focused

Memories:

Times:	
Kindergarten	Elementary Sch.
Middle School	High School
Higher Educ.	Military Service
Early Work Exp.	Vacations
Places:	
Homes	Religious Orgs.
Neighborhoods	Travel
School campuses	Friends' homes
Work sites	
Roles:	
(Grand)Parent	Artist
Teacher	Scientist
Caregiver	Researcher
Religious Leader	Maintenance
Hobbyist	Politician
Sibling	Financier

Values:

Achievement	Materialism
Aesthetics	Politics
Affiliation	Position
Beauty	Poverty/Asceticism
Charity	Power
Compassion	Professionalism
Creativity	Renunciation
Education	Romance
Entertainment	Safety
Escape	Scholarship
Family	Security
Friendship	Service
Healing	Spirituality
Health	Sport
Hedonism	Tolerance
Learning	Wealth
Maintenance	

scribed how the arms and legs of humans, when outstretched at various angles, would fall on the perimeter of either a circle or a square, nature's two perfect figures. Not until Leonardo da Vinci penned "Vitruvian" man was the architect's idea rendered in a way that lasted. I do not pretend to try to rival the work of either Vitruvius or da Vinci, but I do wish to take the idea of the human form as a basis for describing the raw materials of self.

In Figure 6.0, you will see a kind of stick, or box, figure with head, two arms, trunk, and two legs. What it lacks in da Vincian aesthetic it gains in practical content! The head area contains 18 mental tools, the arm on the left contains 8 talents, the arm on the right contains the Big Five supertraits

Figure 6.1   Pierce's Palette

Mental Tools:

Semantic STM	~~Presentation~~
~~Procedural STM~~	Imagination
~~Semantic LTM~~	Fluency
~~Procedural LTM~~	Elaboration
~~Organizing~~	~~Learn from Context~~
~~Planning~~	~~Judgment~~
Evaluating	~~Processing Speed~~
Critical Thinking	~~Time to Mastery~~
Composition	Time Span

Mental Talents:

Language	~~Kinesthetic~~
Numbers	~~Interpersonal~~
~~Visual~~	~~Intrapersonal~~
Hearing	Taxonomies

Physical Characteristics:

~~Height~~	Sensitivity of skin to sunlight
Skin quality	~~Sensitivity of eyes to light/dark~~
~~Nails~~	Sensitivity to noise
~~Weight~~	Muscular/skeletal
~~Speed~~	Sensitivity of touch
~~Tics~~	Sensitivity to odors
~~Figure~~	Taste preferences
~~Date of puberty~~	~~Ease of falling asleep~~
Visual acuity	~~Predispositions for diseases~~
~~Strength~~	~~Sensitivity of digestive system~~
~~Dexterity~~	~~Sleep requirements~~
~~Balance~~	Hand-eye coordination
~~Teeth Endurance~~	~~Hair~~
Allergies	Eyes
~~Flexibility~~	
~~Reaction time~~	
~~Handedness~~	
Tendency to motion sickness	

Behavioral Traits:

~~N- Resilient~~	N= Responsive	~~N+ Reactive~~
~~E- Introvert~~	E= Ambivert	~~E+ Extrovert~~
~~O- Preserver~~	O= Moderate	O+ Explorer
~~A- Challenger~~	A= Negotiator	~~A+ Adapter~~
~~C- Flexible~~	C= Balanced	~~C+ Focused~~

Memories:

Times:	
~~Kindergarten~~	~~Elementary Sch~~
~~Middle School~~	High School
Higher Educ.	Military Service
Early Work Exp	Vacations
Places:	
Homes	Religious Orgs
Neighborhoods	Travel
School campuses	Friends' homes
Work sites	
Roles:	
(Grand)Parent	Artist
Teacher	Scientist
Caregiver	Researcher
~~Religious Leader~~	Maintenance
Hobbyist	~~Politician~~
Sibling	~~Financier~~

Values:

Achievement	~~Materialism~~
Aesthetics	~~Politics~~
Affiliation	~~Position~~
~~Beauty~~	~~Poverty/Asceticism~~
~~Charity~~	~~Power~~
~~Compassion~~	~~Professionalism~~
Creativity	~~Renunciation~~
~~Education~~	Romance
~~Entertainment~~	~~Safety~~
~~Escape~~	Scholarship
Family	~~Security~~
~~Friendship~~	Service
~~Healing~~	~~Spirituality~~
~~Health~~	~~Sport~~
Hedonism	Tolerance
Learning	~~Wealth~~
~~Maintenance~~	

(three levels of each), the torso contains 32 of the more salient physical characteristics, the leg on the left contains 27 salient types of memory, and the leg on the right contains 33 values. The items that comprise this palette are by no means exhaustive, but they should at least get us started. You may ask why a certain trait or physical characteristic is not included, and I would say "Add it, by all means." This is not like the three primary colors of red, yellow, and blue, plus white and black, from which thousands of subtly different derivative colors might be made. Instead of only five colors, people are made of thousands of elements, only a handful of which are listed here. However, they are a very important handful, as determined by centuries of research.

So, how are they to be used? I am going to show you two ways to use them. First, if you will look at Figure 6.1, you will see "Pierce's Palette." I have taken the palette from Figure 6.0 and marked through the items that I do not wish my life to build on. This requires some explanation. Marking through an element does not necessarily mean that I do not like it, it bores me, or that it is a weakness, just as *not* marking through an element does not necessarily mean that it is a strength, that I like it, or that it excites and energizes me. So what does it mean? Marking through an item means that the item is not an important consideration in evaluating the goodness of fit between my environment and me. For instance, I have marked through the "Visual" talent (Visual). Why? I do not think that I have much visual talent. I do not draw very well. My PowerPoint presentations are generally not as visually impressive as those of others around me. While I appreciate visual beauty, whether in a fine museum, a well-toned human body, or an architectural and landscaping wonder, I can live without them for long periods. It is not important for my workplace or my homeplace to be visually arresting. But just like chocolate and cognac, I do enjoy a little visual beauty from time to time. The kind of visual beauty I most enjoy is the wonder of nature—watching Ken Burns' PBS series on the national parks was a spiritual experience for me, and when Jane and I drove the Blue Ridge Parkway in June amidst the purple rhododendrons and orange flame azaleas, my spirit soared. But for me, visual beauty is a plus, not a requirement. To have a beautiful spouse has been a gift to me, but Jane's mind and manner are the reason I'm with her.

On the other hand, I left the "Hearing" talent standing, i.e., not marked through. This is because my auditory world is vitally important to me 7-24-365¼. I react strongly and negatively to noise pollution in a way that I do not react to visual pollution. I like quietness, meaningful conversation, the hum of mechanical processes, or the kinds of music I've grown to prefer. I've walked out of restaurants and other venues whose cacophonous clamor brought me near to a headache. I've walked out of concerts whose performers played or sang badly (unless they were relatives!). I find that the most unwanted sound in my life is a television, radio, or other kind of conversation within earshot, but I am not focused on it. I like command of my auditory space the way others like command of their visual space. I dream longingly from time to time of a larger home (like the one I grew up in!) where I can get far enough away from television, card games, and idle chatter so that I can have quiet. I have a "white noise" machine at the office so that, when needed, I can drown out bothersome chatter with, say, the gentle patter of rain, or maybe the sounds of a tropical rainforest. I am blessed at the office with a corner room that rarely lets unwanted noise in, but in the event there's noise nearby, I can close my door, or, of course, turn on the white noise machine. I get feisty in movie theatres and other venues that turn the volume too high—surely the knobs are controlled by youth who have significant hearing loss from years of high-volume amplified music. And, finally, I am a musician who loves to play and sing and make my own music, my own "noise."

So Hearing is of constant importance to me, while Visual is an occasional treat. If a job were to call on my auditory acuity, it would be a natural fit. If it were to call on my visual acuity, it would be unnatural. I defer to others' visual taste or judgment, but I do not defer to others' auditory taste or judgment.

The behavioral traits to the right of the torso have five rows, with each row containing three levels of the trait. I have lined through the levels that do not describe me. So, I am neither extraverted nor introverted, but ambiverted. Basically this means that I like a balance of both introversion and extraversion. In about two hours, I will have been introverting here at my computer preparing this manuscript for about five hours. Then, Jane and I are off to take dinner to a friend recovering from knee surgery, and an evening of scintillating conversation. She and her visiting sister are avid travelers and social critics; so we're never at a loss for energetic dialog. At work, I spend half my time introverted with my statistics, reading, research, and writing, while the other half goes into teaching, meetings, consulting, and chat-rooming. A nice balance. And this is important to me, as spending most or all of my time in either extreme would be unnatural for me. A job or family situation that required me to be extraverted most of the time would be aversive, as would be a job or family situation that required me to be alone most of the time.

Another trait that is very important to me is the Explorer, and you'll notice that the two items to the left of it are lined through—Preserver and Moderate. This means that most of my time and energy need to be devoted to creative pursuits. As Managing Director of Research and Development, this is a perfect fit for me, as most of my time is spent developing new products, designing research projects, and creating new models for use in the world of work. At the lower end of this dimension, the Preserver, would come activities such as proofreading. Unfortunately, I must do a certain amount of this detailed and (for me) tedious task, as much of my production can only be poofed [sic!] by me. However, where possible, I am able to have other team members who are good at proofreading and who have the natural energy to enjoy it (and, I might add, who delight in finding my errors!) to do some of my proofreading for me.

Note under "Memories" that I have lined through Kindergarten but not through Neighborhoods. This does not mean that I have bad memories of Kindergarten, or that I didn't attend. On the contrary, I did attend a private kindergarten (public schools in N.C. did not yet provide education prior to the first grade), but was expelled when I cut off one of Virginia Dixon's pigtails. She was sleeping so soundly at nap time, and I just couldn't go to sleep, and those construction scissors were just yearning to have some use. It is just that my Kindergarten experience did not produce memories that shape my decision-making today. On the other hand, my childhood neighborhood conditioned me to thrive on wide streets, good sidewalks, greenery and blossoms everywhere, and a canopy of shade trees. Unfortunately, we had a yardman. So I became dependent on a nice yard and neighborhood without acquiring the habit of doing the maintenance to keep it so livable. Yes, I learned to mow the grass and weed the rose garden, but only enough to get the merit badge! So, today, we have a nice yard and neighborhood, but also a yard service. If and when I can no longer afford a yard service, I suppose it will be time to move into an apartment or some such that requires no yard maintenance. But, hopefully, the apartment will be in a neighborhood that has shade trees and walking paths.

In some cases, I have left items standing (i.e., not lined them through) because they are things that I strongly want to avoid. For example, I left "Sensitivity to Odors" standing under "Physical Characteristics" (the torso of Howardian Person). This sensitivity for me is a two-edged sword. I relish the fragrance of honeysuckle in May, magnolia blossoms in June, rosebuds in July, and so on. But being close to someone wearing strong, non-natural perfumes or colognes (Jane and I call them "petrochemical factories") turns my stomach, burns my nose, and typically ends up with me relocating myself. Fortunately, Jane does not use fragrances other than soap and shampoo. I would quit a job before I would work for longer than an hour beside a person reeking of some monstrous petrochemical concoction.

So the first use of "The Palette of Who We Are" (Figure 6.0) is for you to line through the items that are not important to you in having a good fit with your work and family. You might make copies of Howardian Person and try completing them for you and your significant others, and having some dialog around the results. It is a delightful way of getting to know each other: "I didn't know that was so important to you!" or "I really didn't know you felt that way." However, you may find that you need some definitions of these elements before you begin lining through items. In that case, simply keep reading, as I next will define the traits and abilities, even though briefly. Once you have studied the definitions, you might try returning to Figure 6.0 and marking through the items that are irrelevant to your sense of good person-environment fit.

So, the second use of the items in Figure 6.0 is a checklist that I have prepared for you. Before we fill out the checklist based on Howardian Person, I will provide you with some definitions of the abilities and traits, as just mentioned. The physical characteristics, memories, and values are self-explanatory, so I will not define each of them. Instead, I will provide brief overviews. However, for the mental abilities and behavioral traits, I will offer brief definitions of each.

Traits—There's no such thing as a bad trait. Many subtraits comprise the Big Five supertraits that I defined in Chapter 1. For example, extraversion doesn't really exist. Rather, it is a blend of different subtraits. To call someone more extraverted is a shorthand way of saying that they are warm, sociable, active, and so forth. To call someone more introverted is a shorthand way of saying that they are more aloof, solitary, sedentary, and so forth. In fact, "extravert" and "introvert" are stereotypes, in that the qualities that comprise them do not always occur together. While most extraverts are sociable *and* active, some extraverts are one and not the other. So, the more precise way to describe ourselves is to use the subtraits and not the supertraits.

Different models of personality and different personality tests divide up the supertraits in different ways. You are welcome to use one of the many different models that are available (see some of them in Appendix C). For the purposes of this book, I will limit our discussion to the 23 subtraits that I use with the WorkPlace Big Five Profile™ (and also the SchoolPlace Big Five Profile™). Table 6.0 defines the 23 subtraits that give definition to the WorkPlace Big Five Profile™. Each subtrait is defined by two anchors, one that describes one extreme of the trait and one that defines the other extreme, with the understanding that persons who would "score" in the middle area of the continuum would represent more of an equal blend of the two extremes. Keeping in mind that there is no "right" place to locate yourself on any of these 23 scales, put an "X" on each scale that best describes your typical behavior. If you're one way at work and another at home, then you likely belong in the middle area.

   Abilities—Too many are generally better than too few. Once you have placed your 23 X's on Table 6.0, move to Table 6.1, where you will find the 18 mental Tools, and then on to Table 6.2, where you will find the eight mental Talents. Tools are like the operating system on a computer (e.g., Windows, OS X), while talents are like a computer's application programs (e.g., Word, Excel). Tools include basic procedures used in all of the various application programs, like memory and syntax, while talents represent relatively distinct domains of performance, each of which uses all of the tools. In the complete model of mental ability that we are developing at the Center for Applied Cogntive Studies, we are assuming—based on research of course—that an individual could be stronger at one talent than

Table 6.0   The 23 Subtraits of the WorkPlace Big Five Profile™ Defined by Anchors at the Extremes

Need for Stability (N)
Usually at ease...Frequently worries
Usually calm...Quicker temper
More optimistic..Less optimistic
Rapid rebound time..Longer rebound time
Extraversion (E)
Holds down positive feelings..Shows a lot of positive feelings
Prefers working alone...Prefers working with others
Prefers being still or in one place...................................Prefers to be physically active
Prefers being independent..Enjoys responsibility of leading
Is skeptical of others..Readily trusts others
Speaks more directly..Carefully selects right words
Originality (O)
Implements plans..Creates new plans and ideas
Prefers simplicity...Seeks complexity
Wants to maintain existing methods......................................Readily accepts changes
Attentive to details...Prefers broad view
Accommodation (A)
More interested in self needs......................................More interested in others' needs
Welcomes conflict..Seeks harmony
Wants acknowledgement...Uncomfortable with praise
Usually expresses opinions..Keeps opinions to self
Consolidation (C)
Low need to continually refine/polish...........................Continual need to refine/polish
Comfortable with little organization....................................Keeps everything organized
Satisfied with current achievement..................................Craves achievement
Shifts easily between tasks..Completes tasks before shifting
Operates in spontaneous mode......................................Develops plans for everything

another. We also assume that an individual could be stronger on one tool in one talent area than they are on the same tool but in another talent area. For example, I am stronger at the auditory talent (I'm a musician with very good auditory discrimination) than at the visual talent. I do not perform at comparable levels in those two talents. Moreover, my long-term memory for auditory information is stronger than it is for verbal information—I can remember more of a Handel sonata that I memorized previously than of a Shakespeare sonnet that I memorized previously. Hence, we don't just recommend assessing individuals for short-term memory in general, but for short-term memory in specific contexts.

   In Table 6.1, we list the Mental Tools, similar to the components of a computer operating system, like Windows or OS X. Note that in this self-assessment we have offered a scale that goes only

Table 6.1   The 16 Mental Tools (adapted with permission from Howard and Howard, 2011)

Mental Tool:	Definition:	Self-Rating:		
1. Semantic Short-Term Memory (STM)	Ability to retain factual information (names, telephone numbers, faces, chess board configurations, what cards have been played from each suit, dates, figures, facts, and so forth) for short periods of time, such as over the course of a few hours or even a day.	|----------------------|----------------------| About Average	Somewhat Stronger	A Definite Strength
2. Procedural Short-Term Memory (STM)	Ability to retain procedural (also called "episodic") information (sequences/steps, as in how to open, operate, or shut down a piece of equipment, how to bisect an angle, how to find the way to a new friend's house, how to find something online).	|----------------------|----------------------| About Average	Somewhat Stronger	A Definite Strength
3. Semantic Long-Term Memory (LTM)	Ability to recognize and recall semantic information (i.e., facts) for a longer period of time, such as over the course of years, without daily or frequent review (e.g., a phone number, a poem, a friend's birth date, which coin is still missing from your collection).	|----------------------|----------------------| About Average	Somewhat Stronger	A Definite Strength
4. Procedural Long-Term Memory (LTM)	Ability to recognize and recall procedural information for a longer period of time, such as over the course of years, without daily or frequent review (e.g., how to tie a bow tie, how to make a proper caramel icing, how to play a card game, how to train a puppy, how to knit, how to ride a bike, how to swing a baseball bat).	|----------------------|----------------------| About Average	Somewhat Stronger	A Definite Strength
5. Organizing (Spatial Arrangement)	Ability to sort (i.e., categorize) various kinds of information into two- or three-dimensional space. Content could be either concrete (e.g., marbles grouped by size, recipe ingredients arranged in order of use), abstract (e.g., elements of an essay, a series of mathematical expressions), semantic (e.g., different kinds of marbles—aggies, steelies, etc.), or procedural (rules for different kinds of games using marbles). Organizing includes identifying emergent categories (e.g., conducting triage in an emergency room or disaster scene [who is ok, who is hurt a little, and who needs immediate help] or creating categories of folders for storing emails). Organizing additionally includes selecting from a list containing distractors (e.g., in studying for a test or preparing for a research paper, sorting available information into "highly relevant," "moderately relevant," and "irrelevant").	|----------------------|----------------------| About Average	Somewhat Stronger	A Definite Strength
6. Planning (Sequential Arrangement)	Ability to sort various kinds of information into a logical sequence according to time, urgency, hierarchical relationship, linearity, importance, and so forth. Includes both concrete content (e.g., the steps involved in making something) and abstract content (e.g., the steps involved in negotiating).	|----------------------|----------------------| About Average	Somewhat Stronger	A Definite Strength
7. Evaluation of Information	Ability to inspect a body of information (e.g., text, spreadsheet, diagram, photograph) and identify errors, omissions, and changes (e.g., proofreading, editing, comparing an original painting to a copy).	|----------------------|----------------------| About Average	Somewhat Stronger	A Definite Strength
8. Critical Thinking	Ability to examine a body of information (e.g., text, spreadsheet, diagram, photograph) and then identify assumptions, spot logical fallacies, see causal relationships, select logical conclusions, and solve problems (e.g., preparing for a debate, writing a critical review, giving someone feedback on a presentation or performance, preparing a presentation, editing what we have each written in a book).	|----------------------|----------------------| About Average	Somewhat Stronger	A Definite Strength

Table 6.1, cont.

Mental Tool:	Definition:	Self-Rating:		
9. Composition	Ability to create an effective composition on the fly (e.g., speech, spreadsheet, diagram, game plan, improvisational dance, clever excuse for "lost" homework).	|----------------------|----------------------| About Average	Somewhat Stronger	A Definite Strength
10. Presentation	Upon being given the text/script/steps/music/diagram for a presentation (prepared by oneself or by another), ability to present the material effectively (e.g., speech, dance, song, athletic maneuver).	|----------------------|----------------------| About Average	Somewhat Stronger	A Definite Strength
11. Imagination	Ability to come up with an idea that is both novel and effective (e.g., a new way of saying something such as a slogan, a new mathematical expression to show a relationship among variables, a new movement pattern to accomplish an unusual physical challenge, an interesting way to graph data, a new strategy for trying to persuade a person in power to agree with you).	|----------------------|----------------------| About Average	Somewhat Stronger	A Definite Strength
12. Fluency	Once a novel suggestion has been made for #11, brainstorming ability to generate a number of additional suggestions, regardless of novelty or effectiveness (e.g., come up with a dozen new slogans that express the same meaning, a dozen strategies for persuading a person in power).	|----------------------|----------------------| About Average	Somewhat Stronger	A Definite Strength
13. Elaboration	Ability to take a basic body of information (e.g., text, spreadsheet, diagram) and develop modifications, additions, deletions, and spin-off bodies of information (e.g., take a spreadsheet designed for one purpose and adapt it for another purpose, take a speech written for an all-male audience and adapt it for an all-female audience, take a sports analogy and apply it to politics).	|----------------------|----------------------| About Average	Somewhat Stronger	A Definite Strength
14. Learning from Context	Ability to determine the meaning of an unfamiliar symbol or object (e.g., word, phrase, formula, gesture, piece of equipment) by using contextual or environmental clues (e.g., read a description that contains an unknown/unfamiliar word substituted for a familiar word and figure out from context what the nonsense word is, i.e., what the original familiar word was; study a mathematical formula with a novel symbol and figure out its function from context; study a football play or dance movement that contains a novel symbol and figure out its meaning/function).	|----------------------|----------------------| About Average	Somewhat Stronger	A Definite Strength
15. Judgment	When facing a problem requiring good judgment, the ability to select accurate alternative responses and to exhibit flexibility in selecting types of responses (changing yourself, changing the other person, or changing the situation). For example, you are convinced that a teacher is grading you low for personal reasons; you are given 15 possible strategies to pursue in order to improve the relationship, and you must select the best three strategies to implement.	|----------------------|----------------------| About Average	Somewhat Stronger	A Definite Strength
16. Processing Speed	Ability to complete any of the above mental tasks (1 to 15) quickly, adjusted for accuracy (e.g., how quickly you can think up a new slogan, how quickly you can recall a memory).	|----------------------|----------------------| About Average	Somewhat Stronger	A Definite Strength
17. Time to Mastery	Given a novel skill to learn, how long it takes to attain mastery (e.g., how long it takes to accurately learn some basic vocabulary and grammar in a new language or to accurately use some made-up mathematical symbols in a college admissions test).	|----------------------|----------------------| About Average	Somewhat Stronger	A Definite Strength

Table 6.1, cont.

Mental Tool:	Definition:	Self-Rating:		
18. Time Span	The amount of time one can work independently without significant help from a boss, teacher, parent, or other expert (e.g., build a computer simulation over a three-year period; start a school club or a business venture and run it for three months before needing major help; design a special community service project, implement it, and be interviewed about it in your local newspaper so you can use it for your college application; work alone for one year on a science project; write a novel over a two-year span).	|--------------------|---------------------| About Average	Somewhat Stronger	A Definite Strength

from average to way above average. What happened to "below average"? Well, you've probably read or heard that most people think that they are average or better at everything. So, rather than waste space on these scales that will not be used for the most part, we just assume that everyone will be comfortable rating themselves as average, somehwat stronger than average, or definitely strong. If you have the audacity (and honesty!) to rate yourself below average, simply put a mark to the left of "About Average."

Now, review Table 6.1 and rate your level of strength on each of the 18 mental tools.

The Eight Talents

The eight talents that we define in Table 6.2 are based on the "multiple intelligences" (MI) research of Howard Gardner (1983). While we only cite one book here, a huge literature has grown up around Gardner's MI theory. School curriculum experts have developed programs that use the content of these eight areas to teach basic skills. This approach is based on the understanding that any given child will excel in at least one talent area, or, if not excel, will have at least one talent area that is stronger than other areas. In a school setting, the goal is to use a child's talent—their area of greatest interest/ability—for learning the basic skills such as reading and mathematics. For example, if a child's

Table 6.2   The Eight Talents: A Self-Assessment

Talent Area:	Definition:	Self-Rating:		
1. Language	Fluency and comprehension in the use of language involves grammar, phonology (ability to understand and produce shades of difference in the sound of speech—this overlaps with the Auditory talent), rhetoric (matching language to audience), vocabulary, composition, and presentations. Example: J. R. R. Tolkien, British author of *The Hobbit* and *The Lord of the Rings*.	|--------------------|---------------------| About Average	Somewhat Stronger	A Definite Strength
2. Numbers	Capability in mathematical and logical operations involves basic computations, use of math and logic symbols, understanding of calculational formulas and how numbers relate to each other in spreadsheets. Example: Bill Gates, founder of Microsoft.	|--------------------|---------------------| About Average	Somewhat Stronger	A Definite Strength
3. Visual	Accurate perception (detecting similarities, differences, and meanings) of two- and three-dimensional objects involves the ability to rotate them mentally and recognize them from nonobvious perspectives. Example: Steven Spielberg, producer/director of innumerable movies from *E.T.* to *Saving Private Ryan*.	|--------------------|---------------------| About Average	Somewhat Stronger	A Definite Strength

Table 6.2, cont.

Talent Area:	Definition:	Self-Rating:		
4. Hearing	Ability to produce and discriminate between a variety of sounds involves sensitivity to pitch, rhythm, timbre, and volume, both in musical and other (e.g., machines) settings. Example: Alicia Keys, rhythm and blues vocalist and winner of multiple Grammy Awards.	|-----------------------|-----------------------| About Average	Somewhat Stronger	A Definite Strength
5. Kinesthetic	Ability to understand, execute, control, and coordinate a wide variety of bodily movements involves eye-hand coordination, speed, balance, depth judgment, stamina, and principles of physical health and endurance. Example: LeBron James, NBA phenomenon.	|-----------------------|-----------------------| About Average	Somewhat Stronger	A Definite Strength
6. Interpersonal	Ability to recognize and manage the feelings, needs, and opinions of others involves body language, social graces, techniques to influence, conflict management, and delegation techniques. Example: Oprah Winfrey, television host famous for her ability to empathize with and help others.	|-----------------------|-----------------------| About Average	Somewhat Stronger	A Definite Strength
7. Intrapersonal	Ability to recognize and manage one's own feelings, needs, and mental processes involves self-control, objective analysis, blind spots, risk evaluation, and hidden agendas. *Example:* the Dalai Lama, exiled spiritual leader of Tibetan Buddhism.	|-----------------------|-----------------------| About Average	Somewhat Stronger	A Definite Strength
8. Taxonomic	Ability to survey a part of the natural world (e.g., a body of knowledge, an industry, an organization, a type of product or service) and create/understand/manipulate/use a taxonomy that organizes the area in a way that portrays how all of the elements are related. Example: George Washington Carver, Tuskegee Institute professor who, among other achievements, discovered 300+ uses for the peanut.	|-----------------------|-----------------------| About Average	Somewhat Stronger	A Definite Strength

greatest talent happened to be Kinesthetic, then the teacher would employ movement activities for learning mathematical operations and facts. In the world of adults, the emphasis is on finding employment that builds on one's stronger talents. Or, at least make sure that one's stronger talents somehow find some form of expression, whether at work, at home, or in the community.

Let's proceed with identifying your level of ability on all eight of Gardner's "talents." After each definition in Table 6.2, we suggest a famous person who exhibits the specific talent. Rate yourself as anywhere from "About Average" to "A Definite Strength."

Physical characteristics—They are what they are. Physical characteristics can place significant limits on the activities that we pursue. I am highly subject to motion sickness, for example, so it would make no sense for me to pursue a career as a deep-sea fisherman. And while I dearly love driving through the mountains with my family, I need to be the driver, for if I get nauseous as a passenger. I am also severely nearsighted; so my depth perception is subpar. I had several accidents as a junior-high baseball player because of my shortcomings in judging the time of arrival of a baseball. My skin is super-sensitive to the sunlight. When I was in summer camp as a 10-year-old, I went sailing on a sunny day and ended up in the camp infirmary for the better part of a week with severe burns on my upper body. I'd worn no shirt! So, when you review the list of physical characteristics, both on Howardian Person (Figure 6.0) and on the Person-Environment Checklist (Table 6.3), simply mark through any items that do not need to be taken into consideration, but leave unlined any characteristics that you either a) definitely enjoy and would want to build on, or b) definitely want to avoid. For example, I left "Taste preferences" unmarked because I would not like to commit myself to a situation in which I had to accept a constant diet of bland foods and beverages. I do like my herbs, sauces, spices, and variety of flavors in general. When I took my older sister Eleanor to New York City a decade ago, we went to a different ethnic restaurant for every meal, leading my sister to meekly request as we began our return to North Carolina, "Little brother, could we have some American for lunch!" She'd had enough variety and was ready for a grilled (American) cheese with ice tea.

Values—It's what's important that counts. "Values" is a term thrown about in political campaigns (family values, American values, etc.), managerial philosophy (value-based leadership), and a variety of other venues. A value, in its most widely understood meaning, is whatever is important to you. So, how do we gauge importance? The American Management Academy once defined "business strategy" as a "pattern of resource allocation. In other words, if business spent relatively more time, money, staffing, and other resources on improving the packaging of their product than one might normally expect, then "improve packaging" was clearly a business strategy for them, using this definition.

I suggest we use the same definition for defining our individual values. Where do we spend our time, money, and effort? What is our personal "pattern of resource allocation?" From what I spend on sheet music, musical instruments, and concerts, and from the time I spend in practicing and performing, it would be an easy conclusion that at least one of my values is music, or more generally, aesthetics, pursuing the world of art and beauty. Also, from the time and money I spend on reading, one could easily infer that another value of mine is learning. In the list of values in Table 6.3, as well as on Howardian Person's right-most leg (Table 6.0), select the values that are most important to you. Try to select no more than 11—that represents 1/3 of the total of 33 values listed. I tried to set a good example by lining through all but 11—it was not easy!

In his book-now-movie *The Pursuit of Happyness* (2006), Chris Gardner wrote, "I am healthy, have raised two children as a single parent (blessed with a village of support) that have become outstanding young people, and I'm in a position to do work that reflects my values. That's my definition of wealth." Or happiness. Gardner states succinctly the importance of building your life out of what is most important to you. Make what you do fit who you are. It is often said that we are not what we do. However, what we do, if it is based on who we are, should in fact be who we are.

Memories—Our past pleasures shape our current choices. It is often said that those who do not learn from history are doomed to repeat it. That informs the inclusion of "memories" in Howardian Person. The objective here is to identify those memories that represent things either that we want to build on or avoid. For example, I crossed out "Kindergarten" because I do not associate any memories from kindergarten either with pleasurable activities or circumstances that I want to replicate or with unpleasurable activities or contexts that I want to avoid. Kindergarten memories are just not relevant to me as I consider my options in life. On the other hand, "Early work experiences" was left standing. My first real job was with the U.S. Army. I worked as a special agent in the Army Intelligence Corps, sort of like being an FBI agent, but limited to working within the Army. I worked in a three-person office that prided itself on getting its job done well, no matter how long or short it took. We enjoyed both work and play, and my officer in charge, though military through and through, was personable, flexible, creative, and fair. He has been my model of professionalism. And the independence of working in a small office in the Bavarian Alps spoiled me! I get the heebie-jeebies when I think of having to work in a large, bureaucratic organization. Even though I was in the U.S. Army, I felt as though I were a young entrepreneur on a very long leash.

As you review the kinds of memories from your past that are suggested in Howardian Person and the Fit Checklist, cross out the irrelevant ones and enjoy the salient ones. Feel free to add kinds of memories that I've neglected.

Howardian Person—A checklist for assessing person-environment fit.

This monster checklist contains abbreviated versions of the elements of fit that we have just enumerated. You may need to refer back to their fuller, more defined versions from time to time. Otherwise, you will find all of the personal qualities listed in the first column of Table 6.3. The purpose of this checklist/worksheet is to determine where your qualities do and do not fit the various contexts of your current life. I suggest you proceed as follows:

1. Based on your earlier work crossing out qualities that are irrelevant, transfer all of your "left standing" items to Table 6.3. You will not need to pay further attention to the rows that you mark out.
2. Review the four headers (Current Job, Future Job, Home, Other) and modify them to reflect your current situation. For example, I would change mine to: Current Job, Marriage, Choir, and Family Reunion Committees, as these make up over 90% of my time commitments at present.
3. Now, work either row-by-row or column-by-column.
4. Enter a plus (+) or check (✓) for each column in a row where the environment is compatible with the personal quality you have left standing in column one.
5. Enter a minus (-) or an x (✗) for each column in a row where the environment is incompatible, or inhospitable, or otherwise a bad fit, for the personal quality associated with that row.
6. Ideally, you would have a plus or check in all remaining cells. That would mean that the four contexts you've chosen are all perfect fits with your personal qualities. If that is the case, you are fortunate indeed!
7. The reality is that some cells will have a minus or x, an indication that there is something about a context in your life that is not a good fit with the quality associated with that row. For example, I would have an "x" in the row for the Hearing talent in the Current Job column, because it does take advantage of my auditory ability. On the other hand, my current job is quiet and respectful of my need for quiet; so I could also put a check in the same box (✓/✗), indicating both good and bad fit in that case.
8. After you've completed your self-assessment, review your worksheet and highlight or circle any cells with an x or minus that you would like to do something about. In the next section, we will discuss causes of bad fit, and you come up with some ideas about how to improve the fit. Otherwise, you might decide to discuss some of the bad fits with your partner (business, home, or community) with the purpose of finding a way to ameliorate situations where your qualities are incompatible with your environment.

Table 6.3   The Person-Environment Checklist and Self-Assessment

Environments / Personal Qualities	Current Job	Future Job	Home	Other
Mental Tools				
Semantic STM				
Procedural STM				
Semantic LTM				
Procedural LTM				
Organizing				

Table 6.3, cont.

Environments / Personal Qualities	Current Job	Future Job	Home	Other
Personal Qualities				
Planning				
Evaluating				
Critical Thinking				
Composition				
Presentation				
Imagination				
Fluency				
Elaboration				
Learn from Context				
Judgment				
Processing Speed				
Time to Mastery				
Time Span				
Mental Talents				
Language				
Numbers				
Visual				
Hearing				
Kinesthetic				
Interpersonal				
Intrapersonal				
Taxonomies				
Traits (The Big Five)				
Need for Stability (N)				
At ease.......Worries				
Calm...........Temper				
Optimism.........Pessimism				
Slow rebound.....Fast Rebound				
Extraversion (E)				
Holds feelings...Shows feelings				
Alone..............With others				
Still.................Active				
Independent.....Leading				
Skeptical.........Trusting				
Direct..............Tactful				
Originality (O)				
Implements.....Creates				
Simplicity........Complexity				
Status quo......Change				
Details.............Broad view				
Accommodation (A)				
Self needs.......Others' needs				
Conflict............Harmony				
Proud..............Humble				
Assertive..........Reserved				
Consolidation (C)				
Casual..............Perfectionist				
Low Organized......Organized				
Satisfied............Ambitious				

Table 6.3, cont.

Environments / Personal Qualities	Current Job	Future Job	Home	Other
Shifts tasks....Completes tasks				
Spontaneous......Methodical				
Physical Characteristics				
Height				
Skin quality				
Nails				
Weight				
Speed				
Tics				
Figure				
Date of puberty				
Visual acuity				
Strength				
Dexterity				
Balance				
Teeth				
Endurance				
Allergies				
Flexibility				
Reaction time				
Handedness				
Motion sickness				
Sensitivity of skin				
Sensitivity of eyes				
Sensitivity to noise				
Muscular/skeletal				
Sensitivity of touch				
Sensitivity to odors				
Taste preferences				
Sleep quality				
Specific diseases				
Digestive system				
Sleep requirements				
Hand-eye coordination				
Hair				
Eyes				
Memories				
Times:				
Kindergarten				
Middle School				
Higher Education				
Early Work Experience				
Elementary School				
High School				
Military Service				
Vacations				
Places:				
Homes				
Neighborhoods				

Table 6.3, cont.

Environments / Personal Qualities	Current Job	Future Job	Home	Other
School campuses				
Work sites				
Religious Organizations				
Travel				
Friends' Homes				
Roles:				
Parent/grandparent				
Teacher				
Caregiver				
Religious Leader				
Hobbyist				
Sibling				
Artist				
Scientist				
Researcher				
Maintenance				
Politician				
Financier				
Values				
Achievement				
Aesthetics				
Affiliation				
Beauty				
Charity				
Compassion				
Creativity				
Education				
Entertainment				
Escape				
Family				
Friendship				
Healing				
Health				
Hedonism				
Learning				
Maintenance				
Materialism				
Politics				
Position				
Poverty/Asceticism				
Power				
Professionalism				
Renunciation				
Romance				
Safety				
Scholarship				
Security				
Service				
Spirituality				
Sport				

Table 6.3, cont.

Environments Personal Qualities	Current Job	Future Job	Home	Other
Tolerance				
Wealth				

Obstacles to Good Person-Environment Fit

The effects of poor fit over time are physical and detrimental. It behooves us to find the cause of poor fit and attempt to eliminate the damage we do to ourselves therefrom. Let me give a couple of examples of poor fit and their physical consequences, and how addressing the cause arrested the damage. A highly successful physician at age 40 developed high blood pressure. He couldn't understand why: He had a successful practice; he loved his work; he had three delightful children and a loving, independent wife; he exercised regularly; drank red wine moderately…. So why the high blood pressure? The cause was poor fit: He was an introverted (E-), creative (O+), and focused (C+) caregiver in a clinic that called for an extraverted (E+), noncreative (O-), and spontaneous (C-) physician. He was the opposite of the ideal on three out of the Big Five supertraits. The stress of having to be someone he was not was taking its toll on his body. The cortisol pulsed through his veins daily and became life-threatening. He decided to move to the mountains and join a multidisciplinary diagnostic team that typically took three full days to study one child. That was fit made in heaven—he was able to be more solitary, creative, and focused. He was so successful that the high blood pressure went away, and after 10 years he had a hospital wing named after him.

The second example of the ill effects of poor fit was a plant manager who had developed ulcers and high blood pressure. This introverted (E-), creative (O+), kind (A+), and spontaneous (C-) worker had started with the company as an assembly worker. He received all promotions, ultimately becoming plant manager, the most prestigious position in his small community and his only way to increase his income with the employer. However, plant management called for his opposite on three out of the four traits just enumerated (his creativity served him well). When poor fit was identified as the cause of his health problems, company officers invited him to move his family to the headquarters city where he could become Vice President for Research and Development. This new position was a perfect fit for his temperament. He flourished as he waved his health problems goodbye.

Not all instances of poor fit are as easy to diagnose as these two. In order to improve an instance of poor fit, we need to understand the causes of poor fit in the first place. Some of these causes are within our control, and some are not. My tendency to motion sickness in combination with traveling on the Atlantic Ocean was not really under my control when in 1964 I headed for Bremerhaven aboard the USAT General William O. Darby. Well, seemingly not under my control. I found three things I could do to minimize the seasickness: I avoided eating greasy foods, I spent my off-duty time on deck near the galley's exhaust fans, which kept me warm and enwrapped in pleasant odors, and I volunteered (horrors!) for work as a clerk-typist. The latter was delightful. The sergeant in charge of us 800 troops bellowed during my first 15 minutes on board, "I need a volunteer who is MOS 971 Clerk Typist!" I jumped up and ran to the sergeant, knowing that I was not MOS 971 but that I could type, and typing sounded like a pleasing distraction from rising, falling, rising, falling, rising, falling…. I ended up producing the ship's daily newsletter, not only typing but interviewing and writing articles. So, you never know how much control you have over poor fit until you try to make it better.

Let's explore nine kinds of obstacles to good P-E fit. You may recognize one or more of them at work in your life. Recognition of the obstacle is a first step towards its removal, or at least its minimization. The nine that we will discuss are:

- partners
- timid goal setting
- experience
- false self (covering)

- low self-esteem
- necessity
- culture
- the wrong context
- certain (self-defeating) traits

Partners. One of the most common obstacles to good P-E fit is one's partner, whether marriage, business, or otherwise. The research suggests that opposites attract for the short term, similars for the long. When short-term attraction of opposites evolves into long term, the opposite qualities have the potential to prevent one or both partners from feeling comfortable being themselves. If a naturally skeptical person partners with someone who is naturally trusting, then whose instincts prevail? Jane is more skeptical than I am; so when we negotiate a business deal with a third party, this difference causes both of us stress. She laments that I am too trusting, while I lament that she needs to be more trusting. So, the bad news is that I cannot be my trusting self without some grief from her, and she cannot be her skeptical self without some reproof from me. However, the good news is that we might get snookered without her skepticism, and without my trust we might alienate the third party. In this case, the trick is to value the two different perspectives that each of us brings to a situation.

McGill University stress researcher Hans Selye once used "racehorses and turtles" as a metaphor for how partners handle differences, such as Jane's and my trust differences. Selye says there's nothing intrinsically wrong with being a racehorse (or at one end of any given trait continuum, such as low in trust), nor is there anything intrinsically wrong with being a turtle (or at the other end of that continuum, such as high in trust). Both the racehorse and the turtle provide value in certain situations. Or, as Emerson says, "Every individual nature has its own beauty." The problem, says Selye, is when the racehorse exhorts the turtle to speed up and be more of a racehorse, and the turtle tries to be more of a racehorse, which is against its nature. Or, when the turtle urges the racehorse to slow down and be more of a turtle, and the racehorse tries to slow down and be more of a turtle. This is a major cause of stress. In summary, partners become an obstacle to P-E Fit when one tries to get the other to change temperament in some way, and the other goes along with the request. We don't mean little habits, like sticking chewing gum behind one's ear—it is OK to try to change that! We're talking about trying to change traits, abilities, and values. All partnerships should begin by accepting the other with the traits, abilities, and values the person brings into the partnership.

Ickes (2009) summarizes this research as follows:

The evidence clearly suggests that global personality similarity, when assessed as a profile correlation computed across a number of personality traits, is indeed predictive of the degree to which couples are satisfied with their marriage relationships. And these data, in turn, complement the data reported by Watson and his colleagues, which show that married couples are more likely (than chance would predict) to have similar personality characteristics (e.g., similar ages, attitudes, values, and IQ scores) at the time they get married. In summary, "birds of a feather" (couples with similar characteristics) are not only more likely to "flock together" (that is, to select each other as marriage partners), but are also more satisfied with their relationships to the extent that their personality profiles are globally similar. (loc. 1980).... Although "odd couples" (those with globally mismatched personalities) may occasionally find each other and form committed relationships as well, the statistical odds of these "odd couples" being satisfied with each other tend to work against them. In contrast, the statistical odds for the success of committed relationships involving "not-so-odd couples" (those with globally similar personalities) are substantially better. (loc. 1,994)

It should be noted, however, that not all of the Big Five traits are equally important in determining satisfaction in the relationship, particularly with respect to marriage. McCrae et al. (2008) reported on the results of a large, assortative, mating study involved couples in the U.S., the Netherlands, the Czech Republic, and Russia. They found that while similarity on all five supertraits was associated with satisfaction in all five countries, two stood out as having larger effects than the other three—Originality (also called Openness) and Accommodation (also called Agreeableness). In all four countries, people apparently give preferential treatment to expressing their creativity and power by marrying persons with similar levels. Creatives marry creatives, complex marries complex, simpler marries simpler, innovatives marry innovatives, status quos marry status quos, detailers marry detailers, assertives marry assertives, reticents marry reticents, competers marry competers, prouds marry prouds, humbles marry humbles. Why? Because people value these qualities in themselves and want to make sure that their life partner values them also. They don't want to have to soft-pedal personal qualities that are core. This is the essence of P-E fit, that I do not have to restrain myself in behaviors that are important and natural to me. The constraint that one can feel from one's partner's effort to control us is well expressed by William Blake's little gem "Eternity":

He who binds to himself a joy
Does the winged life destroy
But he who kisses the joy as it flies
Lives in eternity's sunrise.

Timid Goal Setting. We will say more about goals in the next chapter. For the moment, however, let's consider how goals affect P-E Fit. I think David Shenk (2010) says it best when he writes that "The problem isn't our inadequate genetic assets, but our inability, so far, to tap into what we already have." (loc. 149-150) Said more simply, nothing ventured, nothing gained. You can't get into college if you don't apply. You can't get into a good college if you don't apply. You can't get into a great college unless you apply. You can't get a date with the one that's best for you unless you ask. You can't start a business unless you prepare a business plan, ask for a loan, and take the plunge. You can't perform in public unless you decide on a venue and just do it, with or without permission, as appropriate.

Playing it safe is not going to harness your wagon to a star! In order to build on our finer qualities, we need to set goals that build on our strengths. Carol Dweck (2006) writes of the "fixed mindset" whereby a person tends to see themselves as being capable of no more than they currently have demonstrated. Hence, they tend to set goals based on doing a repeat of something already done. This is timid goal setting that is likely to entail goals that fail to build on strengths. It is through "growth mindsets" that persons set goals on the assumption that they can learn new knowledge and skill to accomplish goals hitherto not thought possible. A creative person in a noncreative job will feel thwarted until they set a goal that engages their creativity, whether it is to invent, create, innovate, or start a new business. This dogged determination to use one's strengths to serve ever more challenging goals is best summed up by the board member of Greg Mortensen's Central Asia Institute when she announced that "I want to be used up when I die." Indeed.

Experience. Having too little experience can keep one from getting the opportunity one needs to show what one can do. The frustrating "five years experience required" could deter one from ever applying for such work, even though it might be a perfect fit for them otherwise. The solution to this situation might come in one of several different forms. One could attempt to bypass the experience requirement by making a case that one has the equivalent of five years experience. For example, one might create a portfolio that showcases one's accomplishments that are relevant to the job in question. Or one could learn about the experience requirement as early as possible and attempt to gain equivalent experience through internships, summer jobs, volunteer work, and so forth.

Too much experience, on the other hand, can be just as much of a handicap. To apply for a job that you really want could be met with a "you're overqualified." All too often this means we don't want to pay you what you're worth; so we'll get someone with less experience.

False Self (Covering). Kenji Yoshino is Chief Justice Earl Warren Professor of Constitutional Law at New York University. As a homosexual, early in his career he was faced with the dilemma of presenting his true self or a false front to the public. He has not been alone in this dilemma. My brother-in-law was a decorative painter—flowery designs on curtain boxes and doors. He was fearful of his corporate associates learning of this unmanly (to him) hobby; so he never invited any of his work associates into his home. I have a passionate interest in medieval music, including an instrument collection, CDs, sheet music, and performance groups. I hide this interest from some people for "political" reasons lest they brand me as academic, impractical, unbusinesslike, artsy, outdated, or some such [if they are reading this now, so be it—there, I'm uncovered!]. My brother-in-law and I have engaged in what Yoshino (2006) calls "covering," intentionally preventing others from knowing something about us that we fear might threaten our career or relationship. Yoshino identifies (pp. 79 ff.) four aspects of covering:

- Appearance—finding a way to mask how others perceive us with the five senses, as in a heavy person wearing baggy clothes, or a person with a strong dialect using a more mainstream pronunciation.
- Affiliation—the degree to which we identify with a particular culture, through choice of neighborhood, clubs, and so forth.
- Activism—the degree to which we maintain a public advocacy position, through letters to the editor, money raising, demonstrating, and so forth.
- Association—the degree to which our friends, colleagues, lovers, and other close associates are fully in on our "secret."

Covering, or presenting a false self, is the ultimate example of bad P-E fit. Yoshino advocates letting go of our covers in order to be authentic in our relations with others. He writes (2006, pp. 184-185) of the work of psychoanalyst D. W. Winnicott:

Winnicott defines health according to the degree of ascendancy the True Self gains over the False one. At the negative extreme, the False Self completely obscures the True Self, perhaps even from the individual herself. In a less extreme case, the False Self permits the True Self "a secret life." The individual approaches health only when the False Self has "has its main concern a search for conditions which will make it possible for the True Self to come into its own." Finally, in the healthy individual, the False self is reduced to a "polite and mannered social attitude," a tool available to the fully realized True Self." The True Self is who we are when we feel real, that we are being spontaneous and authentic, while the False self feels fake, like acting, unreal, not lasting, futile. The False Self typically involves some form of covering.

Low self-esteem. Low self-esteem is typically defined as a blend of two related conditions: not respecting oneself and not having confidence in one's abilities. To suffer from low self-esteem is a common cause of poor P-E fit. Good fit requires that one stand up for oneself and find situations that could benefit from having one's strengths employed therein. When a person suffers from low self-esteem, they have trouble making requests, much less demands, in their own behalf, and they subsequently settle for less than optimal P-E fit.

William James pointed out a century ago that high self-esteem was dependent on selecting a reference group in which one felt secure, and abandoning reference groups where one's light dimmed by comparison. As a medieval musician, my self-esteem is rather high. As an opera singer, my self-esteem is shockingly low. While I can play an assortment of 16th century instruments with the best of them, I wilt with envy when I hear Thomas Quasthoff sing opera arias and art songs. Low self-esteem arises when one is unable to stop comparing oneself to others who perform far above them.

While I envy doctors, lawyers, and opera singers, I must resist the impulse to feel inadequate in their midst, but rather only to feel appreciative of them. In order to preserve some self-esteem, I must do three things. First, I must select a reference group to which I can bring something of value. Second, I must continue to increase the value that I bring to them through practice, study, and aggressive goal-setting. In essence, I must select a reference group with whom I can be in "flow" and continue to work my way up the flow channel by increasing my skills and, should they not increase theirs, eventually find a new reference group skilled enough for me to be in flow with them. Third, I must stop comparing myself to reference groups with which I cannot compete. At a minimum, I could always begin a hobby that I really enjoy, such as collecting statues of frogs (I know someone who does), and bask in the knowledge that I have a collection that I'm proud of. Who cares what others think!

Necessity. Sometimes it is necessary to accept work or associates that are not of one's choosing, whether out of financial or some other necessity. In military service, in prison, in school, when the client is paying, one doesn't always have the freedom to use one's traits and abilities to the fullest. However, one always has some degree of choice in these situations. When I was in the hold of the troop ship Darby headed for Bremerhaven, I had the choice to volunteer as a typist for the ship's newsletter. While that was not very creative, it suited me more than the alternatives. And, before I knew it, I benefitted from a lazy lieutenant who decided to delegate story-writing to me so he could drink coffee and play solitaire all day! Ah, br'er rabbit, don't throw me in that briar patch!

When I joined up with Uncle Sam's army, my friends warned me: "Never volunteer for *anything*!" On my first day at Fort Jackson, South Carolina, I sensed that their advice was not right for me. I abhor regimentation, and I was eager to find ways to escape days full of hut, two, three, four…. I realized that if I volunteered for *everything* that my routine would be a thing of the past, or at least minimized. So for the next eight weeks, every time the First Sergeant asked for volunteers my arm shot up without waiting to hear what I was volunteering for. I ended up with a wide variety of activities from kitchen patrol to hauling boxes of ammunition and working in warehouses, all of which were better than hut, two, three, four…. On these voluntary assignments, the sergeants typically felt somewhat sorry for us and gave us frequent breaks. Nothing quite like sipping a cola in the shade of long-leaf pines at Fort Jackson and playing chess (I always carried a chess set in my pocket)!

Culture. Culture can put quite a damper on persons who try to engage their traits, abilities, values, and physical characteristics in personally satisfying ways. Eric Weiner (2008), in observing that Japanese culture embodies the warning that "The nail that sticks out gets hammered down," quipped that in the United States "we are a nation of protruding nails." (p. 180) Individualists in collectivist cultures will clearly feel some pressure to "cover" or something like that. In the old South, blacks felt the pressure of Southern culture to limit P-E fit to their own part of town. In that same old South, my wife, Jane, felt the cultural pressure to prepare for one of the only three careers deemed respectable for a submissive Southern Baptist woman: nursing, teaching, or secretarying. As a talented singer yearning for the New York stage, she deferred to culture and got her teaching certificate. She spent a year teaching junior high school choral music, moved away from the deep South, and ultimately became liberated from their expectation, earning her M.B.A. and becoming a (horrors!) management consultant. Had she the opportunity to do it all over again, perhaps she would have rejected her culture and packed her bags for Manhattan. When our older daughter told us she was going to take her college degree and head for Broadway, Jane was openly supportive and inwardly jealous! Incidentally, Mary Belenky and others (1997) wrote *A Woman's Way of Knowing* as a testament to this phenomenon of traditional U.S. women not being encouraged in their youth to find their own voices. Rather, these young women are encouraged, even forced, to accept the voices of their elders. Belenky and her cowriters urged the universities to assist young women in learning the skills of critical thinking and learning how to develop their own points of view.

Culture can be insidious. Barbara Ehrenreich (2009) writes about a website that urges folks to "get rid of the toxins in your life." She characterized this message as the positive psychology movement gone postal. Some of the verbiage on this site (a blog) reveals a scary intolerance of individual differences:

- If you have negative people in your life, you need to get rid of them or, at the very least, insulate yourself from them.
- If it doesn't support you, get rid of it.
- Your environment and everything in it need to support you in being your best.
- If you have negative people, environments, or even things in your life that do not support you in being your best, get rid of them.
- You deserve to be supported, loved and nurtured by everyone and everything in your life. If you're not receiving this support, you will be drained of your vital life energy. Life simply is too short to allow anyone or anything to steal it from you.

While I agree with this crusading blog-vangelista that we all need supportive environments, I would caution that other people are not always to blame. In the case of this blog-vangelista, it sounds like a world of wholesale divorces and no marriage counseling! The thoughtless "get rid of it" needs to be tempered with the spirit of problem solving. If it doesn't support you, start by having a good talk and giving some feedback. Don't just throw something away because your first encounter with it is unpleasant. Maybe you did something that affected it.

If culture is holding you back from enjoying the engagement of your traits and abilities, then you have two options: Either stand up to your culture or change cultures. In the best of all possible worlds, we stand up to the culture that wrongly constrains us. Women drivers of Saudi Arabia, unite!

The Wrong Context. Every skill set can be applied in multiple contexts. If you love your skill set but hate your current context, find a new context. You might have a medical degree with a specialty in surgery. That does not mean that you have to be a surgeon in a big city hospital. You could also teach, become a missionary, become a medical illustrator for a publisher, be a researcher, write textbooks, start a neighborhood health clinic, specialize in sports medicine, and so on. Once a sports journalist came to me for counseling. He produced live, televised, National Basketball Association games for a cable television company. The games typically ended in the late evening, and he was so nervous he couldn't get to sleep until hours later. I tested him and found that he scored very high on Need for Stability. We realized that he just couldn't take the high-stress situation of everything having to be perfect in real time. There was no margin for error, and he was a nervous wreck at the end of a basketball game. The solution was simple. Move his television sports production skills into a context that was not real time. In fact, he ended up working for a sports production company that did documentaries. So, instead of working with no margin of error, he had lots of margin for error, as he could simply edit out all the bad stuff.

Where there is ability, there is an appropriate outlet for that ability. I've known introverted lawyers who ended up miserable as court attorneys, but who found satisfaction in moving to other legal contexts that were more solitary (teaching, copyrights, and so forth).

Certain (self-defeating) traits. Finally, some personality traits make it difficult for one to enjoy good P-E fit. The most obvious trait is Accommodation. Its very nature is to submit to the desires and needs of others. When that submissive temperament is employed as a receptionist, nurse, or social worker, it is likely a good P-E fit. But when parents convince that same accommodating person to take a job that requires an extraverted temperament, and that person is introverted, then the high Accommodation is self-defeating. Other traits could also put one at risk for poor P-E fit:

- Low Consolidation: These folks are not naturally goal-focused, and their tendency to spontaneity and multi-tasking can distract them from pursuits that are the most satisfying.
- High Consolidation: These folks, once they have committed to a goal, are going to pursue it until they achieve it. That in and of itself is fine, but what if they happen to select a goal that proves to be unsatisfying, a poor fit? Their disciplined ambition and goal focus are likely to keep them in pursuit of a goal for which they no longer have passion.
- High Originality: Excessive curiosity can lead one down paths that are interesting but that dissipate one's energy from more satisfying paths. Persons high in Originality have a hard time resisting the allure of a new idea, a new cuisine, a new anything.

In summary, flow and person-environment fit are closely related. It is unimaginable that one could be in flow unless the activity represented a good fit. And it is also natural that when one experiences good fit, that one will also frequently experience flow. In the next chapter, we will explore how our behavior around goals can affect both flow and fit.

Composing Your Next Chapter

Review your highlights and notes from this chapter on fit. Below, indicate your strong attributes that are either underused or not used at all, and how you might incorporate them into your ongoing goals. Then indicate weaknesses that are relied on too much and suggest how you might decrease their presence in your life.

_____

_____

_____

_____

_____

_____

_____

_____

_____

_____

_____

_____

STATEMENT OF
PERSONAL PRIORITIES

FLOW | FIT | GOALS | COMMUNITY | ALTRUISM

Happiness Boosters
(Choice)

Happiness Downers
(Choice)

119 Minor Adjustors

(more within personal control)

(more outside personal control)

HAPPINESS SET POINT

Happiness Boosters
(Circumstance)

Happiness Downers
(Circumstance)

Continuum of Trait Happiness

Perennially Happy (N- E+) .... Occasionally Happy (N + E-)

7

Goals

Maintaining a Clear Sense of Progress

> "She felt happy. That was strange, wasn't it? Thousands of Kingsbridge people had died of the plague, and Tilly had been murdered, but Caris felt hopeful. It was because she had a plan, of course. She always felt better when she had a plan."
>
> --Ken Follett, *World Without End* (p. 825)

Guide to this chapter:

- What is a goal?
- Attributes of effective goals
- Kinds of goals
- Goal generation strategies
- Deciding which goals to pursue
- The role of optimism, grit, and stress in goal pursuit
- Case studies in goal pursuit

Ken Follett grew rich and famous while writing spy thrillers. Yet this master storyteller privately yearned to write a book about cathedrals—about their design, about their construction, and about their resulting social vortex. He eventually wrote two such novels. The first, *Pillars of the Earth*, described the cathedral's construction over a century during the Middle Ages, while the second, *World Without End*, took the story forward in time, including an invasion by the bubonic plague. In the chapter epigraph above, the character Caris—not a "Happer" by birth—provides an example of how having a goal and making progress towards that goal is as good or better than natural happiness. In spite of murder and mayhem, she had a plan and felt the better for it. This chapter is about the contribution made by having goals, and making progress towards them—the contribution made to our sense of being In Gear, of being engaged, as a way to achieve a sense of well-being.

What is a goal?

"Goal" is the more businesslike word for the phenomenon we have in mind. Other more everyday words are dreams, visions, passions, desires, yens, ambitions... The Middle English *gol* referred to a limit or boundary, the outer edge of something. It has come to mean literally the end of something, as in the end of a race, or the end of a series of football plays, or the end of a basketball possession, or the end of a business negotiation. The goal is what you're trying to reach in a race or a game. And possibly reach it repeatedly, as Ohio State did against Akron on the gridiron this afternoon!

To be without a goal of any kind is to be stuck in time and space, either idle like a couch potato or in constant motion like a mouse in an exercise wheel. Whether immobile or busy, to be without a goal results in suboptimal mood. Activity becomes meaningful when it is harnessed to one or more goals. As Lewis Carroll's Cat says to Alice: "If you don't care where you want to go, then it doesn't matter how you get there." In a similar vein, Rev. Joan Watson in a March 29, 2011, sermon referred to a poster on her first office wall: "If you don't have a goal for where you want to go, then you might end up somewhere else." Or, goals by default! To be without goals is to follow paths of least resistance. To be without goals is to miss out on the satisfying feeling of making progress towards a goal. To have a goal and to make progress towards that goal is what "empowerment" is all about (Cattaneo & Chapman, 2010). To be without goals is to be unempowered. Without goals, decisions are wearisome and difficult. Tal Ben-Shahar (2007), Harvard's famous happiness professor, points out that "The proper role of goals is to liberate us, so that we can enjoy the here and now." (p. 70) Otherwise, we are more likely to anguish over every decision—goals are clarifying. By having our goals clearly in mind, choices become easier. If a choice enables progress towards a goal, then embrace it. Otherwise, eschew it. Says Ben-Shahar: "The emphasis in my approach is not so much on *attaining* goals as it is on *having* them." (p. 70) This is similar in spirit to my favorite Quaker philosopher Bernard Phillips' comment that "the search will make you free." The search is energizing. Making progress towards goals is energizing. Reach a goal and the first thing you want to do is fix the next goal firmly in mind. The satisfaction of achieving a goal is bettered only by the satisfaction of pursuing a goal.

Attributes of effective goals[1]

Some goals are more attainable than others because they are formulated better. Since effective goal formation is so important to making progress towards goal attainment, I will list now what research has shown to be the characteristics of effective goals. Most of what we know about effective goal-making comes from three sources: Latham and Yukl, 1975; Gollwitzer, 1999; and Locke and Latham, 2002):

1. **Any goal is better than no goal at all**. This assumes that 1) it is good to be productive, and 2) it is good to experience progress towards achieving something important to us.

2. **Difficult goals produce the highest levels of effort and performance** (i.e., difficult goals are better than easier goals). This assumes that one has the patience and perseverance to tackle something that doesn't come easy, or that at least one is willing to deal with their lack of patience or perseverance. Some prefer easier goals that result in lower levels of performance. And that is OK. If every goal were difficult, we would stay exhausted. Some goals need to be easier ("I think I'll thaw some frozen pizza for supper" rather than "I think I'll try a new recipe by Julia Child tonight") in order to allow adequate energy for goals that are more important and more demanding of us ("I will work on this book for several hours after dinner tonight; so perhaps I'll not wear myself out learning a new recipe.")

3. **Specific goals lead to higher performance** than the general exhortation to "do your best." Setting a goal of "having a better quality relationship with my child" is too general and permits settling for less than would be the case if the goal were more specific—"I will spend at least one hour a week one-on-one

---

[1] This section draws heavily from the third edition of my *The Owner's Manual for the Brain* (2006), pp. 674-680.

with my daughter in a way that permits conversation and spontaneity." Even more specific would be to commit to an ongoing project, such as building, making, or creating something together.

4. **People with higher self-efficacy** (i.e., feeling capable in a specific domain) set higher goals than those with lower self-efficacy, are more committed to assigned goals, find and use better strategies, and respond more positively to negative feedback. William James once commented that he had high self-esteem as a psychologist, but that if he were to compare himself to baseball players (i.e., someone in a field where he was not proficient) he would likely feel low self-esteem. In order to feel self-efficacy, we need to pick goals in domains where we can compete successfully. This means that a) we must choose a content that we are good at (e.g., playing the recorder) and b) we must choose a context in which we stand at least a 50/50 chance of success (e.g., playing recorder with those at or slightly above our current level of proficiency). I would not feel capable as a recorder player if I were to compete with the Dutch professional Michala Petrie (at least, not today!), but I would feel capable if I were to attempt to play with persons at my level or slightly above. The same goes for gardening, cooking, and debating: Pick your points of comparison so you stand a chance of feeling successful in a particular domain, and don't worry about other domains.

5. **Goals influence performance** in four ways: fostering focus and minimizing distractions, providing energy for the task (higher goals generate more energy and effort), yielding greater persistence and more time on task, and   entailing pursuit of greater task-relevant knowledge and strategy. In short, committing to a goal has a way of making it easier to say "no" to rival activities that might otherwise drain your resources and energy for the primary goal.

6. **For very large or complex goals, it helps to set learning goals** (i.e., create or identify ways to approach the performance goal). This involves thinking through all of the implications of large, complex goals: what materials I will need, what permissions, what books to read, what persons to consult with, what bodies of knowledge will be required, what budget I must set aside, how I will make the necessary time available, and so forth.

7. **Goals must be mutually accepted** by manager and associate, by self and partner, and by self and significant other(s). I know two architects—the managing partner of the firm and his successor/assistant—who meet once a year for a weekend to set goals for the coming year, and then they meet monthly for lunch and report on their progress. Neither persists with a goal that the partner does not embrace. They become cheerleaders for each other.

8. **Assigned goals are just as effective as participative goals** *if* the rationale has been explained, but less effective if peremptorily assigned: "Here, just do it." When someone imposes or strongly urges me to take on a goal, I am more likely to accept it and do an excellent job if the purpose is clearly explained, and I acknowledge the value of the stated purpose. When my business partner says I need to do something in order to preserve relationships with an important client (whom I also want to preserve!), then I am likely to take on the goal with alacrity. When my wife asks me to install a new light fixture in order to make it easier on me for future maintenance, then I'm less likely to grumble than if she simply said, "Here's the fixture—get it done."

9. **The benefit of participating in goal setting is cognitive**, inasmuch as participation creates more information sharing, e.g., around strategies. In other words, two heads are better than one. When you engage someone else in formulating your goal(s), you gain the benefit of their perspective, both in shaping the nature of the goal and in coming up with strategies for approaching the goal.

10. **Money offered works best for goals of moderate difficulty.** The more money offered, the more commitment to goal attainment with difficult goals, but if it is all or nothing, people will quit when

attainment seems hopeless; money is more effective when the goal is only moderately difficult or when paying a piece rate for performance.

11. **Leaders can increase the self-efficacy of followers** by providing necessary training, providing models, and communicating belief in the worker. This is related to the growth mindset discussed in the next section, whereby those who assume they have a set, fixed amount of ability tend to avoid stretch goals. Nudge them towards stretch goals by offering training, models, and other forms of support.

12. **Goals with feedback are more effective** than goals alone. Built into a goal should be indicators of progress. This could be anything from a tutor or teacher/trainer who gives periodic confirmatory ("You are becoming more consistent with the new stroke.") or corrective ("You are taking your eyes off the ball too early.") feedback, to having a personal model to compare one's work against. When I learned to play the recorder, I had no teacher. However, I did have "Music Minus One" recordings that allowed me to hear my tone in comparison to the tone of masters of the instrument. Over time, I could hear my tone getting closer and closer to theirs.

13. **After attaining a goal, people typically set a higher goal**. Or a different kind of goal. After all, as we have said earlier, the satisfaction of progressing towards goal attainment is greater than the satisfaction from goal attainment itself. I think I can, I think I can, I think I can, I think I can.... I did!

14. **For complex goals or tasks, proximal goals are effective** (i.e., setting incremental goals for quicker, small victories en route to the larger, more distant goal). This has been called the "salami" approach. One cannot attack a whole salami at once, but rather one slice at a time. This is also called "incrementalism." Jared Diamond (1997) in his Pulitzer-Prize winning *Guns, Germs, and Steel* points out that most major inventions—the telephone, television, light bulb, cotton gin, steam engine, and so forth, did not suddenly appear on the scene. Rather, they represented the final stage in a series of improvements that made an originally costly, inefficient, and unmarketable product more attractive both to manufacturers and to consumers. He called it invention by creep, not by leap. Thomas Edison got lots of credit for major inventions, but he definitely benefitted from standing on the shoulders of others. He found ways to make others' unmarketable devices marketable.

15. **People who attain lower goals are more satisfied than those who attain higher goals** because the latter are more self-critical. To achieve the goal of redecorating my living room is more satisfying than achieving the goal of designing and building a new house. This is not because the higher goal of home design/building is intrinsically less satisfying, but because the kind of person who would take on such a large goal tends to be more self-critical than others. This is related to the research of Kruger and Dunning (1999), who found that the most talented in a given field tend to be keenly aware of their shortcomings, while the second tier—those merely above average—tend to bask in their achievement unaware of their flaws or shortcomings, or at least unbothered by them.

16. **In selection interviews** where the candidate is asked to set goals based on a scenario, **the tendency to set more ambitious goals is a good predictor of higher goal setting and attainment after employment**. Said more glibly, those who talk a good game in an interview tend to walk the big talk after coming on board. While being cautious of those who talk of big dreams, don't reject them outright, as dreamers are generally producers. One way to differentiate the capable dreamer from the idle dreamer is to invite them to outline how they would accomplish their dreams—i.e., to sketch out their plan.

17. **When individual goals are consistent with group goals, group goals benefit**; if they are inconsistent, the group goals suffer. This is a form of synergy, such that when individuals pursue goals without regard to how the goals relate to the welfare of the overall group (family, team, work group) welfare, the individuals are more likely to spend discretionary effort on personal goals. In a church we once belonged to, a new minister arrived with goals to increase membership/attendance. He did so according to his own

notions of what might create a rise in numbers, with minimal input from members about how they could contribute to the overall goals. As a result, individuals (including me) focused more on personal goals (e.g., more a cappella singing) without regard to the larger goal. Leader's goals should build on the abilities and desires of followers.

18. **Feedback to associates** on their progress helps them attain goals. People can't learn without feedback, and people often are not aware of making progress unless they receive explicit feedback. I once taught a performance management workshop. When I got to the part about giving feedback, a participant left the class and returned five minutes later. At break, she told me that she had called her plant and arranged to meet a few days later with an employee she supervised. She realized she'd been hoping for the subordinate's improvement without giving specific feedback as to what needed improving. Once a friend complained to me that his wife used his razor to shave her legs. It *really* bothered him. I asked simply, "How have you asked her to stop?" He responded despondently, "I haven't. She just oughta know better!" Well, people don't just "know better"—they need feedback.

19. **Goals framed as positive achievements** are more achievable than ones formulated as negatives or things to avoid or prevent (e.g., "Respond with humor" rather than "Respond without getting angry").

20. **Goals are more achievable when persons can remove seductive distractions and competing goals.** Being in "flow," as we saw in Chapter 5, not only feels good but brings productivity improvement. To the degree that one can remove distractions (I've learned to do without Mozart or Bach wafting in my work area in order to get more done during a given span) and defer rival goals (I want to write a biography of my grandparents, but I'm waiting until this manuscript is finished before starting. That doesn't mean I can't make notes from time to time, however). Once when my wife, Jane, was recuperating from surgery in our small house, her drugs made her drowsy and made focused attention difficult. So, rather than her accustomed reading, she tended to watch mindless cooking programs that required little sustained attention. However, in our small house, the sound of the television prevented me from reading or writing. Solution: I bought a wireless headset for her. Problem solved.

21. **A goal is more achievable when conjoined creatively with another, synergistic goal**—for example, "Build a deck *and* get to know my neighbor (by asking for help)." In the goal-setting arena, synergy might be defined as having one activity serve two (or more) purposes. For example, I want to have something tasty for supper tonight (goal #1) AND I want to create more time for reading during the coming week (goal #2). What is an activity that could serve both masters? Easy: Prepare too much of a dish and have the leftovers throughout the week. We do a lot of that! Or, read novels for enjoyment (goal #1) and create new products for work (goal #2). Solution: While reading novels, highlight passages that make instructive points for the workshops I teach and collect the passages into some kind of handout to be used in an activity. In fact, I've done that, and my collection of "instructive" passages is now about 50 pages long.

22. **Announce your goal to others with a target date, and you're more likely to achieve it.** Publicly proclaimed goals are more likely to be attained than secretly held ones. There is something about sticking your neck out there and letting others know of your intentions that makes you hunker down and hitch your wagon. Just as my architect friends had an annual goal-setting session and supported each other's goal pursuit, my wife and I have goal-setting discussions and support each other's goals. If someone wants to drive down the road, it helps if I know it in order for me to get out of their way! But not only does announcing one's goals increase the possibility of support from others—it also serves as a reminder to ourselves. I put reminders up in both my workplace office and my home office as to my four superordinate goals—my four passions—so that I frequently refer to them and try to keep all four in balance, with one not overshadowing the others, and finding opportunities for synergy when possible. I'm looking at a note by my monitor right now. It proclaims:

"Am I involved daily in...
1. Translating research into practice,
2. Learning something new,
3. **Developing friendships,**
4. Experiencing sensory pleasure,
   ...or something better?!"

The third one is bolded, as I tend to give it the least time. Bolding it is a way of reminding me to take more initiative in having time with friends and family, and in doing things that they like me to do for or with them. I could easily live the rest of my life in a library in the pursuit of love of learning. But I really enjoy it when I come up for air and take time with friends—and I need to remind myself of that.

If the preceding conditions describe prerequisites for effective goal setting, what do we know about circumstances when goal setting does not work? The research suggests that goal setting does not work when:

- goals formed are not consistent with how performance is measured; e.g., asking a salesperson to write a policy manual, even though they are evaluated by their volume of sales;
- initial commitment to the goal is not obtained;
- the relationship of the goal to personal goals is not considered;
- knowledge of how to accomplish the task is not shared;
- performance goals (i.e., number of widgets made per hour) are used when learning goals (i.e., how to make widgets) are needed;
- proximal (i.e., short-term) goals are missing (in an uncertain or complex environment); and
- goals are too difficult for the individual involved.

New York University psychology professor Peter Gollwitzer (1999) goes into some depth on the subject of what he calls *implementation planning.* It is not enough, he says, to set a goal: One must also plan how to reach it. In a series of experiments, he shows that goals are more likely to be attained when the goal-setter identifies the steps required—that is, formulates a plan. He demonstrates that attainment is more likely when the goal-setter deals with potential distractors by formulating a plan to ignore them, rather than simply redoubling effort in the presence of a distractor. The more strongly they believe in the goal ("I really, strongly want to write a book on X"), and the more strongly they believe in the implementation plan ("I really, strongly want to spend three hours on Monday and Thursday nights at the library researching the book"), the more likely they are to reach their goal. Now, let us look at the research on implementation planning and on handling distractors.

For implementation planning, it is not enough just to say, "I want to write a book." Although this statement has several of the qualities of a good goal (specificity, difficulty, desirability), it is more likely to be attained if the goal-setter specifies the "what, when, and where"—specific behaviors necessary to get the job done. Gollwitzer asked some of his college students to write him a letter within 48 hours after December 24 describing their Christmas Eve experiences. Half of them were asked to specify precisely when and where they would do the chore. In that group, 3/4 successfully completed the assignment. Only 1/3 of the other group wrote him. Gollwitzer cites experiment after experiment, each one showing the dramatic effects of simply specifying when and where one would perform a task. Some groups presented a special challenge. Working with a group of drug addicts in withdrawal, he asked them to write a résumé by a certain time; half were asked, in addition, to specify when and where they would write the résumé. Those who did so were disproportionately successful.

Gollwitzer identifies two ways to address potential distractors: task facilitating and distraction inhibiting. For the goal "Lose 10 pounds in two months," the implementation plan might include "Keep high-fiber cereal with me at all times for snacking." A potential source of distraction would be pastries offered at the many meetings one attends. A distraction-inhibiting implementation plan would be something like "Ignore pastries—they are imaginary and not really there." A typical task-facilitating implementation might be, "Focus really hard on visualizing your body 10 pounds lighter, and redouble your commitment." Gollwitzer finds that the latter is much less effective than the former. Focus your energy on avoiding the distractor rather than on redoubling your goal effort.

The effectiveness of implementation planning is founded on the belief that the plan triggers one or more psychological processes (e.g., a "schema"—a pattern of behavior that comes naturally for a person) that make goal-directed behavior more natural or automatic. To think it is to do it, or at least to increase the likelihood that one will do it. It is important, in order for the implementation plan to actually trigger the schema, that the plan contains specific environmental cues. For example, for the goal "I will stop misplacing my keys," one might formulate a plan for, upon entering the door of one's home, placing the keys in a bowl on the front hall table, then checking the bowl whenever passing it to ensure that the keys are there. Like the traditional string tied around one's finger, the bowl becomes a memory trigger: Upon entering the house, seeing the bowl reminds one to place one's keys in it. There is, of course, one important difference: the string is nonspecific (it could be used for any of a number of goals), but the bowl is goal-specific.

Kinds of goals

Goals vary in eight ways. Each of them can be understood as a continuum defined by two extremes. Each goal can be placed somewhere along each of the first seven continua, with the eighth continuum being a summary of the other seven. The ways in which goals vary are:

- **Area**—Do all of your goals fall into one area of endeavor, or are they spread out evenly among all of your areas of endeavor?
- **Origin**—Did you think up the goal, or was it imposed, or somewhere in between?
- **Survival**—Is the goal necessary for your survival, or merely desirable?
- **Generativity**—Will its achievement have an impact on future generations, or is it limited to your lifetime?
- **Stretch**—Does the goal require mastering something that you've never done before, or does it use familiar knowledge, skills, and abilities? This includes competitive goals, such as being #1 in your class globally, as well as simply completing an activity for its own sake.
- **Time to Completion**—Are we talking years to completion, or just hours?
- **Complexity**—Does the goal require a wide variety of knowledge, skills, and abilities, or is it confined to a single body of knowledge, skill, and/or ability?
- **Balance**—Does your personal set of goals represent only one end of each of the preceding six continua, and/or only one area of importance to you? Or do they represent multiple points on the continua, or all of the areas of importance to you?

Let's take a closer look at the definition of these eight ways in which goals may vary. At the conclusion of these eight definitions, I'll provide a worksheet for you to use in evaluating your personal set of goals.

Continuum #1: Areas of Endeavor

Most Clustered in One Extreme/Area--------------Moderate Balance--------------------All Areas Equally Represented

Area. Each of us has areas of endeavor that are important to us. They are like sections of a library, rooms in a building, or departments in a business or school. These areas could be described in various ways: as values (status, service, health, spirituality, and so forth), as spheres of activity (such as work, family, community, and personal), and so forth. To determine a handful of areas is helpful as a way of monitoring one's balance. Many self-help gurus have proposed such sets of areas. Steve Covey uses the metaphor of saw blades, urging one to "sharpen the saw" blades of one's physical body, one's mind, and one's spirit. The three areas serve to remind one to do something each day or week to keep body, mind, and spirit equally keen and fresh, as in exercising, reading, or meditating. Other gurus are less structured. The "passion test" folks, Chris and Janet Bray Attwood, urge you to think of all the things that you love to do and that are important to you, things for which you have a lot of energy or passion. Then, their process guides you to narrow the dozens of things you're passionate about to four or five main areas. I tried going through the process and ended up with the four aforementioned areas of learning, translating research into practice, developing friendships, and experiencing sensory pleasure. I keep these four areas posted as a reminder to insure that I do continue to create goals in each of these areas, and, hopefully, some goals that synergistically allow one activity to serve multiple goals. Here are some other examples that you might end up with as major areas for creating a balanced set of goals:

- generativity (e.g., making a cradle for a grandchild, making a scrapbook),
- health,
- spiritual,
- educational,
- personal (e.g., hobbies),
- family,
- professional,
- altruism,
- the 5 modes of this book (flow, fit, goals, community, and altruism),
- boosters and downers,
- adjusters (discussed in Chapter 11),
- creativity,
- awards,
- publishing,
- competitions,
- sport, and
- political.

Each of us has different priorities and must select areas or categories for goal-setting that cover these priorities. Then, we use these areas to assist in maintaining a balance in our goals. It has been very helpful to me to keep my four areas posted by my computer monitor, for that is where I tend to spend most of my time. The note serves as a reminder to establish short- and long-term goals to spend more time with family and friends, be it a dinner party with friends, or a tour of the national parks with grandchildren.

One way to assess balance among one's goals is to compare one's efforts at accumulating wealth with one's efforts at non-financial goals. Derek Bok (2010) writes that college students in the mid-20th century tended to espouse nonfinancial goals, but

> by the mid-1970s, their priorities were completely reversed. Making "a lot of money" was now "very important" for 75 percent of entering students, while acquiring a meaningful philosophy of life remained a major goal for only 40 percent. Since then, aspirations have stayed at about these levels, with making money continuing to be the pre-eminent reason for attending college. This is hardly cause for rejoicing. Much research has shown that people who set great store on becoming rich tend to be less happy than those who have other goals. If that is the case, a majority of freshmen arriving at college are already on the wrong path to a full and satisfying life. (loc. 2,785)

Each person has one goal area that tends to be of primary importance. For some it might be loyalty, in one or all of its various forms. For others, it might be competition, or artistic expression, or, as for me, learning. Bok is urging us to consider something non-financial for our overarching goal. Management philosopher Peter Drucker is famous for having declaimed that making a profit should not be one's reason for doing business—it rather is a consequence of doing business well. Such is the case with financial goals. They should not be our driving force, our overarching goal, but should be the consequence of doing our nonfinancial goals well. This overarching goal becomes the core of one's Statement of Personal Priorities (SPP; discussed in Chapter 10). So, the core of my SPP is: To share my love of learning. The SPP should integrate values, abilities etc. into a phrase. What is yours?

Tal Ben-Shahar (2007) writes:

> Summarizing the research on goals and happiness, Kennon Sheldon and his colleagues write, "People seeking greater well-being would be well advised to focus on the pursuit of (a) goals involving growth, connection, and contribution rather than goals involving money, beauty, and popularity and (b) goals that are interesting and personally important to them rather than goals they feel forced or pressured to pursue." (p. 71)

The best goals, then—the goals that result in the greatest personal satisfaction, happiness, well-being, flourishing, or whatever we call it—are nonfinancial in nature and internal in origin.

Continuum #2: Origin

Intrinsic--------------------------------------Partially Internal/Partially External-----------------------------------Extrinsic

Origin. Speaking of origin, this continuum positions extrinsic (external origin) at one end and intrinsic (internal origin) at the other. Chapter 2 explained these terms. Let it suffice here to recall that extrinsic goals are imposed or urged or suggested by others and based on their wants and needs, while intrinsic goals arise from within and are based on our personal wants and needs. This is closely related to the concept of locus of control—the degree to which we feel that things are happening because of our own efforts and abilities (internal locus of control), as opposed to things happening because of factors beyond our personal control, such as luck, favoritism, and the like (external locus of control).

Shawn Achor (2010, p. 128) writes that the "feeling that we are in control, masters of our own fate, is one of the strongest drivers of well-being and performance." It is the difference between feeling like an improvisational actor who creates a spontaneous role from within, based on personal urges, wishes, and instincts, as opposed to being a puppet who only executes the wishes of others. Achor further points out that "How much control we think we have is more important than how much control we actually have…. People who believe that power lies within their circle have higher academic achievement, greater career achievement, and are much happier at work. Internal locus of control lowers job stress and turnover, leads to higher motivation, organizational commitment, and task performance."

So, for this second continuum, we evaluate each of our goals with respect to its origin. Writing this book originated from within for me, but taking our grandson Liam to Washington DC last summer was an external goal—he asked if we would take him! Because we thought it a great idea, it should not be at the opposite/extrinsic end of the continuum, but certainly not totally intrinsic. By accepting his goal as our own, we in essence shared ownership of it. For Liam, it was purely intrinsic, while for Jane and me it was more towards the middle of the continuum. For me, an extrinsic goal was when my office staff decided to move from one office location to another. I was perfectly content with the old location and saw no benefit in moving. Still don't. Out of my control—extrinsic goal. I helped with the move, although without the relish that I've put into other, more mutual goals. I do grudgingly admit, however, that the new location has two benefits: lower costs and a handy snack bar downstairs.

Continuum #3: Survival

Nice but not Necessary----------------------Nice and Somewhat Necessary-------------------Necessary for Survival

Survival. The third continuum for evaluating our goals is the degree to which a goal is necessary for survival versus merely nice. Said another way, it is the difference between a must and a want: something we must accomplish versus something we merely want to accomplish. One of my goals is to prepare for retirement—that is a must, as it is necessary for survival, unless our daughters come to us with a proposal to finance our retirement! I don't think that's going to happen. Another similar goal is to rebuild the fence in our backyard. Not necessary for survival, but eventually necessary to sell our house. So I'd call that one midway on the continuum—necessary to sell the house, but otherwise just cosmetic. And, the house could be sold without the fence—just for not as much.

Survival-type goals include goals that are necessary for the survival of others. These goals entail commitments that we might make in order for others to survive. The University of North Carolina at Chapel Hill's commitment to study brain concussions in sports and to minimize them is a goal taken on by sports neuroscientists in behalf of the survival potential of all athletes in contact sports.

Continuum #4: Generativity

Impacts Me----------------------------Impacts Me and Future Generations--------------Impacts Future Generations

Generativity. It is natural for one to think about one's legacy. What will I leave for future generations to remember me by? The most common form is financial, as in inheritances, trusts, endowments, scholarships, and other ways that one might be remembered long after one's demise. To finance my retirement impacts only me, but to endow a professorship or orchestra chair (e.g., the Gov. James B. Martin Tuba Chair of the Charlotte Symphony Orchestra) creates a legacy that will keep your name and memory alive long after your passing. But financial legacies are only one format for being remembered. Others include writing books, creating family scrapbooks, creating memorial gardens, building everything from dollhouses to monuments, creating works of art or craft, and so on and on. To build a model railroad has impacted only my grandchildren and me, but hopefully when I pass they will take over the train board and remember me thereby. Legacies can also be intangible, such as attitudes, values, sayings, habits, and the like.

Continuum #5: Stretch

Assured of Success--------------------------------Moderately Challenging--------------------------Extremely Challenging

Stretch. Michelangelo set the stage for future centuries of ambitious goal-setters when he wrote that "The greater danger for most of us lies not in setting our aim too high and falling short, but in setting our aim too low, and achieving our mark." Carol Dweck (2006) expands on Michelangelo's admonition when she writes about two kinds of "mindset"—fixed and growth. Fixed mindset assumes that one is limited to one's current skills and abilities. Because one's personal resources are "fixed" (i.e., constant and unchanging), one tends to prefer goals that do not require new skills and abilities. Persons with a fixed mindset thus tend to play it safe by choosing goals in which they are sure to succeed. Growth mindset assumes that one's potential is unknown, possibly even unlimited. Thus, one with growth mindset is more likely to embrace stretch goals, goals that require taking a risk by attempting to master new skills or abilities. Others (e.g., Ames, 1992) have called these "performance" and "mastery" goals. When one wants to emphasize performance quality (i.e., to look good), then one tends to play it safe with performance goals based on a fixed mindset. When one wants to emphasize mastery of a new skill, ability, or body of knowledge, then one tends to take on stretch goals that require exploring the unknown.

I am reminded of our thespian daughter's distinction between great actors and mere stars. She characterized great actors as those who continually accepted roles that demanded different emotional, cognitive, and physical elements than heretofore required, while mere stars tended to prefer new roles that closely resembled earlier roles—not really new at all. Examples include Bruce Willis, who tends to take on roles that all have the same qualities of swagger, violence, smirkiness, and action—the same character underlying many roles. Anthony Hopkins, on the other hand, not only takes on new dialects (as in his portrayal of President Richard Nixon), but assumes the visages of new characters who completely obscure his street self. I recall watching the film *Amistad* and looking forward to seeing Hopkins act. After about 30 minutes, I mentioned to Jane that I was surprised he hadn't appeared yet. She gently suggested to me that perhaps I hadn't recognized him in the role of U.S. President John

Quincy Adams! He'd been there all along. Such is the identity of an actor who takes on mastery goals based on a growth mindset. Who knows what their limits are?

David Shenk (2010) writes that "people who believe in inborn intelligence and talents are less intellectually adventurous and less successful in school. By contrast, people with an "incremental" theory of intelligence—believing that intelligence is malleable and can be increased through effort—are much more intellectually ambitious and successful." (loc. 1,343-1,345) Clearly the limits of knowledge are unknown. Every time we read a blog, a book, or a person's facial expressions we take in new knowledge, and when we recall the content of the blog, book, or face we take a step towards entrenching that knowledge in our long-term memory. The limit of such memories is unknowable but has been estimated at something around the equivalent of 10 million books of 1,000 pages each. However, the limit of our abilities and skills is less obviously unknowable. Some say if you don't have musical ability, language-learning ability, or the skill to operate a television remote, that you'll never have that ability or skill. That is a fixed mindset. As we will see later in this chapter, the evidence comes down hard that extraordinary practice can in fact produce previously unconceived abilities and skills. Shenk (2010) concludes: "Science has demonstrated unequivocally that a person's mind-set has the power to dramatically affect both short-term capabilities and the long-term dynamic of achievement." (loc. 1,505-1,506)

Continuum #6: Time to Completion

A Day or Less-----------------Days or Weeks------------------Months---------------------Years--------------------Decades

Time to Completion. To take on the goal of replacing the fixture in the upstairs bathroom means a time of completion of less than a day—probably less than one hour. To take on the goal of organizing my home and office libraries, days or weeks. To take on the goal of planning and implementing a family reunion, months. To write this book, years. To win the U.S. Open Tennis Championship (or Australian, French, or Wimbledon), decades. Longer, more complex goals require different personal temperaments than shorter, simpler goals. Some might opine that to engage in only shorter, simpler goals to the exclusion of longer, more complex ones may not reflect on one's willingness to take risks, but rather on one's limited mental abilities. However, that is not the case. With proper support, even those of limited intelligence can pursue lifelong, complex goals. For example, family friends of ours have a daughter with Down's syndrome. Her favorite hobby: She does ongoing research on the assassination of John F. Kennedy in an effort to determine whether it was one person acting alone or more than one. It does help that her parents are a professor and an artist who are highly supportive, but this gal genuinely pursues her intrinsic goal that will take decades to complete. What's your decades-long goal? I have several including compiling 11 related, family photo albums using PowerPoint, conducting research on the Five-Factor Model of personality, and striving to be a worthy parent. Again, the recommendation here is that each of us has a balance of goals requiring shorter and longer times to completion, from preparing a gourmet meal to pursuing the Holy Grail (or its equivalent!).

Continuum #7: Complexity

Simple--Moderately Complex---Highly Complex

Complexity. To the degree that a goal requires a single person, location, ability, skill, body of knowledge, or type of material, then that goal might be said to be simple. So, playing solitaire requires one person, one location (unless you have a global game online!), one material (a deck of cards or a smart device), and one skill. At the other end of the continuum would be a goal such as directing a video production (film, television program, and the like), which in its full-blown version could include thousands of people, dozens of locations, multiple materials (sets, landscapes, buildings, furniture, cameras, sound equipment, air conditioning trucks, food service equipment, and so on and on), and a myriad of skills, abilities, and knowledge, from period knowledge (such as knowing all about the culture of ancient Rome, from apparel to politics) to visual composition. Again, balance is the key. To only embrace complex goals would likely result in burnout, for one needs the mental rest from time to time of goals that are simpler and require little or no mental effort. But to embrace only simple goals would result in stagnation, poor mood, and underachievement.

Continuum #8: Balance

Most Clustered in One Extreme/Area----------Moderate Balance---------All Six Continua & Area Set Show Balance

Balance. So, we have seven other continua. For this final continuum, we ask ourselves to now review how our many goals are distributed on each of the other seven continua. In Table 7.0, I provide a worksheet for doing this self-study. Appendix E is a blank version for your use. I have entered some of my goals (there is not space here for all of my goals!) so that we might see how to use the worksheet. For the first seven continua, I have entered each goal seven times, once under each continuum and placed from left to right according to the anchors provided in the continuum. The first continuum, Areas of Endeavor, is not truly a continuum, but I have treated it as such, just to keep things simple. Notice that in this first "continuum," a goal may be entered more than once. For example, I have entered both "Natl Parks" and "Psalm 150 Project" twice. My national parks project stems from Jane's and my enthrallment with Ken Burns' series on public television. We have decided that we would like to take our grandchildren to all of them eventually. That would fall under both "building relationships" and "sensory pleasure." Our first such trip will be this fall, when we plan to go to the Congaree National Park near Columbia, SC. The Psalm 150 Project stems from our visit to the Opera ("workshop museum") of the Duomo (cathedral) in Florence, Italy. Therein rests a series of marble reliefs called the *Cantoria* (singing loft), sculpted by Lucca della Robbia between 1431 and 1438. The 10 reliefs depict verses of the well- known Psalm 150. I have always wanted to create a multi-media show that combines these 10 images, as well as depictions of Psalm 150 by other visual artists, with musical interpretations of the same psalm. This project leads me into some uncharted territory but contains visual and auditory beauty, so I have listed it twice, once under "new learning" and once under "sensory pleasure."

Table 7.0   Worksheet for Evaluating Balance of Goals (Based on the author's current goals)

(Note: A blank version of this worksheet is available as Appendix E.)

Continuum #1: Areas of Endeavor[2]

| Area 1: New Learning------Area 2: Translating Learning into Practice----------Area 3: Building Relationships------------Area 4: Sensory Pleasure |

Chinese history   Values Test   Natl Parks   Natl Parks

Psalm 150 Project   Globus   Tsinghua PPP   Replace DBR Fixture   Motet Group

                                        WP-4 CFA   Psalm 150 Project

Continuum #2: Origin

| Intrinsic--Partially Internal/Partially External--Extrinsic |

Values Test   Chinese history   WP-4 CFA

      Globus   Natl Parks   Tsinghua PPP   Replace DBR Fixture

Motet Group   Psalm 150 Project

Continuum #3: Survival

| Nice but not Necessary------------------------------------Nice and Somewhat Necessary------------------------------------Necessary for Survival |

Chinese history   Psalm 150 Project   Motet Group   Values Test

Natl Parks   WP-4 CFA

Replace DBR Fixture   Tsinghua PPP   Globus

Continuum #4: Generativity

| Impacts Me--Impacts Me and Future Generations----------------------------------Impacts Future Generations |

Motet Group   Chinese history   Psalm 150 Project   Values Test   Globus

Replace DBR Fixture   Tsinghua PPP   Natl Parks   WP-4 CFA

Continuum #5: Stretch

| Assured of Success--Moderately Challenging------------------------------------Extremely Challenging |

Chinese history   Values Test   Motet Group   WP-4 CFA   Globus

Natl Parks   Tsinghua PPP

Replace DBR Fixture   Psalm 150 Project

Continuum #6: Time to Completion

| A Day or Less------------------Days or Weeks----------------------------------Months----------------------------------Years----------------------------Decades |

Replace DBR Fixture   Tsinghua PPP   Chinese history   Values Test   Natl Parks

                                                                                 WP-4 CFA   Globus

                                        Psalm 150 Project   Motet Group

Continuum #7: Complexity

| Simple--Moderately Complex--Highly Complex |

Chinese history   Replace DBR Fixture   Values Test   Globus

Natl Parks   WP-4 CFA

                              Motet Group   Tsinghua PPP   Psalm 150 Project

Continuum #8: Balance

| Most Clustered in One Extreme/Area------------------------Moderate Balance------------------------All Six ~~tinua~~ & Area Set Show Balance |

---

[2] Note: "Areas of Endeavor" is not—strictly speaking—a true continuum. However, we treat it as though it were. Rather than having opposite terms at each end, we place the names of our own unique areas of endeavor along the continuum. Then, we can place each goal under its proper area. Some goals address two or more areas simultaneously, and so should be entered more than once, as appropriate.

Perhaps you will find it instructive for me to discuss some of my other goal placements in Table 7.0. For example, "Chinese history" is listed midway under origin. This is because Jane and I have been asked to travel to China for a two-week work assignment. That makes the goal externally imposed. However, I have taken it upon myself to study Chinese history, language, and biographies in preparation for the experience. It is not required, and the desire comes from within. So this goal, or project, is both intrinsic and extrinsic in origin. The Psalm 150 Project will give me great pleasure, but it also will remain for others after me to enjoy, so I have placed it somewhat towards the right on the generativity continuum. The three goals listed as necessary for survival (the far right on Continuum #3) will not put food on the table for me or thee in the foreseeable future. However, their successful completion will enhance the value of our company, a condition necessary for our being able to retire at some point!

Overall, on Continuum #8 (Overall Balance) I have evaluated my goal distribution along the seven other continua as more balanced than not. I only have one goal that is extremely challenging, and one that is highly complex. But that goal, Globus, is huge and will take many people besides me and a very long time to complete. In fact, it will never be complete. In short, it is a new, comprehensive assessment of mental ability administered online using multimedia.

I suggest that now you might try listing your goals and then placing them on a worksheet similar to Table 7.0. You may copy Appendix E if you like and use it as a guide. Now we will turn our attention to ways of generating new goals. Some of us have so many goals that we don't see the need for any new ones! However, for the sake of those who want to thoughtfully consider possible new goals, let's explore some common goal generation strategies.

Goal generation strategies

This section is aimed in part at people who say, "I'm bored. I can't think of anything to do." It is likely such folks haven't taken the time to set specific goals. That is not to say that people with clear goals are never bored. Some people get bored with their own goals! Goal generation is for everyone. Even those of us with lots of goals benefit from taking time periodically to generate a fresh list of possible goals, and then select new goals and possibly abandon other goals that have not proven to be satisfying. I call it weeding the garden. I get to the point that I have so much on my plate that less satisfying goals are clamoring for my resources that I'd prefer to put on more satisfying goals.

Goals should be grounded in our personal infrastructure: our traits, our abilities, our values, our physical characteristics, and our memories. Keep in mind that financial goals have a way of resulting in deficient mood and energy levels (Ben-Shahar, 2007, p. 72); so keep them to a minimum. Try one or more of the following ideas for coming up with new goals. The purpose of pursuing goals is linked to your values. For some, goals lead to greatness or stardom, while for others goals lead to learning or health or heightened spirituality. If you value power or achievement, your goals will be different from those who value learning or relationships. However, some value power *and* learning, and perhaps set a goal to be chair of a university department or even president/chancellor. Or someone might value achievement *and* relationships, and set a goal to get their Ph.D. in counseling. Review the list of values presented in Figure 6.0, The Palette of Who We Are. Write your strongest-held values on a piece of paper and keep it in view as you try to generate a list of goals.

Strong Points. Begin by making a list of your strong points. These are the traits, skills, abilities, physical characteristics, and memories that comprise The Palette of Who We Are (Figure 6.0). Keep these salient features of yourself (outgoing, verbal, altruistic, etc.) in front of you as you consider the following ways to create goals. Whatever goals you embrace, they should build on your strong points, the characteristics that make you you, the qualities that you can engage in naturally and with almost unlimited energy.

Inventory. Many self-help books include some kind of process for using activities from your past as a way to shape your goal-setting for the future. One of the more popular ones is *The Passion Test* (Attwood & Attwood, 2006). The process that I'll walk you through here is an adaptation and combination of features from many different approaches. Its simplicity is appealing and effective.

1. **Make a list**. Begin by making a list of everything that you can do. Go for length—think of as many things as possible. In a sense, this is a catalog of every kind of activity that you have ever engaged in. Each activity should be generic. For example, you might write "making up stories for children" rather than listing all the different contexts, such as "making up ghost stories around campfires," "making up stories for bedtime," "making up stories to pass the time on long trips," and so on. When I made my most recent list, I came up with about 100 activities, from playing the trumpet to reading philosophy.

2. **Underline your enjoyments**. Now, review your list and underline the activities that you enjoy doing. You might have written that you were a gardener, but perhaps you do it out of necessity or for someone else's sake and don't really enjoy it—if so, don't underline it! Only underline the activities that entail pleasant feelings while you are doing them. When I reviewed my most recent list, I underlined about half. The other half were not necessarily unpleasant—I just didn't delight in them.

3. **Circle your favorites**. Now, review your list one more time and circle the underlined activities that you would never tire of doing—activities that you feel passionate about, that you look forward eagerly to doing, that you have fire in the belly for, that you feel proud of, that you do well. For my list, I circled about 20.

4. **Find the pattern**. Now, review your circled activities with the objective of finding a pattern among them. In the same manner, this is how I came up with my list of four areas of endeavor: new learning, translating theory into practice, sensory pleasure, and building relationships. Earlier I offered a brief list of areas of endeavor under "Continuum #1." You might review that list to see if it gives you some ideas of what your patterns might be. The objective here is for you to reduce your life to four, five, or six primary areas of activity. Each area will likely be related to a value, as these areas represent activity that is important to you.

5. **To Do List**. Now, make a "To Do" list for each of your areas of endeavor. In other words, make a list of everything you are doing at present or in the near future for each area of endeavor. The objective here is to determine whether your current activities are balanced among the areas of endeavor that are important to you, that make you feel good, that you likely would never tire of doing.

6. **Identify over- or under-served areas**. Perhaps there is an area of endeavor that you have enjoyed in the past but now find yourself missing. This becomes the source for you to create some new goals. No time for new goals? Then, you'll need to back off of some activities in the over-served areas or of activities that take your time but don't fall under any of your top areas of endeavor.

7. **Share your results** with someone significant to you. The act of sharing your primary endeavor with a partner or some other close friend, associate, or family member serves three purposes: upping the stakes on your commitment by making them public, encouraging support from others by letting them know your priorities, and inviting assistance in clarifying your thinking and how best to implement your priorities.

Dissatisfaction. Dennis Prager (1998) talks about the need to "distinguish between two types of dissatisfactions—necessary and unnecessary."(p. 18) A necessary dissatisfaction is like normal constructive criticism of self, others, and the world in general that suggests areas for development or improvement. For me, necessary dissatisfactions would include my ramshackle backyard fence and my unorganized collection of about 2,000 books. I want to do something about both of them—I am dissatisfied, even embarrassed, that my aging, pitiful fence is an eyesore for the neighborhood, and I mutter to myself every time I spend time looking for a book—time I wouldn't have to waste searching if the books were organized. On the other hand, a dissatisfaction is unnecessary when it is about something that is *unchangeable* (or, at least, unchangeable by me, such as my inheritance from my parents, where my grandchildren live, and so forth) or *unimportant* (at least, unimportant to me, such as the state of my wardrobe or how my hair looks). I am reminded of the well-known serenity prayer—"Give me the courage to change what I can, the grace to accept what I cannot, and the wisdom to know the difference. We would benefit from abandoning goals about things that cannot be changed or that are unimportant, and instead place our resources in the service of sources of dissatisfaction that are important to us and that we can do something about. Recall that William James commented once that self-concept is based on how we see ourselves in certain selected areas of activity, and that we should not compare ourselves to others in spheres that are unimportant to us and in which we tend to be inept.

In sum, make a list of everything in your life with which you are dissatisfied. Then, mark through the things either that you don't really care that much about or that you cannot do anything about. You will be left with sources of dissatisfaction that you can do something about and that are important to you. You can then pursue some goals to eradicate (or at least minimize) these sources of dissatisfaction.

Bucket List. Another popular method for coming up with a list of goals is the bucket list. My first encounter with the concept was through the 2007 film *The Bucket List*, in which Jack Nicholson and Morgan Freeman play two cancer patients who take off on a trip with the intention of accomplishing some long-wished-for goals before they die (i.e., "kick the bucket"). I learned afterward from friends that many have a list of 100 or so things they would like to do in their lifetime. Their lists include vacationy-type things such as climbing Mt. YouNameIt, writing a book, visiting a country or region or city never before experienced, meeting someone, building something, learning a new skill…. In short, the bucket list is a long-term To Do list of things one would like to do (as opposed to *have* to do).

The reason for the list is the same reason we recommend making goals in the first place: Having a goal makes it more likely that you will accomplish it. So just the act of making a bucket list makes it more likely that you will accomplish many of the things on the list. I have my own bucket list, and it includes everything from job-related dreams (such as building a new assessment of intelligence) to vacation dreams (such as camping in the Puget Sound area and eating fresh salmon while there). If this is not enough information for you to make your own bucket list now, then try reading *Creating Your Best Life: The Ultimate Life List Guide* (Miller & Frisch, 2009). Believe it or not, the entire book is devoted to reasons for having a bucket list and how to get started developing one. At any rate, I keep my bucket list in a computer application called Evernote, so that whenever I add something to the list, or check something off, it automatically synchronizes with my laptop, desktop, iPhone, and iPad. Evernote exists in the "cloud," so you can access it from anywhere. From time to time, I open Evernote and review my bucket list.

Moderation. Perhaps this is a strange thing to say when we are talking about goal generation methods, but here goes. Be selective in your goal-setting. Some goals entail the drive to be first in something, to be the best at something. Wisdom suggests, however, that one should limit the number of arenas in which one aims to be first. A person who is, or aims to be, first in everything they do is insufferable! Hear Samuel Butler's (1903) small essay on such people from *The Way of All Flesh*:

> It is involved in the very essence of things that rich men who die old shall have been mean [i.e., moderate]. The greatest and wisest of mankind will be almost always found to be the meanest--the ones who have kept the "mean" best between excess either of virtue or vice. They hardly ever have been prosperous if they have not done this, and, considering how many miscarry altogether, it is no small feather in a man's cap if he has been no worse than his neighbours. Homer tells us about some one who made it his business always to excel and to stand higher than other people. What an uncompanionable disagreeable person he must have been! Homer's heroes generally came to a bad end, and I doubt not that this gentleman, whoever he was, did so sooner or later. (loc. 1,181)

Butler's musing reminds me of Machiavelli's warning to leaders in *The Prince*. He observed that many leaders attempt to be all-or-nothing with respect to leadership straits: always confident, always brave, never fearful, and so forth. Machiavelli observed that people do not respect leaders who are *always* anything. People like to see the soft side of their leaders. Sometimes fearful, if only of their favorite baseball team not being able to make the playoffs. Sometimes self-doubting, if only showing low confidence in being able to succeed at a non-critical task, such as training the family dog. Sometimes cowardly, if only of not feeling potent against a non-threatening menace. U.S. President Barack Obama experienced some of this in the first half of his administration when followers lamented his sustained periods of remaining rational and calm, thinking instead that he should have shown more emotion.

In short, we are suggesting that someone who tends to be strong at everything might consider actually setting a goal to hold back in some areas so as not to be hated or resented for having no apparent weaknesses. A husband might defer to his wife to handle finances, while a wife might defer to her husband to handle the baking.

The goal-less. Some people have no goals. They may or may not be depressed. They may have led a busy professional life and find themselves unable to get going in retirement. I remember my own father's retirement. Every workday (Monday through Saturday) he toiled from 5 a.m. until 5 p.m. in his store, came home to eat, read the paper, and went to bed early. Upon retirement, he began watching mindless television shows: quiz shows, reruns, and so forth. I don't recall him ever starting a project after retirement. It was as though his store had provided total structure for his life, and he was unable to find a way to structure his time without the daily rhythm of orders and deliveries.

My retired psychiatrist friend, who lives in a retirement center, tells the story of a fellow retiree who had no goals. He had been the CEO of a major utility, and he entered retirement like a pilot who had no airplane. Mark suggested that the ex-CEO commit to the goal of living to be 100, and to plan and execute what it would take to do so. That goal kept him keen and upbeat for some time. For people who are depressed, homebound, isolated, etc., and can't muster the energy, or desire, or know-how, to come up with a goal, this simple goal of living until a milestone becomes a source of energy for making progress day by day. Jane's father had a goal of being the first member of his family to live until he was 90 (he missed it by a few months).

In fact, the ex-CEO lived to celebrate his 100th birthday. Then he grew listless. Mark suggested that he set a new goal of living to be 101. And so he did, and continues to do so. Also, he might consider goals that relate to his age, such as studying the lives of others who've made it to 100, making a list of those who have lived to 100, and selecting to outlive specific persons at each succeeding age: 101, 102, etc. He might also correspond with persons his own age or write an autobiography, or annotate photos. Make an oral history of self and family with an audio recorder. Develop a relationship with a schoolkid, and form a mutual goal that both work on.

Gap Analysis. Some professionals estimate that as many as 90% of U.S. Fortune 500 companies use some form of 360°, multi-rater feedback assessment. This assessment is not typically used for performance appraisal and salary determination, but is used for helping employees identify areas of their job—competencies—in which they are doing well, in addition to areas where they stand in need of improvement. In its most common form, an individual, their boss, their peers, and their subordinates (if any) answer specific questions about their day-to-day performance. It is as though the individual were at the center of a circle, with boss, peers, and direct reports forming a circle around them. Hence, the term "360°." In response to the statement "Leads meetings effectively," the raters might rate the individual as a "3" on a 1 to 5 scale, while in response to the question "How important is this behavior to the person's current job?" the raters might answer with "5." The 2-point difference between Importance (= 5) and Performance (= 3) is called a "gap" between performance and importance, suggesting that, in this case, leading meetings is an area this individual might consider setting a goal for improvement.

For organizations that use such multi-rater feedback instruments, this is the primary way that individual employees set goals for professional development. If you think that this would be a helpful way for you to get some developmental feedback, ask your human resources manager about resources that might be available to you and the organization. Or, if you have no HR manager, you could always get in touch with a local member of the American Society for Training and Development, the International Coach Federation, the Organization Development Network, or a faculty member of any university's business, management, or organization behavior department. You could also check the global consulting network of my company, the Center for Applied Cognitive Studies. We have consultants listed on our website at http://www.centacs.com/services/consultant-directory/. All of these professionals would know who in your community to turn to for assistance in having a 360° assessment done for you. Or, you might consider retaining the services of a "coach"—they use not only 360° feedback instruments with their clients but other methods as well to assist them in personal and professional goal-setting.

Volunteering. Offering your services to a community agency is an excellent way to generate goals. It is also an excellent way to get a boost in well-being. The options here are staggeringly close to limitless:

- Homeless shelters need persons willing to sleep over, to prepare meals, to eat and converse with residents, and so on.
- Check with the volunteer coordinator at United Way.
- Explore being a museum docent or helper.
- Ask family and neighbors what they need or want that your skills could achieve.
- Elementary schools need volunteers to help extend the eyes and hands of the classroom teacher, whether through reading to children, helping with projects, or assisting with recreation and field trips.
- Recreation departments need volunteers to coach and assist in a variety of leagues.
- Hospitals need a variety of helpers, from receptionists to visitors.

Religion. Places of worship have a variety of opportunities through which you could establish goals. From childcare to office help, from teaching religious education to working with youth, from driving buses and vans to playing handbells—find a suitable congregation and make yourself available.

Politics. Every residence in the United States is assigned to a political district. Check if the political party of your choice has an organization in your district. This district political organizations need a variety of help, from leadership to taking minutes, from doing research to electioneering (standing at the polls on an election day). In addition, these district political organizations feed upwardly to the city, state, and national organizations.

Civic Club. Civitan, Elks, Kiwanis, Lions, Optimists, Rotary, Sertoma, apartment associations, homeowners associations, neighborhood associations. The list goes on. Houston, Texas has an online database of upwards of 700 civic clubs: http://www.houstontx.gov/cao/civicdir-a.pdf . Each of these clubs is a fertile opportunity for developing goals to accomplish either on your own or with friends and neighbors—from public art projects to garden and landscaped areas, from neighborhood watch groups to holiday festivals. Get involved and set goals with likeminded associates.

Book Club. Here's an idea: Join (or create) a book club and set a goal to read a book each month and discuss it with friends. Don't know how to get started? Visit this website: http://www.book-clubs-resource.com/ . If there's no book club nearby, start your own—the website tells you how to do that. Or, try an online book club—the website is helpful there also. Or similarly, start a scrapbooking club and meet regularly to share ideas on how to organize and present material while enjoying a partner working beside you.

Music Group. Musical? Find a group to play with. This web site (http://boerger.org/c-m/com-mother.shtml) lists over 1,300 nonprofessional bands and orchestras around the country (three are listed for my hometown). Or find a small group to play with (chamber music, rock band, madrigal group, and so forth), or start your own. Enoch Pratt Free Library in Baltimore has a database of hobbyists in music and other areas with each person rating themselves as beginner, intermediate, or advanced, with an invitation to contact them to make music (or other activities) together. If you are past your prime vocally and can't or don't want to sing with younger voices, then start your own senior vocal group. Our friend Danny Sue Kidd tells the story of a church in Greensboro, NC that started a choir of seniors who had "graduated" (maybe retired is better) from their church's chancel choir that sang Sunday after Sunday. It was a low-pressure group that sang only on special occasions.

Counseling. If none of my ideas work for you, and you feel as though you just don't know how to set a meaningful goal for yourself and get involved in pursuing that goal, then I suggest that you invest in some counseling for the express purpose of helping you formulate some goals and develop plans to accomplish them. Or, if you don't wish to go to a professional counselor, then ask a family member, colleague, or friend to assist you.

Roles versus Goals. Marshall McLuhan once wrote about the difference between role-oriented people and goal-oriented people. For example, being a good parent would be a role, while getting your oldest into Harvard would be a goal. Many of my suggestions in this section will seem more like roles and not like goals at all. That is OK. In the larger sense, a role is a goal. The conscious commitment to being a parent is not only a role but a worthy goal. It is something that you do (role) as well as something that you aim for (goal). Among other things, I am a musician. I try to practice daily. That is a goal. Whether my being a musician is a role or a goal is splitting hairs, as far as I am concerned. Whenever you or I make up our minds to do something, whether it is to be a vegetable gardener (role) or to create a vegetable garden (goal), then that is a goal. What is NOT a goal is to commit to a role without any idea of how to implement it. Implementation is goal pursuit.

Deciding which goals to pursue

Often our choices are obvious. Given two or more rival goals, we rely on our instincts to select the one that resonates the most with us. This is supported by brain research. The so-called decision-making apparatus—the prefrontal cortex and environs—is attached to the seat of the emotions—the amygdala and environs. Persons whose connections to the amygdala have by some means become severed, as in the famous case of Phineas Gage, are unable to make decisions. A railroad spike explosively penetrated his skull and separated amygdala from frontal cortex. His normal intellectual functioning was not appreciably diminished as a result, but he had trouble managing his emotions and making decisions. Damasio (1994) pointed out that we have emotions attached to our memories. For example, I had a painful experience with sunburn when I was a child. Ever since, I have no trouble deciding *not* to spend lots of time in the bright sun. Every time the option is again available to me, the negative emotions attached to my childhood memory at Camp Morehead make it easy for me to say no. It is not a rational decision. I know I could use sunscreen. On the other hand, I had an exhilarating experience growing up with 18 nieces and nephews. When I was in my teens, during major holidays the house was filled with kids ranging from newborns to three years my junior. As a result, whenever I have the opportunity to play with children, my positive emotions associated with memories of play with children make me favorably disposed to deciding in favor of those decisions. Again, it is not rational but is rooted in strong emotional associations.

So, the lesson here is to trust our instincts, to trust the feeling that one choice or goal might have stronger positive emotional associations than another. But what should one do when our emotional cues are unable to send a clear message that one option is superior to another? What if I am stymied between building a deck or building a fence, between writing a novel or writing a biography, between learning a foreign language or learning calculus? Here is my recommendation: Make a matrix of rows and columns. The rows could be your choices, the columns, your strongest personal qualities (from the Palette of Who You Are, Figure 6.0). Then, estimate how well each choice engages your strongest personal qualities. In Table 7.1, I have shown how I might do this for the choice of what I should write my next book about.

Table 7.1   How to Decide When Stymied Between Possible Goals

Criteria / Options	Novel about consulting	Biography of Papa and Danken
Relationships	*	****
Learning		**
Generativity	*	***
Imagination	***	*
Complexity	***	**
Personal Desire	*	*
Aesthetics	*	
Pleasure	*	*
Mental Challenge	**	*
Total:	13	15

The criteria column includes elements from my Palette as well as some additional criteria, like Personal Desire (i.e., how strongly do I want to do it?), Learning (one of my four passions), Relationships (another of my four passions), and Generativity. In reviewing my marks, writing a novel about the world of consulting would, in my judgment, contribute little to my desire to spend more time developing my relationships with friends and family, while the biography of my paternal grandparents would contribute quite a bit—from interviewing family members to providing a record to future generations of their ancestry. On the other hand, I gave three stars to the novel for drawing more heavily on my imagination. For learning, however, as I never knew my paternal grandparents, writing about them would definitely involve learning lots that I didn't know before. Looks like the biography of Papa and Danken wins out! Ben Franklin called this process a "moral calculus," in the sense of helping decide what one "should" do. There are more complex variations on this theme. If you are interested in a more thorough treatment of this method of decision-making, take a look at Kepner & Tregoe (1981) and Plunkett & Hale (1982), both of which have chapters on how to use this kind of matrix. They call it rational decision making.

The role of optimism, grit, and stress in goal pursuit

The impact of achieving one's goal ranges from the local and humdrum, as in weeding one's garden, to the global and extraordinary, as in achieving world class status in your field (Michael Phelps' 14 gold medals for swimming in the 2004 and 2008 Olympics comes to mind). I celebrate both extremes and everything in between. The point is to set goals and pursue them, no matter how ordinary or extraordinary. In this section, we want to talk about three personal dispositions that affect one's ability to pursue a goal—optimism and its bedfellow hope, plus grit and its bedfellow practice, and stress and its bedfellow resilience.

Optimism and Hope[3]. It is the very nature of optimism that those who possess it are more likely to attain goals. Optimism typically leads to self-efficacy, while pessimism leads to despair. In between, realism provides a balance: either optimism or pessimism as the circumstances suggest. Martin Seligman, in his book *Learned Optimism* (1991), describes how rats and humans learn to be helpless. When they learn they have no control over their environment, they give up trying to exert control. Whether the bothersome stimuli are electroshocks or noise, unsuccessful attempts to stop them are followed by defeatist despair. Seligman has found three ingredients of this learned helplessness among humans, which he contrasts to learned optimism. The three ingredients are personalization, permanence, and pervasiveness.

> "There are two mistakes one can make along the road to truth...not going all the way, and not starting."
> --Buddha
> (Hindu Prince Gautama Siddharta, the founder of Buddhism, 563-483 B.C.)

Table 7.2 Seligman's Explanatory Styles

Explanation of Adversity	
Optimist:	**Pessimist:**
It's someone else's fault *(external personalization)*. It's only temporary *(not permanent)*. It won't affect other areas of my life *(limited pervasiveness)*.	It's my fault *(internal personalization)*. It's gonna last forever *(permanent)*. It'll affect every area of my life *(universal pervasiveness)*.
Explanation of Success	
Optimist:	**Pessimist:**
I made it happen *(internal personalization)*. This is one in a line of many successes *(permanent)*. The effect will ripple throughout my life *(universal pervasiveness)*.	Someone else made it happen *(external personalization)*. It'll never happen again *(not permanent)*. It won't help me in other areas of my life *(limited pervasiveness)*.

---

[3] The section on optimism draws heavily from Chapter 37 of the 3rd edition of *The Owner's Manual for the Brain* (Howard, 2006).

Depending on how we typically respond to success or adversity along these three dimensions, we are described as optimistic or pessimistic. In Table 7.2, I have summarized the healthy, more motivated explanatory style and the less healthy, unmotivated explanatory style.

Seligman concludes from his research that the optimistic explanatory style is associated with high motivation, success, achievement, and physical and mental health. The pessimistic explanatory style is associated with the opposite traits. He also finds that certain pessimistic people who constantly ruminate about their misfortune in life and brood about the pessimistic aspects of personalization, permanence, and pervasiveness are at high risk for depression.

Notice that the preferred explanatory styles are opposite in their response to success or adversity: the more healthy (optimistic) explanatory style for success (internal, permanent, and pervasive) is in fact unhealthy (pessimistic) as a way to explain adversity. Conversely, the more unhealthy (pessimistic) way to explain success (external, temporary, and limited) is in fact the healthy (optimistic) way to explain adversity. In figure 7.0, I illustrate this model as a flowchart.

Figure 7.0   Martin Seligman's Model of Explanatory Style

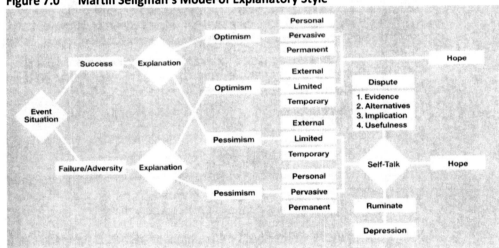

Current brain research suggests that explanatory style needs to be understood as overlaying the process discussed earlier of memory and emotion in the amygdala linking to decision-making in the frontal cortex. When faced with explaining success or failure, we need to challenge the first associations that our memories provide us—challenge in the sense of eschewing questionably pessimistic explanations in favor of demonstrably sound optimistic explanations. If I experience failure in pursuit of a goal, I may immediately question my ability to master its demands. That is pessimism. Seligman suggests that we challenge such a pessimistic explanation and search for a more optimistic and healthy explanation that has some merit. So, rather than explain failure with concern for my ability, I could link failure to my inadequate opportunity to practice. Lack of practice is something that I can do something about. It is temporary and definitely fixable, while saying I lack ability tends to sound permanent and unfixable—especially to someone with a "fixed" mindset.

Seligman has codified this self-questioning process in what he calls the ABCDE method. The "A," "B," and "C" concern how we react negatively to success or adversity; "D" and "E" represent ways we can rethink the pessimistic reaction into an optimistic one. The letters are defined as follows:

A   *(Adversity)* Recognize when adversity hits. For die-hard pessimists, successes are a form of adversity; they say, "It won't last," "I was just lucky," or "Too little, too late."

B   *(Beliefs)* Be aware of what you believe about the adversity.

C   *(Consequences)* Be aware of the emotional and other consequences of your belief about that adversity.

D   *(Disputation)* Question whether your beliefs are the only explanation. For example, ask:
- What is the evidence for my beliefs?
- What are other possible explanations for what happened?
- What are the implications of my believing this way, and do they make it worth holding onto my beliefs?
- How useful are my beliefs? Do I or others get any benefits from holding onto them, or would we get more benefits from holding other beliefs?

E   *(Energization)* Be aware of the new consequences (feelings, behaviors, actions) that do or could follow from a different, more optimistic explanation or set of beliefs.

Here is an example of the ABCDE model as I applied it to a specific situation. My train of thought went like this:

1. I didn't finish this chapter by the end of the Thanksgiving holiday, as I promised my wife and myself I would do. *(Adversity)*
2. I'm an incurable procrastinator, and I will never meet my goals. (*Beliefs*: a personal, pervasive, and permanent explanation, which is therefore pessimistic)
3. I might as well abandon this project and settle for a life of less ambitious projects. That way, my wife won't be disappointed with me when I miss deadlines. *(Consequence)*
4. Wait a minute! Lots of writers set unrealistic deadlines. Besides, my wife and I did several things together and with her parents that had a very positive impact on our relationship. And if sticking to my schedule were so all-fired important to her, she could have insisted on doing some of those things without me. *(Disputation)*
5. I'll talk about my schedule with her and get her input on whether the remainder of the schedule is important to her. If not, I'll push my deadlines back. If so, I'll ask her assistance and cooperation in finding ways to make more time for writing. I really don't want to give up this project. It's exciting, even if it is a little behind schedule. *(Energization)*

A word of warning: The goal of understanding explanatory style is not to create a world of Pollyannaish optimists. Too much optimism, like too much pessimism, is typically counterproductive. Excessive pessimism, however, has a negative impact on health that excessive optimism doesn't. Psychologists Katri Raikkonen and Karen Matthews of the University of Pittsburgh School of Medicine report that people with more pessimistic outlooks have an average blood pressure that is about five points higher (both systolic and diastolic) than that of optimists. Among people who have suffered one heart attack, pessimism predicts a second, more lethal heart attack more accurately than physical condition. And a University of Michigan research team headed by Christopher Peterson has reported that people (especially males) who "catastrophize" events, seeing them as part of a worldwide pattern of evil and pain, tend to die before age 65 and are more likely to die by suicide or accident (*Psychological Science,* March 1998).

One of hallmarks of pessimism is resistance to letting go of past failure. Laura King and Joshua Hicks (University of Missouri—Columbia) define maturity as complex ego development (King & Hicks, 2007). According to their theory, one considers all of one's lost goals, failures, missed opportunities, successes, achievements, and so forth and composes a progressively more complex life story, as opposed to someone who remains stuck in the past, stymied by lost goals and unengaged in the present: "The failure to disengage from lost goals is associated with lowered well-being." (p. 629) Maturity is predicated on acknowledging one's losses or limitations (promotion, death of loved one, personal or family health issues, etc.) but nonetheless emerging from them totally engaged in present goals. This necessitates letting go of one's old self and embracing one's new self. The temperament for developing in this manner requires acknowledging that one has erred or experienced trouble or loss, while remaining capable of being surprised (as opposed to being something of a know-it-all who takes everything in stride knowingly), showing humility at not being totally in control, and having the courage to explore new goals and risk new losses/failures. This involves cutting one's losses, learning from them, and moving on. Failure to do so results in what some call "escalation of commitment," or pouring good money or energy after bad. Globally, escalation of commitment looks like the Vietnam War, where resources were continually committed in spite of clear evidence that losses should be cut and move on. The researchers declare that "mindful acceptance on one's life, 'warts and all'" is essential to maturity, and that "Lingering engagement in lost possible selves is negatively related to happiness." (p. 634) In calling one's life a work of art, they conclude that

> The happy, complex person's palette is one that contains a rich array of color, and the mature artist, though genuinely marked by life, maintains an enthusiasm to put paint to the canvas of life in remarkable ways. (p. 634)

Grit and Practice. I want to talk now about two concepts that are inseparable: grit and practice. Grit is the quality of staying with a goal until it is completed. Persons who have grit tend to exhibit two core components: the capacity to resist distractions from the goal at hand, and the capacity to bounce back after setbacks. (Duckworth & Quinn, 2009) The quality of grit predicts finalists in the national spelling bee, graduating from the military academies, higher grade point average, and fewest hours of television watched. Brown & Fenske (2010) write about people who have a "goal laser"—people who have one tend to excel because they, in comparison to their less focused peers, take specific measures to remain focused and thus achieve their goals. Such a goal laser would fit the meaning of having a "yen" for something. It is interesting to note that the English word "yen" comes from the China's Guangdong region where *yīn-yáhn* comes from *yīn* (opium) + *yáhn* (craving), or a craving for opium. Hence the modern "yen" suggests an intense craving, and this notion of a goal laser certainly suggests a kind of addiction to one's major goal(s). This would be a person who is high in the traits of perfectionism, order, ambition, concentration, and methodicalness. Persons low in these traits can also achieve goals but they lack the natural laser, being more spontaneous and distractible. They need to compensate for lack of a laser. For example, I do not have such a laser—I am not perfectionist, I'm comfortable with relative disorder, I don't aspire to be a star, and methodicalness to me is like a straightjacket. But I nonetheless achieve goals that are important to me—I've written eight books, created two significant psychological tests, and am hard at work on this new book. How do I manage to make progress when I lack the natural temperament?

I thought you'd never ask! I have many crutches. First and foremost, I tell a lot of people what I am going to do, which increases the pressure on me to deliver. Second, I create an environment that minimizes distractions—I come home from the office most days at 4 p.m., and write until Jane gets home. That is usually a nice three-hour stretch. While I am writing, I burn a big, fat candle—a reminder to me that I am trying to stay focused and a symbolic inspiration to me to cherish the illuminating effect of writing. I post a quote by Sir Francis

> "Whatever you can do, or dream you can, begin it. Boldness has genius, power and magic in it."
>
> -- Johann Wolfgang von Goethe

Bacon as further inspiration: "Reading maketh a full man, conference a ready man, and writing an exact man." In order to "bring home the Bacon," I must resist devoting all my time to reading and talking and devote equal or more time to writing. I have learned to view reading and talking as easy and in a sense selfish, while writing provides balance by being more effortful and more giving to others.

The difference between persevering until you accomplish your goal (grit) and true excellence is your amount of practice. Practice involves commitment to putting in the hours necessary to repeatedly perform something until the desired standard is reached. Florida State University psychology professor Anders Ericsson has turned the world on its ear by discovering his rule of 10,000 hours. To wit, practice something for 10,000 hours over a period of 10 years, frequently introducing difficulties and variations (like practicing the piano blindfolded, or practicing tennis with a smaller racquet), and you should achieve a world class level of expertise. (Ericsson & Charness, 1994) That amounts to about three hours, seven days a week, with two weeks of vacation, or four hours, five days a week, again with some vacation. Ericsson's research on expertise has established this principle across a wide variety of disciplines, from music and sports to science and technology. Again, it is not just 10,000 hours of practice over 10 years—it is 10,000 hours of *deliberate* practice. You can't do the same thing time after time with no variation. Introduce difficulties, variations in the practice routine that lead to new neural pathways and new insights into the skill itself.

Ericsson's findings lead inevitably to the conclusion that inherited talent is neither required nor sufficient to achieve extraordinary expertise. Music historians, for example, have studied Mozart's early life and concluded that, in fact, he did not begin creating compositions with compelling allure until he had put in his 10,000 hours of deliberate practice. David Shenk (2010) points out that scholarly research "on the heritability of acquisition of elite sports achievement failed to reveal reproducible evidence for any genetic constraints for attaining elite levels by healthy individuals (excluding, of course, the evidence on body size)." (loc. 3,695-3,697) Shenk continues:

> In study after study, of composers, basketball players, fiction writers, ice-skaters, concert pianists, chess players, master criminals … this number comes up again and again. Ten thousand hours is equivalent to roughly three hours a day, or 20 hours a week, of practice over 10 years.… No one has yet found a case in which true world-class expertise was accomplished in less time. It seems that it takes the brain this long to assimilate all that it needs to know to achieve true mastery. (loc. 3,706-3,709)… But the new science tells

us that it's equally foolish to think that mediocrity is built into most of us, or that any of us can know our true limits before we've applied enormous resources and invested vast amounts of time. (loc. 163-165)

As we have mentioned earlier (cf. Kruger & Dunning, 1999), one of the things that separates the truly great performers from the merely excellent is the unrelenting dissatisfaction with one's current level of performance—the certain knowledge that one could have done better. The merely excellent performers appear to be satisfied with less than perfection and/or to have little or no clue as to their own errors, even though their typical audience member might also be clueless as to their errors. Martha Graham expresses this state of mind:

No artist is pleased. There is not satisfaction whatever at any time. There is only a queer, divine dissatisfaction; a blessed unrest that keeps us marching and makes us more alive than the others.' (Prager, 1998, p. 20)

This sense of noble dissatisfaction does not mean that one is unhappy in any sense, but rather that one is keenly aware of opportunities for improvement. This presupposes that these same individuals are also keenly aware of the progress that they have already made and that they take satisfaction in past progress. They just do not rest on their laurels. The persistence associated with grit and 10,000 hours was expressed tersely by Albert Einstein when he quipped that "It's not that I'm so smart. It's just that I stay with problems longer." (Shenk, 2010, loc. 1,877-1,878)

On the political front, Shenk (2010) offers this March 24, 2009 statement from U.S. President Barack Obama:

That whole philosophy of persistence ... is one that I'm going to be emphasizing again and again in the months and years to come, as long as I am in this office. I'm a big believer in persistence. I think that ... if we keep on working at it, if we acknowledge that we make mistakes sometimes and that we don't always have the right answer, and we're inheriting very knotty problems, that we can pass health care, we can find better solutions to our energy challenges, we can teach our children more effectively ... I'm sure there'll be more criticism and we'll have to make more adjustments, but we're moving in the right direction. (loc. 1,934-1,939)

Shenk (2010) summarizes the research on deliberate practice in this way:

For those on their way to greatness, several themes consistently come to light: Practice changes your body. Researchers have recorded a constellation of physical changes (occurring in direct response to practice) in the muscles, nerves, hearts, lungs, and brains of those showing profound increases in skill level in any domain. Skills are specific. Individuals becoming great at one particular skill do not serendipitously become great at other skills. Chess champions can remember hundreds of intricate chess positions in sequence but can have a perfectly ordinary memory for everything else. Physical and intellectual changes are ultraspecific responses to particular skill requirements. The brain drives the brawn. Even among athletes, changes in the brain are arguably the most profound, with a vast increase in precise task knowledge, a shift from conscious analysis to intuitive thinking (saving time and energy), and elaborate self-monitoring mechanisms that allow for constant adjustments in real time. Practice style is crucial. Ordinary practice, where your current skill level is simply being reinforced, is not enough to get better. It takes a special kind of practice to force your mind and body into the kind of change necessary to improve. Short-term intensity cannot replace long-term commitment. Many crucial changes take place over long periods of time. Physiologically, it's impossible to become great overnight.... (loc. 864-877) How does deliberate practice actually improve one's skills? In a nutshell, our muscles and brain regions adapt to the demands that we make of them. (loc. 890-893)

Stress and resilience. As we have said elsewhere, stress occurs when something interferes with your goal attainment. These "somethings" are called "stressors," or things that cause stress by interposing themselves between you and a goal that is important to you. People misunderstand stressors to be bad or undesirable things. Stressors may be intrinsically bad (e.g., being ill and thus not able to perform) or intrinsically good (e.g., your child/grandchild/neighbor wants you to play with them but you have work to do), but their intrinsic nature is not what makes them stressors. They are only stressors in the sense that you feel stressed as the result of their keeping you from progressing towards a goal. For example, let's say that your partner wants to "play around." In and of itself, playing around has no automatic association with goals or with being a stressor. However, in a particular situation, playing around could be a stressor (by keeping you from being on time to an important meeting), a promoter (by adding value to the relationship), or neutral (by simply humoring the partner because there's nothing better to do and you are indifferent to the relationship).

If stress is what we feel when obstructed from continuing progress towards our goal, then resilience is the quality that enables us to bounce back from a setback and continue where we left off. This is easier for some of us than for others. Some can shake off setbacks like a dog shakes off water, while others need sustained nurture in order to get over a setback. If getting over a crisis or setback is not easy for you, I suggest that there are three things you can do to promote greater resilience:

- **Make up your mind** that it is OK *not* to mope, OK *not* to take a long time to get over things. Some of us might feel, for example, that we are being disloyal or insensitive if we do not take time to recover after such crises. The non-resilient commonly lament, "How can you think about or do anything after what has just happened?" One can, with some effort, decide that quick recovery is not only permitted but in fact necessary.
- **Flush the toxins** from your system that the crisis has ushered in. Stress pumps cortisol and other toxins into your system. They interfere with your body/mind's optimal functioning. The only way to flush these toxins is with aerobic exercise (e.g., a good run, brisk walk, bicycle ride, and so forth). Of course, ridding your body of these toxins is only half of the task: You also need to stop producing them. For this you need to practice some form of relaxation that is natural for you (yoga, reading, grooming the family pet, having a latte with a friend).
- **Occupy your mind** by becoming absorbed in pursuit of your goal. Remove sources of distraction, even if it means isolating yourself. Again, Shakespeare says it best: "The labor we delight in physics [heals] pain." (Macbeth, II, iii)

In short, be *hope*ful for success, *focus* on goal pursuit, and *get over it.*

Case studies in goal pursuit

I want to close out this chapter with several examples of goal pursuit. The first is a negative example from Ray Bradberry's *Fahrenheit 451* in which the firemen have taken upon themselves the task of distracting the populace with entertainment so that they don't accomplish meaningful goals:

> If you don't want a man unhappy politically don't give him two sides to a question to worry him; give him one. Better yet give him none. ...Chock them so damned full of 'facts' they feel stuffed but absolutely 'brilliant' with information.... Don't give them any slippery stuff like philosophy or sociology to tie things up with. That way lies melancholy. ...So bring on your clubs and parties, your acrobats and magicians, your daredevils, jet cars, motorcycle helicopters, your sex and heroin, more of everything to do with automatic reflex...solid entertainment. ...The important thing for you to remember, Montag, is we're the Happiness Boys, the Dixie Duo, you and I and the others. We stand against the small tide of those who want to make everyone unhappy with conflicting theory and thought. We have our fingers in the dike. Hold steady. Don't let the torrent of melancholy and drear philosophy drown our world. We depend on you. I don't think you realize how important *you* are, *we* are, to our happy world as it stands now." (pp. 61-62)

The second example is a positive story in which David Shenk (2010) describes baseballer Ted Williams' "goal laser" in action:

> But all that innate miracle-man stuff—it was all "a lot of bull," said Williams. He insisted his great achievements were simply the sum of what he had put into the game. "Nothing except practice, practice, practice will bring out that ability," he explained. "The reason I saw things was that I was so intense ... It was [super] discipline, not super eyesight." (loc. 76-79)
>
> But someone forgot to tell Ted Williams that talent will out. As a boy, he wasn't interested in watching his natural abilities unfurl passively like a flower in the sunshine. He simply wanted—needed—to be the best hitter baseball had ever seen, and he pursued that goal with appropriate ferocity. "His whole life was hitting the ball," recalled a boyhood friend. "He always had that bat in his hand ... And when he made up his mind to do something, he was going to do it or know the reason why." At San Diego's old North Park field, two blocks from his modest childhood home, friends recall Williams hitting baseballs every waking hour of every day, year after year after year. They describe him slugging balls until their outer shells literally wore off, swinging even splintered bats for hours upon hours with blisters on his fingers and blood dripping down his wrists. A working-class kid with no extra pocket change, he used his own lunch money to hire schoolmates to shag balls so that he could keep swinging. From age six or seven, he would swing the bat at North Park field all day and night, swing until the city turned off the lights; then he'd walk home and swing a roll of newspaper in front of a mirror until he fell asleep. The next day, he'd do it all over again. Friends say he attended school only to play on the team. When baseball season ended and the other kids moved on to basketball and football, Williams stuck with baseball. When other boys started dating girls, Williams just kept hitting balls in North Park field. In order to strengthen his sight, he would walk down the street with one eye covered, and then the other. He even avoided movie theaters because he'd heard it was bad for the eyes. "I wasn't going to let anything stop me from being the hitter I hoped to be," Williams later recalled. "Looking back ... it was pretty near storybook devotion." In other words, he worked for it, fiercely, single-mindedly, far beyond the norm. "He had one thought in mind and he always followed it," said his high school coach Wos Caldwell. Greatness was not a thing to Ted Williams; it was a process. This didn't stop after he got drafted into professional baseball. In Williams's first season with the minor league San Diego Padres, coach Frank Shellenback noticed that his new recruit was always the first to show up for practice in the morning and the last to leave at night. And something more curious: after

each game, Williams would ask the coach for the used game balls. "What do you do with all these base-balls?" Shellenback finally asked Williams one day. "Sell them to kids in the neighborhood?" "No sir," replied Williams. "I use them for a little extra hitting practice after supper." (loc. 86-109)

Knowing the rigors of a full practice day, Shellenback found the answer hard to swallow. Out of a mix of suspicion and curiosity, he later recalled, "I piled into my car after supper [one night] and rode around to Williams's neighborhood. There was a playground near his home, and sure enough, I saw The Kid him-self driving those two battered baseballs all over the field. Ted was standing close to a rock which served as [home] plate. One kid was pitching to him. A half dozen others were shagging his drives. The stitching was already falling apart on the baseballs I had [just] given him." (loc. 110-114)

In 1941, his third season with the Boston Red Sox, he became the only major league player in his era—and the last in the twentieth century—to bat over .400 for a full season. (loc. 124-126)

Shenk (2010) also helps clarify the origin of Mozart's genius at composing:

"People make a great mistake who think that my art has come easily to me," Mozart himself once wrote to his father, as if to make this precise point. "Nobody has devoted so much time and thought to composition as I." (loc. 940-941)

Over about ten years, Mozart voraciously incorporated different styles and motifs and developed his own voice. Critics consider his Symphony no. 29, written ten years after his first symphony, to be his first work of real stature. His first great piano concerto is widely considered to be the no. 9, "Jeunehomme," written at age twenty-one. It was his 271st completed composition. "Idomeneo," his first operatic master-piece, written three years later, was his thirteenth opera. The most notable thing about his teenage years is not the quality of his work, but his breathtaking output. Given that, the quality seemed to—in due course—take care of itself. Looking at Mozart's works chronologically, there is a clear trajectory of increas-ing originality and importance leading up to his final three symphonies, written at age thirty-two, which are generally considered his greatest. (loc. 946-952)

In John Irving's *A Prayer for Owen Meany* (1989), Owen's best friend and the book's narrator, John Wheelright, converses about a basketball maneuver that entails the dwarfish Meany (whose freakish voice is suggested by writing in ALL CAPS) jumping to the waiting arms of Wheelright and then "dunking" the ball through the hoop (they call it "the Shot"). Their goal was to practice repeatedly until they beat their own previous time of execution.

He had sunk the shot in under four seconds!
"YOU SEE WHAT A LITTLE FAITH CAN DO?" said Owen Meany.
The brain-damaged janitor was applauding. "SET THE CLOCK TO *THREE* SECONDS!" Owen told him.
"Jesus Christ!" I said.
"IF WE CAN DO IT IN UNDER FOUR SECONDS, WE CAN DO IT IN UNDER THREE," he said. "IT JUST TAKES A LITTLE MORE FAITH."
"It takes more *practice*," I told him irritably.
"FAITH TAKES PRACTICE," said Owen Meany. (p. 304)

There we have it: faith and practice, or set your goal, believe in your capacity to achieve it, and work as though no one else will be helping you. Or as Bear Bryant is quoted: "If it is to be, it is up to me."

The Owner's Manual for Happiness

Napoleon Hill (2005) tells the story of Edwin Barnes. Wanting passionately to work with Thomas Edison, he forked over his last money for a train ticket to East Orange. Hill reports the great inventor's reaction:

> He stood there before me, looking like an ordinary tramp, but there was something in the expression of his face which conveyed the impression that he was determined to get what he had come after. I had learned, from years of experience with men, that when a man really *desires* a thing so deeply that he is willing to stake his entire future on a single turn of the wheel in order to get it, he is sure to win. I gave him the opportunity he asked for, because I saw he had made up his mind to stand by until he succeeded. Subsequent events proved that no mistake was made. (p. 2)

Composing Your Next Chapter

Review your highlights and notes from this chapter on goals and list below the areas of importance to you in which you would like to accomplish more, and then indicate specific goals with deadlines.

_____

_____

_____

_____

_____

_____

_____

_____

_____

_____

STATEMENT OF PERSONAL PRIORITIES

FLOW | FIT | GOALS | COMMUNITY | ALTRUISM

Happiness Boosters
(Choice)

Happiness Downers
(Choice)

119 Minor Adjustors

(more within personal control)

(more outside personal control)

HAPPINESS SET POINT

Happiness Boosters
(Circumstance)

Happiness Downers
(Circumstance)

Continuum of Trait Happiness

Perennially Happy (N- E+) .... Occasionally Happy (N + E-)

Community

8

Staying Connected to Your Lifeline

> "Look to the companion before the road."
>
> --Arab proverb

Guide to this chapter:
- Community, Relationships, and Social Capital
- One-on-One Relationships—Building Intimacy
- Small Group Relationships—Building Support
- Large Group Relationships—Building Community

Community has its roots in the Latin *communis*, meaning public, or shared by all (or at least most!). The opposite of community is the individual. The last three chapters have focused on the individual—flow, fit, and goals. Now we turn more outward to those around us. In this chapter, we cover the value of relationships and how to maximize that value, while in the next chapter we cover the value of altruism and how to get the most out of our altruistic activity.

Contemporary Muslim scholar Abdal-Hakim Hurad has expanded on the Arab proverb at the head of this chapter: "The companions before the road, the road before the destination." We might paraphrase this in the spirit of this book by saying: "Establish your primary relationship, your companion for life, before you make your career path final, and once you have both firmly in place, then commit to your major long-term goal. One's long-term goal, then, should be compatible with one's primary relationship and career path. In fact, one's mate and one's career working in synchrony with you as a unique human being provide the most positive basis for deriving major goals. For me, the spirit of Sheikh Hurad's saying does not dictate a sequence, but rather the need for synchrony among the three elements of career, mate, and goal. To the degree that the three work together, one should experience maximum possible psychological benefit.

Eric Weiner (2008) in *The Geography of Bliss* writes about the small country of Bhutan, where officials track gross national happiness (GNH) rather than gross national product (GNP). He quotes the philosopher of Bhutan's culture, Karma Ura, as asserting that "Happiness is relationships." (p. 92) Have satisfying relationships, according to this philosopher, and the rest falls into place. Weiner continues with "the phrase 'personal happiness' makes no sense to them or, as Karma Ura told me, 'We don't believe in this Robinson Crusoe happiness. All happiness is relational…. There is no such thing as personal happiness. Happiness is one hundred percent relational.'" (p. 75) Weiner concludes that, according to the Bhutanese, "happiness is not a noun or verb. It's a conjunction. Connective tissue."

Community, Relationships, and Social Capital

The sense of community is about the quantity and quality of relationships that we maintain, whether through work, family, neighborhood, or a multiplicity of social organizations and other outlets. Harvard University political scientist Robert Putnam (as well as other writers) refers to this as "social capital," which he contrasts to personal capital (education and so forth) and material capital (money and possessions). In his *Bowling Alone: The Collapse and Revival of American Community,* Putnam (2000) describes an average 30% decline in "social capital" over the last half of the 20th century. This is the same as an increase in social isolation. This decreased social capital was accompanied by increases in suicide rates, reports of depression, decreased immune function, and general malaise, particularly among the younger cohorts. For example, teenagers in the 1990s report fewer (in comparison to earlier, midcentury teenagers) friends, weaker friendships, and more frequently changing friendships, along with spending an average of 3½ hours alone each day. (p. 264)

The primary causes of increasing social isolation are:

- Generational Change. Accounts for about 50%--attributed mostly to growing up after two world wars where social solidarity was rampant, and being exposed to a succession of socially unstable eras—Vietnam, women's rights, integration, and so forth--leading to decreased faith in government and institutions and rampant individualism.
- Change in Work Patterns. Accounts for about 10%--especially two worker families.
- Sprawl. Accounts for about 10%--primarily urbanization and resulting long commutes.
- Technology. Accounts for about 25%--especially television, which the average American and Brit watches 3 ½ hrs. daily.
- (Leaving a small portion around 5% unexplained at the time of writing.) (pp. 283-285)

Putnam writes (p. 289):

Social capital also operates through psychological and biological processes to improve individuals' lives. Mounting evidence suggests that people whose lives are rich in social capital cope better with traumas and fight illness more effectively. Social capital appears to be a complement, if not a substitute, for Prozac, sleeping pills, antacids, vitamin C, and other drugs we buy at the corner pharmacy. 'Call me [or indeed almost anyone] in the morning' might actually be better medical advice than 'Take two aspirins' as a cure for what ails us.

Social capital is equal to the number and diversity of healthy relationships maintained by an individual. It is measured by:

- number of civic or social organizations, per 1,000 population, the person joins;
- attendance at civic, religious, nonprofit, school (e.g., PTA), political, fraternal, athletic/sports; professional, and other kinds of clubs;
- taking positions of responsibility in such clubs (holding office, serving on committees);
- voting in local through national elections;

- speaking out by writing letters to editors/political representatives, giving speeches, and so forth;
- level of trust (measured by survey answers such as "I believe that most people can be trusted");
- volunteer work (e.g., Habitat for Humanity, disaster assistance);
- informal socializing (visiting with friends, entertaining, going to restaurants with others);
- being married.

The research documenting the value of high social capital is dramatic, such as the work of James House, which Putnam cites. According to House and his research team, social capital impacts health positively to the same degree that cigarettes, obesity, high blood pressure, and the couch potato syndrome impact health negatively. Shawn Achor (2010, p. 177) reports that social isolation can raise an adult's blood pressure by 30 points. Putnam writes (p. 327):

Finally, and most intriguingly, social capital might actually serve as a physiological triggering mechanism, stimulating people's immune systems to fight disease and buffer stress. Research now under way suggests that social isolation has measurable biochemical effects on the body. Animals who have been isolated develop more extensive atherosclerosis (hardening of the arteries) than less isolated animals, and among both animals and humans loneliness appears to decrease the immune response and increase blood pressure. Lisa Berkman, one of the leading researchers in the field, has speculated that social isolation is 'a chronically stressful condition to which the organism respond[s] by aging faster.' ... Over the last twenty years, more than a dozen large studies ... in the United States, Scandinavia, and Japan have shown that people who are socially disconnected are between two and five times more likely to die from all causes, compared with matched individuals who have close ties with family, friends, and the community.

Some other provocative conclusions from Putnam's work, in his words:

- [If one participated in social-capital activities,] moving from a state with a wealth of social capital to a state with very little social capital ... increased one's chances of poor to middling health by roughly 40-70 percent.... [T]he researchers concluded that if one wanted to improve one's health, moving to a high-social-capital state would do almost as much good as quitting smoking. (p. 328)
- As a rough rule of thumb, if you belong to no groups but decide to join one, you cut your risk of dying in half during the next year. If you smoke and belong to no groups, it's a toss-up statistically whether you should stop smoking or start joining [but don't join a group that encourages smoking more; better yet, join a group that discourages smoking]. These findings are in some ways heartening: It's easier to join a group than to lose weight, exercise regularly, or quit smoking. (p. 331)
- In round numbers, getting married is the 'happiness equivalent' of quadrupling your annual income.... Civic connections rival marriage and affluence as predictors of life happiness. (p. 333)
- Virtually no cohort in America is more engaged or more tolerant than those born around 1940-45. They are the liberal communitarians par excellence. Their parents were as engaged, but less tolerant. Their children are as tolerant, but less engaged. For some reason, that cohort inherited most of their parents' sense of community, but they discarded their parents' intolerance. (p. 357) Perhaps the sense of community engendered among those who grow up during World War II might be attributed to the deep national sense of community associated with rallying together to win the war against Nazism.
- For North Carolina [ranked 41 on SAT scores] to see educational outcomes similar to Connecticut's [ranked 9], according to our statistical analysis, residents of the Tar Heel State could do any of the following: increase their turnout in presidential elections by 50%; double their frequency of club meeting

attendance; triple the number of nonprofit organizations per thousand inhabitants; or attend church two more times per month. These may seem like daunting challenges...[but it would be even harder] for North Carolina to match Connecticut's performance simply through traditional educational reforms—by decreasing class size, for example. (p. 301)

Putnam's summation includes a 1914 quote from Walter Lippman: "We have changed our environment more quickly than we know how to change ourselves." (p. 379) Our society has changed over the last 50 years, but our institutions have not. The old organizations such as labor unions, Boy/Girl Scouts, the NAACP, and Hadassah, do not speak to youth of the new social order. We need new organizations that also attract Latinos and Asians; multiracial organizations (like a local, ethnically-based congress); multifocused, interrelated community centers (school, recreation department, health department, daycare [adult and child], social services branches, police, and so forth). In fact, a rising school of architecture and city planning called the New Urbanism is at work trying to make these kinds of things happen. We must make workplaces more family friendly.

Now that we have established the profound contribution of social capital—of relationships, of community—to well-being, we will take a look at three different contexts for relationship building: one-on-one (as in marriage, friendships, relationship with a work associate, partnerships), small groups (as in families, work teams, boards, sports teams), and large groups (as in organizations, neighborhoods, towns, regions, countries, professional associations). It is not enough to simply add more relationships to our plate: we must also understand and incorporate the ingredients that contribute to the positive quality of these relationships. First, we look at dyads, or one individual relating to another individual.

One-on-One Relationships—Building Intimacy

The primary goal in anyone's life is to build at least one high-quality relationship. This entails four phases:

1. Start right.
2. Establish a positive consistency.
3. Achieve trust.
4. Experience intimacy.

> "If every individual in the world would commit to one high-quality relationship, we would be guaranteed world peace."
> --Attributed to Dag Hammarskjold.

The first two phases involve effort, while the last two phases are the reward for doing the first two well.

1. Start right.

"Starting right" means selecting someone you like for a friend. It is that simple. No matter how many relationship-building gimmicks you employ (marriage enrichment weekends, dating rituals, sending flowers or cards, giving gifts, going on a safari together), if you don't like each other, you're doomed to a mediocre relationship at best, or an unmitigated disaster at worst. A marriage counselor once told a couple, "I'm here to help you folks learn to communicate better. But, you are already excellent communicators! However, you just don't like each other. I can't help you!" On another occasion, I hired a consultant to do some team building for my department at work. His first question was, "Do you like each other? For, if you don't, you are wasting your money on me."

To the extent that there is a science of what makes people "click," the Brafman brothers, Ori and Rom, have codified that science in their 2010 book *Click: The Magic of Instant Connections.* According to these California brothers, two people click when a magical moment finds them sensing an intensely intimate connection with one another. It may be romantic or not. It is likely to be lifelong. Physically it is defined by heightened dopaminergic activity and an accompanying heightened arousal and alertness. The Brafmans identify five conditions that are associated with permitting two people to click. They serve as gatekeepers as it were, or, what they call "accelerators" (perhaps accelerants would be better). The five are vulnerability, proximity, resonance, similarity, and a strong shared experience.

Vulnerability. A strong façade that shows no weakness is off-putting. Clicking is minimized for those of us who come across as know-it-alls who never hurt or otherwise come up short. Perhaps showing vulnerability triggers the other person's desire or need to nurture, protect, aid, or otherwise complete us in some way. I can help you. We can be good for each other. As opposed to "You're so strong you don't need me or anyone else for that matter." People who click share emotionally sensitive concerns, and sharing such weakness builds strength in the connection. Showing vulnerability is a prerequisite for trust, and trust is essential for clicking. This does not mean that strong people can't click, only that strong people need, on occasion, to show some vulnerability, some humanity, in order for another person to be let into their emotional door. I'm reminded of Machiavelli writing about the ideal leader in *The Prince* where he wrote that leaders who are *always* brave are hated, not admired. We must know when to open our floodgate.

Proximity. The Brafmans identify this factor as the most critical influence on clicking. Sensory cues are important, especially touching, smell (both conscious and unconscious, as in pheromones), and sight. The ensemble must be pleasing and, according to older lines of research, whether or not the sensory cues are pleasing is largely dependent on strong emotional associations we develop in our childhood. Given compelling sensory cues, the two must be physically close: down the hall from one another, not geographically dispersed. (However, increasingly easy Internet and other electronic communication already has increased "physical" proximity, collaboration, and even romantic entanglements between people thousands of miles apart.) The Brafmans report that scientists are 25 times more likely to collaborate with colleagues housed on a common floor than with colleagues on a different floor of the same building. Proximity is essential for spontaneous communication, as in bouncing ideas off of each other. Even a simple, "Have you got five minutes?" helps solve problems.

Resonance. One may resonate with another (or with a group for that matter) when two conditions are present: flow (see Chapter 5) and "presence" (or, as Baba Ram Dass would say, "Be here now"). I can resonate with someone when 1) we perceive each other as capable and sufficiently challenged by each other's presence, and 2) paying undivided attention to each other, as evidenced by attentive listening, knowledge/memory of the other's interests (How're the kids?), needs (How's your childcare problem working out?), hurts (How's your back doing?), and so forth. I remember a client with whom I clicked some 30 years ago—Ernie Morrissey. I never once felt rushed or unimportant in his presence. He paid me undivided attention, and I returned it, asking after his favorite hobbies (his aviary and his square-dancing group). Being truly present with another person is a function of one's mirror neurons, deficiencies in which will affect the ability to click. Also, when a friend is terribly superior or inferior to you in some important way, the gap in performance can kill the relationship. If one of you consistently beats the other at tennis, for example, perhaps you'd best suspend that aspect of your relationship. Unless, of course, you can find a way to handicap one or the other of you.

Similarity. Whether we allow ourselves to click with another person is a function of the degree to which we see each other as similar: both admire Mozart, check; both like pizza, check; both like National Public Radio, check; both like spy novels, check…. All it takes is a few significant dissimilarities, regardless of what they are, to put the thaw in the clicking process: they don't like garlic (what's wrong with them), they don't like chamber music (not my kind of person), they love rock and roll (I think I need to change the station)…. I recall vividly when our daughter met our first exchange student: One adored Prince (the musician/entertainer) and the other rejected him. That's all it took. They never clicked. Points of similarity form the basis of a common bond, without which clicking is unlikely.

A common, intense experience. This is not just being in the same physical space—that would be proximity. This is being in the same circumstance. Persons who share a special experience—especially difficult experiences—form strong bonds. And the more difficult the experience, the stronger the bond. The space occupied during the experience forms a kind of frame in which the other four accelerators may operate. I can think of persons with whom I click, with whom I feel a special bond, and the shared adverse experiences come freshly to mind. With one, it was another singer who went through unsuccessful and painful vocal cord surgery at the same time I did and with the same inept doctor. Or with one fellow, we escaped nightly for eight weeks from our barracks during basic training and read while sitting in the nearby chapel listening quietly to classical music on the local NPR station in Columbia, SC. With another, it was sharing resources during an extended neighborhood power outage due to a major hurricane. With another, it was getting lost together on a system of Appalachian mountain trails. With another, it was going through marital divorce at the same time. With yet another, it was starting a business together. I suspect that US Airways Flight 1549 (the "miracle on the Hudson" landing on the Hudson River) produced much clicking, as have wars, famines, natural disasters, and financial or business reverses.

Why bother about whether we click with others? The Brafmans conclude that the primary benefit of clicking is that our personal performance level increases when we are in the presence of one or more with whom we click. We outdo our personal bests when we are with our clicks. With how many of your friends do you truly click? What can you do, by way of manipulating one or more of the Brafmans' five accelerators, to nurture relationships with those who click with you? Maybe it is something as simple as Skyping (calling, plus face time) rather than a traditional phone call. Or taking on a long-term project together.

Clicking is related to flow. Perhaps we could say that clicking is for relationships what flow is for tasks. Flow requires that we be neither frustrated nor bored. In the case of a relationship, that means that when we are with that other person, we feel neither bored nor frustrated, but engaged and in the moment. Apparently, when we first meet someone, we tend to make an instant judgment as to the likelihood that we will experience flow with another person. Princeton psychologist Susan Fiske (Fiske, Cuddy, & Glick, 2007) finds that, across cultures, we look for two things as we size up each other: warmth and competence. Our mind tends to be made up within a matter of seconds. From an evolutionary point of view, this relates to judging newcomers as friend or foe: warm and capable is an effective ally, warm and weak is a mere cheerleader, cool and capable is a potential enemy, and cool and weak is neutral. But from a relational perspective, what we look for in this first moment is how well we match up on these two dimensions. If I sense that the other is warmer than I, I may feel somewhat crowded. If I sense that the other is more competent at a mutual skill, I may feel somewhat uneasy with my inferiority. Conversely, I may sense potential boredom if I feel superior, potential disappointment if I feel warmer. For the long term, similarity in traits, interests, abilities, values, and physical characteristics is optimal for satisfaction in relationships.

2. Establishing a positive consistency.

"Establishing a positive consistency" is how you maintain a relationship over time. To click with someone from the beginning of a relationship is wonderful, but just as a new car is also wonderful, both need maintenance. Robert Frost was writing darkly about the short life of beautiful things when he penned "Nothing Gold Can Stay." But relationships are not doomed to misery. The flippant riddle—"How are marriage and a tub bath similar? After a while, neither is very hot."—is unthinkingly cynical. We can with effort maintain our relationships so that infatuation and romance lead to deep, sustaining love and companionship. We can with effort maintain friendships so that the initial feeling of "clicking" leads to lifelong mutual anticipation of being in each other's presence. For some of us, it takes more effort than others. But what kind of effort?

Confucius recognized the nature of this effort some 2,500 years ago when he taught the importance of kindness and respect in relationships. Dacher Keltner (2009) has translated Confucius' concept of *jen* into a modern construct that he calls the "jen ratio," or the balance between kind and unkind actions. Others (Fredrickson, 2009; Fredrickson & Losada, 2005; Losada & Heaphy, 2004; Waugh & Fredrickson, 2006) refer to this as the Losada ratio. Their research has found that one-on-one relationships, groups, and organizations that exhibit optimum jen/Losada ratios tend to flourish, while those exhibiting suboptimal ratios tend to languish. At a minimum, all agree that the ratio should be positive, i.e., more positive emotional events (PEEs) than negative emotional events (NEEs) in any given situation. The rule of thumb for an optimal ratio is that PEEs should outnumber NEEs in a ratio of no less than 3:1 and no more than 12:1. When the ratio over time is less than 3:1, the relationship cannot withstand the amount of negativity.

> "We cannot tell the precise moment when friendship is formed. As in filling a vessel drop by drop, there is at last a drop which makes it run over; so in a series of kindnesses there is at last one which makes the heart run over."
> --James Boswell, *The Life of Samuel Johnson, LL.D.* (1791), entry for September 19, 1777.

When the ratio over time is greater than 12:1, the relationship is not dealing adequately with unpleasantries. Said another way, very high ratios indicate a kind of Pollyannaish attitude, a pattern of denial and refusal to acknowledge and deal with unpleasant matters.

In one sense, what these folks are saying is that negative emotional events tend to kill or negate the benefits of positive emotional events. A harsh word negates a pat on the back. A harsh word negates *several* pats on the back. We have to offset negativity with positivity. With respect to marriage, the researchers suggest that a ratio of less than 3:1 (equivalent to three pats on the back and one harsh word) will, over time, result in divorce. A common rule of thumb is to aim for a 5:1 ratio of PEEs to NEEs. The equivalent of five pats for every pinch, five smiles for every sneer.

The researchers say that, while negativity may be called for in some situations, over time it is debilitating. Frederickson (in Seligman, 2011) once commented that "a negative Losada ratio might make an effective lawyer...but it may have a huge personal cost. Law is the profession with the highest depression, suicide, and divorce rates. If your colleagues take that office ratio home, they are in trouble." If we must be negative, so be it. But that does not mean that we have to be negative *all* of the time! We can segment our negativity, just as we can segment our perfectionism or our sociability. We can't always be perfectionist or always be sociable. Sometimes we have to be more casual about standards. Sometimes we have to shut the door and be solitary. As we have indicated earlier, to become rigid in any one behavior is to invite mental illness.

With respect to minding our PEEs and NEEs, consider the most extensive research ever conducted on what people most desire in a life partner. David Buss (reported in Keltner, 2009) studied 10,000 individuals in their early 20s in 37 different countries, asking them what was important in considering a mate. The highest priority for both sexes in all countries was kindness. As a way of implementing Buss's finding, let me suggest a healthy habit to develop: ACORNs! Plant acorns to grow trees. Plant ACORNs to grow relationships. I am referring to a way of responding to others that Shelly Gable (described in Seligman, 2011) calls "active and constructive responding." Get it? I created the term "ACORNS" from "**A**ctive and **CO**nst**R**uctive respo**N**ding." ACORNS. Gable created a two-dimensional model that describes how we most typically respond to others. I have summarized it in Table 8.0. In each of the four examples, you see a response to a situation in which one's partner has just informed the other that they have received a raise at work. Gable maintains that the kind of response that is associated with

Table 8.0   **Shelly Gable's Model of Interpersonal Responses**

	Active	Passive
Constructive	Active responding involves engaging in a conversation that typically results in elaborating on what one's partner has just said, as in finding out more information. It amounts to being supportive, being curious, and wanting to know more. Being constructive means that you are encouraging, approving, offering to help. Example: "You got your raise! That's great! Tell me all about it! Where were you when you found out? How did they communicate it to you? What were you thinking and feeling when you found out? Let's celebrate!" Positive emotion and nonverbal response (constructive) coupled with showing interest (active).	Passive responding offers no elaboration, no curiosity. It is a simple acknowledgment. Example: "You got your raise! That's great! Woohoo!" Positive emotion and nonverbal without showing much interest.
Destructive	Destructive responding finds a way to be critical, to rain on the other's parade, to burst their bubble. And active destructive responding won't let it go, keeps finding fault. Example: "You got your raise? Well, it is about time. If you were better at what you did, you would have gotten it a long time ago. And, if you would only have played nice to your boss more, you would probably have gotten more of a raise. Moreover, you're probably going to go spend it all on yourself, and the rest of us won't get any benefit from it." And so on and on. Negative emotions and nonverbals accompanied by a tirade.	Passive destructive either ignores what has been said and, for example, changes the subject, as in "What's for dinner?", or it offers a brief deflation, such as "Well, hell will freeze over before you ever get another raise." Negative emotion and nonverbals.

strong relationships is the "active constructive response" that I have dubbed "ACORNs" and have described in the upper left quadrant in Table 8.0. As a way of practicing the ACORN approach, while watching one of your television programs (or some other suitable human drama!), latch onto a response and evaluate which of the four quadrants it belongs. If it is not an ACORN, try rewording to become an ACORN. This could become a family exercise. Clearly not every response is or should be an ACORN—they take a bit more time and thought, and we simply couldn't get through the day. But in the spirit of maintaining a healthy PEE to NEE ratio, one good ACORN should count for several PEEs, not just one. Gable's makes the point that the quality of celebration in a relationship is more important than the quality of fighting. The ACORN (my way of describing it!) approach is designed to celebrate one's partner's victories.

Keep in mind that I am describing a four-phase process of relationship building: starting right, maintaining with kindness and the PEE:NEE ratio, establishing trust, and experiencing intimacy. We have been focusing on the ratio of positive emotional events (especially kindness) to negative emotional events. The two techniques we have mentioned for achieving optimal PEE:NEE have been simply counting these events over time and monitoring your ratio, and the ACORN technique for celebrating good outcomes for each partner. Let's take a look at several other ways of achieving optimal PEE:NEE.

First, let's consider the role of rituals in relationships. Rituals—a call home to say you've safely arrived somewhere, grace before meals, a kiss upon parting, cards sent on event days—are habits that perhaps at first were effortful and spontaneous, requiring some thought and energy, that over time become automatic, perhaps even thoughtless. However, the meaning behind the ritual remains, and partners expect the ritual as a way of renewing the meaning, as a way of saying "I care" or "I'm thinking of you" or "Don't worry" or some such. Eduard Punset (2007) writes about the havoc entailed by failure to observe appropriate rituals. In fact, observation of ritual is deeply engrained in our evolutionary heritage. Temple Grandin (& Catherine Johnson, 2005) in *Animals in Transition* tells the story of poultry producers who had bred roosters to be large and get quickly to the act of copulation with hens. However, it turned out that the roosters were mauling the hens. Why? The genetic manipulation was accompanied by the roosters' failure to perform the accustomed ritual dance preceding mating, and the hens were programmed to receive only after the ritual. In the absence of the proper "foreplay," the hens fought rather than received, with disastrous results. Message: Don't skip the rituals in your relationships!

Another way of keeping the PEEs in charge of the relationship is to observe the need for balance between what Easterners call yin-yang, or what in the West we refer to as Agency and Communion. In brief, agency is what we do to complete *tasks* (building something, winning something, selling something, creating something, fixing something, and so forth), while communion is what we do to nurture our relationships (listening, touching, spending time with, helping, celebrating with, and so forth). Conventional wisdom suggests that these two be in balance. The most familiar example of these two being out of balance is spending excessive time "at the office." One way to strive for balance is to do some tasks together. A crossword puzzle done alone is "agency," while a crossword puzzle done together is "communion." A meal cooked by one person is agency, while a meal cooked by two is communion. Unless, of course, you bicker with each other while working together!

Let's look for a moment specifically at marriage. Sonja Lyubomirsky (2008) writes that John Gottman's book (with Nan Silver, 1999) *The Seven Principles for Making Marriage Work* is "the best marital advice manual on the market by far." (p. 141). Gottman's guidelines on what to emphasize and what to avoid in marriage is based on his having studied some 650 married couples in his Seattle Love Lab. Over several days together in the lab, the couples were videotaped (except in the bathroom and after a certain hour in the evening). The most significant overall finding from observing these interactions was what he calls "repair attempts." Gottman refers to them as the secret weapon of successful marriages/relationships. It is not the total amount of conflict in and of itself that hurts a marriage, but whether or not the couple attempts to repair the effects of things having gone sour.

In the spirit of PEEs and NEEs, Gottman identified nine negative interactions that predict divorce and seven principles that signal strong relationships. The nine harbingers of bad times are these:

- *Harsh startups*: "You're a no-good, sorry-ass so-and-so who doesn't care about me," versus "I'm ticked off/hurt/etc. at being left out of the loop."
- *Criticism* (versus complaint): "You're trying to undermine me" vs. "My feelings got hurt."
- *Contempt*: Sarcasm/cynicism is the most toxic, as it communicates disgust.
- *Defensiveness*: Doesn't work, is actually a veiled form of blaming. "I was only trying to help" means "You didn't know what you were doing and I was trying to CYA."
- *Stonewalling*: Shutting down; giving the cold shoulder; hiding; taking flight.
- *Flooding*: When dialog becomes one-way/lecture/berating/unrelenting; often known as getting on one's high horse.
- *Body language*: Increased heart rate, sweating, cringing, gesticulating, pointing, waving, slapping hands; in general, tense versus relaxed, fidgeting vs. still, immediate vs. remote.
- *Failed repair attempts.* This includes giving up too quickly on trying to repair a bad moment.
- *Bad memories.* Bad memories obviously are NEEs. However, one may loosen their grip by trying to recreate the experience as a good one. Unseat the bad memory with a good version. "Let's try that over again!"

The seven principles of behavior that point towards strong relationships are these:

- *Love maps.* Knowing the landmarks of each other's hot buttons, both for PEEs and NEEs. Knowing one's partner's turn-ons and turn-offs and observing them as you navigate the relationship—emphasizing the turn-ons (cards, touches, taking out the garbage) and avoiding the turn-offs (hold the farts until in another room, don't talk about the other's weight in front of others).
- *Expressed care*, respect, admiration
- *Turn towards*, not away. He says "Look at that!" and she "turns toward" by saying "Wow" rather than turning away by saying just "Uh-huh."
- *Let the other have a say*, influence you. You don't always have to have your way or always have to be right. My mother's favorite toast at wedding receptions was a takeoff on an Ogden Nash quote: "When you're wrong, admit it; when you're right, fergit it!"
- *Solve problems* that are solvable. Don't let them smolder and cast a dark cloud—guaranteed daily doses of NEEs.
- *Accept unsolvable problems.* Failure to accept unsolvable problems is a form of gridlock. We must learn to accept and forget about the unsolvable problems and avoid continually bringing them up to beat the proverbial dead horse.

- *Create shared meaning.* Shared meaning originates in shared experiences. One of Jane's and my favorite ways of sharing meaning out of separate experiences is when each of us reads a novel independent of the other. So, if I read a novel first, then when she begins reading it, I continually ask her, "Whas hapnin?" This little game is amusing and serves to create shared meaning out of two otherwise separate experiences. Another way to create shared meaning is to review special moments after some time has passed, as in "Remember the time when we…" and then linger on the memory by asking each other open-ended questions about the experience, thus making it continue to live. This notion of shared experiences is very much what Joseph Campbell (1991) was referring to in this interview with Bill Moyers:

> Campbell: "I would say that if the marriage isn't a first priority in your life, you're not married. The marriage means the two that are one, the two become one flesh. If the marriage lasts long enough, and if you are acquiescing constantly to it instead of to individual personal whim, you come to realize that that is true—the two really are one."
>
> Moyers: "So marriage is utterly incompatible with the idea of doing one's own thing."
>
> Campbell: "It's not simply one's own thing, you see. It is, in a sense, doing one's own thing, but the one isn't just you, it's the two together as one." (pp. 6-7)

All of these suggestions should get us well on our way to proper maintenance of something that began well. Use as your guideline the ratio of five positive emotional events (a touch, a smile, a laugh, a joke, a word of praise) for every one negative emotional event (an impatient comment).

There is one caveat in all of this, and that is the matter of sincerity. Two studies caution us against unauthentic behavior. Lemay, McFerran, & Laven (2011) were interested in the effect of "counterfeiting," or expressing only positive emotions and suppressing negative emotions. They were particularly interested in the effect of counterfeiting on chronically insecure partners. In other words, does holding back negative feelings enhance an insecure person's satisfaction in a relationship? They concluded that counterfeiting does not work, that both secure and insecure partners experience a decrease in satisfaction when counterfeiting occurs over time. If Partner A suspects Partner B of having unexpressed, negative emotions then Partner A becomes suspicious, distrusting, and increasingly more fragile, rather than increasingly less fragile, as was Partner B's usual intent. Said another way, the researchers found that suppressing negative feelings doesn't protect one's partner. In a similar investigation, Mauss et al. (2011) were interested in the effect of positive emotional statements when accompanied by positive emotional states, as opposed to being accompanied by vacant or even negative emotional states. In other words, is the effect of an authentic positive emotional statement (e.g., saying you like something when in fact you do like it) any different in its effect from an inauthentic positive emotional statement (e.g., saying you like something when in fact you do not like it or have no opinion). They concluded that authentic statements (appropriately expressed) increase well-being and the sense of social connectedness, while inauthentic statements decrease well-being and the sense of social connectedness. So, in this sea of positive and negative emotions, while trying to maintain a positive balance, be careful:

- Do not suppress negative feelings, but get them out in as kind a manner as possible (e.g., non-accusatory) and be open to problem solving, and
- Do not express positive feelings when you don't actually feel them.

In summary, to hone your awareness and skills at the PEE:NEE ratio, practice counting positive and negative events when you are not otherwise mentally engaged. For example:

- standing in line at the post office (bank, stadium, etc.) listening to others converse,
- sitting in a pew listening to a sermon,
- listening to a talk-show host interview a guest,
- perusing a string of text messages with one particular friend,
- eavesdropping on a conversation (e.g., while on a long flight or in a waiting room),
- watching a television program or movie or play that you're having a hard time staying interested in, or
- biding your time at a party or other gathering where you are not mentally engaged.

And, of course, don't just count—look for patterns:

- Do the sermons you find more satisfying have higher, lower, or optimum (i.e., around 5:1) PEE:NEE ratios?
- Is the overall content of a conversation reflected in the PEE:NEE ratio (e.g., if the conversation's content is optimistic and friendly, is the ratio accordingly 5:1 or higher?)
- Can you tell when a talk show host varies their ratio according to their interviewee?
- Do parents in sitcoms use the same ratios with each other as with their children? With what effect?

3. Achieving trust.

"Achieving trust" is the third phase of relationship building. When we start well and maintain the relationship over time with a positive PEE:NEE ratio, at some point we begin to trust one another. Trust in a relationship is the feeling that we can rely on the other person to be kind, constructive, respectful, and accepting. Trust is established over time. We must establish a habit, a pattern of responding in a way that builds the other person up rather than tearing them down. To trust one is to feel psychologically safe with them. Trust takes time to build, and even more time to rebuild once it is broken.

4. Experiencing intimacy.

"Experiencing intimacy" is the reward for succeeding at the first three phases. These phases build upon each other: it is much easier to maintain a relationship that started well, where both partners "clicked," and it is only possible to establish trust when each partner senses a pattern in the other of positive responding. Similarly, it is only possible to experience intimacy when one trusts the other. Intimacy is opening one's innermost feelings—insecurities, doubts, fears, longings, disappointments, joys, points of pride, resentments. Sadly, many people report in surveys that they do not have a friend whom they could call in the middle of the night to discuss an urgent concern. These are people who do not have a friend with whom they experience intimacy. They do not have a "go to" person when needed.

Nicholas A. Christakis of Harvard University and James H. Fowler of the University of California, San Diego, write (2009) in *Connected: The Surprising Power of Our Social Networks and How They Shape Our Lives* that "the average American has just four close social contacts, with most having between two and six. Sadly, 12 percent of Americans listed no one with whom they could discuss important matters or spend free time. At the other extreme, 5 percent of Americans had eight such people." (p. 18)

The intimacy of which we speak is not the same as sex—that is, physical intimacy. We are talking here about emotional intimacy. No secrets—being totally known by the other. Emotional intimacy means you're never afraid that you'll be judged poorly when you share a sadness, a pride, a fear, a joy, a shame, an achievement, an anger—in short, with an intimate friend, a go-to friend, you don't have to hold anything back. You are confident that what you reveal will be accepted without judgment and responsibly dealt with as necessary. All too often such opening up to others is off-putting, with the other person listening to you being uncomfortable or even repulsed by your having opened up. In that case, you have not built a relationship based on the three previous phases. If you had gone through the first three, the likelihood is that this person would be there for you, and you for them, come hell or high water, and would bounce back for the next round that life brings on.

Before we move on to talk about groups, I need to mention some interesting recent research that assesses the capacity of social networking media (e.g., Facebook) to substitute for face-to-face relationships. Sheldon, Abad, & Hinsch (2011) concluded that Facebook and its ilk are particularly attractive to those who report feeling or being socially disconnected. The good news is that joining an online social network increases everyone's sense of connectedness, regardless of whether an individual feels more socially connected or less socially connected. On the other hand, they found that joining an online social network does not solve real-world relationship issues. So, if an individual continually engages in self-defeating behavior (such as a high NEE to PEE ratio) in the real world, being active in the virtual world will not change those behaviors. However, I suggest that online networking is the perfect place to practice ACORNs! In the real world, it is often hard to recognize opportunities to spread ACORNs— they come and go so quickly, and we regret all the missed opportunities. However, in the virtual world, i.e., on Facebook, we can scan our friends' posts in order to find something that merits a well-thought-out ACORN, e.g., perhaps one of our "friends" posts that they just won a local opera audition. Rather than just clicking on "Like!", make a well-thought-out comment such as: "Wow! I'm really proud to know you! Wish I could have been there. What did it feel like when you heard you won? Who was with you? Where's the next stage of competition?" Over time, as you practice offline and then send comments, you will find it increasingly more natural to respond to others' good news with ACORNs.

Small Group Relationships—Building Support

In committing to increase our individual social capital, keep in mind that we need to be engaged on three fronts: developing one-on-one relationships/friendships, developing memberships in small groups, and getting connected to the community, even the world, at large. In this section, we will focus on how we work with small groups. Cultivating relationships is the core skill on all three fronts. Ultimately, our associations with small groups and the community at large are both based on one-on-one relationships. Not everyone in one's bridge club will be that kind of go-to person with whom we are able to be emotionally intimate. But they might be. In a sense, our friendships comprise an A-list and a B-list. The A-List contains the go-to friends with whom we can tell all, while the B-List is friends whose company we enjoy but with whom we would not feel free to let it all hang out. The C-List is simply acquaintances, not friends. People nice to be around but whom we do not necessarily seek to spend time with. Every person we know could be located on a continuum from intimate confidante to casual acquaintance. Similarly, the groups in our lives—family, club, class, support, service, professional, hobby, arts, social— also have a general gradation: intimates, friends, and acquaintances.

University of Chicago sociologist Yang Yang (cited in Weiner, 2008) reported on interviews with around 28,000 folks from 18 to 88. He found that old people are the happiest group, 33% of them at age 88, compared to 24% in their late teens. Among the many reasons for increased happiness, Yang noted the link between happiness and high-quality individual and group relationships. The unhappiest group was baby boomers—folks who are still in the rat race and who are not making time for relationships outside of work. Yang concludes that increased happiness is mostly attributable to increased individual and group activities—increased social connectivity—with relationships that last over time and survive hardships.

Robert Putnam (2000) writes:

> Statistically speaking, the evidence for the health consequences of social connectedness is as strong today as was the evidence for the health consequences of smoking at the time of the first surgeon general's report on smoking.... People who are socially disconnected are between 2 and 5 times more likely to die from all causes, compared with matched individuals who have close ties with family, friends, and the community." (p. 327)

The ideal new group is one composed of persons whom you know, plus some who are new to you. Northwestern University sociologist Brian Uzzi found (as reported in Christakis & Fowler, 2009, p. 163) that new groups composed of people who had already known each other lacked the kind of vitality associated with an abundance of new ideas. Hence, they made little progress. However, they were fun to be in, just not particularly productive. On the other hand, groups composed of strangers were more creative but rootless and more likely to fail. The best, most stable, harmonious, productive, and creative groups are composed partly of friends and partly of strangers who bring new ideas, skills, and experiences. Don't hold out to join a group until you find one in which you know all members. So long as you have a few anchor friends, the effect of the new folks will be less uncomfortable.

I am not a "groupie," a person who loves to join groups just for the sake of joining a group. For me, groups are ways of expressing my passions. At this point in my life, I am a member of about a dozen groups:

- my immediate family of 10 (six in Charlotte, four in New York City);
- my church choir of about 50 (averages two get-togethers weekly);
- my brass sextet (averages one get-together a week);
- my work team (10 members);
- the authorship team for a new book I'm working on (five members);
- the advisory board for my business (ten members);
- the leadership team (i.e., the partners) of my business (four members);
- two local professional associations, each with about 50 members;
- the faculty at Queens University's McColl School of Business, where I teach a couple of graduate courses and do some student advising (my department has about eight members);
- several groups on Facebook and LinkedIn that are comprised of former employers, schoolmates, and family members.

In my past, many groups have come and gone. As my needs change, and as the makeup of the groups change, my participation may increase, decrease, or stop all together. I've dropped one professional group and picked up another. I've been a member of dozens of different music ensembles over the years and have now settled on only two (there may be a third in the offing!). I join these groups because I can do things with them that I can't do alone—choral singing, chamber music, discussion of ideas, keeping up with all that is new in my field, running a business, and so forth. There are many things that I do alone, without a group, that others might do with a group. However, these activities—reading, cooking, camping, crafts, dining out—are things that my wife and I enjoy doing spontaneously, alone or together. I don't need a book club to make me read, or a dinner club to cook a fancy meal, while others may very much need or enjoy having a book or dinner club to incite them to read and gourmet cook. Each of us must do alone what is satisfying alone, and search for groups to do those things that we find more satisfying when done with a group of familiar others.

One special form of group that has gained popularity in the last 50 years is the "support group." These come in both face-to-face and online meetings of persons afflicted with the same disease or disorder.. They are called support groups because, like Alcoholics Anonymous, persons attempting to deal with the same issue find both emotional and cognitive (i.e., informational) support from fellow sufferers. Just Google a personal problem area or affliction (e.g., stuttering, procrastination, Asperger's syndrome) along with the phrase "support group" and you are sure to find an ongoing support group. If not, start one!

Another kind of group is the "special interest group" or SIG. Professional associations, religious communities, schools, neighborhoods, and other large collections of loosely connected individuals (e.g., Facebook!) often encourage the formation of SIGs so that individuals interested in the same topic (a hobby, a philosophical idea, a game—such as Go, winemaking, and so forth) might get together periodically and share information, techniques, resources, tips, and even engage in an activity related to the topic. I have belonged to SIGs dealing with leadership, statistics, organization theory, and cognitive science. My favorite SIG was one housed at a local university and was comprised of faculty and community members interested in brain science. We were psychologists, biologists, linguists, philosophers, and information scientists. The English author and academic C. S. Lewis (*The Chronicles of Narnia, The Screwtape Letters*) had a SIG that met regularly at the Eagle and Child Pub in Oxford. They dubbed themselves "The Inklings" and discussed religion, literature, writing, and, well, wherever the "spirits" led them. Such SIGs may be pursued for the sheer enjoyment of the experience of meeting with like-minded others, while others may cherish them as incubators of ideas and insights that may be used productively in one's career or other pursuits.

One controversial kind of group is the cancer patient support group. In 1989, David Spiegel published in *Lancet* the results of studies that ascribed a curative value of support groups for cancer patients. However, in 2007, *Psychological Bulletin* published a review of the literature led by James Coyne. He found no evidence that experience in cancer support either cured the cancer or increased life expectancy. Certainly some patients experience comfort from being in such groups. But, as Barbara Ehrenrich (2009) writes, "Psychotherapy and support groups might improve one's mood, but they did nothing to overcome cancer." The emphasis on optimism and seeing the positive side of having cancer (makes you tougher, etc.) was like a sugar pill. It felt good, and was supposed to positively influence the body's healing, but it didn't. The primary problem with most of these groups was that they were not composed of meaningful friends, rather just of random assortments of patients with no prior history. As mentioned earlier, new groups comprised of strangers tend to founder. Spiegel later published a retraction of his earlier claims.

One last issue with small groups is that, in addition to engaging in optimal PEE:NEE behavior, small groups need certain additional behaviors to be functional. Small-group theory has identified a variety of roles that help groups accomplish their mission, as well as other roles that hinder a group. Here are some of the helpful roles, included under the first two bullets "Task" and "Maintenance," followed by several hindering roles under the third bullet:

- Task: Roles that are critical to getting the job done.
    - Information Provider: Offers information relevant to the group's task or interests,
    - Information Seeker: Draws information out of others,
    - Procedure Initiator: Suggests how the group might get unstuck, how to proceed,
    - Summarizer: Pulls together all of the main points made until that moment, and
    - Opinion Giver: States pro- or anti- how they feel about particular items.
- Maintenance: Roles that make being a part of the group more enjoyable, but that do not necessarily promote the task at hand.
    - Gatekeeper: Insures that all group members get to have their say—someone who opens the gate for those unable to open it for themselves, as in, "Let's hear what Erskine has to say on this subject,"
    - Humorist: Relieves the tension with appropriate humor,
    - Storyteller: Relates relevant experiences, but not to excess,
    - Recognizer: Praises the contributions of others as appropriate, and
    - Conflict Manager: Attempts to mediate conflicts between individuals or factions.
- Hindrances: Roles that hinder the group from realizing its purpose.
    - Blocker: Prevents the group from moving ahead, as when someone knocks down every suggestion because it violates a not-so-important criterion,
    - Dominator: Takes more than their share of air time (sometimes, if one individual has all or most of the information or experience, then it may be appropriate for them to dominate),
    - Distractor: Frequently brings up points that do not relate to the task at hand,
    - Personal Agenda Pusher: Urges consideration of personal requirements or interests that do not contribute to the group's needs or interests, and
    - Non-Participant: Withdraws from participation—might as well be absent.

Every group—whether a work team or a family council—needs more behavior in the first two categories and minimal behavior from the last one. The first two categories represent PEEs in a group context, while the third category represents NEEs in groups. I have not exhausted the possibilities for group roles—Google "group roles" and you'll find dozens more in each category. However, you get the idea. In the typical group, no one individual performs all of the task or maintenance roles—they are spread out among the group members. It is good to have a sense of which of these roles we perform most naturally, and that we take some pride in offering these roles when we find ourselves in a group. Clearly, the more of the task and maintenance roles that you can play, the more valuable you will be to a group.

The difference in small groups and large groups is that we typically experience small groups when all members (or most) are present. There is a continuity of membership from get-together to get-together. In large groups, although bound by some common purpose or interest, we seldom if ever meet with the entire membership. We will turn now to a consideration of such large groups, and how they might provide social capital.

Large Group Relationships—Building Community

Pairs, groups, and communities—these are the three contexts in which relationships play out for good or ill. In all three contexts, the PEE:NEE ratio indicates the quality of the experience. And to the degree that PEE dominates, each of the relationship contexts flourishes. Large organizations comprising thousands of individual relationships behave essentially the same as a pair of friends or marrieds. University of North Carolina at Chapel Hill psychologist Barbara Frederickson describes (in Seligman, 2011) how she measured the ratio in organizations and how the ratios related to organizational performance:

> "Here's our latest finding," Barb explained to the thirty-five students and five faculty members, all of us now on the edge of our seats. "We go into companies and transcribe every word that is said in their business meetings. We have done this in sixty companies. One-third of the companies are flourishing economically, one-third are doing okay, and one-third are failing. We code each sentence for positive or negative words, and then we take a simple ratio of positive to negative statements. "There is a sharp dividing line," Barb continued. "Companies with better than a 2.9:1 ratio for positive to negative statements are flourishing. Below that ratio, companies are not doing well economically. We call this the 'Losada ratio,' named after my Brazilian colleague Marcel Losada, who discovered this fact. "But don't go overboard with positivity. Life is a ship with sails and rudder. Above 13:1, without a negative rudder, the positive sails flap aimlessly, and you lose your credibility." (loc. 1257)

As demonstrated by Putnam, social connectedness translates to higher performance of individuals, groups, and organizations. But as Erickson has pointed out, not all connectedness is equal. To be in a toxic group—one in which negativity dominates—is to be in a less productive group, a group in which the individuals are not experiencing well-being, a group with higher employee turnover and shorter life expectancy as an organization. Wherever possible, individuals in such toxic groups self-select out of the group. I belonged at one time to a chamber music group in which one individual member was a sourpuss. Even though I enjoyed the company of the other players, I quit the group. And on the national level, I belonged to a professional organization whose executive director proved to be paranoid. I didn't remain with them. Even though Putnam (2000) does not explicitly control for positivity and negativity in social connections, the power of social connectivity to improve society must clearly be based on ongoing positive experiences within in those social connections. The more we are connected to elements of our community, the healthier our community, assuming that the quantity of social connectivity is evidence of the quality of those connections.

Putnam's measure of social capital includes membership in political, religious, educational, sports, civic, artistic—in short, all manner of organizations. Girl Scouts, Boy Scouts, Rotary Clubs, political party precincts, professional associations, community college continuing-education classes, religious education classes, bowling leagues, religious congregations, town bands, basketball leagues—to the degree that a community has greater participation in these and similar areas, the results are widespread:

- higher educational attainment (Putnam, 2000, p. 306);
- lower levels of crime (p. 308); Baumeister (2011, loc. 2524) writes about the "warehousing" effect, such that if people are attending school or other positive community organizations, then they are off the street and less likely to contribute to crime levels; similarly, if one is attending AA meetings, then they are not drinking—Baumeister suggests that being with other people may be more preventive than the 12-step method and its belief in a higher power—"They may even be the higher power." (loc. 2539);
- greater life expectancy (Putnam, 2000, p. 135);
- greater well-being (p. 326);
- fewer colds, heart attacks, strokes, cancer, depression, and premature deaths (p. 326);
- greater job satisfaction (p. 90);
- higher levels of philanthropy (p. 120; joiners give roughly 10 times more money to social causes than nonjoiners; social capital predicts philanthropy better than financial capital!);
- lower unemployment levels (p. 321; more than half of all people get their jobs through a friend or relative).

Why join large organizations? Why not remain satisfied with family and friends, and maybe a few small groups—maybe a bowling league and a bridge club. Well, just as with small groups, people join groups, large or small, in order to do things that they can't do alone. To the degree that our large groups are wisely chosen, they will in fact decrease our social isolation and increase our sense of well-being. I experience most of my small groups daily or weekly. My large groups I experience less frequently, although now with the Internet, I can experience some of them almost as frequently as my small groups. Facebook and LinkedIn have helped regional, national, and global organizations reinvent themselves. At present, I am a member of these regional, national, or global groups:

- my siblings and their descendants (around 60—we get together every other year as a full (as possible) group. However, we keep in touch—mostly by Internet—in between meetings;
- my first cousins and their descendants on my mother's side (about 50; meet every other year);
- my first cousins and their descendants on my father's side (about 100; meeting next month for the first time in 10 years);
- my state professional association (about 150 members; three meetings a year);
- my primary national professional association (about 5,000 members; one meeting a year);
- Several "virtual" organizations on Facebook and LinkedIn—we've never met face-to-face and probably never will, but we feel highly connected with one another as resources to one another;
- my business associates around the world—Singapore, Mexico, Finland, Spain, India, China, the Czech Republic, Canada, Ireland, Netherlands, Saudi Arabia, Brazil, Pakistan, Switzerland, Australia, Austria, Germany, Japan, and throughout the U.S. Skype and the Internet do in fact bring us closer together. The inexpensive, high quality VOIP (voice over Internet) technology is helping me to build a global network of colleagues;
- my clients. We have an annual "users' conference." At that meeting, our customers from all over the world join in one location to learn from each other and from my team of professionals. Although we only have that one annual get-together, they describe it as a "community." I think one thing that contributes to that community feeling is having the Internet to keep us in touch throughout the year.

Just as one-on-one relationships and small groups need maintenance over the long term in order to remain satisfying, so do large organizations and communities. In addition to the PEE:NEE ratio at the community level, there are other, perhaps not-so-obvious factors that can influence the quality of a large organization.

- Putnam (2000) makes the interesting point that people who have friends at their place of work are also happier at work (p. 90). Some organizations I have known actively discourage making friends with work associates and strongly frown on fraternizing with work associates "after hours." This policy is contrary to what we know about effective organizations. Make friends where you find them. When you click with someone, stick with them.

- Weiner (2008) points out that tropical locations tend to score lower on happiness indexes than do temperate and frigid zones. He attributes this to the "Get-Along-or-Die" Theory (p. 143), which states cooperation and interdependence are more crucial to survival in the less tropical zones. In the tropics, where food falls from trees, lack of social connectivity has not quite so dramatic an impact. This interesting contrast underscores the benefits of connectivity—one can simply accomplish more when one acknowledges their interdependence and works on the quality of their relationships. Says John Donne, "No man is an island."

- Some try to build social capital by offering money. Just as "you can't buy my love" (according to popular songs), you can't buy the social good will of the needy. For that reason, working shoulder to shoulder constructing a Habitat for Humanity home or gardening elbow to elbow with volunteers and the needy at a food pantry's homegrown vegetable project produces greater social capital than just writing a check to either cause (not to say that the checks are not nice to get—they are just not enough). Arms-length altruism creates less social capital than arms-around altruism.

- Putnam (2000, p. 21) emphasizes that trust is the sine qua non of social capital. Without trust, social capital simply cannot accumulate. Weiner points out that in the lowest-scoring countries on the happiness scale, people do not trust their government, their businesses, their neighbors. They fend for themselves. People who trust tend to be those who take the first step in building social capital. Putnam writes that "the haves are typically more trusting than the have nots in most all societies," (p. 138), and it is the haves who must take the first step in building social capital. When there is no bridge to cross the chasm, there is no hope for making it across the chasm. When bridge builders construct bridges to cross the chasm, then one learns over time to trust the bridge, to trust the bridge builder, and to restore hope to the have nots.

- When you want to get something done, give it to someone who does not have the time to do it. As Putnam (2000) points out, "People who have the heaviest time pressures are more likely to participate in community projects...." (p. 191) Why is this true? Putnam (p. 192) says that "busy people tend to forgo the one activity—TV watching—that is most lethal to community involvement." In the age of the DVR, it is easy to record our favorite television programs so that we can engage in community activities when needed. The TV programs will be there when we find time to kick back and enjoy them. I have found that, with a 40-hour time limit on my DVR, I tend to delete recordings that do not have as great an appeal as others. In effect, not having time to watch programs when they are regularly scheduled serves as a way to force higher quality programs to the surface and to send lower quality programs packing. There is not enough storage space to accommodate low quality! And, by watching the recording, I can skip portions of programs that hold little interest for me—commercials, introductions, and so forth. Some people take three hours to watch a football game on television. By skipping to the good parts, it takes me only about 15 minutes! For a REALLY good game, maybe 45 minutes!

- We tend to become more like the people in the groups we join. Associate with fatter people, we tend to stay heavier. Associate with readers, we tend to read more. Baumeister (2011) writes about this principle as it relates to smoking:

> Smoking researchers have been especially intrigued by places where very few people smoke, because the assumption was that these remaining few must be seriously addicted. Indeed, one popular theory was that more or less everybody who can easily quit smoking has already done so, leaving behind a hard core of heavily addicted smokers who could not kick the habit for love or money. But wave after wave of evidence has contradicted this theory. While some people will go on puffing all by themselves, smokers who live mainly among nonsmokers tend to have high rates of quitting, indicating again the power of social influence and social support for quitting. Studies of obesity have detected similar patterns of social influence.... (loc. 2593)

The lesson here is to select our friends and groups wisely. The familiar "Be like Mike" (or, perhaps more *au courant*, "Be like Lebron") applies to more endeavors than basketball. We tend to acquire the standards and habits of our salient peer groups. Or as child development researcher Judith Rich Harris (1998) emphasizes, we tend to minimize the differences between us and those we identify with. Peer pressure is not peers making us conform—rather, it is us putting pressure on ourselves to be more like our favorite peers.

A final comment on religious groups. In his definitive work on willpower, Roy Baumeister (2011) attempts to enumerate the factors that are most supportive of self-discipline, or willpower—the factors that minimize impulsiveness and other self-defeating behaviors. Towards the end of his book, he includes this thoughtful passage on the relative absence of impulsiveness in religious organizations:

> Michael McCullough (who isn't religiously devout himself)...looked at more than three dozen studies that had asked people about their religious devotion and then kept track of them over time. It turned out that the nonreligious people died off sooner, and that at any given point, a religiously active person was 25 percent more likely than a nonreligious person to remain alive. That's a pretty hefty difference, especially when the measure is being alive versus dead, and that result (published in 2000) has since been confirmed by other researchers. Some of those long-lived people no doubt liked to think that God was directly answering their prayers. But divine intervention was not the kind of hypothesis that appealed to social scientists, if only because it was so tough to test in the lab. They have found more earthly causes. Religious people are less likely than others to develop unhealthy habits, like getting drunk, engaging in risky sex, taking illicit drugs, and smoking cigarettes. They're more likely to wear seat belts, visit a dentist, and take vitamins. They have better social support, and their faith helps them cope psychologically with misfortunes. And they have better self-control, as McCullough and his colleague at the University of Miami, Brian Willoughby, recently concluded after analyzing hundreds of studies of religion and self-control over eight decades. Their analysis was published in 2009 in the *Psychological Bulletin*, one of the most prestigious and rigorous journals in the field. Some of the effects of religion were unsurprising: Religion promotes family values and social harmony, in part because some values gain in importance by being supposedly linked to God's will or other religious values. Less obvious benefits included the finding that religion reduces people's inner conflicts among different goals and values. As we noted earlier, conflicting goals impede self-regulation, so it appears that religion reduces such problems by providing believers with clearer priorities. More important, religion affects two central mechanisms for self-control: building willpower and improving monitoring. As early as the 1920s, researchers reported that students who spent more time in Sunday school scored higher on laboratory tests of

self-discipline. Religiously devout children were rated relatively low in impulsiveness by both parents and teachers. We don't know of any researchers who have specifically tested the self-control consequences of regular prayers or other religious practices, but these rituals presumably build willpower in the same way as the other exercises that have been studied, like forcing yourself to sit up straight or speak more precisely. (loc. 2614)

This association between religion and self-control invites the questions: Which came first, the chicken or egg, the behavior or membership in the religious organization? Are less impulsive people more likely to join religious organizations? Do more impulsive people join in hopes of acquiring more self-control? Or is impulsivity control a product of the religious experience and/or group? Regardless of the answer(s), the fact that we see so many positive behaviors associated with well-being in religious organizations certainly is an argument in favor of membership. Whether the "warehousing effect" or some other principle is in effect here, the relationship holds. However, it should be clear that what we are after is a sense of well-being, and there are many contexts in which that sense is possible.

In summary, Putnam (2000) pleads that "We Americans need to reconnect with each other. That is the simple argument of this book." (p. 28) We must examine our lives and determine whether we are more socially isolated than we should be, or whether the organizations that we engage with are as satisfying as they could be. In addition to simply joining a new group or dropping out of one group in order to find a better one, I suggest two resources for improving one's existing group:

- First, Peter Block's 2008 book, *Community: The Structure of Belonging*, is a how-to guide to community transformation: how to take your community and bring it to new life. It builds on the works of Putnam and many others.
- Second, David Cooperrider (& Whitney, 2005) developed a process he dubbed "Appreciative Inquiry." An entire industry has emerged around this simple but powerful tool. Here it is in a proverbial nutshell: If your organization is suboptimal, go with some members of your group to visit a similar but flourishing organization in a non-competing location. Through careful observation, find out the policies and practices that 1) differ from yours and 2) clearly lead to their success. Then go back to your organization and implement your findings.

Scott Peck (1987) tells the story of a medieval French monastery that had fallen from its former greatness—novitiates were not applying, crops were failing, morale was poor, the coffers were empty. In short, they were doomed to close without a change of fortune. Having heard of a wise rabbi in Paris, the monks suggested that the abbot travel to the rabbi and seek his advice. After a long walk, the abbot met the rabbi and described the dire situation. The rabbi pondered, then responded: "I do not know what to tell you in order to reverse your monastery's fortunes, but I can tell you this: One of you is the Messiah." The rabbi was both shocked and disappointed. As he walked back to the rural monastery, he was both sad at having no hopeful advice to give his brothers, and puzzled about who might be the Messiah, as suggested by the rabbi. "Is it Brother Solomon? No, I don't think so. Brother Francis? Possibly. Myself? Certainly not." And so he considered each member of his community at the monastery. Upon his return, the brothers were eager to hear the rabbi's advice. The abbot apologized for having no advice for helping their situation, and followed by sharing the rabbi's comment that one of them was the Messiah. All were disappointed, but they resumed their routines. Each began to wonder who among them might be the Messiah, not being able to get the rabbi's prediction out of their minds. Just to be on the safe side, each began to treat the others as though they might be the Messiah. Over the next several months, the crops began to thrive, the novitiates resumed their interest in joining the monastery, the coffers overflowed, and the morale blossomed.

Without intending to do so, Peck has told a story that illustrates the effect of a positive PEE:NEE ratio. Perhaps a key to successfully adhering to a positive regard for others is to join in the kind of role-play that Peck's monks played out. Or, we might take the Quaker William Penn's statement to heart, that "there is that of God in every person." We must only be open to discovering it.

In the next chapter, let us turn our attention to the fifth and final of our five modes of positive mood: altruism.

Composing Your Next Chapter

Review your highlights and notes from this chapter on community. Then, list the relationships and groups that you wish to strengthen or begin, and some suggestions as to how you might go about that.

_____

_____

_____

_____

_____

_____

_____

_____

_____

_____

STATEMENT OF PERSONAL PRIORITIES

FLOW | FIT | GOALS | COMMUNITY | ALTRUISM

Happiness Boosters
(Choice)

Happiness Downers
(Choice)

119 Minor Adjustors

(more within personal control)

(more outside personal control)

HAPPINESS SET POINT

Happiness Boosters
(Circumstance)

Happiness Downers
(Circumstance)

Continuum of Trait Happiness

Perennially Happy (N- E+) .... Occasionally Happy (N + E-)

Altruism

9

Generativity and Your Legacy

> "Service is the rent that we pay for our room on earth."
>
> --Charles Lindley Wood, 2nd Viscount Halifax, British ecumenist

Guide to this chapter:

- What is Altruism?
- The Characteristics of Effective Altruism
- The Kinds of Altruism
- The Universal Declaration of Human Rights
- The Charter for Compassion

Charles Wood makes service sound somber, more like a duty than a joy. However, just as paying the rent enables us to be right with the world and to get on with our work and play, so do acts of service enable us to feel right with the world and to enjoy our work and play to the fullest. Altruism is perhaps the proper family name for the set of behaviors that are associated with doing things for others. Synonyms include service, benevolence, charity, humanitarianism, magnanimity, philanthropy, good deeds, public spirit, and so forth. I use the term altruism to include all of these. Altruism comes from the Latin alter meaning "other." In its most basic meaning, then, altruism is acting in behalf of others. The definition of altruism is the opposite of egoism, the pursuit of self-interests. However, in 1830, Auguste Comte, the French philosopher and founder of the school of positivism proposed that altruism actually complements egoism because feel-good altruism ultimately is in one's self-interest.

Pleasure through giving has been dubbed the "Bishop Butler Paradox of Hedonism." Butler was an 18th century moral philosopher who observed that those who most pursue pleasure in and of itself are less likely to experience lasting pleasure than are those who pursue the genuine service of others. Or, that chasing happiness typically leads elsewhere. The great American psychologist and physician William James based his moral philosophy on the Butler paradox, concluding that the only way to insure a personal sense of well-being is to commit oneself to serving a purpose higher than oneself. In the noblest of blends, one builds on one's personal strengths in order to serve the greater social good.

What is altruism?

Mohammed calls it compassion for the poor, while Jesus calls it "doing unto others what you would do for yourself." The irony of altruistic behavior is that it feels good. Making others feel better makes us feel better. The National Institutes of Health's Jorge Moll and a team of researchers studied the fMRIs of 19 individuals who were making decisions whether or not to give real money to a variety of causes they liked. Those choosing to give money showed increased activity in the pleasure area (the midbrain ventral tegmental area [VTA]-striatum mesolimbic network), which is the area that is activated by engaging in sex, using drugs, eating tasty foods, and receiving money. In addition, activity increased in the social attachment area (the subgenual area) that is associated with oxytocin and attachment with others, both romantic and parental. (Moll et al, 2006) Thinking and acting in consideration of others clearly increases our sense of well-being.

> "Those who are happiest are those who do the most for others."
> --Booker T. Washington

The characteristics of effective altruism

But not all altruism is equal. University of California, Riverside, psychologist Sonja Lyubomirsky (2008) has committed her career to the scientific study of altruism. One of her interests is why the giver gets longer-lasting pleasure from some acts of charity than others. She found that two factors produce longer-lasting effects:

- Prolonged acts concentrated on one point in time, as opposed to brief acts spread out over time. This is not to say that, for example, random acts of kindness are not pleasurable for the giver—it is just that the sense of elation for the giver is brief. Contrast this to a day spent building a Habitat for Humanity home, or volunteering to conduct a planning retreat for a nonprofit organization. Just as couples who share meaningful experiences together benefit from the glow of these experiences for a long time, so do individuals who share meaningful altruistic experiences with others benefit for a long time from the satisfaction that ensues.

- Acts that are varied, compared to acts that are similar and repeated. Again, this is not to say that shoveling an infirm neighbor's snow whenever needed is not satisfying—it is just that the repetition is typically less satisfying than embarking on a different act of charity—cleaning their gutters, mending their fence, taking them a fresh casserole, and so forth.

Lyubomirsky does not discuss how the individual differences among altruistic people might affect the impact of repetition and concentration. For example, one important personality trait is Originality—the degree to which people like novelty and change, versus those who prefer the familiar. People differ on this quality along a continuum, whereby some folks love variety, others love the familiar, and still others are in-between, preferring a mixture of the novel and the familiar. Individuals also differ in the Consolidation trait, or the degree to which folks prefer to focus on one task until it is completed, as opposed to being more spontaneous and skipping from one task to another. Clearly spontaneous folks will find less concentrated acts of charity more satisfying than will more focused folks. Similarly, folks who love the familiar are more likely to find repetitive altruistic tasks more satisfying than would folks who love variety.

The kinds of altruism

Building houses is not for me, and playing chamber music is perhaps not for thee. However, you might take great pleasure in giving your time to build a Habitat for Humanity home, and I would certainly take great pleasure in playing a chamber music concert at a retirement home. Each of us has our ways of giving that are genuine, that spring from who we are. I have identified 33 different ways that people can be, and are, altruistic. They appear to fall in five categories, or affinity groups:

- Thoughtful Communication (six ways) primarily involves the use of language.
- Positive Regard (seven ways) primarily involves how we regard others with our attitude.
- Generous Affection (eight ways) primarily involves how we express our love and friendship to others.
- Helpful Giving (five ways) primarily involves the giving of time, money, skills, and other resources to others.
- Beneficial Relief (seven ways) primarily involves doing things that reduce others' stress.

As I describe each of the 33 ways of being altruistic, be aware of those that would feel natural for you to engage in. Also be aware that two more kinds of altruism from across the categories might appear together in a single altruistic act. Combining two or more kinds of altruism in a single endeavor can only intensify the effectiveness of the act itself.

33 Ways of Being Altruistic:

1. Thoughtful communication (using language six ways)

Apologies—taking the time to let someone know that you are sorry for a wrong that you have done them, and that you seek their forgiveness, ideally both in writing and face-to-face. Once a friend who had betrayed my trust sent me a letter of apology. In the letter, they asked if they might come for a visit so that we could talk the matter through. They expressed no expectation that I would be obliged to forgive them—they just wanted to express their bad feelings, get them off their chest, and hopefully lay them to rest. The effect of the visit was indeed a sense of forgiveness on my part, and we have continued to keep up with one another by having lunch together about once a year.

Crediting—not just thanking someone, but taking the time to describe exactly what it is that they did, and what the positive consequences were, whether to you or others. I learned this format for crediting, or recognizing, or patting on the back, from the Interpersonal Management Skills (IMS) course offered decades ago by Xerox Learning Systems. I have tried to find a current commercial version of it without success. According to the IMS program, when you praise someone, in order for the message to have maximum impact, two ingredients are necessary:

- describing exactly what the person did, so that there will be no doubt what you are referring to; and

- identifying the positive consequences on you or others for which you or they are grateful.

In this manner, the receiver of the credit knows precisely what they did of note, and why it mattered. If I quip "Thanks for cleaning up" to a babysitter as she runs off to her home, she has no idea what I am referring to. She may think I mean that she washed her face! Or that she picked up toys in the living room. Better: "Thanks for washing the dishes from supper that we had left out. As a result, I will get to bed 30 minutes earlier than I would have and will get a much better night's sleep. I've a big meeting tomorrow, and a good night's sleep will make a big difference on my sharpness. You go, girl!"

Itemized Response for Constructive Feedback—when you need to tell someone that they have done something wrong—sometimes called constructive criticism, sometimes called negative feedback. The IMS program based its formula for this communication task on research into what makes people most receptive to such feedback. They found that "itemizing" your response to them—saying not only what they did wrong but also what they did right—makes them less resentful or defensive and potentially even appreciative. It takes more effort to itemize your response, and typically such effort is appreciated. The IMS approach has two components:

- describe what the person has done correctly in the situation in question, and
- describe, without using judgmental language, what they did incorrectly.

"Your holiday memo is very clever. You do need however to double-check your spelling—it is Grinch—capitalized and with an 'i', not grench!" As opposed to, for example, "You screwed up the spelling of Grinch—fix it."

Managing Conflict—taking the time to help two conflicted parties to understand and resolve their differences. The conflict can be between you and another person, or between two other persons. In either case, you are serving as a facilitator of the process. The IMS approach to conflict management involves five steps:

1. *Summarize the conflict*: "You want to go out to dinner, and I want to stay home. Right?"
2. *Identify what is important to each person*—what lies behind the stand they are taking:
   You: "What is important to you about wanting to go out to dinner?"
   They: "I haven't been out to eat in three weeks. I'm getting cabin fever."
   You: "What's important to me is that I wanted to kick back and watch my ball game."
3. *Explore possible actions that could satisfy both needs*: "Well, we could go to a sports bar, or to a restaurant with a television, or go wherever we want to and watch it on our iPad."
4. Agree on one course of action, if a mutually agreeable one is possible.
5. If no mutually agreeable action is possible, then you have to accept the right to disagree, and stand your ground.

On-the-spot Recognition—remarking spontaneously on someone's noteworthy behavior, as in "That was very thoughtful of you to help that old man across the street" or "I'm impressed that you still have such a radiant smile at 4:45 p.m. on Friday!"

Thank You's—writing thank you notes (handwritten preferred over emailed, but better either than neither!), especially in a timely manner (i.e., not months later!). Be sure to mention specifics.

2. Positive regard (seven attitudes)

Compassion—awareness of the suffering of others and attempting to help in relieving that suffering. Compassion has both a knowledge and an action component: educating oneself as to the specific details about the suffering of an individual or group, and then acting in your own way to relieve some aspect of the suffering, whether it be through providing money, pressing governments and other agencies to provide relief, a shoulder to cry on, physical labor, offering expertise, giving shelter, or some other action. A friend's wife died of cancer some dozen years back. On her deathbed, she asked me to "Take care of him." A week or two after her passing, I asked him what the hardest time of the day/week/month was. He quickly replied "Friday nights—we used to go dancing every Friday night, and I miss that terribly." So for the next several months, every Friday night we did something together to replace that emptiness.

Nonverbal positive energy—directed at supporting the efforts of others. In his 1993 novel *The Celestine Prophecy*, James Redfield described the practice of providing nonverbal support when someone you care about is in the spotlight in some way. When your business partner is making a speech or leading a meeting, you offer abundant eye contact, smiles, appropriate head nods, and in general pay attention and react in a supportive way, as opposed to shaking one's head, frowning, doodling, and other nonsupportive gestures. You are in effect being a silent cheering section for the person you value.

Optimism—giving both others and self the benefit of the doubt, when appropriate. As we saw in Chapter 2, optimism a) views successes and good news as attributable to individual effort that will spill over into other areas of one's life and continue for a lifetime and b) sees failures and disappointments as due to bad luck that is limited in time and scope. Pessimism, not surprisingly, is the opposite: seeing successes as due to good luck and limited in scope and time, and failures as due to one's effort and likely to spread to other areas of one's life for quite some time. Without becoming Pollyannaish and always being optimistic about one's close acquaintances, one can at least give the benefit of the doubt to one's close acquaintances by being optimistic when circumstances permit. When your friend loses a promotion, unless there is clear evidence to the contrary, try something like: "Your time will come, and hopefully sooner than later! You've earned it, but the competition is fierce. Patience—you'll get there."

Prayer—conscious, positive thoughts for the purpose of improving the lot of others, whether religiously framed or otherwise. Prayer is a refusal to ignore one's own or another's needs, and to beg, entreat, request, or ask for those needs to be addressed. From the Latin *precari* and the proto Indo-European *prek*, this long established word for begging is both secular and sacred in its usage. In my liberal definition of "prayer," many of the acts of altruism that I am listing also might be considered an act of prayer. In effect, sending a "Get well!" card is just as much of a prayer as "Lord, look over my friend Roberto and help him to a speedy recovery." Whether on your knees with hands clasped, eyes closed, and words directed towards your god, or sitting at your desk writing a note of encouragement to someone in travail, you are praying.

> "Everything will be all right in the end. So, if it is not all right, it is not yet the end."
> --Unknown origin; a line in the film *The Best Exotic Marigold Hotel*

Smiling and Casual Touching—making a conscious effort to be pleasant, as in a genuine smile or an appropriate touch, especially to someone not necessarily accustomed to such, e.g., a bus driver, sanitation worker, librarian, police officer, and so forth. This is similar to the "non-verbal positive energy" mentioned earlier.

However, here I am not talking about sustained focus aimed at being supportive of someone over time, but rather a quick smile or touch (to shoulder, elbow, top of hand, or some other appropriate "hard" and non-threatening spot) to indicate acknowledgement of the other person's existence and value as a human being. In one study, library patrons who were casually touched (e.g., fingers brushing against one another when handing over a book) by the circulation desk staffer upon checkout rated their library experience significantly more positive than did those patrons who were not casually touched. Just don't allow the casual touch to linger, as delight can transmogrify into offense.

Visualization—repeatedly imagining your partner or other associate framed and exhibiting their most positive aspect. Author Ann Patchett wrote in *Prevention* (April 2010) of her attendance at a meditation workshop. The leader asked her to hold her hands in front of her and to make a frame, then to visualize her loved one (in this case, husband) in his most positive aspects. For "homework," she was to repeat this visualization exercise for 11 minutes daily. Over time, she felt a growing appreciation for him, a gratitude for his finer qualities, plus her increasing overt regard for him was returned with his increasing self-respect by working out more, helping others more, and feeling better about work.

Zaniness—giving the gift of spontaneous positive energy, such as tap dancing briefly or jumping up and kicking one's feet. I enjoy making a duck-quacking sound around kids, particularly when they are giving their parent(s) a hard time. The quacking distracts them, as they giggle and gaze while I ask, "Where's that duck?" A friend has an act he does from time to time whereby he pretends to trip badly, but with quick recovery. Always good for a rapid, "Oh no!...Ha ha!" I have a friend with chronic fatigue syndrome. Laughing boosts his morale and energy; so every chance I get, I try to do a funny around him—a new joke, a bawdy observation...whatever comes to mind.

3. Generous affection (eight expressions of it)

Chattiness—offering your gift of gab to someone you don't know but who looks like they might benefit from not being ignored yet again, as in chatting about sports, the weather, a rude customer, etc., with a gas station attendant or a sanitation worker. This is a way of being friendly with someone who is not actually a friend. It is also surprising how often such apparently superficial conversation yields interesting information. Once Jane and I were taking a cab from Greater Rochester (NY) International Airport to a Holiday Inn near the office building where we were to consult the next day. The driver appeared to be from the Asian subcontinent, an area whose cuisine appeals to both of us. I asked where he was from. India. So we started talking about Indian food, as we love to both cook and eat it. The snow was thick and fast, and we had resigned ourselves to room service at the inn. I asked him if by chance there were a good Indian restaurant near the hotel. No there was not, but his brother had a very nice Punjabi restaurant about 20 minutes away. He offered to drive us to the restaurant at no extra charge, and he would play with his nieces and nephews while Jane and I dined! What a delightful evening it turned out to be, all because of just being chatty.

Friendship—making the time to get to know and do things with close friends, including being available when they call upon you. The inertia of going back and forth from home to work with errands and a few activities thrown in has a way of minimizing our time with friends. It is too easy to just do everything with one's partner and/or one's workmates. It takes extra effort to make time to call or email a friend (who might also be a relative) and find a time for taking breakfast or lunch together to just "catch up." Just yesterday I emailed our daughter to suggest a father-daughter lunch. Today we lunched, and timely it was, as I learned important information that I wished I'd learned much earlier!

Gratefulness—expressing your gratitude to someone, either in writing or in person, or both. This is different from "thank you's" mentioned earlier. Thank you comes after a specific gesture, such as opening a door, picking up lunch, or collecting a neighbor's paper while they're out of town. Here we are referring to gratitude for an extended period of service by someone towards us: gratitude towards a teacher for being patient throughout the year with our child, towards a teammate who has consistently been reliable in completing every task we've asked of them in a timely and professional manner, towards a former college or high school teacher whom we haven't seen in 20 years but who taught us things no book could, and so forth. Robert Emmons and Michael McCullough (2004) find that keeping a daily gratitude journal—listing five things daily for which one is grateful—leads to an increased sense of well-being.

Love—Agape, often defined as charity, or love for humanity in general. C. S. Lewis in his *The Four Loves* (1960) described this kind of love in theological as well as secular terms. He emphasized its unconditional nature. A minister friend of mine learned this definition from a professor at Princeton University Divinity School: "the unconditional acceptance of the singularity of another person." This sense of unconditional acceptance is a prerequisite for Lewis's explanation—he says this kind of love is the love for those who are unlovable—the sick, the deranged, the incarcerated. In effect, agape—charity—is the love for everyone, of humankind. I have often lamented the failure of theologically minded friends to define the concept of grace. Lewis would have it defined as the notion that God loves all creatures, warts and all, the lovable along with the unlovable. This theological ideal form of love becomes an aspiration for humans—to develop the capacity to love everyone—to give the gift of love to everyone. The other three forms of love are *Eros*, *philia*, and *storge*, and are explained in the next three paragraphs. In his 1956 novel *Till We Have Faces*, C. S. Lewis illustrates the four loves using different characters.

Love—Eros, an emotional longing between two partners, or what Lewis calls the feeling of "being in love." Lewis describes being in love as total surrender of one person to another, and of preoccupation with the other person. Biblically, this sense of surrender has been misunderstood by those who say men are head of their family like Jesus is head of the church. The corrupt interpretation is that the wife is the servant of the husband as the church is the servant of Jesus. However, Lewis points out that it is two way—the husband is servant to the wife also, surrendering to her as Jesus is servant to the church. Pure two-way love is pure two-way servitude. When in love, one would prefer misery with one's beloved than alternate arrangements. In its extreme form, Eros is renunciation, whether religious (as in taking religious orders and being "married" to the church) or secular (as in the *Bible's* Ruth saying, "Whither thou goest, I will go"). In its most extreme form, Eros becomes demonic, where one martyrs oneself to one's beloved, and one's love becomes nothing less than idolatry. In such a state, one lives under the illusion that being in love justifies wrong behavior, as in cults.

Eros is typically understood to mean erotic love, or physical intimacy between two partners. However, Lewis reserved the term "Venus" to refer to the physical component. In more common usage, I understand this form of love for Lewis to be romantic love in all of its dimensions, but with an emphasis on giving pleasure to the other, rather than selfishly focusing only on one's personal emotional or erotic needs. There is a passage in D. H. Lawrence's 1920 novel *Women in Love* in which the sisters Gudrun and Ursula Brangwen compare lovers. One argues for the strong bull of a man, the other preferring a man who is receptive, listening, sensitive, and attentive, with the result that he focuses on her needs and likes and continually learns from her verbal and nonverbal cues. He is the opposite of the arrogant, egotistical male lover who is a "bip-bam, thank you ma'am," kind of lover who plows into lovemaking with the sensitivity of a bull in a china shop, riding slipshod all the way, clueless as to his partner's likes and dislikes. The word I remember most is a man's "receptivity" to a woman's signals, in contrast to the macho man's cold disregard of them. All about *me* versus all about *thee*, with the latter resulting in a better *we*.

Love—Philia, a strong friendship formed between two persons springing from a common interest. It is freely chosen, in contrast to being accidentally thrown together in the next kind of love—storge. Lewis captures the moment of recognizing someone as a friend with this quip: "What? You too? I thought I was the only one." (p. 65) This is what we described earlier as "clicking." Philia is intentional, wherein two persons choose to be friends. Intentional friendships include affection, loyalty, familiarity, equality, and virtuous behavior around each other. Philia differs from Eros in a couple of important ways: Eros is two people in love only with one another, while philia/friendship can include more than two—it can be a coterie. Those in Eros love are consumed with one another, while those in philia love are consumed by their common interest, whether it is rebuilding engines, building an organization, or plotting to destroy something. Yes, philia/friendship can serve good or ill. Or as Lewis writes, "It makes good men better and bad men worse." (p. 80)

> Mattie: "Are you happy?"
> Caris: "I wasn't born to be happy. But I help people, I make a living, and I'm free."
> --Ken Follett, *World Without End* (2007)

    I am sure you have occasionally heard someone say that they have no friends. Lewis comments that absence of deeply satisfying friendships is common among persons who do not have a strong personal interest in something. Where one's interests are strong, they are likely to attract persons who share them. Lewis writes, "Those who have nothing can share nothing; those who are going nowhere can have no fellow-travelers." (p. 67) The greatest risk of these deep friendships based on a common interest is that they form a mutual admiration society where pride makes them feel unique, superior, and characterized by exclusivity, self-righteousness, and intolerance.

Love—Storge, is a fondness or affection that grows out of familiarity with another family member or friend whom one does not intentionally choose but whom one has simply found oneself on the same "stage" with in life. By virtue of being a part of the same family, work team, club, or the like, one grows fonder towards some than others—not a deep philia-type friendship but a less intense but nonetheless positive regard. This has sometimes been called an "avuncular" love, like uncles and aunts with nephews and nieces. Lewis describes storge as old, long-lasting loves that we take for granted but miss when absent. They are modest loves of which we do not boast, where there are kisses of affection that are less intense than kisses of Eros. Kissing cousins, as it were. This is a love of circumstance, the result of being thrust together by blood or employment, whereby two people discover over time that the other has value. Jocularly referring to time working its storge-like love magic, Lewis quips that "Dogs and cats should always be brought up together...it broadens their minds so." (1960, p. 36) The ally of storge is what Harold Kelley (& Thibaut, 1978) calls interdependence, whereby both parties share in the drudgery required to maintain a relationship, while the enemy of storge is change, whereby one party takes up a radically new interest that separates them from the other over time. As for persons who lament that no one feels affection towards them, Lewis suggests that they may be candidates for owning a pet. The prerequisites for earning the affection of one's acquaintances are "common sense and give and take and 'decency.'" (p. 54) On the relation of storge to Eros and Philia, Lewis quips that "Without Eros none of us would have been begotten and without Affection [Storge] none of us would have been reared; but we can live and breed without Friendship [Philia]." (p. 58)

Respect for the Environment—Among many methods such as recycling, here's one of my favorites: continually finding ways to reduce one's carbon footprint, or the quantity of carbon emissions for which you are responsible. Find a website that takes you through the steps required to compute your carbon footprint. This involves calculating car, electricity, natural gas, airplane, and food emissions per year. One such calculation guide is at www.motherearthnews.com/Healthy-People-Healthy-Planet/Carbon-Footprint-Calculator.aspx. Then, set a goal to reduce your footprint, and identify some changes required in order to meet your goal. This could involve anything from taking the bus to installing solar panels. Jane and I have been happy with our decision some years ago got rid of our second car. When schedules conflict, I take the bus.

4. Helpful giving (five ways).

Charity—giving money, goods, or services to the needy. I restrict my use of the word "charity" to mean gifts to the poor. Sending money to aid the famine-stricken, taking a portion of one's crops to the kitchen at a homeless shelter, and staffing a soup kitchen once a week would all be examples of charitable acts, each focused on the impoverished. I once read with interest that the techno-thriller novelist Tom Clancy gave his time to help staff a homeless shelter—an act of charity.

Donations—giving money or goods to a cause where the benefit is more to others than to you. I restrict the use of "donation" to mean giving money or goods to a cause that one deems worthy, but not necessarily aimed at the poor. A donation also might go toward items such as building a multi-million-dollar symphony hall. Charity or donation can include the practice of "tithing," or committing a fixed percentage of one's income to donate to one's religious organization or some organization that looks after the needy. The word comes from the Old English word for "tenth," so tithing is traditionally 10% of income or crop production or other output.

Generativity—leaving something for the use, enjoyment, and benefit of future generations. The use of the word "generativity" in this sense was first proposed by the German-Danish-American developmental psychologist and psychoanalyst Erik Erikson in 1950. Erikson proposed eight critical phases of human development. Generativity (as opposed to stagnation) was the seventh stage, and it typically occurs, or is the focal point, in one's life between the ages of 25 and 65. Each of us has different ways of contributing to the welfare of future generations. Typically it is based on our strengths: a financial wizard endows a university professorship, a carpenter leaves furniture, a writer leaves her books, a social activist leaves his followers their newly won rights, and a singer leaves the joy of song. The object of one's generativity may be specific (as

> "…so your soul has somewhere to go when you die."
> --Ray Bradbury, *Fahrenheit 451* (2007)

for one's grandchild) or general (as Martin "Little Mikey" Luther King, Jr., and Mohandas "Mahatma" Gandhi each left a legacy for the millions). Ray Bradberry (1950) writes of generativity in *Fahrenheit 451* when he portrays Granger (who has memorized books in order to preserve them) trying to comfort Montag (who admires Granger):

> Everyone must leave something behind when he dies, my grandfather said. A child or a book or a painting or a house or a wall built or a pair of shoes made. Or a garden planted. Something your hand touched some way so your soul has somewhere to go when you die, and when people look at that tree or that flower you planted, you're there. It doesn't matter what you do, he said, so long as you change something from the way it was before you touched it into something that's like you after you take your hands away. The difference between the man who just cuts lawns and a real gardener is in the touching, he said. The lawn cutter might just as well not have been there at all; the gardener will be there a lifetime. (pp. 156-7)

Gifts—The unsolicited, unexpected gift (as in flowers to cheer someone, or giving a book because you thought someone would especially like it) is more in the spirit of altruism than is the expected gift (as in holiday gift exchanges, birthday gifts, and the like), which is more like fulfilling a duty than giving a gift. Ralph Waldo Emerson wrote that "rings and jewels are not gifts, but apologies are gifts. The only true gift is a portion of thyself." According to Emerson's criterion, the highest form of gift-giving entails an item or gesture than expresses your effort, talent, time, and thought, and that fits the interests or needs of the other. For me to give a recording of my church choir to someone who detests choral music would be an inappropriate gift, but giving note cards I made myself from linoleum block prints to my mother—who loves to write notes to folks and is always having to replenish her supply—well, that would qualify as a "portion of [my]self."

Pro Bono—(short for *pro bono publico*, "for the good of the people") originally referred to lawyers providing free legal services to those who could not afford it. Now it refers to anyone providing such a free service (consultants, plumbers, doctors, and so forth) when you normally would ask a fee, as you do it for a living. . When a lawyer takes no fee for helping a charitable organization set up its charter, that is acting pro bono publico, for the good of the public.

5. Beneficial relief (seven actions).

Connecting People—for their mutual benefit, as when a friend needs a job and another friend may have a job opening. Many of us are so busy that the very notion of taking time to introduce two people who can be of benefit to one another is painful. We just don't have time. When, however, we take a deep breath and say to ourselves that we need to make the time to let jobless Mary know about our friend Caryn who is hiring people with Mary's qualifications, then we are altruistically connecting people.

Good Samaritan—stopping to help someone in need of assistance, as in taking a hurt bird to a nature museum or calling an ambulance for someone in distress. My son-in-law recently told me that he and our grandsons were driving to an appointment with no time to spare when they spied a hawk that had been apparently hit by a car and was futilely trying to fly. He circled the block with the intention of picking up the stricken bird and taking it to a nearby nature museum for care. By the time he returned to the scene of the accident, the bird was already being assisted by someone who'd beat him to it! Good Samaritanism is alive and well.

Neighborliness—as in offering to do a chore (taking the trash out, mowing the grass, collecting newspapers) for a neighbor who is ill, infirm, out of town, or otherwise not able to stay on top of things around the domicile. My sister Virginia lived alone in her 90s in the Mt. Lebanon neighborhood of Pittsburgh. Unable to keep her walkway and driveway clear of snow, neighbors filled in without being asked, and continued doing so until she moved into a retirement home several years later. In the same neighborhood, when she decided to learn to use a computer at age 92, a teenage boy who had heard of her daring venture decided to drop in one or two afternoons a week and help her learn the ins and outs of email, printing, and the like.

Service—participating in a project that primarily benefits others rather than self, as in helping to paint a group home or to build a Habitat for Humanity house. I once joined four other guys in building a harpsichord (from a kit) for our choirmaster. That was not true service, as I/we were the beneficiaries of the new harpsichord, as we could then make music together with the new instrument. Some years before that, I joined a dozen other folks in my Charlotte Civitan Club to paint, inside and outside, a group home at a sheltered workshop that housed a dozen individuals with Down's syndrome. I hate to paint. I did not know the residents then. I do not know them now. *That* was an act of service. It needed to be done; so do it we did.

Random Acts of Kindness—spontaneously engaging in a kind act towards someone else. The dictionary definition of kindness is an act that is thoughtful, considerate, tender, or generous. The word "kind" comes from the Old English word for "kin," which suggests that kindness is treating others like family you love. The many ways of being kind include giving your coat to a shivering friend, letting a child have something of yours that they have been admiring, offering to carry a heavy object for someone struggling with it, or offering a pitcher of ice water to someone working in your yard.

Respite Care—offering to relieve (as in babysitting, sitting with demented elder) a caregiver so that they may have some personal time (to shop, go to a movie, etc.). The Senior Care Network (see more at www.senior-carenetwork.com) is an organization that, among other things, enlists volunteers to relieve caregivers. Let us say that you are caring for a parent with severe dementia. You accept this role willingly, but you nonetheless need relief in order to shop for groceries, run errands, and even go to a movie now and then. Senior Care Network (SCN) is organized to send someone to relieve you for several hours in order for your parent to have uninterrupted care while you take care of needs that must be addressed outside the home. This is an institutional response to a need that is everywhere. We do not have to be registered with SCN in order to provide respite care to a friend or even acquaintance who is providing care 7/24 and who needs relief from time to time. All we have to do is offer to help.

> "Happiness is a perfume you cannot pour on others without getting a few drops on yourself."
> --Ralph Waldo Emerson

Volunteering—in hospitals, schools, etc. Most volunteering is straightforward: You go to your neighborhood elementary school and offer to read to young children or otherwise be a teacher's helper, go to your hospital of choice and be a regular visitor, or contact your favorite politician to let them know you're available to help with anything from envelope stuffing to research for position papers. However, volunteering in the U.S. has become quite a production. With the Internet, linking your interests and skills with needs in the community has become relatively painless. For example, go to www.volunteermatch.org. Enter your zip code, then enter a keyword that describes the activity you would like to volunteer to perform. I just went to the Volunteer Match website and typed in my zip code and the term "tutoring." The site then identified 17 organizations that could use my services. What a powerful way for the Internet to link us as individuals to others who need our talents and time. And, there are even more online sites where you can find ideas about satisfying opportunities for volunteer work.

The Universal Declaration of Human Rights

On December 10, 1948, the United Nations General Assembly declared in Paris that the document entitled "Universal Declaration of Human Rights" (UDHR) was the common standard for defining and protecting the fundamental human rights of all people and nations. The document (see http://www.un.org/en/documents/udhr/) holds the Guinness World Record for the Most Translated Document. As of February 2012, 383 translations are available.

Led by then First Lady Eleanor Roosevelt and her U.S. Department of State advisors, a team that included H. G. Wells proceeded with the composition of a litany of basic human rights in the hope that their acceptance would avoid anything like the two world wars from which they had recently emerged. I have included below the U.N.'s "plain language" version that eliminates any legalese from the 30 articles:

1. When children are born, they are free and each should be treated in the same way. They have reason and conscience and should act towards one another in a friendly manner.

2. Everyone can claim the following rights, despite
   - a different sex
   - a different skin color
   - speaking a different language
   - thinking different things
   - believing in another religion
   - owning more or less
   - being born in another social group
   - coming from another country
   It also makes no difference whether the country you live in is independent or not.

3. You have the right to live, and to live in freedom and safety.

4. Nobody has the right to treat you as his or her slave and you should not make anyone your slave.

5. Nobody has the right to torture you.

6. You should be legally protected in the same way everywhere, and like everyone else.

7. The law is the same for everyone; it should be applied in the same way to all.

8. You should be able to ask for legal help when the rights your country grants you are not respected.

9. Nobody has the right to put you in prison, to keep you there, or to send you away from your country unjustly, or without good reason.

10. If you go on trial this should be done in public. The people who try you should not let themselves be influenced by others.

11. You should be considered innocent until it can be proved that you are guilty. If you are accused of a crime, you should always have the right to defend yourself. Nobody has the right to condemn you and punish you for something you have not done.

12. You have the right to ask to be protected if someone tries to harm your good name, enter your house, open your letters, or bother you or your family without a good reason.

13. You have the right to come and go as you wish within your country. You have the right to leave your country to go to another one; and you should be able to return to your country if you want.

14. If someone hurts you, you have the right to go to another country and ask it to protect you. You lose this right if you have killed someone and if you, yourself, do not respect what is written here.

15. You have the right to belong to a country and nobody can prevent you, without a good reason, from belonging to a country if you wish.

16. As soon as a person is legally entitled, he or she has the right to marry and have a family. In doing this, neither the color of your skin, the country you come from nor your religion should be impediments. Men and women have the same rights when they are married and also when they are separated. Nobody should force a person to marry. The government of your country should protect you and the members of your family.

17. You have the right to own things and nobody has the right to take these from you without a good reason.

18. You have the right to profess your religion freely, to change it, and to practice it either on your own or with other people.

19. You have the right to think what you want, to say what you like, and nobody should forbid you from doing so. You should be able to share your ideas also—with people from any other country.

20. You have the right to organize peaceful meetings or to take part in meetings in a peaceful way. It is wrong to force someone to belong to a group.

21. You have the right to take part in your country's political affairs either by belonging to the government yourself or by choosing politicians who have the same ideas as you. Governments should be voted for regularly and voting should be secret. You should get a vote and all votes should be equal. You also have the same right to join the public service as anyone else.

22. The society in which you live should help you to develop and to make the most of all the advantages (culture, work, social welfare) which are offered to you and to all the men and women in your country.

23. You have the right to work, to be free to choose your work, to get a salary which allows you to support your family. If a man and a woman do the same work, they should get the same pay. All people who work have the right to join together to defend their interests.

24. Each work day should not be too long, since everyone has the right to rest and should be able to take regular paid holidays.

25. You have the right to have whatever you need so that you and your family: do not fall ill or go hungry; have clothes and a house; and are helped if you are out of work, if you are ill, if you are old, if your wife or husband is dead, or if you do not earn a living for any other reason you cannot help. Mothers and their children are entitled to special care. All children have the same rights to be protected, whether or not their mother was married when they were born.

26. You have the right to go to school and everyone should go to school. Primary schooling should be free. You should be able to learn a profession or continue your studies as far as wish. At school, you should be able to develop all your talents and you should be taught to get on with others, whatever their race, religion or the country they come from. Your parents have the right to choose how and what you will be taught at school.

27. You have the right to share in your community's arts and sciences, and any good they do. Your works as an artist, writer, or a scientist should be protected, and you should be able to benefit from them.

28. So that your rights will be respected, there must be an 'order' which can protect them. This 'order' should be local and worldwide.

29. You have duties towards the community within which your personality can only fully develop. The law should guarantee human rights. It should allow everyone to respect others and to be respected.

30. In all parts of the world, no society, no human being, should take it upon her or himself to act in such a way as to destroy the rights which you have just been reading about.

It seems to me that these 30 articles form the ultimate pool of causes to which one could harness their altruistic energy. Whether you choose to pick one or more article and then address it through letter-writing, blog-posting, lobbying, political action, fund-raising (such as Bono and George Clooney), physical labor (as in Greg Mortenson's schools for girls in Central Asia), or pro bono work (as in my niece's free availability as a physician to women's clinics in India and Kenya three months a year), this list is the first reference when one considers how to give one's time and resources. One couple who has devoted their lives to addressing violation of these rights is Nick Kristof and Sheryl WuDunn (editorial writers for *The New York Times* and winner of two Pulitzer Prizes). This couple's recent book *Half the Sky* (2009) documents abuses of women around the world. Nick's weekly columns provide timely information and opportunities for altruistic action. Their lives serve as a call to action for the rest of us. If in doubt where to focus your altruistic energy or to send your money, follow Nick and Sheryl on twitter (@NickKristof).

Make copies of the UDHR, either the plain language version or the original at the website indicated above. Use it as a resource for evaluating countries and cultures (including the United States) that interest you. Use it as a basis for school curriculum, religious school lessons, book discussion groups, sermons, letters to the editor. Keep it in the forefront of yours and others' attention.

The Charter for Compassion

A more recent effort to challenge the world community towards greater regard for others is that of former Roman Catholic nun and current religion scholar Karen Armstrong. In an interview with *The Charlotte Observer* (July 1, 2011), she described how she issued a "Charter for Compassion" for the purpose of urging religious leaders around the world to cooperate for peace. She defined compassion as the Golden Rule, or doing for others what you would like them to do for you. She traced the origin of this concept to Confucius and points out that it is core to all religions. Armstrong emphasizes works over faith, the traditional Christian dilemma whereby some argue that one is more important than the other: What good is having faith without performing good deeds, or what good is doing good without having a strong faith? The interviewer confronted her with, "Here in the South, many evangelical Protestants say it's not about good works, it's about faith. And they can recite chapter and verse from the Bible. What do you say to them?" Her reply:

I would quote back: "I could have faith that moves mountains," it says in Paul, "but if I lack charity, it will do me no good at all."

Interviewer: So are they misreading the Bible when they stress "being saved" by Jesus?

Armstrong: This is a form of Christianity that developed quite late. This preoccupation with being saved yourself is a bit on the egotistical side. I think religion is about giving yourself away to others. We are at our best when we give ourselves away. As the Buddha said, "A good life is to live for others." The kingdom of heaven is a Jewish way of talking about the kingdom of God—this is a Jewish concept. And that was not something with clouds and angels up there. It was something that's going to happen on earth. The whole world will come, as the prophets said, to the rule of God. That's what Jesus is working for."

And, I would add, so did Buddha, Mohammed, and so forth. She concludes that "Compassion means get rid of your ego and it means working for other people, working selflessly for others... Service is a universal religious practice... I don't mind what people believe or how they think of God as long as it leads them to be compassionate and kind to others. 'By your fruit, you shall know them' (as the Bible says)."

Armstrong's goal is for everyone to agree to the charter. To date, 30 translations are available. Her website (http://charterforcompassion.org/share/the-charter) asks for visitors to affirm the statement with signature and email address. As of June 8, 2012, 86,932 had signed. Here is the text:

The principle of compassion lies at the heart of all religious, ethical and spiritual traditions, calling us always to treat all others as we wish to be treated ourselves. Compassion impels us to work tirelessly to alleviate the suffering of our fellow creatures, to dethrone ourselves from the centre of our world and put another there, and to honour the inviolable sanctity of every single human being, treating everybody, without exception, with absolute justice, equity and respect.

It is also necessary in both public and private life to refrain consistently and empathically from inflicting pain. To act or speak violently out of spite, chauvinism, or self-interest, to impoverish, exploit or deny basic rights to anybody, and to incite hatred by denigrating others—even our enemies—is a denial of our common humanity. We acknowledge that we have failed to live compassionately and that some have even increased the sum of human misery in the name of religion.

We therefore call upon all men and women to restore compassion to the centre of morality and religion, to return to the ancient principle that any interpretation of scripture that breeds violence, hatred or disdain is illegitimate, to ensure that youth are given accurate and respectful information about other traditions, religions and cultures, to encourage a positive appreciation of cultural and religious diversity, to cultivate an informed empathy with the suffering of all human beings—even those regarded as enemies.

We urgently need to make compassion a clear, luminous and dynamic force in our polarized world. Rooted in a principled determination to transcend selfishness, compassion can break down political, dogmatic, ideological and religious boundaries. Born of our deep interdependence, compassion is essential to human relationships and to a fulfilled humanity. It is the path to enlightenment, and indispensable to the creation of a just economy and a peaceful global community.

Consider asking your religious organization, your workplace, and your club, to officially affirm the Charter for Compassion. Use it in planning programs and speakers. Post it prominently. And follow its progress on www.charterforcompassion.org.

It's Not About You

In his annual column to exhort college graduates towards greatness and fulfillment, *The New York Times* editorial writer David Brooks lamented (May 31, 2011) that graduates were wrongly encouraged to follow their passion selfishly. He continued, "Today's graduates enter a cultural climate that preaches the self as the center of a life." Brooks challenges this view by insisting that the typical young person builds on opportunities that knock them off center, by problems they choose to solve that weren't a part of their dream at all. He perorates with "The purpose in life is not to find yourself. It's to lose yourself."

I agree with the thrust of Brooks' point but differ in a major way. First, I agree that most of us do not set a career goal and then go achieve it. Rather, we are presented by a challenge or problem and our successful grappling with it becomes the basis of our career. I chose a career as a supervisor of English teachers, and in my first assignment I ended up taking a 180° lurch into becoming an industrial and organizational psychologist! So, yes, I agree with Brooks that most of us lose control of our initial goals and by becoming sidetracked into a different challenge, we surrender ourselves to a larger, perhaps more worthy, need, and certainly a need or goal that we had not anticipated.

Yet I respectfully disagree with Brooks that it is not all about me/us! While I lost sight of my original goal and surrendered myself to a new master, I in fact chanced upon a goal that suited my temperament better. By abandoning my original goal, I was able to latch onto a new goal that suited me better. My traits, my values, my mental abilities, my physical characteristics, and my experiences all lent themselves better to my new career. It is as though we set out in our 20s to pursue a goal for some reason other than how well it uses our gifts, but then we intuitively recognize replacement goals that better suit the stuff of which we're made. It is still all about me, but in the sense of using me in the service of others. Brooks meant that wanting to be a superstar athlete or a rich doctor is "all about me." That is true. But "all about me" also means knowing my strengths and recognizing appropriate opportunities for using them to help myself and others.

Perhaps the most engaging portrayal of the bad form of "all about me" is the 1993 film *Groundhog Day* staring Bill Murray as selfish Phil the weatherman. Phil is doomed to spend the same day over and over again, repeatedly, event for event, until he breaks out of his selfishness by taking a genuine interest in others. A nice parable for modern times.

Composing Your Next Chapter

Review your highlights and notes from this chapter on altruism. List below some behaviors, guidelines, practices, and skills that you would like to include in the next chapter of your life. Pay attention to how altruistic acts can build on who you are (i.e., good fit), engage your mind (i.e., flow), assist in making progress towards a short- or long-term goal, and get you more involved in relationships that are important to you.

_____

_____

_____

STATEMENT OF PERSONAL PRIORITIES

FLOW | FIT | GOALS | COMMUNITY | ALTRUISM

Happiness Boosters
(Choice)

Happiness Downers
(Choice)

119 Minor Adjustors

(more within personal control)

(more outside personal control)

HAPPINESS SET POINT

Happiness Boosters
(Circumstance)

Happiness Downers
(Circumstance)

Continuum of Trait Happiness

Perennially Happy (N- E+) .... Occasionally Happy (N + E-)

10
Putting It All Together

A Template for Your Statement of Personal Priorities

> "Nature, Mr. Allnut, is what we are put in this world to rise above. "
>
> -- Katharine Hepburn, in *The African Queen* (1951)

Guide to this chapter:
- The Importance of All Five Elements
- The Art of Composing a Statement of Personal Priorities
- Creating a Personal Optimization Plan

When Katherine Hepburn's character Rose Sayer says to Humphrey Bogart's character Mr. All-nut that we are put in this world to rise above our nature, she does not mean that we are meant to be something different than who we are—our palette of traits, abilities, and so forth. What she means is that we are not meant to be inertial creatures who set no goals and always follow the path of least resistance. Our natural condition is not an excuse for selfish, lazy, immoral, or self-defeating behavior. We may be born to racism, but we can choose to rise above it. We may be born to aristocratic privilege, but we can choose to eschew it. We may be born to a culture of superstition, but we can choose to look at evidence to the contrary. We have the power to choose to rise above the circumstances in which we find ourselves. In order to succeed in that effort, we must use and rely on our strengths. In other words, we must use our nature to rise above nature—we must use our personal strengths to accomplish our goals.

Ronald Fischer (2011) surveyed 420,000 individuals spanning 63 countries to determine how wealth and a sense of choice affected a person's sense of well-being. He found that having a sense of personal autonomy—the freedom to choose a life partner, career, residence, political representative, religion, or how to spend one's leisure—was much more closely associated with a sense of well-being than was level of income. The suggestion here is that not only do we need the freedom to choose, but we must exercise that choice wisely in order to feel in gear, to feel that we are moving forward with our life in a way that we feel good about.

The Importance of All Five Elements

In this chapter we are going to build and practice the habit of linking all five modes of positive being—flow, fit, goals, community, and altruism. In order to experience the satisfaction that ensues from any one of the five modes, we need to pay attention to the other four. We may have a stirring goal, but stress and dissatisfaction will occur if we pursue that goal with poor fit between our personal characteristics and tasks we choose to do in pursuit of that goal. We may experience intense flow day in and day out, but if that flow does not serve a greater purpose, we will feel empty and unfulfilled. We may have a perfect fit between our personal characteristics and the work we do, but if we do not develop intimate relationships along the way, we will end up lonely. We may have a rich network of friends and family with whom we have supportive, intimate relationships, but if we do not select tasks and activities wisely, we may end up being bored or frustrated and using our relationship network primarily as shoulders to cry on. We may serve charitable causes in the noblest of style, but if we do not have goals, we will feel as though we are treading water.

In his novella *Family Happiness,* Leo Tolstoy (1859) described the feelings of the 17-year-old girl Mashechka, who had married a much older family friend. She had naively entered the relationship with the certainty that all one needed in life for "family happiness" was service to others. As the consequences of her decision became apparent, she pondered her situation:

> Once it seemed so plain and right that to live for others was happiness; but now it has become unintelligible. Why live for others, when life had no attraction even for oneself?

I think Mashechka is describing the consequence of embracing altruism without fit or flow. She is clearly an outgoing, sociable young woman who is stuck alone in the country, a creative inquiring mind who is without books or other forms of mental stimulation. She is an example of how unwise altruism can create a suffering servant. For the remainder of the chapter, we will look at how to link all five modes so that one does not suffer for lack of the others.

The Art of Composing a Statement of Personal Priorities

The purpose of composing a Statement of Personal Priorities (SPP) is to create a reminder for how to focus our energy in order to stay in gear. The SPP has five elements: flow, fit, goals, community, and altruism. In its most abstract form, the SPP for all of us might read like this:

> "To achieve something (goals) that benefits others (altruism) in a way that builds on my strengths (fit), develops my relationships (community), and keeps me appropriately challenged (flow)."

At the end of the last five chapters, we provided space for you to make notes on the highlights of each of the five areas of positive mood. Now you can refer back to the end of each of those five chapters and use your notes as an aid for building your SPP. In Table 10.0, I use myself as an example.

Table 10.0   Identifying Highlights from the Previous Five Chapters (author as example)

Area:	Items to Include in my SPP:
Flow	I am currently experiencing relatively little frustration but rather more boredom than desirable. I attribute this to an excess of activities that are insufficiently demanding. So, I need to take on **greater challenges**, particularly musically, family-wise, pleasure-wise.
Fit	The personal qualities that I most want to build on are: -**music**al ability -valuing **family** All of my other abilities, values, traits, physical characteristics, and memories are rather well taken care of; so for the foreseeable future these are the two I want to focus on.
Goals	I want to set goals in four areas: 1. New Learning 2. Translating Theory into Practice 3. Experiencing Sensory Pleasure 4. Developing Friendships Of these four, **friendships** and **pleasure** are the least addressed.
Community	My principle deficits, relationship-wise, are in two areas: **couples** who share Jane's and my interests, and **male friends**.
Altruism	After reviewing each kind of altruism, the ones I'd like to focus on are the ones I tend to do less frequently, and less naturally, than others: -protecting the **environment** -expressing **gratitude** -**neighborliness**

Notice that I have reviewed my entries in the five areas above and bolded the focal points. Here is my stab at writing a SPP that incorporates them into a single statement: "To find musical, environmental, gratitude, family, and sensory pleasure challenges that will build relationships with couples and male friends." Now, the task is to take this high-level SPP and convert it into specific plans. I called this step the creation of a Personal Optimization Plan (POP), or a plan to make optimum use of my natural energies.

Creating a Personal Optimization Plan

A good starting point would be with my bucket list. These are things that I want to do before I die; so clearly it would be lovely if I could find things on the list that would address the issues in my SPP. Let's take a look at my list (not all my verbal shorthand will make perfect sense, but you'll get the idea I have a big bucket full of wishes):

Camp and eat salmon at Puget Sound.
Complete Globus mental abilities assessment.
Write book on Globus model.
Write novel based on world of consulting.

Write book on mental abilities.
Write Owner's Manual for Coaching.
Take grandchildren camping.
Be part of a motet/madrigal group.
Have a Florida porch (fresh air, shade, no bugs).
Cross the pond with Papa.
Cross the pond with Other Mama.
Cross the pond with Henry Johnson.
Finish Happiness Book.
Write a textbook for Personality Assessment at Work.
Write a textbook for Applied Research, Critical Thinking, and Statistics.
Travel in South America.
Visit Ray in Austin, Texas.
Take Rowan on a trip.
Take Stella on a trip.
Take AJ on a trip.
Visit all national parks.
Get off the power grid.
Berlin.
Prague.
Spain, Barcelona, Le Segrada Familia.
Build whaling ship model.
Build 19th century sailing vessel model.
Buros for SP and WP.
Integrated report for Globus.
Coacher.
Selector.
Text for Critical Thinking.
Big Five User Conferences in Asia, Europe, West Coast.
Psalm 150 Project.
Sing/perform Missa Luba.
Eat at Stinking Rose in San Fran.

I reviewed my list to see which bucket items—things I really want to do—happen to satisfy elements of my SPP. They are in boldface above. In the Table 10.1 below, I indicate my thinking. It is certainly interesting to note that each item is capable of addressing more than one issue in my SPP. The best activities to pursue are those that address multiple needs.

Table 10.1 How Bucket Items Address Personal Priorities (author as example)

Be part of a motet/madrigal group.	*This would address my need for greater musical challenges, for increased sensory pleasure, and possibly for developing friendships with couples and males.*
Cross the pond with Papa (i.e., determine how/when his ancestors came over from Europe).	*This and the next two items would address family and gratitude (to my parents and miscellaneous other family members who've done things for me over the years).*

Table 10.1, cont.

Cross the pond with Other Mama.	"
Cross the pond with Henry Johnson.	"
Take Rowan on a trip.	*This would address family and gratitude (to our daughter).*
Get off the power grid.	*Environment, and possibly developing a male relationship*
Spain, Barcelona, Le Segrada Familia	*Sensory pleasure, music, and gratitude (to Jane, for visiting countries I was more interested in; she speaks Spanish but has never visited Spain)*
Psalm 150 Project	*Music, sensory pleasure, and possibly building relationships if I find a partner/s for the project.*

Now I need to come up with a simple plan for each item. The plan needs to keep in mind how I might keep all five of the modes of positive being uppermost. Since each item is in fact a goal, I don't need to worry about having goals, but I do need to make sure that I maintain a balance of goals across all of my values, needs, and interests. In addition, I need to plan each item so that it maximizes the elements of my SPP. Table 10.2 is my first pass at outlining a plan for each item, and evaluating it against the modes and SPP elements:

Table 10.2   Forming a Plan for Bucket List Items (author as example)

Goal:	*Planning Criteria:* **Flow, Fit, Altruism, Relationships, Music, Environment, Gratitude, Family, Sensory Pleasure, Relationships with Couples, Male Friends**
Be part of a motet/madrigal group.	In the past, these groups have had weak members whom I could not get rid of once the group was formed. I was too impatient to get started and invited folks to join before I knew whether they had sufficient skill. So, this time, we must resist the urge to move fast. We must find a couple that contains a tenor and a soprano (as Jane and I are alto and bass). If the result of an evening of singing, wine, and good food proves edifying, then we can add persons one at a time. This addresses all of the planning criteria but three (Env, Grat, Fam). We will not be in flow if the group contains persons with inadequate skill in reading music—this is the major point to keep in mind.
Cross the pond with Papa.	I have already begun this project using ancestry.com, DNA reports, and a research firm in Salt Lake City. I think I know which of my paternal ancestors crossed the Atlantic, what year, from what city in England, and where they landed in Virginia. Now I need to prove it. This is a solitary activity. However, if I think it through, I can use it to get to know some members of my family better by soliciting their participation in the project.
Cross the pond with Other Mama.	I never knew any of my grandparents—they all died before I was born. I wrote a biography of "Other Mama" (my maternal grandmother) several years ago, and now I feel as though I know her. All of the interviews and other information-gathering activity and then the writing caused her to come alive in my mind. Now, if I can determine when her ancestors came from Europe and who they were, I will complete the process of getting to know her, as well as provide a service to other members of my family.
Cross the pond with Henry Johnson.	HJ is my maternal grandfather. He died early, in his 20s. No one in my family knows anything about any of his ancestors. This one is a real challenge.

Table 10.2, cont.

Take Rowan on a trip.	We have taken Rowan's older brother Liam on a nice trip to Washington, DC. We need now to take Rowan on a similar trip. We've been waiting for him to be a little older so that he can be more independent, as in being able to read.
Get off the power grid.	Here is an item that could possibly help develop a relationship with a male friend. I'll have to think about this one—maybe first ask around for someone to think through the project with me. I do have a family member I could ask, but he lives elsewhere.
Spain, Barcelona, Le Segrada Familia	I can smell this one! Jane has to teach a class in Barcelona later this year, so I think I'll tag along and do some writing in the hotel room while she's with the client. Then we can enjoy the culture and indulge our musical and other sensory delights.
Psalm 150 Project	As I review my items, the glaring omission is things that would promote the development of relationships with couples. Maybe I could do that here. Jane and I could identify a couple with similar aesthetic sensibilities to help us develop a PowerPoint show that coordinates musical settings of Psalm 150 with the Cantoria of Luca della Robbia. I need to find other visual settings of Psalm 150 besides that of della Robbia.

I will now print this table and share it with my wife. We'll make some decisions about how to proceed.

Now, try your hand at developing your own SPP and POP. These are the steps that I suggest you follow:

1. Review your notes at the ends of Chapters 5 through 9. Make a table like the one below and enter key points to include in your Statement of Personal Priorities:

Area:	Items to Include in my SPP:
Goals	
Altruism	
Fit	
Flow	
Relationships	

2. Highlight the key points in this table. Then take a stab at writing your SPP. Use mine as a model, if you like.
3. Now, if you have not made a bucket list, this is a good time to do so. Go for length—a hundred or more things you would like to do before you quit this earth.
4. From your bucket list, select items that address the issues you specify in your SPP. Make a table like mine above and, for each bucket-list item, jot down in the right hand column the aspects of your SPP that the item addresses. Be clear how each item chosen will satisfy your needs for flow, fit, relationships, and altruism.
5. If any element of your SPP is not addressed in your bucket list, think of a goal that would address that element. When I reviewed my bucket list earlier, I had nothing that addressed "respect for environment," so I added "get off the power grid" to my bucket list. That is something I've dreamed about doing, but it had never occurred to me to add it to my bucket list.
6. Rough out a plan for each item, discussing the details with your partner or someone significant to you.

My bucket list and my subsequently chosen goals will not look like those of a younger person. At 70 years of age, I'm not thinking about achieving degrees or licenses, building a home, having children, writing a book, or singing in one of the grand cathedrals of Europe—I've done all those things! My list reflects a lifetime of checked-off items, and I still have a lot left to do. Also, the eight items I've singled out above are in addition to everything else I've got going on. These are eight items, however, that address aspects of my SPP that all the other activities in my life are not adequately addressing. Hence, successful attention to them should increase my sense of well-being, and make me feel that much more in gear.

In the next chapter, I'm going to introduce you to 119 "minor adjustments" that can make life more satisfying. These adjustments are different from the five major modes in this sense: The five modes of goals, flow, fit, relationships, and altruism work for everyone, regardless of individual differences in personality. The adjustors, on the other hand, do not work the same for everyone. You might make an adjustment that, should I do the same thing, would make me miserable and you happy! The five modes that we have been discussing are standard for everyone, whereas the four dozen adjustments are customized for the individual.

Part Three

Ongoing Maintenance—
Tools for Staying In Gear

STATEMENT OF PERSONAL PRIORITIES

FLOW | FIT | GOALS | COMMUNITY | ALTRUISM

Happiness Boosters   **Happiness Downers**
(Choice)   *(Choice)*

119 Minor Adjustors

(more within personal control)

(more outside personal control)

HAPPINESS SET POINT

Happiness Boosters   **Happiness Downers**
(Circumstance)   *(Circumstance)*

Continuum of Trait Happiness

Perennially Happy (N- E+) .... Occasionally Happy (N + E-)

11

119 Minor Adjustments

...that Make a Big Difference

> "If I had my life to live over, I'd dare to make more mistakes next time. I'd relax, I would limber up. I would be sillier than I have been this trip. I would take fewer things seriously. I would take more chances. I would climb more mountains and swim more rivers. I would eat more ice cream and less beans. I would perhaps have more actual troubles, but I'd have fewer imaginary ones...."
>
> -- Nadine Stair, at age 85

Guide to this chapter:

- The Relation of Individual Differences to the Minor Adjustments
- The Minor Adjustments

As I have asserted several times, proper attention to the five major modes will contribute to everyone's sense of well-being. We all feel as though our personal engine is in gear and heading in a meaningful direction if we are experiencing flow for much of the time; having good fit between our personal qualities and the demands made on us by our work; making progress towards goals, home, and community; developing satisfying and intimate relationships; and engaging in altruism.

The minor adjustors, on the other hand, are related to our unique personal qualities—our traits, abilities, values, experiences, and physical characteristics. In this chapter, we will review several dozen such opportunities for making adjustments in how we live our lives. In one sense, I am offering you an opportunity to write your own poem after the style of Nadine Stair's famous "I'd pick more daisies." While it is generally agreed that the sentiment expressed in the poem originated with Ms. Stair, humorist Don Herold (1889-1966) published a close version in the *Reader's Digest* in October 1953. See www.devpsy.org/nonscience/daisies for both versions. In effect, "I'd pick more daisies" is a testament to the perils of extreme behavior: too much solitude, too much society, too much worry, too little worry, too much trust, too little trust, too much reading, not enough reading, too much movie-going, not enough movie-going, and so forth.

Extremes in behavior are natural. People who score high on the trait of sociability tend to spend more time around other people and less time alone, in comparison to those who score lower. However, the danger is that we can overdo it. We can become so comfortable in indulging our natural extremities that we do not use what capacity we have for their opposites. A very sociable person can easily follow the path of least resistance and spend all of their waking time around others, with the result that they wake up one day and find they haven't read a book in years. If they then stop and make time to read a book of their choice, they are likely to be exhilarated at the accomplishment. I have a very sociable teammate who once or twice a year will come up to me and exclaim, "Pierce, you'd be so proud of me—I read a BOOK last week! And it was WONderful!"

> "You're only here for a short visit. Don't hurry. Don't worry. And be sure to smell the flowers along the way."
> --Walter Hagen, golfer, in *The Walter Hagen Story* (1956)

I am not going to go through the laborious process of identifying which of the minor adjustments relate to the hundreds of personal qualities that we identified in Chapter 6 as "Howardian Person." Instead, as you review the several dozen minor adjustments, you should experience a kind of murmur of recognition, a kind of tingling in your brain/body, as though your soul is suggesting to you that, "Yes, yes, this is an area in which you would benefit from an adjustment" from doing more or less of something—the mild shock of recognition that I could do with more or less of that.

List of 119 Minor Adjustments:

The 119 minor adjustments are of two kinds: unidimensional and bidimensional. Bidimensional adjustments are like a balance scale, whereby two opposing qualities present themselves for your consideration. Based on our individual natures, some of us may prefer more of one opposite than the other. For example, "poetry" and "prose" are two bimodal adjustors. So, I would ask myself, "Is the balance between reading poetry and prose in my life at this time satisfying to me? Would I be more pleased with myself if I were reading more of one than I am at present?" The answer for me is "Yes—I'd feel better about reading more poetry. I've let prose take charge of my reading life, and I miss reading a really intense poem." Whenever you find a bidimensional adjustment you'd like to make, use the space below it to make some notes about how you might make that happen. If you have 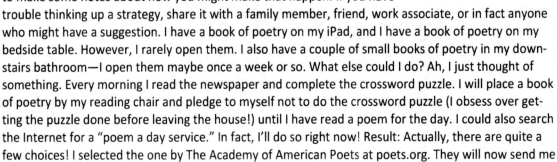 trouble thinking up a strategy, share it with a family member, friend, work associate, or in fact anyone who might have a suggestion. I have a book of poetry on my iPad, and I have a book of poetry on my bedside table. However, I rarely open them. I also have a couple of small books of poetry in my downstairs bathroom—I open them maybe once a week or so. What else could I do? Ah, I just thought of something. Every morning I read the newspaper and complete the crossword puzzle. I will place a book of poetry by my reading chair and pledge to myself not to do the crossword puzzle (I obsess over getting the puzzle done before leaving the house!) until I have read a poem for the day. I could also search the Internet for a "poem a day service." In fact, I'll do so right now! Result: Actually, there are quite a few choices! I selected the one by The Academy of American Poets at poets.org. They will now send me an email every day with a complete, and free, poem. Can't wait for my first one! (Update: I've been re-ceiving poems daily now for several months—some are more engaging than others!)

The other kinds of adjustments are unidimensional. Whereas bidimensional adjustments are like trying to achieve a balance between honey and vinegar in a sweet and sour sauce, a unidimen-sional adjustment would be for just honey, or just vinegar. As in, do I use too much honey in my diet, not enough, or just about the right amount? In this case, you are not trying to balance two opposites or alternatives, rather you are trying to adjust the degree to which you experience some single quality in your life. This is less like a balance scale and more like a linear scale, such as a ruler or thermometer. One of the unidimensional adjustments is "Playing Games." So, I would ask myself, "Do I play too many games, too few, or about enough?" This is an interesting question for me. In my 20s and 30s I played 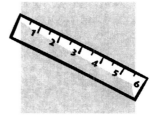 many games, from bridge to chess, from Scrabble to Pac-Man, from charades to Monopoly. For the last 20 years, I've played few games—the occasional game on my iPhone or iPad, every now and then a game of chess or checkers with our grandchildren, "Go Fishing" when our grandchildren were younger. But as a general rule games have given way to reading and writing. Part of this is because of my rela-tionship with Jane, who is just fine with my love of reading and writing. But the two of us seldom play games. When we travel, we will do a crossword puzzle together while waiting in an airport. Recently, I've begun playing "Words with Friends" on my iPad/iPhone. It is the same thing as Scrabble, but online. There is only so much time in the day, and games have taken the back seat. I think it is likely time for me to up the importance of playing games, both with my wife and with my grandchildren. So, what can I do to make this happen? Well, I understand that our local grandchildren have begun to en-joy chess. Our chess set is hidden at the moment; so it never reaches our awareness when they visit. I shall change its location so that it is within plain view. Also, there is an online version of chess, and the grandchildren both love to use iPads/iPhones. So, I will talk with their parents about starting chess games with them online. (Update: My granddaughter Stella and I have played several chess games us-ing the "Chess with Friends" app for iPhone and iPad. Delightful! She is six years old and uses her mother's iPhone to play me. They live in Manhattan—we are in Charlotte, NC.)

I have grouped the 79 bidimensional adjustments into 10 categories:

- Attentional Focus (7 adjustments),
- Entertainment Alternatives (7),
- Goal Types (7),
- Language (8),
- Maintenance (6),
- Money (4) ,
- Outlook (8),
- Physical Mode/State (11),
- Social/Interpersonal (12), and
- Work Style (9).

The 40 unidimensional adjustments comprise seven categories:

- Achievement Areas (8 adjustments),
- Entertainment Levels (16),

261

- Health (1),
- Past Experiences (1),
- Physical Characteristics (1),
- Social (5), and
- Talents (8).

As you proceed through each group, consider the adjustment presented. If you are OK with the balance or degree to which you are experiencing that adjustment, simply check the "OK" box and proceed to the next adjustment. Otherwise, indicate which direction you'd like to move in by drawing an arrow. Then, jot down some notes as to what you'd like to do and how you'll do it. Often, you'll need to stop doing one thing in order to make time for another; so indicate what you'll do less of in order to do more of something else.

Bidimensional Adjustments (79), with the goal of balance:

The first adjustments are what I call "attentional focus." These seven mental states reflect how you choose to focus your attention. In each case, decide whether you would like to spend more time in the state on the left or on the right. Draw an arrow in the direction you would like to spend more time, or simply circle the description you'd like to do more of going forward. Then, in the "Notes" box below, indicate the specific situations you'd like to apply this to. And, indicate what it may take in order to do that.

☐ Check if OK	**Concentrating**	**Multitasking**
	Pure concentration is engaging in one activity with no rivals for your attention. Examples: reading with no other responsibilities (such as children, security monitors, lifeguarding, etc.)	There is really no such thing as multitasking, but rather alternate-tasking—doing two or more things in alternation, such as read a paragraph, then look at the kids, read a paragraph, then check the security monitor, etc.)
	Notes on What and How To:	

☐ Check if OK	**Creative**	**Practical**
	While creative activity is not mutually exclusive with practical activity, they often are considered mutually exclusive. One can make a broom, and that is practical. But one can make an unusual, novel kind of broom, and that is both creative and practical, but only if the broom actually works! If it is novel and doesn't work, then it is just creative!	One can be practical and no-nonsense and never be creative. Being practical means only getting the job done. Some people get bored just being practical, and some don't. In fact some people avoid doing practical things because they get bored with them. Perhaps the solution for them is to find ways of making the practical more interesting.
	Notes on What and How To:	

☐ Check if OK	Details	Big Picture
	Spending time on the details means thinking through all, or most, of the things that need to get done in order for a decision or course of action to be satisfying. For example, one could throw a party with the best of intentions, but it could go awry because of failure to think through such details as who would get along together, how many drinks are likely to be consumed and of which kind, what the weather forecast is, competing activities (how many wedding receptions have been ruined because too many people huddled around a televised ball game?), etc.	I recently had an idea to get some friends together to see a provocative film and have dinner afterwards in order to discuss issues in the film. That was the overall idea. A good one. I found the time of the film, and made a reservation for the dinner. That was as much detail as I wanted to get involved with! However, my experience told me that I needed to pay more attention to details. It turns out that the theatre changed the time of the movie, and if I hadn't double-checked it, we'd have had a botched evening.
	Notes on What and How To:	

☐ Check if OK	Local	Global
	Being local is being active in one's neighborhood or homeowner's association, eating local traditional foods (in my case, fried chicken and barbecue!), keeping the local river clean, enjoying local traditions (in my case car racing), and the like.	Being global is being active in an international association or social networking group, being open to trying dishes from other countries, showing concern for the destruction of rain forests half way around the world, enjoying and respecting traditions from other countries (such as the Indian bindi), and the like.
	Notes on What and How To:	

☐ Check if OK	Online	Offline
	Amount of time spent working at a computer or with computer-like devices—plugged in, regardless of whether one is actually on-line/connected to the Internet.	Gardening, reading (e-readers OK!), writing (not keyboarding), cooking, entertaining, traveling, volunteering, childcare (without devices!), exercising, painting, and the like.
	Notes on What and How To:	

☐ Check if OK	Sacred	Secular
	Activities related to the study or practice of religion.	Activities related to the pursuit of bodily pleasures and non-religious intellectual or social interests.
	Notes on What and How To:	

☐ Check if OK	Specialized	Multi-disciplinary
	Study, work, or play related to one's primary field, such as mathematics or history.	Study, work, or play that incorporates multiple fields, as a project that involves history, art, mathematics, and computer programming.
	Notes on What and How To:	

The next seven adjustments are entertainment alternatives. Indicate whether you are more towards one extreme than you'd like to be.

☐ Check if OK	Acting	Observing
	Being an active participant, like being in a play, playing a sport, throwing a dinner party, planning a reunion, or playing in a concert.	Being in the "audience," as in going to a play, watching a game, eating at a restaurant, attending a reunion, or listening to a concert.
	Notes on What and How To:	

☐ Check if OK	Aesthetic	Ordinary
	Activities that involve the so-called fine arts, which emphasize beauty more than utility, e.g., paintings, sculpture, ballet, chamber music, symphonic and choral music, art songs, fine writing (poetry or prose), theatre, opera, handcrafts (pottery, weaving, woodworking, basketry, etc.).	Activities that place more emphasis on usefulness than on beauty, such as housepainting, Jazzercise, hymn-singing (as used in worship), technical and news writing, cabinet-making, sewing. Clearly, some activities can emphasize utility and beauty equally as in an elegantly designed coffee mug.
	Notes on What and How To:	

☐ Check if OK	Chores	Entertainment
	Washing dishes, mopping, sweeping, paying bills, doing tax returns, cleaning windows and gutters, raking, weeding, running errands, cooking meals, putting kids to bed….	Watching television (usually), going to movies, drinking beer or latte with friends, watching or attending sports events or concerts, reading, going to an amusement park, travel….
	Notes on What and How To:	

☐ Check if OK	Fiction	Nonfiction
	Reading novels, short stories, or plays.	Reading biographies, essays, histories, philosophy, and sundry specific topics.
	Notes on What and How To:	

☐ Check if OK	Watching Fictional TV Programs	Watching Nonfictional TV Programs
	Soaps, dramas, mysteries, thrillers, science fiction, comedies....	News, documentaries, hobby programs, so-called reality shows....
	Notes on What and How To:	

☐ Check if OK	Watching TV with Violent Content	Watching TV with Nonviolent Content
	Shows that portray killings, blood and gore, rape, rough sex, verbal abuse, child and spouse abuse, foul language, war, gang violence, bullying....	Shows that emphasize healthy relationships, family-friendly language, provocative ethical situations, social criticism, a search for truth, an appreciation for beauty....
	Notes on What and How To:	

☐ Check if OK	Work	Play
	Activity required to earn an income, although it is understood that for some people their work feels more like play! Also, housework, volunteer work, maintenance work for a club or other organization.	Activity that you don't have to do in order to earn an income, such as playing catch with a dog or child, playing Words with Friends on the Internet, having a jam session with friends, being silly, playing a pickup game of basketball.
	Notes on What and How To:	

The next seven adjustments are types of goals. If you over-rely on one extreme type of goal at this time in your life, indicate how you'd like to form some goals with different characteristics.

☐ Check if OK	Change	Status Quo
	A new goal is a change goal when it requires something substantially different from the last time you tried a similar goal. For example, painting a piece of furniture blue instead of red is not substantially different, but adding decorative painting to parts of it is. To count as a change goal, it must require a new or different skill or ability, or require a greater effort.	A status quo goal means taking on a task that has essentially the same requirements that it has had every other time you've taken it on. To add a handicap to a customary task would move it from status quo to change, as in deciding to start using your weaker hand to play Ping-Pong with your child. Keep in mind that too many change goals can be draining—status quo goals preserve your energy for the more important change goals.
	Notes on What and How To:	

□ Check if OK	Complex	Simple
	Goals become more complex as you add elements. For example, a goal requiring the management of people is less complex than one that requires managing people, data, things, and ideas. And elements of a goal become more complex as you vary the number or type within an element. For example, managing 20 people is more complex than managing three people, and working with one kind of data is less complex than working with several kinds of data.	Simple goals mean a minimal number of elements—either no other people involved or a very few, only one skill involved, only one body of knowledge involved, only one person to satisfy, and so forth. The goal of building a bookcase for your personal use in your home office is likely to be much simpler than the goal of building a deck and patio for your family's use. Of course, one can complexify a simple project rather quickly!
	Notes on What and How To:	

□ Check if OK	Mastery Goals	Performance Goals
	Mastery goals entail taking on something you've not done before and are not guaranteed success. They are often called stretch goals, or risk-taking goals. The difference between a performance goal and a mastery goal is the degree of risk involved, or the degree of certainty of success.	Performance goals entail taking on something at which you feel you are sure to succeed. To run a marathon for the 10th time is a performance goal, assuming you've successfully completed the other nine.
	Notes on What and How To:	

□ Check if OK	My Agenda	Others' Needs
	A goal that you think up is one that reflects your personal needs, interests, and values, regardless of whether the goal benefits only you or benefits others. I built a model railroad for my grandchildren because I thought they would like it, but it was my idea, and I wanted to do it. I didn't ask whether they wanted it or not.	When others identify a goal that they would like you to take on in their behalf, then the focus is on doing something that others say they need and are asking for your help. For example. For example, I have a friend who agreed to earn a Ph.D. because his partner wanted him to, even though my friend didn't really want to do it.
	Notes on What and How To:	

□ Check if OK	Perfectionist	Casual
	A perfectionist approach means that your quality standards are high and that you will not consider it to be attained until you have met or exceeded those standards. The emphasis is on quality.	A casual approach to goals means that your quality standards are lower, and that you will consider the goal attained if it serves the purpose for which it was originally intended. The emphasis is on utility.
	Notes on What and How To:	

☐ Check if OK	**Short Term**	**Long Term**
	Short-term goals do not take a long time to attain and have relatively immediate payoff. To earn the money to buy a guitar is short term. To find wildflowers and make a bouquet for your partner is short term.	Long-term goals take longer, and the payoff is often not immediate. To commit to learning how to play classical guitar is a long-term goal. To design, plant, nurture, harvest, and continue to maintain a garden of flowers and vegetables is long term.
	Notes on What and How To:	

☐ Check if OK	**Taking Risks**	**Playing It Safe**
	This is similar to Mastery goals, but Mastery goals only entail the risk of success, where this kind of risk could be involved with safety, reputation, health, and financial security. Investing money in long shots is taking a risk, while trying to write a novel is a mastery goal in which success is not guaranteed.	This is similar to Performance goals, but Performance goals only entail taking on challenges that you're sure to succeed at, while here you also insure that the goal will not harm you socially, financially, or healthwise.
	Notes on What and How To:	

Next are eight adjustments that concern our use of language. We don't often think about the way we talk and write, and we may have fallen into some habits or patterns that we'd like to change.

☐ Check if OK	**Native Language**	**Other Language(s)**
	Reading, writing, and talking in the language(s) you were brought up using. A bilingual home would entail equal use of two languages.	Reading, writing, and talking in one or more languages that you did not grow up using. This includes time spent learning a new language, or in increasing one's proficiency in a non-native language.
	Notes on What and How To:	

☐ Check if OK	**Poetry**	**Prose**
	Reading poetry, whether in books, magazines, the Internet, newspaper, going to poetry readings, listening to poetry through various media, and so forth.	Reading prose fiction or nonfiction in all of its various formats, including listening to prose being read through various media.
	Notes on What and How To:	

☐ Check if OK	Simple Vocabulary	Complex Vocabulary
	Some states have Plain English laws that require all legally binding documents to be written in easy to understand language. This typically means, for English, Anglo-Saxon words like "use" or "clear up" in preference to similar words with Greek and Roman roots, like "utilize" or "disambiguate." Typically, the fewer the syllables, the simpler the words.	Complexity is not the same as technical language. To refer to a carburetor is to use a technical word, but it is the only possible word to use! A simpler word doesn't exist. However, to use the word "palimpsest" is obscure and complex, and one could simply use "layers." While more complex words are often more precise, they are not necessarily more communicative.
	Notes on What and How To:	

☐ Check if OK	Talking	Listening
	Running your mouth verbally, whether face-to-face, on the phone, with one person or a large group, whether starting a conversation, interrupting someone else, or responding.	Keeping your mouth shut and focusing on what the other(s) is(are) saying, and only speaking when others have completed their thought.
	Notes on What and How To:	

☐ Check if OK	Technical Language	Plain Language
	Every field has a vocabulary special to its theory and practice. Poets talk about hexameters, physicists talk about black holes, and physicians talk about their stock portfolios (just kidding!).	Technical language is fine when talking with others who have mastered that field, but persons outside the specialty would typically prefer that you not use such jargon and that you find more everyday ways to express yourself. Use "changing your behavior to be like those around you" rather that the psychological term/jargon "self-monitoring."
	Notes on What and How To:	

☐ Check if OK	Words	Numbers
	At one extreme, one's life revolves around words only, as in using numbers only when necessary to say amount ("We're expecting four for supper.") and avoiding arithmetic, algebraic, and higher mathematical operations. This extreme is based on fear, distaste, lack of talent, or just habit.	At the other extreme, one's life revolves around numbers and symbols (as in X's and O's to diagram sports strategy, or shapes to represent geographical features), allowing words in one's life primarily to talk about numbers and to take care of basic necessities.
	Notes on What and How To:	

Check if OK	❐ Writing Letters	Writing E-mails
	Handwritten letters take more time, cost more, and take more effort, but they normally pack more of an emotional punch, assuming they are legible.	Computer-generated letters transmitted through the Internet are quicker and cheaper (almost free!), but lack the personal touch and emotional impact of handwritten letters delivered by a letter carrier.
	Notes on What and How To:	

Check if OK	❐ Polite Language	Coarse Language
	In my world, polite language entails the choice of words I would use around my parents, teachers, religious leaders, most of my customers. Profanity, slang, stereotypes, racial slurs, ethnic put downs, sexual references, bodily functions (and even some body parts, as in "tummy" is more polite than "stomach") are not polite usage.	In my world, coarse language is unrestrained expression as though no one who might care is listening—cussin' like a proverbial sailor, telling bawdy jokes, and the like. In one sense, coarse language is easy language, as it sometimes takes effort to find a way to express something politely.
	Notes on What and How To:	

The next six address issues surrounding maintenance. You can't run a machine indefinitely without performing periodic maintenance. Neither can we run our body-mind for long without physical and mental maintenance. Ignoring needed maintenance invites breakdown. A friend died of a massive coronary while bicycling up a mountain with his family—it was the first time he'd bicycled in 30 years!

Check if OK	❐ Aerobic Exercise	Anaerobic Exercise
	Exercise that moves major muscle groups and elevates heartbeat for some time: running, swimming, stair-stepping, cross-country skiing, brisk walking.	Exercise that does not elevate heartbeat in a sustained and substantial manner: weight- lifting, golf, baseball.
	Notes on What and How To:	

Check if OK	❐ Composing	Performing
	Composing includes creative activity before it is shared with the public: outlining, writing, music composition, choreography, storyboarding, modeling.	Performing takes a creative work to the public: publishing, concertizing, dancing, showing.
	Notes on What and How To:	

☐ Check if OK	Memorizing	Scanning
	When we were in school, we frequently went over and over certain material so that we could recite it pretty much word for word. As adults, we often lament our fading memory, but the truth is that we typically abandon the effort to *try* to memorize. Memory requires rehearsal (practicing), organizing (e.g., mnemonic aids), and intention (consciously deciding that you *want* to remember something).	Most of our reading, listening, viewing, tasting, touching, and smelling occurs like a movie that cannot be stopped and repeated—rapidly experienced without stopping to savor and reflect. One kind of wisdom is knowing when to scan and just catch the essence of meaning and when to stop and savor something with the intention of committing it to memory.
	Notes on What and How To:	

☐ Check if OK	Practicing	Performing
	Management guru Peter Drucker once said something to the effect that time spent in planning is saved in execution. A corollary to that maxim is that time spent in practice is reflected in performance. The violinist Jascha Heifitz once quipped: "If I don't practice for one day, I can tell. If I don't practice for two days, the critics can tell. If I don't practice for three days, the public can tell." On another occasion, a passerby asked him how to get to Carnegie Hall, to which he retorted, "Practice!"	Performing is the goal of practice. However, performing does not mean that you have to be on stage before a large group of people. Performing is what you do with something in order to determine whether you've mastered it. Practicing dribbling and foul shots for hours and days on end can be put to the performance test by engaging in an imaginary end-of-game situation, say, in which you are ahead by four with a minute to go and the other team starts fouling you. Games and concerts are performances, but offstage run-throughs are also performances.
	Notes on What and How To:	

☐ Check if OK	Studying or Preparing	Executing or Performing
	This is another example of the Drucker maxim that time spent in preparation is reflected in execution. The more time and energy you put into preparing a talk, the better the talk will be. The more time you spend studying how to cook a dish and selecting the best ingredients, the better the dish should be.	All the study in a lifetime is worthless until it is applied to a real world situation. Do something with all your preparation. Study the construction of chairs, but build one to test your learning. Read and converse, then put your learning in print, action, song, sport, business, or some other application of choice.
	Notes on What and How To:	

Check if OK	Using	Maintaining
☐	Use your wooden musical instrument, your car, your circular saw... Use your body at work, at play, and for chores...	Sharpen the saw blade, oil it with linseed oil, and take it in for maintenance. Get sufficient aerobic and anaerobic exercise to keep it in good condition.
	Notes on What and How To:	

Now we look at four adjustments that concern our use of money.

Check if OK	Material	Spiritual
☐	Materialism is most often defined as a combination of 1) the maximum accumulation of physical possession plus 2) the pursuit of physical comfort. To simply have or own something is materialistic—to use it is not. Not reading your fine library of leather-bound volumes is materialistic. Reading them is not. Owning a Picasso only for the prestige is materialistic. Using it as an investment tool or admiring it as artwork is not.	Spiritual activity deemphasizes possessions and physical pleasure and emphasizes the life of the mind including meditation, introspection, reflection, analysis, observation, prayer, appreciating or creating art. Just leaving my musical instruments on the living-room wall would be materialistic. When I play them and fill my world with Josquin or Joplin, I am transported into the world of the spirit.
	Notes on What and How To:	

Check if OK	Spending on Things	Spending on Experiences
☐	To spend on a family vacation and then spend no time together (one shops, one goes to the arcade, one plays golf, one reads) is not to spend on an experience, but to spend on things.	To spend on an entertainment center is to spend on things, but to enjoy it as a family and have discussions about its offerings makes it more of an experience.
	Notes on What and How To:	

Check if OK	Spending	Saving
☐	It's the portion of your income that you pay out and will never see again. Sometimes it is necessary, sometimes not. To buy a computer or new car is spending. To buy an antique car, fix it up, maintain it, and let it accumulate value is saving/investing.	It's the portion of your income that you put aside for future use. Depositing in a savings account, certificate of deposit, IRA, etc. is saving. Purchasing stocks, gold, silver, artworks, and real estate for future redemption is saving.
	Notes on What and How To:	

☐ Check if OK	Traveling	At Home
	Traveling includes any effort to see a part of the local or international scene that you've not seen before, or not seen enough of. To live in a city that has a good museum that you've never seen before and to then go to that museum, that would be small-scale travel. To go abroad to a country you've not visited would be large-scale travel.	To stay at home is to occupy scenes that are very familiar to you: home, workplace, shopping center, place of worship, workout gym, favorite restaurants. To venture to new shops, new restaurants would be small-scale travel.
	Notes on What and How To:	

The next eight adjustments reflect our general outlook towards life and others in general.

☐ Check if OK	Personal Focus	Community Focus
	Focused on my immediate environment and my immediate needs related to work, family, and other current commitments	In addition to my immediate concerns, following varied sources of information about conditions around the globe and universe.
	Notes on What and How To:	

☐ Check if OK	Ornamented	Plain
	In personal attire, interior decorating, landscaping, and/or other aspects of my life, attempting to decorate, trim, garnish, adorn, prettify, or add to. Where one bauble is good, 10 baubles are better.	Insisting on pure functionality and not going beyond that. No garnish on the mashed potatoes. No earrings (or at least they are very small, relatively unnoticeable). No frills. Not necessarily austere (as in sleeping on boards), but certainly minimal—a mattress, but no frilly dustcovers.
	Notes on What and How To:	

☐ Check if OK	In the Foreground	In the Background
	Time spent being highly visible, as in meeting the press, being on television, acting in a drama, performing onstage in some capacity, making presentations, leading meetings, making calls on people.	Time spent behind the scene, as in preparing statements for people who meet the press, being stage manager, preparing presentations, planning, making various preparations, and generally staying out of the limelight
	Notes on What and How To:	

☐ Check if OK	Optimistic	Pessimistic
	A tendency to take responsibility for good outcomes and to see poor outcomes as only temporary and limited in scope.	A tendency to disclaim responsibility for good outcomes and to see poor ones as a direct consequence of your flawed participation.
	Notes on What and How To:	

☐ Check if OK	Proud	Humble
	Openly taking pride in one's accomplishments, abilities, demeanor, and general station in life.	Downplaying one's accomplishments and abilities and accurately deflecting the responsibility for accomplishment to the efforts of others.
	Notes on What and How To:	

☐ Check if OK	Romancing	Taking for Granted
	Not just meant for one's romantic partner, but rather a general tendency to do the little things that make people feel flattered, important, or cared about, as in sending flowers, sending cards, buying chocolates or donuts, cutting out clippings of interest to them, showing an interest in their family's welfare (or their favorite sports team, movie star, etc.).	Being what might be called tough and no-nonsense, with the outlook that a fair day's wage for a fair day's work is all that others should need to feel cared about. Resisting the time, money, and effort required to do what might seem to you like pampering others.
	Notes on What and How To:	

☐ Check if OK	Seeking Recognition	Recognizing Others
	Showing others the results of one's labor and efforts and asking what they think. Showing no reluctance in self-promotion.	Shying away from self-promotion and preferring instead to point out how others' accomplishments merit praise and recognition.
	Notes on What and How To:	

☐ Check if OK	**Serious**	**Light**
	My sister once accused me of not being able to take a joke. She was saying I was too serious, that I took things too literally and seriously. The contrast being serious and light is highlighted in the eponymous movie in which the female lead accuses the male lead of an "unbearable lightness of being" in the way he cavalierly dismisses the gravity of the soviet invasion of Prague in 1986.	G. K. Chesterton once said, "A characteristic of the great saints is their power of levity. Angels can fly because they can take themselves lightly." Shakespeare's tragedies have comic relief, and surgeons joke in the operating room—both do this to keep the seriousness of the moment from becoming oppressively stressful.
	Notes on What and How To:	

Now let us look at 11 adjustments that deal with our physical self.

☐ Check if OK	**Active**	**Sedentary**
	This is similar to being a participant versus being an observer. However, "active" means one is physically active, as in walking and moving about, which could include jogging, cooking dinner, gardening, and playing basketball. Microwaving dinner and watching basketball are not active, but sedentary!	In this sense, sedentary refers to activities that involve sitting or reclining. People who are naturally more physically active, but who need to be more sedentary (as in reading, doing computer work, and other desk/lap work), often choose to use a "standing desk" tall enough so one can stand while doing desk work.
	Notes on What and How To:	

☐ Check if OK	**Being under Pressure**	**Being Free of Pressure**
	Pressure means being held to an exacting standard with enormous consequences for failure to meet that standard, as in having to meet a deadline with scarcely enough time and resources to achieve the desired standard and one's job or reputation being on the line.	Freedom from pressure means that one has a rather wide margin of error for successfully completing an assignment, with ample time and resources for getting the job done properly. The standards can still be exacting, but without the erstwhile pressure.
	Notes on What and How To:	

☐ Check if OK	**Cooking**	**Eating**
	Cooking is a way of being both active and participating, with some folks never even sitting down to eat, but attending to food preparation, serving, and cleanup while others eat.	Eating is taking a seat and enjoying a meal from beginning to end, whether at home or out.
	Notes on What and How To:	

☐ Check if OK	Fast Foods	Slow Foods
	Purchasing meals that are prepared in quantity (and usually in advance), cheaply, and able to be served quickly, e.g., McDonald's Happy Meal. Emphasis is on speed, convenience, and simple tastiness.	Purchasing meals that are prepared only after the order is submitted. In its extreme form, as in the "Slow Food" movement, everything is prepared from ingredients in their naturally occurring form, as in the movie *Babette's Feast,* with one meal taking up to several weeks to prepare. Emphasis is on complex taste and nutrition.
	Notes on What and How To:	

☐ Check if OK	Hard at Work	Relaxed
	One person's work is another's relaxation. For one, gardening is work, for another relaxation. For me, cleaning the house, maintaining the yard, doing home repairs, preparing presentations, proofreading, doing pushups, and doing repetitious tasks all are work.	For me, reading, writing, study, music practice and performance, walking, preparing for a dinner party, doing genealogical research, and model railroading are all relaxing. You must determine whether you want more of the activities that feel like work to you, or of the ones that feel relaxing.
	Notes on What and How To:	

☐ Check if OK	Number of Activities Scheduled in the Day	Amount of Unscheduled Time
	Some don't know what to do with themselves when they have nothing on the calendar to do after the current activity concludes. That is not a bad thing, but when one schedules all of their time, they often end up not having time for personal pleasures such as reading, crafts, and music. Some take craft classes and join book clubs because they would not do the crafts or reading if it were not scheduled.	How many times have Jane and I exclaimed, "Ah, an unscheduled weekend! Don't commit to anything with anyone! Let's enjoy it." I love those few days when I arrive at the office, and I have no appointments on the calendar—not one! It is not that I then do nothing, but that I can choose what I want to do with the time--things that take long stretches to accomplish, such as writing, analysis of complex data, product design, and such.
	Notes on What and How To:	

☐ Check if OK	Physical	Mental
	Physical is planting and weeding a garden. ...building a model railroad ...exercising ...acting in a Gilbert & Sullivan musical ...distributing political brochures door to door	Mental is planning a garden. ...planning the railroad layout ...reading an exercise physiology book ...learning the lines and notes for the musical ...researching a position paper for a politician
	Notes on What and How To:	

☐ Check if OK	Plant-based Diet	Animal-based Diet
	Consuming a diet that comes exclusively from plants, as proposed in the documentary film (and book) *Forks over Knives.*	Consuming a diet that is plant and animal based, whereby one gets most of one's proteins from animal products.
	Notes on What and How To:	

☐ Check if OK	Quiet	Loud
	Working or relaxing in a place where there is no sound—no music, no people talking or making noise, no traffic, no construction noise, just quiet.	Being in the thick of the action with people talking and doing, machinery going, vehicles operating, nature singing, music pulsing.
	Notes on What and How To:	

☐ Check if OK	Savor	Engorge
	To savor is to take in something sensually—taste, vision, hearing, touch, or smell—and to focus on that perception, letting it linger, not rushing to add another perception. Two examples—to smell a flower and recall all of the previous places you've taken in that fragrance before, to imagine the kind of person who planted it and how they went about it, and how it differs from other fragrances; or to take a bite of chocolate and let it sit on various places on your tongue, seeing how long you can make it last, while comparing it mentally to other chocolates, where you tasted them, and so forth.	The opposite of savoring is seeing how much sensation you can experience in a given amount of time, as in 17 cities in 21 days, or a hot-dog eating contest, or hurrying through the Louvre to see if you can get a quick glimpse of every work of art therein before you leave, or a beer chug-a-lug contest. The emphasis is not on sensation but on consumption. In *Walden Two,* B. F. Skinner proposed that music concerts offer only one work for a program—that would be savoring, not multiple works as is the norm, which is really engorgement.
	Notes on What and How To:	

☐ Check if OK	Scratch Cooking	Quick Cooking
	This really refers to making anything from raw materials rather than from mostly prepared materials. In cooking, it would be using flower, eggs, butter, vanilla, salt, milk, etc. to make a cake. In making models, it would be obtaining plain unshaped pieces of balsa wood, sheets of paper, coils of wire, etc. to make model airplanes, cars, and so forth. In furniture making, it would mean building a table from sheets of plywood or other woods that have not been cut to size for assembly.	This refers to anything made from a kit. In cooking, it means making a cake from a mix. In model building, it means making a model from a kit in which all parts are molded plastic and only assembly is required, with maybe a little painting or application of decals. In furniture making, it would mean buying a table kit in which the legs have already been turned on a lathe, and all the other pieces have been cut to size, so that only sanding, assembly, and finishing are required. The ultimate "quick cooking" is buying something already made.
	Notes on What and How To:	

The next 12 cover social, or interpersonal, practices.

☐ Check if OK	Encouraging	Reprimanding
	This is a version of the PEE to NEE ratio. Encouraging is emphasizing the merit in what one has done and expressing confidence that any shortfalls can be successfully dealt with. "You've only got another three seconds to shave off of that race before you qualify for the Olympics. I think you can make it up in the middle part of the third lap."	Reprimanding is focusing on where others fall short of success and omitting the merit in their work. "You keep falling short by three seconds. That'll never make the Olympic cut. You're not trying hard enough."
	Notes on What and How To:	

☐ Check if OK	Alone	Around Others
	Solitude means working and living with no other people in the immediate environment. In the U.S., the number of people living alone by choice has increased dramatically in the last two decades.	Being around others means there is always at least one other person, often more, in the house, the car, the playground, the office.
	Notes on What and How To:	

☐ Check if OK	Busy	Available
	This is a question of accessibility. Busy people typically say "no" when asked if they have five minutes or if they can have an appointment.	Available people have enough flexibility in their schedule that they can typically work in a brief or relatively short visit without a lot of notice.
	Notes on What and How To:	

☐ Check if OK	Committed	Tentative
	Many areas of our life require a commitment—making a promise to oneself or to others and keeping that promise. Examples of commitment include agreeing to marry someone and sticking to the marriage vows, agreeing to pursue a college degree and completing it, agreeing to serve on a board and fulfilling all of the duties expected of you therefrom, and agreeing to lose weight and sticking to the plan.	The opposite of commitment is good intentions without the follow-through of devoting the required time, energy, and resources. Being tentative in this way is stressful, as one tends to think less of oneself when one makes a promise and doesn't follow through. The solution is to remove the promise from the tentative category and either make a firm commitment or let go of it—take it completely off of your plate—say "No" to it.
	Notes on What and How To:	

☐ Check if OK	Competing	Cooperating
	Some of us try to win at everything we do, whether it is entering a sales competition or playing Go Fishing with a child. For these folks, it is more important to say "I won" than to say we had a good time. Some have not competitive spirit—perhaps you would enjoy being more competitive in some situations.	Perhaps you and others would benefit by your being less competitive. There are two ways to be less competitive. One is to handicap yourself, so that you can still try to win but are less likely to win the majority of the time. The other way is to change to an activity not involving winning, e.g., building a model with your grandchild rather than playing cards.
	Notes on What and How To:	

☐ Check if OK	Following	Leading
	Some of us naturally like to take charge of situations and be the leader, while some like others to lead. In the two church choirs Jane and I used to sing with, we tended to be the leaders with respect to initiating opportunities to go out to eat/drink after rehearsals and concerts. We often wished that others would take such initiative. We now are singing with a choir in which a long-established tradition of going out to eat/drink finds us no longer having to be the ones to arrange things. I like being in situations where others take the lead, so long as I like their choices!	If others make choices for you that violate your values or in other ways are not enjoyable for you, then you might consider taking the initiative yourself and planning events that would be more suitable to you. If it is to be, it is up to thee! Or as Alabama football Coach Bear Bryant said, "Make something happen!" Or, if you just really don't like being the leader, perhaps you could find someone else to take the responsibility. You'd just need to ask around.
	Notes on What and How To:	

☐ Check if OK	Formal	Casual
	Are you always formal? When do you let your hair down? Often enough? Consider that excessive formality might feel good to you while being off-putting to others. Review the settings of your life and consider those in which you might enjoy being more or less formal.	Are you always casual? I really like to be casual, both in clothing and language. However, many other people see my time and efforts at formality as a sign that I care about them. So I bite the bullet and wear starch shirts on occasions, especially when Jane suggests it! I try not to concede grudgingly.
	Notes on What and How To:	

☐ Check if OK	Tactful	Direct
	Tact is a form of empathy—it is about "walking in another's shoes" in order to sense how they feel about your words and gestures. Being more tactful means using words and gestures that are not offensive to others. Putting "spin" on an issue is a form of tact, just as "political correctness" is a form of tact. Tact is doing as the Romans do while in Rome, within reason.	Being direct means telling it like it is, letting it all spill out without prettifying it. "I have to go to the bathroom," rather than "I have to go powder my nose." The danger of excessive tact is that people may not understand your meaning when you in fact want them to. When communication is primary, use directness. When avoiding unpleasant feelings is primary, use tact. One of my sisters had an aversion to the word "pee," so I didn't use it around her. But I used it around most others, unless I sensed I was talking with a clone of my sister!
	Notes on What and How To:	

☐ Check if OK	Taking Charge	Leaving Alone
	When something is not right, you can try to fix it or you can ignore it. The issue here is "choosing one's battles." Clearly, if one were to fix every wrong one encountered in one's day, one would not only fail to achieve one's goals—one would be regarded as neurotic!	Sometimes we must allow imperfections, mediocrity, and mistakes to go uncorrected or unimproved. On the other hand, if we always ignored them, we would be seen as not caring, as having no standards. For me, I ignore average food when I'm a guest, but I criticize it when I'm paying, or when I'm cooking. I try to ignore ineffective parenting, unless a child's safety is involved.
	Notes on What and How To:	

☐	Time for Me	Time for Others
Check if OK	We all need to take time for ourselves in order to "fill up our tank." We can give our time to others only so much before we become ineffective. I need to make time for exercising, reading, practicing, and doing maintenance on things that matter to me. The easiest way to insure such time for self is to make a ritual out of it. For example, I come home from the office every day at 4 in order to write. However, when I reach the house after my bus ride and walk, I spend 10 minutes working crosswords and another 10 minutes practicing one of my musical instruments. Only then will I permit myself to start putting pen to paper (or rather, fingertips to keyboard).	Just as rituals help insure that we make time for ourselves, rituals also help us make time for others. At work, my weekly "Touch Base" meeting with my two partners is such a ritual. The temptation is to skip the meetings and to continue working on "my stuff." However, I know it is important for us to have this time together to share, analyze, plan, and so forth. Another way is to have internal "rules," as in not letting a month go by without having our two local grandchildren for a sleepover, and not letting a year go by without spending a long weekend with our New York grandchildren (including a sleepover in our hotel!)
	Notes on What and How To:	

☐	Trusting	Skeptical
Check if OK	There are some people and things in our life we need to trust more, and some we need to trust less. I tend to be more trusting; so my task is to determine situations where I need to be more skeptical. Jane is less trusting; so her task is to determine situations where she needs to be less skeptical. For example, if she is not asked to do something with a friend, she would benefit by assuming they are busy and not that they are angry.	I tend to trust most of the time: trust my typing to be accurate, trust the waiter to tally the bill properly, trust the machine to operate without proper maintenance. Oops, it sounds like my "trusting" may be more a matter of laziness! I need to make a habit of poofreading [sic!].
	Notes on What and How To:	

Check if OK	Warm and Outgoing	Cool and Silent
	Some of us smile, laugh, and touch naturally, while others need to remember to do so. Part of being warm and outgoing is being talkative, and being too smiley and too talkative are equally off-putting. In a meeting, I use the rule of thumb that, barring an unusual situation, no one should speak more than the number of minutes in the meeting divided by the number of participants. Five people meeting for 50 minutes ideally have 10 minutes each, but not necessarily in a solid chunk. And, when I'm describing a pain, that is normally not an appropriate time to be smiling at me!	I remember my first experience at a Quaker silent meeting, and how moved I was at the effect of keeping my mouth shut for 60 minutes! To become comfortable with silence is a part of growing up. Other signs of maturity are showing appropriate emotion and speaking when necessary, especially to help others—some people lack the confidence, background, or caring to do so.
	Notes on What and How To:	

The final bidimensional adjustments comprise nine aspects of our work style.

Check if OK	Composing	Editing/Proofing
	Composing is manipulating a symbol set for some purpose. Composing includes writing words (as in essays, memoranda, books, manuals, poems), writing music, painting pictures, sculpting, choreographing, designing (interiors, landscape, sports strategies), sketching, mathematics (formulas, spreadsheets), computer programming….	A composition almost always needs revision, e.g., editing writing for style and accuracy, as well as proofing for errors. Many who excel at the creative act of composition either fail to follow up with revision or can't stop revising. Sometimes revisions such as editing and proofing can be delegated, but all too often the only person who can revise is the composer.
	Notes on What and How To:	

Check if OK	Improvising	Following Structure
	Improvising involves extemporaneously using known and/or new elements. Cooks improvise by not using a recipe. Musicians improvise by not using printed music or music they've memorized. Athletes improvise by not using a standard play or strategy. Actors improvise by not following a script. Lawyers improvise by not using a plan, or by departing from it. When you improvise, you are winging it, following your instincts.	The opposite of improvisation is adhering to a plan or some other kind of organized, step-by-step approach to a task. One could make a model ship by buying a kit and following the directions, or by assembling materials and making it up as they go along. The danger of excessive improvisation is shallowness, while the danger of excessive adherence to structure is boredom.
	Notes on What and How To:	

☐ Check if OK	Managing	Doing
	Some people prefer planning and organizing the work of others, directing them in how to accomplish it, giving them feedback on their performance, and monitoring their progress. A business manager who does not like to manage others needs to have mature workers who need little to no supervision.	Other people prefer doing tasks aimed directly at providing a service, building a product, or in doing tasks designed to support the providing of products and services. The higher positions in an organization typically progressively do fewer tasks and more managing of personnel.
	Notes on What and How To:	

☐ Check if OK	On Stage	Off Stage
	"On stage" is a metaphor that refers to any activity in which one has an audience. This is similar to the earlier "In the Foreground" category. On stage could include acting on stage, performing music for an audience, giving a talk or lecture to a group, playing a game (either mental or physical) before spectators, facilitating or leading a discussion, or making a face-to-face sales call. The more people you have doing the task with you, the less it feels like being "on stage." To sing a solo is more "on stage" than singing soprano in a chorus with 100 others. To sing a solo is more on stage than singing in a quarter. It is a matter of degree.	"Off stage," similar to the In the Background category earlier, is a metaphor that refers to any activity that is conducted out of sight or hearing by audience. In a play, the stage manager, set builders, costumers, and so forth do not perform their tasks in such a way that an audience can see them at work. To write a poem by oneself is "off stage," while to read a poem to a group is "on stage." To prepare a PowerPoint presentation is off stage, while speaking to a group with the Power Point presentation as an aide is on stage. Some people are more comfortable being on stage; others more comfortable being off stage.
	Notes on What and How To:	

☐ Check if OK	Organized/Files	Unorganized/Piles
	Being completely organized involves all of one's books to be grouped by categories, for all of one's clothes to be separated into a logically arranged system, for all of one's computer files to be easily and quickly located in logically clear folders, for all of one's papers and pictures and other documents to be filed for ready accessibility, for all of one's tools to have "home" and to stay there when not in use, and so forth.	Some folks prefer to spend time looking for things over spending time organizing them, and keeping them organized (e.g., putting things back where they "belong"). Most of us are neither completely organized nor totally unorganized. We rather choose the areas of our lives where we prefer organization/neatness and those areas where we are comfortable with clutter.
	Notes on What and How To:	

☐ Check if OK	Planning	Executing
	Management guru Peter Drucker once wrote something to the effect that time spent in planning is saved during executing. A good example of how lack of planning can protract a task is the Iraq War following the bombing of the World Trade Center. Failure to take into consideration the aftermath of war resulted in costly (both time, money, and other resources) follow-up needs. Planning involves specifying all of the steps necessary for effective pursuit of a goal. PERT charting and Gantt charting are planners' tools.	Some of us enjoy creating the plan, while others are impatient with planning, preferring either to let others do the planning, or to not use a plan at all and just "get it done." Certainly excessive planning can delay goal attainment, but lack of planning can result in costly errors, unanticipated resource unavailability, and other snafus that planning can alleviate.
	Notes on What and How To:	

☐ Check if OK	Spontaneous	Methodical
	Being spontaneous means going with the flow, going where the spirit moves you, following your instincts, reacting to what's going on at the time. In short, it means not feeling obligated to stick with what one is currently doing. I am being spontaneous if, while I am reading a book, you ask me to play chess, and I agree. (However, the game of chess itself is not spontaneous, but methodical, where I must abide by rules.)	Being methodical means that I have a plan, I do not deviate from my plan, I resist distractions, and I keep my eye on the immediate goal. After I have achieved it, then I might be "spontaneous" and accept a request to play chess. When two close partners include one who is spontaneous and the other methodical, resentments can ensue. They need to know the kinds of issues to bend their preferences for.
	Notes on What and How To:	

☐ Check if OK	Teaching	Learning
	Teaching includes anything from showing someone how to use a corkscrew to teaching a university course. Teaching is sharing what you know and have learned. Teaching could involve mentoring, coaching, speaking, demonstrating, giving feedback, evaluating, counseling, writing, or any other activity that helps others learn about something.	Learning is what you do to acquire a new body of knowledge, a new skill, talent, behavior, habit, attitude, job, or relationship. You may learn by reading, observing, practicing, mimicking, trial and error, memorizing, studying, surfing (the Internet), asking/inquiring, interviewing, listening, smelling, touching, tasting, looking at how others respond to you, asking for feedback, and so on.
	Notes on What and How To:	

☐ Check if OK	Working with Hands	Working with Mind
	The obvious example of working with one's hands is carpentry. Also, plumbing, electronics, gardening, landscaping, organizing, physical tasks (e.g., tennis, making bread, flower arranging). This category involves activities that are more physically active than sedentary.	The obvious example here would be reading essays by the Greek philosophers! Also, reading in general, conversing, analyzing, planning, computing (including many various devices), calculating, practicing sedentary tasks (e.g., chess, decorative painting), board games, playing cards, word games, and so forth.
	Notes on What and How To:	

Unimodal adjustments (40), with the goal of optimal level:

Now we turn to the unidimensional adjustments. Each is a single kind of thing. The question here is whether you have too much of that thing at this point in your life, too little of it, or about the right amount. If you are satisfied with the amount of the thing under consideration, simply check the box at the left. On the other hand, if you would like to have more of it, circle the descriptor at right that says "More X" (e.g., "More Breadth"). Or, if you would like to have less of it, circle the descriptor to its left that says "Less X". Then, in the "Notes" box, make some notes as to how you might go about this: what you might have to give up or what you might need to add to your plate, for example.

The first group entails eight areas of achievement.

☐ Check if OK	Breadth of Education	
	Less Breadth (keeping up with fewer subjects or bodies of knowledge or skills)	*More Breadth* (learning more subjects or bodies of knowledge or skills)
	Notes on What and How To:	

☐ Check if OK	Depth of Education	
	Less Depth (keeping up with fewer, as in reading fewer journals or books, going to fewer professional meetings, and so forth)	*More Depth* (learning more about the fields I currently master, through reading, experimenting, interviewing, taking classes, and so forth)
	Notes on What and How To:	

☐ Check if OK	Level of Education	
	Stopping My Formal Education (You may feel that you have advanced in your education as much as you need to in order to lead the kind of life you want to live.)	**Continuing My Formal Education** (You may feel that you want to complete your current degree or certificate program, and perhaps to continue beyond that, in order to lead the kind of life you want to live.)
	Notes on What and How To:	

☐ Check if OK	My Level of Achievement in Special Areas	
	Less Achievement (You may want to back off of your pattern of entering competitions, publishing, holding office, gunning for promotions, earning certificates/licenses/awards, and so forth.)	**More Achievement** (You may feel that, in order to lead the kind of life to wish to live, you need to increase your efforts to win awards, and get promoted, elected, published, and so forth.)
	Notes on What and How To:	

☐ Check if OK	My Status at Work	
	Less Status at Work (Status at work involves attention on you, responsibility for managing other people, responsibility for financial and material resources—in general, responsibility and risk. You may feel that you've accepted such status but that you'd prefer relinquishing it in favor of being more of an individual contributor and/or more in the background.)	**More Status at Work** (You may feel that you have a strong appetite for status and responsibility, and that you welcome increases in status associated with promotion and greater responsibility.)
	Notes on What and How To:	

☐ Check if OK	My Status in the Community	
	Less Status in the Community (You may feel proud of having achieved status in your community through volunteering, elections, service activities, pro bono work, and the like, but that you are overcommitted and have too little time for self, job, family, or friends, and need to cut back.)	**More Status in the Community** (You may feel that you have adequate time and resources to offer more to the community through the various ways of getting involved, and that increasing your visibility and status would be good for the kind of life you want to live.)
	Notes on What and How To:	

☐	Level of Generativity	
Check if OK	**Less Generativity** (You may feel that you have focused too much on what you leave to future generations—that perhaps your legacy is in good shape and that you can relax more or work on other priorities in the here and now.)	**More Generativity** (You may feel that your legacy is weak—that you would like to leave more for future generations to remember you by, such as financial arrangements, works of art, landscaping, construction projects, and such.)
	Notes on What and How To:	

☐	Level of Specific Skills	
Check if OK	**Less Skill at Something** (You may feel that increasing your skill in a specific area—through practice, entering competitions, seeking instruction—is no longer desirable, and that it is time to rest on your current skill level, perhaps to make time for other things.)	**More Skill at Something** (You feel that you have the capacity and desire to increase your skill at something—through practice, learning, raising your standards, or taking on greater challenges or competition.)
	Notes on What and How To:	

Next are 16 different levels involving entertainment.

☐	Experiencing Sensuous Pleasure	
Check if OK	**Less Sensuous Pleasure** (Perhaps you would like to cut back on the pleasures of the senses in some way—less chocolate and brandy, less fine dining, in favor of simpler and/or more spiritual pursuits.)	**More Sensuous Pleasure** (On the other hand, perhaps you feel that you have been denying yourself unnecessarily and that it is time to pick more daisies and savor more flavors.)
	Notes on What and How To:	

☐	Having Fun	
Check if OK	**Less** (Perhaps you feel you're overdoing it with merely having fun and that you wish to spend relatively more time in activity that, while it is neither un-fun nor fun, would be productive and satisfying.)	**More** (You may have heard someone say, "Lighten up and have more fun." You are ready to take them up on their suggestion. I was once told I was too serious, and my efforts to move somewhat in the other direction have been, well, fun!)
	Notes on What and How To:	

☐ Check if OK	Pursuing Intellectual Interests	
	Less Intellectual Activity (For some of us, intellectual activity may have lost some of its meaning and we need to balance our intellectual life with things like playing with kids, playing with a band, or building model ships.)	*More Intellectual Activity* (We may feel a yearning for mental challenges that stretch us out of our comfort zone and into new areas of the mind, whether it is learning a new language or rereading the great philosophers.)
	Notes on What and How To:	

☐ Check if OK	Reading	
	Less Reading (Perhaps we feel that we've lapsed into the habit of too much solitary reading and would benefit from enjoying some other hobbies, interests, and skills or some of our relationships with family and friends.)	*More Reading* (Go from one newspaper a day to two. Go from one book a year to one a week. One of my professors read a book a day in college and never did his assigned reading, and he ended up earning academic honors.)
	Notes on What and How To:	

☐ Check if OK	Watching/Listening to News Programs	
	Less News Programs (Too much of a news junkie? Cut back from 10 news sources to five!)	*More News Programs* (Being caught uninformed? Add at least one daily news source to your routine.)
	Notes on What and How To:	

☐ Check if OK	Watching Reality TV Programs	
	Less Reality Television (Hooked on a bushel basket of reality TV and feeling addicted? Pick one [or none!] to follow and stick with it.)	*More Reality Television* (Feeling like an old fogey for not watching any reality TV? Sample several and pick one to watch steadily, or watch highlights online.)
	Notes on What and How To:	

☐ Check if OK	Watching Television	
	Less TV (Set a goal for reducing hours per day and reward yourself for sticking to it.)	*More TV* (Watching TV is a way of lightening up, of getting informed, of escaping—perhaps there are programs that would serve you in one of these ways.)
	Notes on What and How To:	

☐ Check if OK	Watching TV Arts Shows	
	Fewer Arts Shows (Too much opera and art history? Set a limit and use the extra time to go to a museum or an opera, or read an art history book, or undertake a painting yourself.)	**More Arts Shows** (Not attracted to TV art shows because of poor TV quality? Maybe it is time to upgrade your equipment. Ask some of your artist friends to recommend TV arts programs they watch.)
	Notes on What and How To:	

☐ Check if OK	Watching TV Crime Dramas	
	Less TV Crime Drama (Rank your crime drama shows from highest quality to lowest, and eliminate the lowest one. Repeat this with some frequency until you feel really good about the one, or few, that you are watching. Use the extra time to read, exercise, build something for your grandchildren, or some such.)	**More TV Crime Drama** (I have a hard time supporting this option! If you really must add another, do your research and only add one that meets your criteria. Watching episodes online takes less time than watching on TV; watching highlights online takes even less time.)
	Notes on What and How To:	

☐ Check if OK	Watching TV Documentaries	
	Fewer TV Documentaries (Just as there are news junkies, there are documentary junkies. If you want to cut back, try eliminating one network, or eliminating all networks but the best one for documentaries.)	**More TV Documentaries** (Documentaries and news programs are television's alternative to reading magazines and newspapers. Extended documentaries somewhat substitute for nonfiction books.)
	Notes on What and How To:	

☐ Check if OK	Watching TV Hobby Shows	
	Fewer TV Hobby Shows (Maybe it is time to watch fewer television shows about cooking or carpentry and spend some time preparing some interesting dishes yourself or building that bunk bed you've been thinking about.)	**More TV Hobby Shows** (Maybe your cooking and carpentry is becoming too repetitive and you'd like to get some new ideas—TV could help with that, as could magazines, the Internet, or talking with friends who have similar interests.)
	Notes on What and How To:	

Check if OK	Watching TV Movies	
☐	**Fewer TV Movies** (Fallen into a habit of watching movies you've already seen, in addition to new releases? Establish a policy for yourself, announce to those living with you and stick to it. Save repeat movies for special occasions, like anniversaries, birthdays, and the like.)	**More TV Movies** (Want to watch more movies on television but don't have the time or access to the right titles? Get a service that gives you access to any movie, any time, such as pay on demand or Netflix. If you feel guilty about watching more, then only select movies that meet your strict criteria, as in "I'm watching every movie that Judi Dench ever made and keeping notes on how she developed as an actress.")
	Notes on What and How To:	

Check if OK	Watching TV Sports	
☐	**Less Televised Sports** (Unless you make an oath to give up all televised sports, establish clear criteria for what you will watch and don't stray. E.g., "I'll only watch my undergraduate team in football and basketball," or [in my case] "I'll only watch the last quarter of any game." Decide what to do with your extra time and avow your joy in having that new productive time.)	**More Televised Sports** (Most people could watch more televised sport if they wished; so not doing so is likely to be a matter of insufficient time or a sense of guilt in so doing. If inadequate time, record your desired events, then watch when it is convenient and fast-forward during slow moments or commercials. If guilt holds you back, determine strict criteria that you and those around you feel good and clear about, as in "I'm going to watch golf tournament championships because being able to discuss them with clients or prospects would help my business relationships.")
	Notes on What and How To:	

☐	Writing	
Check if OK	***Less Writing*** (It is hard to imagine that very many people feel they write too much. However, it could be that one frequently posts on Facebook, blogs, Twitter, YouTube or other electronic media without asking two questions: 1) Is this interesting to others? 2) Am I overwhelming people with too many posts? One's writing may be fluffy, shallow, or false without time spent collecting interesting, true information [preferably from more than one source], whether through research, reading, interviewing, experimenting, and so on.)	***More Writing*** (17th century philosopher Sir Francis Bacon asserted that "Reading maketh a full man, conference a ready man, and writing an exact man." Taking time to put it in writing is an admirable discipline. You may not consider yourself a writer, but there are many activities that you and others could benefit from—a biography of yourself, your parents, your grandparents, your children; a history of your business or organization; a poem for your romantic partner; a letter to the editor; a proposal for funding for a project you'd like to be a part of; a thoughtful online comment; a guest blog post; and so on.)
	Notes on What and How To:	

☐	Pursuing Hobbies	
Check if OK	***Less Time on Hobbies*** (Perhaps you feel you have too many hobbies, or that you spend too much time on one or all of them. Hobbies do have a way of letting the time get away from you. Establish a weekly time limit and decide how you want to distribute it among your interests.)	***More Time on Hobbies*** (Hobbies become more satisfying the more time one puts into them. Remember the 10,000-hour principle of Anders Ericsson? One way to support spending more time on a hobby is to find others engaged similarly and take time with them to discuss your plans and goals, and perhaps even spend some time working together. Maybe a joint project.)
	Notes on What and How To:	

☐ Check if OK	Playing Games	
	Less Time on Games (Whether on an electronic device or a game board or some other venue, give yourself a time limit, or a limit of number of games and/or competitors you will take on in a given week. Addiction to online or offline games requires more measures, including support from someone else. When I play Words with Friends on my iPad/iPhone, I limit my time to four games going at any one time. And, one competitor on Chess with Friends—my granddaughter. I'll play as many games as she has time for herself! If necessary to satisfy her appetite for chess, perhaps I'll cut back on Words with Friends!)	***More Time on Games*** (If you enjoy games but can't fit them in, try some of the many computer-based games that you can play with other persons not physically present—but not games that require you to appear online regularly or participate in prolonged team play. I've always loved games but couldn't justify the time over the last 30 years. Recently I've enjoyed games like Words with Friends, and I can play them at convenient times when no other kind of productive activity is available. I'm afraid describing this further would be TMI. ;-))
	Notes on What and How To:	

The next category addresses issues of health.

☐ Check if OK	My Health	
	Less Attention to My Health (Maybe you feel you're overdoing health-related activity. Confer with knowledgeable persons and set yourself limits in various areas. E.g., authorities say that more than 30 minutes of aerobic exercise five times a week does not increase the health benefit of just 30 minutes x 5/wk.)	***More Attention to My Health*** (Spending more time on health should reflect a reasonable standard. Ask a qualified health professional about your health concerns and behaviors. Don't rely solely on Internet information. It has good but also offbeat, extreme perspectives.)
	Notes on What and How To:	

Now for a look at past experiences.

☐	Building on My Past Experiences	
Check if OK	*Less Concern about Using My Past*	*More Use of My Past Experiences*
	(You don't have to continue to engage in an activity just because you've always done it, or because you've done it before and you feel you ought to continue with it. Consider eliminating activities that you engage in just because you've always done them, but discontinuing them might give you time to engage in an activity you [and possibly others around you] would enjoy even more.)	(You may have played trombone in high school and college, and were reasonably good at it—enough so that you enjoyed it. But you haven't played now for years. Find a community band in your area and joint it or form a group. Get your employers to sponsor a band, orchestra, or chorus comprised of employees—and maybe their friends/family.)
	Notes on What and How To:	

Now we look at the degree to which we over-rely or under-rely on our various physical characteristics. There is only one item to consider here, as everyone's physical characteristics are different, and you'll need to consider just yours. If I listed every possible physical characteristic in this section, it would consume the equivalent of an entire book!

☐	Building on My Unique Physical Characteristics	
Check if OK	*Less*	*More*
	(Perhaps you're tall and have been recruited for a basketball team, but you don't really enjoy it. Stop! Or perhaps you are held back by a physical weakness, such as a sensitivity to noise or light. If so, get earplugs or a glare minimizer for your computer screen, or eyeglasses that reduce glare, or use a yellow background for typing, as I'm doing now!)	(If you're blessed with a strong back, good hand-eye coordination, and skin that doesn't burn easily, then enjoy getting outdoors and helping to build homes with Habitat for Humanity. Other physical characteristics that you might wish to take into consideration are listed in Figure 6.0, "The Palette of Who We Are.")
	Notes on What and How To:	

Here we look at five social practices.

☐ Check if OK	My Carbon Footprint	
	Less of a Footprint (We could all stand to do our part in reducing carbon emissions by studying up on them, measuring our carbon footprint, and making decisions about how we can proceed in a way appropriate to our way of life. Maybe we need to significantly modify our way of life!)	*More of a Footprint* (I should hope that you do not consider this alternative! However, you may have reduced your footprint so severely that you and those and those around you suffer from it. Consider that there are areas you could lighten up on and still be way ahead of the game.)
	Notes on What and How To:	

☐ Check if OK	My Degree of Independence	
	Less Independence (Perhaps you're living too independent a life with minimal interdependence with others. Kelley (1978) describes interdependence as sharing both the fun and onerous chores with one's partner, so that neither partner gets more than their share of undesirable chores, nor less than their share of desirable ones.)	*More Independence* (You may feel tied down so that you have too little time and discretion to enter into activities that would please you. Either negotiate a more equitable distribution of chores with your partner, or find a way to delegate through hiring someone to help you.)
	Notes on What and How To:	

☐ Check if OK	My Ethical Behavior	
	Less Ethical (Perhaps you've been told that you're a stick in the mud or a prude, and you'd like to feel more accepted by your others. Discuss with persons whose judgment you respect and find ways to lighten up on your moral standards.)	*More Ethical* (Ethical behavior is easier to adhere to when those around you are doing the same. Consider a support group, or changing your life in some way so that you are around folks who tempt you less to stray.)
	Notes on What and How To:	

☐ Check if OK	My Power over Others	
	Less Power over Others (Having power over others can breed resentments, be stressful, and cause relationships to deteriorate. Discuss this matter with persons you trust and find areas in which you can begin to lengthen your leash. Consider a support group for persons who seek excessive control.)	**More Power over Others** (Some say that it is easier to decrease control, than to increase control. Nonetheless, sometimes we find ourselves in situations where we have been too lenient and need to reestablish standards, policies, expectations, and consequences of some people around us, whether at home, work, or in the community.)
	Notes on What and How To:	

☐ Check if OK	Stability and Balance between Work and Nonwork	
	Less Balance between Work and Home (You may feel that home requirements, even though they are "normal," are obstructing progress at work, or that work requirements, even though they are just "9 to 5," are adversely affecting your home life. In either case, you will need to negotiate with your partners at home or at work how you might agreeably shift your priorities, either temporarily or permanently, in order to improve your quality of life at home or at work.)	**More Balance between Work and Home** (If excessive home demands are hampering your satisfaction at work, you need to negotiate with your family how you might find more time for work, whether you are an office worker or a virtual worker. Conversely, if work demands are excessive and your home life is suffering, either negotiate changes at work, or find ways to extend yourself at home, as in hiring a nanny or joining some kind of carpooling or work-sharing arrangement.)
	Notes on What and How To:	

Finally, we look at the eight talents, or mental abilities, that we defined in Table 6.2.

☐ Check if OK	Being Introspective and Reflective	
	Less Introspective (Idleness is said to be the devil's workshop, and you may find that you are brooding as the result of too much unstructured time and activity that leads you to daydream and dwell on matters that are depressing. As Shakespeare quipped, "Labor we delight in physics (relieves) pain." So get busy and commit to coaching a kids' sport, joining a choir, taking a community college class, learning a new language, practicing a moderately familiar language, and so forth.)	**More Introspective** (To have a propensity for deep thinking and not to have time to indulge in it may well prevent the world and those around you from benefitting from the exercise of your introspection and reflection. Make time for solitary activity away from other people, as in going for long walks, closing your door on occasion, joining a Quaker silent meeting, meditating, and so forth.)
	Notes on What and How To:	

☐ Check if OK	Creating Order Out of Massive Amounts of Data, Ideas, Things, or People	
	Less Effort at Creating Order (If dealing with complex organizational charts, three-dimensional matrices, multi-system flow diagrams, and taxonomies is stressful for you, then you need to find a way to simplify, such as dividing such tasks into smaller segments, if possible.)	*More Effort at Creating Order* (If you find yourself bored with the simplicity of what you find around you, take on the task of helping it evolve into a more complex, useful system. Or, if you are frustrated with inefficient, incomplete organization, or the lack of organization, then take on the challenge of getting it organized in some meaningful way.)
	Notes on What and How To:	

☐ Check if OK	Executing Well-Coordinated Physical Movements and Tasks	
	Less Demand for Physical Coordination (Many kinds of dance, sport, lab work, construction, and artistic expression require physical coordination and strength. If these demands on you exceed your native ability, and if considerable time spent in them does not appear to be improving your talent in this area, then you may want to opt for alternate activity in the same field that does not require so much strength and/or physical coordination. Rather than ballet, try square dancing. Rather than soccer, try rugby.)	*More Demand for Physical Coordination* (You may find that the current demand on your kinesthetic ability falls short of what you are capable and what challenges you. Take up a physical activity that requires greater strength and/or coordination. From building boat models from kits with plastic molded parts, move to kits made from balsa wood where you must cut to fit and assemble. From weight-lifting, move to the pommel horse.)
	Notes on What and How To:	

☐ Check if OK	Using Images	
	Less Work Involving Visual Imagery (Some of us are stronger at tasks involving depth perception, accurately perceiving multi-dimensional objects, judging the speed of objects moving in space, and other visual/spatial tasks. If you struggle with map reading, navigating, visual inspection, drawing, or other visual/spatial tasks, you may want to find a way to rely less on visual demands and more on talents in which you are stronger.)	*More Work Involving Visual Imagery* (You may find that your skill in visual/spatial perception is underused at work or elsewhere. If this is the case, find a way to use your visual/spatial talent in order both to benefit others and to make life more interesting for you.)
	Notes on What and How To:	

☐	**Using Numbers**	
Check if OK	**Less Math/Logic in My Life** (If you find formulas, calculations, spreadsheets, and code writing to be tedious and stressful, then you may want to find a way to rely less on math/logic and more on a greater strength. For example, if you started as a code writer and find it unsuitable, you might ask to switch to become a technical writer and documenter.)	**More Math/Logic in My Life** (So many people are math-phobic that, if you have skill and enjoyment in mathematical and logical activities, then you and others would benefit from getting the maximum amount of training and taking on challenging tasks that involve logical and/or mathematical ability. On an everyday level, you might volunteer to be a statistician for a youth or school sports team.)
	Notes on What and How To:	

☐	**Using Sounds**	
Check if OK	**Less Reliance on My Hearing Acuity** (If you love music and have chosen to play the violin, but get feedback that you can't play in tune, then you might switch to piano, harp, guitar, or percussion (except tympani), where once the instrument is tuned, you can play in tune forever.)	**More Reliance on My Hearing Acuity** (If you are someone with excellent hearing and can identify a wide variety of sounds easily, then you may want to build on that talent by engaging in more activities that require that skill, such as bird-listening, engine repair, singing, being a security guard, and playing wind instruments, bowed string instruments, tympani, and so on.)
	Notes on What and How To:	

☐	**Using Words**	
Check if OK	**Less Verbal Activity** (If you are being expected to do a lot of writing, reading, speaking, proofreading, and editing, and you find it stressful, then you would benefit from finding a way to spend less time on such verbal activities and more time on one of your stronger talents, whether it is mathematics, working with people, or getting things organized.)	**More Verbal Activity** (Many people are gifted writers who lack opportunities to ply their skill. If you are one of them, or suspect you may be, then volunteer for work that showcases your skill and could lead to people relying on you more for your language expertise. Volunteer to write proposals, memoranda, promotional materials, documentation of procedures, and so forth. Write your autobiography or biographies of family members. Start writing your blog, novel, short story, poem, or pithy tweets.)
	Notes on What and How To:	

Check if OK ☐	Working on Relationships with Others	
	Less Requirement on Managing Relationships (If managing relationships is stressful for you, as in face-to-face sales, leading meetings, coaching and counseling employees, and customer service, then you would be well-served by finding others to take over these tasks and your taking over some of theirs that are less people-oriented. Rather than face-to-face sales calls, for example, you might write proposals for other sales people. Rather than leading meetings, you might let others lead them, while you, the boss, simply make yourself available as a resource and decision-maker. If you're a manager who doesn't enjoy working with people, find a way to get out of your management role and into an individual-contributor role that is more satisfying.)	*More Relationship-Building Opportunities* (If you are naturally a people person who thrives on communicating with others, managing conflicts, helping solve problems, training and orienting others, and so forth, then you would be suited for work in customer service, sales, or management, depending on your other qualities. Many people in roles that require people skills do not have those skills, and there is always a way for you to avail them of your talents.)
	Notes on What and How To:	

Composing Your Next Chapter

Review your notes from this chapter on Minor Adjustments and list below the adjustments you would like to make during the next chapter of your life. Pay attention to how these adjustments can build on who you are (i.e., good fit), engage your mind (i.e., flow), assist in making progress towards a short- or long-term goal, enhance your altruistic gestures, and get you more involved in relationships that are important to you.

_____

_____

_____

_____

_____

_____

Common Techniques

...for Keeping Focused

> "...Man who man would be,
> Must rule the empire of himself; in it
> Must be supreme, establishing his throne
> On vanquished will, quelling the anarchy
> Of hopes and fears, being himself alone."
>   --Percy Bysshe Shelley, Sonnet: Political Greatness

Guide to this chapter:

- Overview of These Last Two Chapters
- Getting Ready by Letting Go
- The Key to Focus—Self-Control
- Who Has Self-Control?
- How Can One Maintain or Increase Self-Control?
- Other Factors Related to Maintaining Focus
- Checklist for Getting Beyond the Blahs

The poet Shelley provides the charge for this chapter: Each of us must resist the anarchy of distractions in our lives and take charge of our energy for realizing our dreams. As the Scottish poet Robert Burns said more plainly, the best laid plans of mice and men often go astray. The most common reason for plans going astray is distractions. Some distractions are minor—yielding to a friend's suggestion to go shoot some hoops when a project deadline is looming, while others are major—caring for a dependent while trying to finish a university degree program. In this chapter, we will explore the major causes for yielding to these distractions and build an understanding as to how we may more effectively resist them. Perhaps the image for this chapter should be that of

Ulysses having tied himself to the mainmast in order to hear the Sirens, yet still be able to resist their allure. Of course, his crew was provided a much simpler and less stressful means for resisting their allure—they placed wax in their ears to nullify the songs' effects.

Overview of These Last Two Chapters

The bulk of this book has addressed the issues required for us to form an appropriate plan that will enable us to experience a maximum sense of well-being—the sense that our mind-body is in gear and engaged in a way of life that feels right for us. Chapters 1 through 11 all feed into the formulation of our plan, Chapter 12 helps us to implement that plan effectively, and Chapter 13 suggests ways that we might evaluate our plan to insure that it continues to express our traits, talents, physical characteristics, memories, and values. This process is cyclical over our lifespan:

> "Nature is often hidden, sometimes overcome, seldom extinguished."
> --Sir Francis Bacon

Periodically—perhaps once a year, or more or less frequently—we evaluate our plan for possible revisions. Things change over time, and our plans need to reflect these changes. In the final chapter of this book, we will consider several options for taking time out and insuring that our plan is consistent with our needs.

While this chapter is all about how to stick to the plan, the next chapter is about how to diagnosis the plan for its continuing soundness. This chapter is about stability, and the next, change.

Getting Ready by Letting Go

This chapter assumes that you have formed your Statement of Personal Priorities and that you have made a series of decisions about how to implement it. In order to establish the conditions that are optimal for achieving your plan's goals, we need to address two issues:

- The need to let go of lost ambitions, and
- The need to neutralize distractions.

First, let's take a brief look at the notion of lost ambitions.

In Chapter 7, we defined goals as one of the five primary modes of positive being. Or, better, *progress* towards goals, for it is not having goals in and of themselves that makes us feel in gear, but rather the certainty that we are making progress towards our goals. To avow that I'm going to have a mountain home (or start my own business, or win a tennis competition, or be an author) is not as satisfying as to have searched the mountains for a site (or to have bought a book on how to write a business plan, or to have contracted with a tennis coach, or to have outlined my short story or book).

Also in Chapter 7, we looked at the research of Laura King and Joshua Hicks of the University of Missouri—Columbia, who identified the linchpin of maturity as the ability to let go of past failures, disappointments, tragedies, and other forms of loss. (King & Hicks, 2007) According to their theory, the mature person considers all of one's lost goals, failures, missed opportunities, and so forth as so much past history, rather than allowing them to achieve a current status as voices that discourage us from seizing upon new goals and opportunities. To allow past adversity to stand in the way of present progress is  immature and self-defeating. When we feel in the grips of such a past, we need help, perhaps even professional (i.e., therapeutic) help, to enable us to let go of a memory's grip. Not let go of the memory—memories are forever, but let go of their grip. Subsequent studies have supported the notion that folks who hold onto regrets tend to suffer prolonged poor mood.

My friend has a brother whose wife died two decades ago. Not only is the wife's memory alive in her widower's mind, but she has as firm a control over his life now as she did in the flesh. While he has met several "perfect" lady friends, he simply cannot establish intimacy with them for fear of being viewed as disloyal to his deceased wife's memory. In other words, he feels guilty when experiencing the desire to get close to another woman, as though he were having an affair, rather than trying to create the next chapter of his life. He has grieved too long. A therapist could help him, not to forget his lost wife, but to reframe a potential relationship with another. Rather than feeling guilty and disloyal, perhaps the therapist could help him feel that his desire to build another partnership was a tribute to the beauty of the first one. Rather than "Boy, I'll never get entangled with a wife again!" it should be "She taught me how to love, and in her absence I will honor her teaching by sharing it with another." Not to cheapen his feelings, but it is almost like refusing to have another sip of wine because one's favorite vintage is no longer available.

The point here is that too many of us allow memory to have a kind of "agency," a kind of godlike quality to monitor and watch us and dictate our choices. Memory tells us which of our past choices have been pleasing and which have been aversive, but memory should not tell us what to do—only advise us. If you have allowed a memory to stymy your capacity to move forward, contract with someone, not to erase the memory, but to dislodge it from the driver's seat of your future.

The Key to Focus—Self-Control

With nothing now preventing us from feeling right about moving forward with our lives, let us now take a look at the most common reason for failure to stay in one or more of the five modes of positive being—distractions. The prototype for distraction is the Sirens of the ancient world. Residents of elusive islands in the sea, their voices and music were so alluring that no human could resist; so they would perish in the sea after jumping ship to get closer. From the lore surrounding this myth, three forms of distraction have emerged. Orpheus played his harp more beautifully and louder than their song and thus escaped harm. This was preventing distraction by neutralizing it, much like using a whitenoise generator to mask background noises. Odysseus wanted to hear their music but respected their reputation for black-widow-like seduction. So, he had his sailors insert wax in their ears, but not his, and tie him firmly to the ship's mainmast. Thus, two more methods for resisting distraction: a) placing barriers (i.e., the wax) between oneself and the distraction—like closing the door so you don't hear a family member running the television, and b) restraints (i.e., tying oneself to the mast)—like leaving one's cash, checkbook, and credit cards at home before going to the mall with a gift card to redeem, as a way of minimizing the allure of baubles along the way.

What we are talking about is the dynamic between goals, willpower, and distraction. It works like this: We have the will to pursue a goal but get distracted. Many psychologists have maintained that there is no such thing as willpower, as in whether one has sufficient willpower to lose weight, or to train for a marathon, or to study for a degree. Florida State University psychologist Roy Baumeister has made an attempt to put this argument to rest in his 2011 book *Willpower: Rediscovering the Greatest Human Strength.* Baumeister maintains that willpower does in fact exist, and he provides both a biological and a psychological explanation for how it works.

First let's look at Baumeister's psychological explanation. In essence, we will define willpower by explaining how it works. Its synonyms are self-control and self-regulation. What they refer to is one's capacity to maintain effortful attention, as opposed to easy attention, e.g.: reading the manual for a new piece of software, as opposed to watching a soap opera; practicing a difficult, not-so-enjoyable assignment, as opposed to practicing a familiar, easy, enjoyable assignment; solving a theorem from Russell and Whitehead's *Principia Mathematica* versus eating a plate of chocolate chip cookies. Attention, or focus, can be placed on a continuum from one end that represents minimal effort to another end that represents maximal effort. Some tasks require little if any effort to pay attention, such as watching a basketball game. However, if you are a scorekeeper, it requires more effort, and if you are a coach diagnosing the game for insights in how to improve, it takes even more effort. What requires effortful attention for one person does not necessarily require the same degree of effortful attention of another. For me, to read a software manual requires prodigious effort to maintain attention, but reading it requires minimal effort by my IT vendor. Effortful attention means, in essence, how hard and unfamiliar a task is for a person, versus how easy and familiar it is. One person's effortful attention is another's piece of cake, or breeze.

Attention is threatened when a distraction invades the space in which you are trying to maintain that attention. Distractions may also be placed on a continuum, from distractions that are highly appealing at one end, to distractions that have minimal appeal at the other. For me, as for most, the aroma of freshly baked chocolate chip cookies is hard to resist—it requires much effort to say no and continue working without caving in. Hearing basketball games played in the park across the street from my house might distract a more active hoopster in my home trying to read a book, but it doesn't faze me. It takes no effort to ignore the dribbling, clanging, and shouting. So we end up with a two-by table as shown in Table 12.0

The numbers one to four indicate the progression from 1 = easiest attention task to 2 = most difficult attention task. The point of all this is that resisting something you don't like and doing something that is familiar tend to take little or no effort, while resisting something you like, doing something novel and unfamiliar, and doing something that you don't like all three require mental effort. We bring to any task a wide variety of resources that can be used to execute the task. Our resources include knowledge, skills, experience, values, physical characteristics, and traits. More complex and unfamiliar tasks require more of these personal resources, and simpler, familiar tasks require fewer resources.

Baumeister's major contribution to the study of willpower involves the discovery of the biological basis of willpower. In short, we run out of fuel when we engage in effortful control. The brain, that is, runs out of glucose.

Table 12.0   Attention as It Relates to Distractions

		Degree of Attention Required	
		Effortless	Effortful
Appeal of the Distraction	Unappealing	1. Effortless Attention + Unappealing Distraction *Painting a wall + Need to wash dishes*	3. Effortful Attention + Unappealing Distraction *Need to write a chapter + Need to wash dishes*
	Appealing	2. Effortless Attention + Appealing Distraction *Painting a wall + Playing with grandchildren*	4. Effortful Attention + Appealing Distraction *Need to write a chapter + Playing with grandchildren*

As we direct the brain's attention towards a task, our central command system searches for familiar cues in the task itself to determine whether we can use neural networks already developed, or whether we must form new neural networks altogether. This is like a French speaker looking at a Spanish lesson as their brain recognizes familiar conjugations and declensions, whereas the same French speaker looking at a Chinese lesson would find very little in their storehouse of linguistic neural processes that they can relate to. Hence, Chinese lessons would require more effortful attention than would Spanish lessons for a French speaker. Effortful attention means establishing brand new neural pathways and relating them somehow to existing pathways. The very act of learning, whether minor learning (as in a French speaker learning a new French word) or major learning (as in the same person learning Chinese) means the formation of new neural pathways. And just as building interstate highways requires energy in the form of food for the human workers, the brain requires energy in the form of glucose for forming its new pathways.

So, whenever the brain sees the unfamiliar, it tends to bring all of its resources to bear until it has wrapped itself around the new material. Brain scans have shown that brighter, quicker persons light up more areas of their brain when initially attacking a problem, but then when they have their "Aha!" the brain areas return to a more restful state. Not-so-bright persons attacking the same problem do not light up as large a proportion of their brain as more intelligent persons, and the less intelligent tend to keep their brains lit for much longer periods of time. In either case, the brain requires glucose in order to go on the attack in order to make sense out of new material.

Baumeister's contribution to our understanding of willpower came when he made the connection between fuel and performance, between glucose supplies and effortful attention. Building on the research of Danziger, Leva, and Avnaim-Pesso (2011), he related the following story of the Israeli judges to larger issues of effortful attention. Danziger's team found a predictable tendency for judges to render lenient verdicts after meals and breaks and to render more stringent verdicts as a court session wore on. In fact, at the peak of the day, judges awarded parole in 65% of the cases presented just after lunch, with parole virtually disappearing a couple of hours later. What was happening was effortful attention was required in order to assess all the dimensions of a case, each case being unique. In order to be fair and objective, judges engaged in effortful attention while considering a case's many ramifications. As the session wore on, their supplies of glucose diminished and the verdicts became harsher. Unable to call on as many resources when glucose was diminished, the judges simply threw the book at them and put them in the slammer.

Subsequent research has confirmed that individuals perform better at complex tasks when glucose supplies are optimal. In addition, individuals are better able to resist distractions when they have more glucose available. Hence, the traditional advice of having a good breakfast before taking a test is good advice. When we run out of fuel, we revert to habits and what is familiar. We stop thinking about things and make the quick, easy decision. We follow the path of least resistance. We tread on tried trails. If we need to make new trails, we need fuel for the brain. While any kind of glucose works, over the long haul the best source of energy is complex, low-glycemic carbohydrates, such as grains, beans, vegetables, and fruits. Baumeister calls the diminished glucose supply "ego depletion." He means by this that the normal cogitations of the self are not available to us when the tank is empty. We are not "ourselves." We are not our normal "ego." Our ego is depleted. To return to our good old ego selves we need fuel. Whether we are trying to resist distractions or to simply continue trying to solve a complex problem or learn a new skill, we need sufficient glucose in our body. Fatigue sets in otherwise, and we veer from the task or succumb to the distraction.

Who Has Self-Control?

Willpower to a certain degree depends on the person and the situation. I have more willpower for certain tasks than you do, and you have more willpower for certain tasks than I do. Willpower is a function of our trait composition. Using the Big Five (see definitions of the Big Five traits in Chapter 1) traits as a way to describe our individual differences in personality, we can see the following relationships between trait levels and willpower:

- Persons low in Need for Stability show greater willpower in situations that are more stressful, while persons high in Need for Stability show greater willpower in situations that are relatively free of stress; persons in between show the most willpower over time if they have a balance of more stressful and less stressful conditions.
- Persons high in Extraversion show greater willpower in maintaining effortful control in activities that involve a large amount of sensory stimulation, while persons low in Extraversion show greater focus in situations that are quieter, more solitary, and relatively free of sensory stimulation; persons in the middle like a balance.
- Persons high in Originality show greater willpower in focusing on activities that are complex, unfamiliar, and creative, while persons low in Originality show greater stick-with-it-ness in situations that are simple, familiar, and practical; persons in the middle like a balance.

- Persons high in Accommodation show greater willpower in situations where they must implement the desires of others, while persons low in Accommodation show greater focus when they are implementing their own personal agenda; persons in the middle like a balance.
- Persons high in Consolidation show greater willpower in situations where they can methodically progress towards a finish, while persons low in Consolidation show greater willpower in situations where they can multitask, moving frequently from one task to another; persons in the middle like a balance.

In essence, persons who work in situations that have the optimal "fit" (see Chapter 6 for a discussion of Fit) are naturally going to have the greatest willpower, as they are engaging in tasks that call upon their behavioral strengths. It would seem then that persons experiencing good fit and persons able to maintain their levels of glucose will have the most willpower. Because poor fit requires greater effort at sustaining attention, it burns glucose more rapidly. People with better fit will burn proportionately less glucose, and hence will experience less fatigue day in and day out, and will find it relatively easier to take on more challenging tasks.

The Benefits of Maintaining High Self-Control (or Willpower, or Self-Regulation, or Focus, or Effortful Attention, or Self-Discipline, or Whatever Name We Call It)

Baumeister cites a series of studies that have identified measurable benefits for persons who have greater Self-Control. One well-known study of self-control (Mischel, Ebbesen, & Zeiss, 1972) was the "Stanford marshmallow study," in which then Stanford professor Walter Mischel (now at Columbia University) experimented with four-year-olds and their ability to delay gratification. If they succumbed to eating a marshmallow in the experimenter's absence, then no more marshmallows. If they held out for the prof's return and resisted eating the marshmallows before them, then they were rewarded with more marshmallows. In follow-up studies conducted decades later, researchers found that the children who resisted:

- earned higher grades and test scores,
- averaged 210 points higher on the Scholastic Aptitude Test (SAT),
- became more popular with peers and teachers,
- earned higher salaries,
- had lower body-mass/less prone to weight gain,
- had fewer incidents of drug abuse,
- showed up for college classes more reliably,
- avoided waiting until the last minute to begin homework, and
- spent less time watching television.

Another study in Australia followed 1,000 children from birth to 32. Self-control was assessed by parent and teacher observations, as well as by the children's self-assessments. As young adults, the children higher in self-control:

- had better physical health,
- evidenced less obesity,
- had fewer sexually transmitted diseases,
- better teeth,

- fewer alcohol and drug issues,
- had better paying jobs,
- had more money saved,
- were better prepared for retirement,
- were more likely to have a stable marriage, and
- were less likely to go to prison.

The data are conclusive: To the degree that we can establish and maintain self-control, the more likely we are to experience a sense of well-being.

How Can One Maintain or Increase Self-Control?

So, what can we do to maximize our willpower, our self-control? What can we do to keep our attention focused on the tasks and activities that we want to stay focused on, and to resist the daily distractions that steal our attention? There are, broadly speaking, three kinds of strategies that we can use to maximize our willpower:

- Development: We can exercise our willpower much like exercising our muscles.
- Compensation: We can compensate for the lack of natural willpower by removing or at least minimizing distractions.
- Support: We can support our efforts to maximize willpower by providing ourselves incentives, such as monetary or nonmonetary rewards and recognition.

Let's take a look at these three kinds of willpower-creation strategies in turn.

Development Strategies:

- **Practice with external distractions.** Ever attended a football game and experienced the home team making thunderous noise while the visiting team quarterback is trying to shout signals to his teammates? Teams prepare for this eventuality by holding practices with their stadium loudspeakers blaring at top volume. Players learn (hopefully) to ignore the distraction and focus on the signal calling. This is a classic example of practicing the discipline of maintaining focus in the face of strong distractions. It clearly requires effortful attention. One must strain mentally and physically to hear signals in the midst of such noise. Baumeister reports a plethora of studies that conclude that such practice with distractions actually develops one's willpower for use in other situations, such as resisting a donut staring at you from a nearby platter while you are reading a book. These examples illustrate how you can train yourself to maintain focus on good tasks that you want to do successfully (i.e., hear signals and read the book) by consciously placing external distraction nearby. One distraction is unattractive but hard to ignore, while the other is attractive and hard to ignore (unless you really don't like sweets!). Even if you are trained to avoid distractions, it is easier to do a task if you can get rid of potential distractions.
- **Practicing with internal distractions.** We may also use internal distractions, such as visualization, to fight temptations. Whenever we see a tasty treat awaiting our consumption

when we have no need for it, we can imagine an image of us (or someone else) in a bathing suit before and after eating donuts. Mischel found that the four-year-olds who were able to resist marshmallows in the Stanford experiments used both external and internal distractions to help them resist—external distractions such as moving to another part of the room and playing with a toy, and internal distractions such as pretending that the marshmallow was a golf ball or Ping-Pong ball. Again, Baumeister reports that voluntarily practicing with either external or internal distractors will help increase willpower when faced with a situation in which distractors are unavoidable.

- **Manage interruptions.** Probably the single greatest distractor for many of us is the interruption. Various studies have estimated that it takes anywhere from 3 to 25 minutes to return to one's previous task after being interrupted. Contract with those around you to minimize interruptions. Contract with yourself to either ignore incoming emails at your computer or simply close your mailbox, checking emails only at some regular interval, depending on the nature of your work. I could easily limit my attention to emails to three times a day, as opposed to looking at every email whose arrival gets flashed at the bottom right of my monitor. If emergencies occur, people should telephone, not email. Apps are available (e.g., Freedom, or Concentrate) to selectively block Internet intrusions.

- **Be high-minded.** Baumeister (2011) reports that persons with lofty, abstract reasons for doing things tend to be more successful in resisting distractions and focusing on challenging tasks, than do those who use more mundane, concrete reasons. For example, resist dessert not to "forego the calories" but to "be around to see my grandchildren marry." I remember playing on the concert stage at Transylvania Music Camp in Brevard, NC. Behind the curtain and high up so only those on stage could see was a sign calling for "Eternal Vigilance," which the wise directors must have known to be more effective than "Support from the Diaphragm" or "Eyes on the Conductor" or some other more concrete and less lofty message.

- **Create synergies.** Find ways to satisfy two or more needs simultaneously or at least close in time. Jane and I have "writing retreats" that are half-the-time working on writing projects, and the other half of the time enjoying walks through the mountains or along the beach and taking in the local cuisines. Or, as in a recent trip, we went to a family reunion near the beach in eastern NC; so we tacked on several extra days and worked on writing projects a few miles down the road at the beach.

- **Enter a competition.** Competitions force one to focus time and energy. The philosopher Friedrich Nietzsche pointed out that competition "was central to [Greek] culture, where rivalries were encouraged not only in sports but also in oratory, drama, music, and politics.... The ancient Greeks turned competition into an institution on which they based the education of their citizens." (Shenk, 2010) However, not all of us respond to the competitive arena. While competitions described by Nietzsche demand that we compete with other people, some of us prefer to compete within ourselves. I am one of those, as I prefer developing my skill and knowledge, not to triumph over others, but to satisfy my own internal urges for mastery and the personal satisfaction of a job well done.

Compensation Strategies:

- **Remove distractions from the good.** St. Paul is credited with "The good I would, I do not; the ill I would not, I do." Paul is referring to the fact that we have intentions to do a good thing but get distracted. The remedy is to be aware of the distractions that keep us from focusing and either eliminate them, neutralize them, or minimize them. Eliminating is easy to understand—when Jane wants to play the television or stereo and I am trying to write or read, she uses a headset that I bought her just for that purpose—to eliminate the distraction (noise for me, but actually a focal point for her). Neutralizing finds a way to mask a distraction, such as the white noise generator I have in my office that I can turn on when my office mates are engaged in animated conversation that makes it hard for me to concentrate. My white noise machine has several options—rain forest, tropical storm, ocean waves, and a literal white noise (i.e., a buzz). My first awareness of the power of white noise was at Wilson Library at the University of North Carolina at Chapel Hill, where I spent much time in a reading room with banks of fluorescent lights. The fixtures made a light buzz of which I was unaware until I read a passage in a psychology book that described white noise! The presence of the white noise minimized my tendency to look up at the sound of footsteps and such—they were masked effectively by the buzz. Minimizing distraction is like closing the door to conversation or television or music—it is still there, but sufficiently muffled that I can't recognize the words or music well enough to be distracted by them.

  Unfortunately, one distraction from the good is other goods. For example, I have two good goals at present: to finish this book and to begin another. If I were to try to work on both simultaneously, I would risk not finishing this book on time, and I would lose my focus and momentum. Better to be firm with my publisher and resist their flattery by saying that I will not spend time on the new book until this manuscript is finished. The effortful control necessary for writing is energy-depleting, and working on two books simultaneously is doubly depleting. Baumeister wisely suggests that "those who try to quit smoking while also restricting their eating or cutting back on alcohol tend to fail at all three—probably because they have too many simultaneous demands on their willpower." (loc. 588)

- **Frequent breaks and appropriate snacks.** I am aided by taking a five minute break about once every hour. One thing I do to force me to take breaks is to drink water throughout the day—that forces me to take a breather periodically—specifically in the direction of the nearest WC. I also keep healthy snacks in my desk—unsalted nuts and dried fruits—that will not easily spoil and that help me resist more unhealthy snacks offered in the company break room. This helps 1) replenish my glucose supply and 2) give my eyes and overall bodily system a break so as to forestall fatigue. It also is wise to get away from your workstation for lunch—people tend to eat too much when eating at their computer, and you don't get the benefit of the break.

- **Modify your environment.** The precise way you might go about modifying your environment to maximize focus really depends on your personality and your kind of work. The library practice of providing study carrels in the stacks is a way of helping students minimize distractions by keeping them away from "traffic." An extraverted worker stationed near a water fountain is likely to be easily distracted by talking with coworkers who use the water fountain frequently—move the extravert to a more remote area of the office and have a more introverted worker use the space near the watering hole. When I taught at the local university full-time, I had a desk/office in a "cube farm." No privacy. Anyone walking by could interrupt me. As a single parent with two kids at home awaiting my attention, I needed to get my work done while at the office. Solution: I rented—permanently—a tape player and headset from the media center and would wear the headset when I really needed to concentrate. I was listening to nothing, but the walkers-by thought I was and left me alone!

Support Strategies:

- **Declare your intentions publicly.** The research evidence suggests that one is more likely to achieve a goal, or at least to make progress towards a goal (not *everyone* who declares to run for President of the U.S. gets to the White House!), if they let the significant persons in their life know of their intentions. If others know your intentions, they are more likely to consciously help you in subtle or not-so-subtle ways. And by committing openly, you are more likely to tap into emotions that would support your following through—pride (not wanting your pride assaulted by not living up to your promise), guilt (feeling embarrassed at breaking a promise), and competitiveness (the inner sense of challenge at meeting or beating your own timetable for completion). Baumeister (2011) calls this "precommitment"—the practice of writing or speaking of your commitment to a "virtuous path" (loc. 2188) in advance. Odysseus precommitted when he roped himself to the mast to resist the Sirens. Next time you head for a party, you might precommit by sharing with your partner that it will be two drinks then switch to water, or that you plan to leave by 10 p.m. in order to get a good night's sleep. You can also use the Internet to precommit by making a "Commitment Contract" with www.stickk.com (yes, that is *two* k's), a website that invites you to state your goal, and then select the "stakes," which could be anything from holding money in escrow that would be permanently lost if you fail your goal, to asking for a slew of emails to bombard you.

- **Announce what and when.** Research suggests that if your announcement includes both *what* you plan to accomplish and *when* you plan to accomplish it, you are more likely to succeed. Recall John F. Kennedy's famous 1961 speech proclaiming that the country would place a man on the moon by the end of the decade. It happened eight years later, in 1969. Staking oneself out to a task and a date of completion has a way of focusing not only one's personal attention and resources but that of those around them.

> "'Tis easy to frame a good bold resolution; But hard is the Task that concerns execution."
> --Ben Franklin

- **Have a plan.** Research has clearly shown—having a stepwise plan dramatically increases the chances of accomplishing the goal associated with that plan. The best plans include a series of steps—what to do first, second, third, and so on, and for each step the three details of 1) what the step is, 2) when it is to begin and end, and 3) what special resources or permissions will be needed to proceed with the step. Note: The so-called Zeigarnik effect refers to the way an unfinished task tends to intrude on your present activity until that unfinished task gets done. Whether you're trying to go to sleep or to concentrate on reading a book or to clean out a closet, other unfinished tasks (e.g., a homework assignment, a project, and so forth) pop into your mind and disturb your current focus. *Unless*, that is, you have a plan for how and when you plan to finish the unfinished task(s). Research shows that having a plan somehow puts your mind at ease, confident that matters will be attended to later. The same kind of phenomenon happens when you try to go to sleep and you think of all the things you want/need to do the next day—that litany of To Do's keeps you awake, *unless* you turn the light on and write them all down. Then the mind, now assured you won't forget, can enter the land of Nod.

John Kotter (1985) recommends a five-step, cyclical process for tackling particularly ambitious goals:

1. Make a list of stakeholders—persons who potentially have a (positive) interest of some kind in your pursuit of the goal.
2. Meet with each stakeholder and share your goal with them (I want to be president of the U.S., I want to open a new business, I want to write a book, I want to build a mountain house, I want to find the cause of a disease, and so forth).
3. As you talk with them, build an agenda for yourself based on their comments, suggestions, cautions.
4. Evaluate their suggestions and execute the promising items.
5. Revise your goal as you see fit, then begin again at Step 1 until you achieve your goal.

I have a friend who wanted to become a college president. I advised him to use this process. It worked!

Time management advisor David Allen (see more at www.davidco.com), known for his "Getting Things Done" approach, has a technique for planning that he calls the "Next Action." It consists of writing a To Do item not in general terms, such as "Plan July family reunion," but in terms of the next thing you need to do with regard to that item, such as "Gather last year's planning notes and draft a new version to send to my committee." By writing down the next step, you don't have to spend time wondering how to get started on something.

- **Have a partner with periodic update/support conferences.** I have mentioned them before, but their discipline is worth repeating. My two senior architect friends meet for a weekend once a year and agree on a variety of goals for the coming year—professional development goals, family goals, spiritual goals, health goals, educational goals, and so forth. (One year the younger partner set the goal of becoming a state senator—and they achieved it). Then, once a quarter (or if time permitted, once a month), they would have lunch off site and share their progress towards their goals. If special support were needed by one from the other, they would identify the need and agree to it.

- **Join a support group or goal-monitoring group.** The Internet has given a fresh lease on life to the support group. You can travel via computer to thousands of support groups. Go to www.supportgroups.com and you'll find online support for everything from abuse to Zoloft, including Internet addiction. Many Internet services permit you to state your goal and periodically report progress. News at www.quantifiedself.com discusses technology to monitor not only your use of technology but your exercise and diet patterns. Want to be reminded how many hours you're spending on websites you'd like to resist—there's an app for that, just like one tracking your daily calorie intake. And you can monitor yourself with sensors you place on your body, such as the "Fitbit" clip (www.fitbit.com) that records steps, sleep, and so forth. This is an area that, if finding assistance in monitoring some area of your behavior appeals to you, you will just need to spend time surfing the Internet researching your personal needs and interests. If you are a runner, for example, you can use Flotrack (www.flotrack.org/) or Nikeplus (www.nikeplus.nike.com/plus/) to record and monitor your workouts.
- **Reward yourself.** Contract with yourself and obvious stakeholders to receive a reward upon completion of your long-term goal. When I finished the third edition of my "brain book," I got for myself (with Jane's permission) an N-scale model railroad kit to build for both my enjoyment and that of our grandchildren. Here's a thought—give yourself an item on your bucket list as a reward for completing a major goal, as in "I'll go to Paris after I finish my degree. And, if I make straight A's, I'll throw in a side trip to Rome."

Other Factors Related to Maintaining Focus

Finally, I'll mention a variety of factors that influence our ability to focus. Most of these are obvious, but they are certainly important to keep in mind:

- **Keep in good shape**. Research suggests that if you cannot reach your ideal weight, you can at least get sufficient exercise so that you can climb a set of stairs without getting winded, and realize most of the benefits of being in overall good shape. But don't stop there. The more you're in shape, the healthier you are.
- **Get a good night's sleep**. If you have to set an alarm to get up, then you're sleep deprived. Ideally, get to sleep in time to wake up on your own.
- **Eat a balanced diet—resist sugar binges**. Sugary intake feels good at first and then we hit a trough, making focus difficult.
- **Females understand luteal glucose depletion**. During the two weeks beginning with ovulation, the female's normal supply of glucose to the brain gets redirected to the reproductive system, with an accompanying decrease in willpower. By understanding this phenomenon, females can take precautions, such as appropriate snacking or removal of distractions.
- **Don't overdo caffeine**. No more than one milligram of caffeine per pound of body weight every seven hours. That's one cup of drip coffee (c. 150 ml of caffeine) for a 150 pound person.

- **Avoid neurotoxins**. See discussion under Neurotoxins in Chapter 2. Especially, for the sake of young boys, avoid plastic food and beverage containers using phthalates. (Sax, 2007); also avoid containers made with BPA.
- **Eliminate boredom**. Boredom is caused by lack of challenge—increase the demands that you and others place on yourself. Doing the same old, same old, is a recipe for boredom. Identify the next level for an area of your life in which you are bored, and then pursue that next level of challenge.
- **Eliminate frustration**. Frustration is caused by lack of skill or resources—either increase your skill and resources or reduce the demands being placed on you. Boredom and frustration are the symptoms of being out of "flow" (see Chapter 5).

Checklist for Getting Beyond the Blahs

On the next page, peruse Table 12.1—a device I came up with several years ago to help diagnose how my life may have gotten out of balance, with the result of feeling the "blahs," or just feeling tired, uninterested in doing anything in particular, unmotivated, just wanting to veg. When you have the blahs, pull out this list and see if you can pinpoint what you need to do restart your arousal system. Keep it near your favorite resting place. On the left side of the table, identify the problem. On the right side of the column, directly across from the problem, is a potential solution.

Table 12.1   *Auto Pilot Restart Checklist, or How to Find What Has Caused the Blahs*

Step One: Quick Restart. Check the five categories to the right to see if one is reponsible for feeling de-energized. If so, how to restart should be obvious. If not, continue with step two below. In general, the blahs are relieved by a change of pace, like stopping reading and taking a walk.	1. One or more of my **passions** is unsatisfied. 2. My **physical** condition is out of whack. 3. My **mental** life is out of whack. 4. My **spiritual** life is out of whack. 5. My **relational** life is out of whack.
Step Two: Extended Restart. Peruse the detailed sources of the blahs below, and find the one that you think is the most likely cause of your current condition. Then check to the right for an idea on what to do about it.	
One or More of My Five Passions is Unsatisfied: • #1 (enter them here) • #2 • #3 • #4 • #5	**Suggestions:** • Back off of an overused passion to make room. • Back off non-passions; delegate if possible. • Rethink non-passion activities so they become passions (housework become relationship work). • Find new ways to express neglected passions.
Some Aspect of My Physical Condition Needs Attention: • Been eating too much • Too much sugar • Too much caffeine/jittery • Too much alcohol • Too little sleep • Too little exercise • Sexual restlessness.	**Possible Remedies:** • Take a nap; go for a walk • Nap; sleep; walk • Walk; calisthenics; drink water • Drink water; walk; nap • Nap; sleep 1 cycle; exercise; fresh air; sun • Exercise of choice • Find your partner
Some Aspect of My Mental Condition is Out of Balance: • Priorities are unclear, feeling overwhelmed • A problem needs solving • A decision needs to be made • A project needs to be planned out • Too much stress • Too much/little socializing • Too much/little sensory stimulation • Too much/little physical activity • Too much/little leadership responsibility • Too much/little creative effort • Too much/little complexity • Too much/little change • Too much/little work with detail • Too much/little perfectionism • Too much/little structure • Too much/little focus on goals • Too much/little concentration • Too much/little adherence to a schedule • Too much/little active engagement (practicing) • Too much/little time spent in my comfort zone	**How to Restore Balance:** • Update my To Do list/focus on top priority for now • Find help to identify cause/solution • Establish criteria; evaluate options • Identify the steps required • Get away from/remove source; aerobic exercise • More/less time alone (e.g., with hobbies) • More/less time quiet and low key • More/less sedentary activity • More/less time doing personally meaningful work • More/less time in routine, practical matters • More/less time simplifying/with simpler matters • More/less time spent with what is familiar • More/less time away from the details • More/less activity that requires only casual effort • More/less pure exploration and spontaneity • More/less time in relaxation unrelated to goals • More/less activity not requiring mental effort • More/less unplanned time alone or with others • More/less passive involvement (listening) • More/less challenging/stretching goals
Some Aspect of My Personal Life is Out of Balance: • Too much/little focus on others • Too much/little physical pleasure • Too much/little time on low-level/maintenance • Time spent on my possessions/things • Time spent preparing my legacy	**How to Restore Balance:** • More/less focus on self • More/less focus on the intellectual • More/less time on higher level/production • Adjust time/energy/resources spent on them • Either get busy on your legacy, or chill for awhile!

Composing Your Next Chapter

Review your highlights and notes from this chapter on willpower and list below some behaviors, guidelines, practices, and skills that you would like to include in the next chapter of your life. Pay attention to how distractions can interfere with who you are (i.e., good fit), how you engage your mind (i.e., flow), your ability to make progress towards a short- or long-term goal, and your relationships that are important to you, and your ability to be of service to others.

_____

_____

_____

_____

_____

_____

_____

Staying Right

13

> "All our lives long, every day and every hour, we are engaged in the process of accommodating our changed and unchanged selves to changed and unchanged surroundings; living, in fact, is nothing else than this process of accommodation; when we fail in it a little we are stupid, when we fail flagrantly we are mad, when we suspend it temporarily we sleep, when we give up the attempt altogether we die...."
> --Samuel Butler, *The Way of All Flesh* (1903, p. 37)

Guide to this chapter:
- The Need for Annual Checkups
- A Challenge of Hope

Novelist Samuel Butler describes a world of constant change where we adapt or die. Every day we encounter at least one change in our surroundings. For each, we must decide whether to accept that change and live with it, ignore that change, fight in hopes of modifying or eliminating it, or reject that change and move away from it. Accept, ignore, fight, or reject. Here are some recent changes some of my associates faced, along with how they reacted, and how their reaction fared over time:

- *60 Minutes* reported that more than 150 grams of sugar a day is toxic.
  Reaction: Accept. He eliminated all cookies, candies, pies, cakes, and other foods and beverages with high sugar content.
  Outcome: Excellent. He has begun envisioning dessert-y type things as poisons. So far, so good.
- My nephew wanted to visit with me on a day I had reserved for writing.
  Reaction: Accept, with modification. I timed my lunch to coincide with his visit, which made the visit less of a distraction from my writing, since I had to eat anyway.
  Outcome: Fine. A pleasant two-hour visit proved to be a good break for me, as I wrote intensely for several hours after he left.
- A colleague received an email asking them to submit news for a professional association newsletter.
  Reaction: Ignore.
  Outcome: Blissful. The older we get, the easier it becomes to say no. Not that one has become indifferent, but that practice has improved one's sense of the unnecessary.
- My granddaughter asked if I would play Internet-based chess with her.

Reaction: Accept. We're about 10 moves into our first "Chess with Friends" game.

Outcome: Fun. My only challenge is how to "let" her win without being obvious about it. Only takes an average about one minute of my time every other day.

- A cousin suggested after rafting a river for an hour that his boatmates change rowing positions just before hitting some rough water.

  Reaction: Accept. With disastrous consequences, as one boater came near death from being bumped into the rapids as a result of the unfamiliar weight distribution.

  Outcome: Poor. They should have resisted the change. The cousin countered initial reluctance with, "I can't believe you all are so resistant to change!" That punched a hot button for folks, as they liked to think of themselves as comfortable with change. They learned that safety is more important than image.

- A client was let go by his employer and asked if my partner would help him with his job search.

  Reaction: Accept.

  Outcome: OK. He didn't need the help, and the time was more needed elsewhere, but the goodwill created therefrom was worth it.

- My doctor said I should eliminate, or severely limit, mammal products from my diet.

  Reaction: Accept.

  Outcome: Excellent. My PSA count (a prostate test) is way down. And except for the occasional cheese, I've found it an easy discipline. I'm also preparing to try nut-based cheeses, and if that is satisfactory, I should be mostly free of mammal products.

- The leadership at a large church made changes that lessened a couple's satisfaction with the music-making there. As music was their primary reason for participation, this caused great angst.

  Reaction: This was in two phases: First, the couple questioned the changes, attempting to reverse them. Second, they rejected the changes and left to join another church music program.

  Outcome: Excellent. The leaving couple was very happy with the new music program they found. It better suited their needs. And, they made new friends, as well as continuing to see their old friends. The church conflict stabilized.

The Need for Annual Checkups

I listed the changes just now to point out that our environments are constantly changing, and to some degree we change along with them. If there were no change, then one could, for example, read this book once, make a plan for life, and never revisit the plan for its aptness. However, because we all experience so much change, it makes sense to take a timeout once a year to make sure that our Statement of Personal Priorities (SPP) and our plans for being in gear with the five modes of positive being still reflect the realities of our circumstances. My favorite metaphor for this kind of personal self-evaluation is the Jewish New Year, or the High Holy Days—the ten days from the beginning of Rosh Hashanah to the end of Yom Kippur. During this time the book of life is held open and the individual prayerfully evaluates their life, with the book of life closing at Yom Kippur and the individual now possessed of new insights and commitments.

My recommendation is that each of us takes time once a year to insure that the focus of our Statement of Personal Priorities still matches the realities of our circumstances. The simplest way to do this is to make a list of all the things we are doing that we really enjoy, that we feel passionate about, that we find energizing and full of meaning and cause us to look forward to waking up to them in the mornings. Then, compare the items on that list with your SPP. You may recall that my SPP from Chapter 10 went as follows:

"To find musical, environmental, gratitude, family, and sensory pleasure challenges that will build relationships with couples and male friends."

Let's say that, in the future, I review my list of things I feel passionate about, and I find that some elements in my SPP are inadequately addressed in the activities I am currently engaged in. That could be because I don't really feel as strongly about that element as I thought I did. For example, I am doing relatively little at the moment with respect to pro-environment activity. So, either I need to let go of that from my SPP, or identify how I might up my activity in that area. Perhaps there is something in my bucket list that I might select, or maybe I could dream up something new altogether. Or, I may find that some new activities that I am engaged in have subtly, or not so subtly, changed what should go in my SPP. For example, our participation in a new church choir has significantly addressed my need for greater musical challenges: I play with a brass sextet, play recorder with Jane and our organist/harpsichordist, and sing with a first-rate conductor. I should eliminate "musical" from my SPP. I could also eliminate "family," as I have been an intimate part of three family reunions in the past year, have scanned thousands of family photos and documents, created 11 PowerPoint family photo albums, increased my involvement with grandchildren, and more. Also, the "couples and male friends" emphasis seems to be better addressed than it was a year ago. My revised SPP could read:

"To find environmental and sensory pleasure challenges that will build relationships."

With this revision, I could then reexamine my bucket list in search of items that focus on my new SPP. I will underline items that I could emphasize in my near future. Also, I will indicate items I accomplished. Here is that now-altered list from Chapter 10:

Camp and eat salmon at Puget Sound.
Complete Globus mental abilities assessment.
Write book on Globus model.
Write novel based on world of consulting.
Write book on mental abilities.
Write Owner's Manual for Coaching.
<u>Take grandchildren camping.</u>
Be part of a motet/madrigal group.
Have a Florida porch (fresh air, shade, no bugs).
Cross the pond with Papa. ✓
Cross the pond with Other Mama.
Cross the pond with Henry Johnson.
Finish Happiness Book. ✓
Write a textbook for Personality Assessment at Work.
Write a textbook for Applied Research, Critical Thinking, and Statistics.
Travel in South America.
Visit Ray in Austin, Texas.
Take Rowan on a trip.
Take Stella on a trip.
Take AJ on a trip.

Visit all national parks.
Get off the power grid.
Berlin ✓.
Prague. ✓
Spain, Barcelona, Le Segrada Familia. ✓
Build whaling ship model.
<u>Build 19th century sailing vessel model</u>
Buros for SP and WP.
Integrated report for Globus.
Coacher. ✓
Selector.
Text for Critical Thinking.
Big Five User Conferences in Asia, Europe, West Coast.
Psalm 150 Project.
Sing/perform Missa Luba.
Eat at Stinking Rose in San Fran.

In reviewing the list, I found two items I can focus on: camping with the grandchildren and building a 19th century sailing vessel model. The former addresses pro-environment and the latter addresses sensory pleasure. I can accomplish the camping within the year, and I will use the 19th century model as a reward for completing the 4th edition of *The Owner's Manual for the Brain.*

A Challenge of Hope

The primary focus of this book has been to encourage the "other eight"—the eight out of nine persons who are not born happy—to consider five alternative modes of positive being that are as good as, or even better, than happiness. I have been collecting some data from a happiness questionnaire that I designed a few years back. I asked folks how important each of the five modes were to them. A "100" means highest importance, and a "1" lowest. I also asked the degree to which they were actually experiencing that mode. Over 100% satisfaction means an excess—they're getting more than they need; under 100% means a deficit—they're experiencing that mode less than they'd like to be. Here are the results of the survey, in order from the most important to the least important, along with the percent to which they were experiencing that mode with respect to its priority:

- Person-Environment Fit: 86   91% Satisfied
- Community: 76   105% Satisfied
- Flow: 74   81% Satisfied
- Altruism (tied):   70   86% Satisfied
- Goal Progress (tied):   70   109% Satisfied

I would suggest these numbers mean that:
- People in general place a high value on all five modes.
- Having a good fit between who you are and what you are doing is the most important mode.
- Most people have at least one aspect of their personality that is either:

- ○ a strength that is not being used enough at home or at work (as in a creative person not allowed to be creative, or a solitary person not permitted to have private, quiet time), or
- ○ a weakness that is being used too much (as in a person weak in interpersonal ability being expected to deal with people all day, or a person weak in mathematics expected to work with spreadsheets most of the time).
- Most people are either bored or frustrated (i.e., not in flow) for a total of about 20% of the time at work and/or at home, and would benefit by either increasing their skill to reduce frustration or increasing their challenges to relieve boredom.
- People would like to be more altruistic than they are at present.
- For many people, the key to satisfying the need for fit, flow, and altruism must come from community (relationships) and goal progress because both are experienced to excess. Either people need to back off of community and/or goal progress in order to pursue the other three, or people need to modify their relationships and goals in order to include more fit, flow, and altruism.
- As a part of this survey, I asked folks how important it was for them to be "busy," or to always "have a full calendar." They placed an importance of 56 to this notion of having plenty of activities scheduled, substantially lower in importance than that ascribed to the five modes. However, when asked about the degree to which they were satisfying their need to stay busy, they gave it a rollicking 129%. I conclude that all too many of us are staying busy at the expense of staying in a positive mood. We need to prune the garden of our many commitments in order for our core plants to grow. Less busy-ness, more business. Fewer activities, more meaning. Less idling, more time in gear.

Our life's garden is well, but not thriving. In order to thrive, we must remove the weeds and superfluous plants and tend those that bring us the greatest sustenance. It is our decision whether we wish to live out our days with weeds and superfluity, or whether we live them with growth and engagement. It is not too much to expect us all to hope that we can be wise enough, and disciplined enough, to tend the garden of our life and keep it growing. Listen to the bird in your head that perennially beckons you to a life of meaning, a life continually in gear, engaged to the optimum. Emily Dickinson described it this way:

> Hope is the thing with feathers
> That perches in the soul,
> And sings the tune without the words,
> And never stops at all....

Yes, never stops at all.

Appendices

A. A Thesaurus of Happiness
B. Three Millenia of Quotes About Happiness
C. Using Other Personality Tests to Obtain N and E Scores
D. Action Items
E. Worksheet for Evaluating Balance of Goals
F. Composing Your Life Story—A Process

Appendix A

A Thesaurus of "Happiness"

In consulting a variety of synonym lists—from Roget's traditional volume to current Internet synonym finders, I came upon 235 words or brief phrases that scholars and pundits regard as synonyms for the word "happiness." I have grouped these words into 18 families, which I label "allelonyms," for lack of a better word. Like alleles in genetics, which are variants on a basic genetic code, allelonyms are variants on a semantic code. Not synonyms, really, but siblings. Closely related, but not substitutable. For each allelonym, I have listed the synonyms within its heading. In some cases, the name of the allonym group is also found as one of the synonyms. In that case, I repeat the name of the allonym group as one of its constituent synonyms.

Group 1: Positive Emotions (29)
Affectivity
Delirious
Ebullient
Ecstatic
Effervescent
Elated
Enchanted
Enraptured
Enthusiastic
Euphoric
Excited
Exhilarated
Expansive
Exuberant
Exultant
Felicitous
Full of gladness
Gratified
Happy as a king
Happy as the day is long
Having positive emotions
Hopeful

In high feather
Joyful
Joyous
Jubilant
Rejoicing
Relieved
Thrilled

Group 2: High Energy (29)
All alive
Animated
Bouncy
Brisk
Brisk as a bee
Buoyant
Frisky
Full of pep
Full of play
Full of puff
Full of spirit
Full of zing
Full of zip
Having vim

Having vim and vigor
Having vitality
High spirited
Inspiriting
Lively
Peppy
Playful as a kitten
Spirited
Spiritful
Sportive
Sprightful
Sprightly
Spry
Vigorous
Vivacious

Group 3: Calmness (20)
At ease
At rest
Authentic
Calm
Complacent
Cool

Group 3: Calmness, continued
Having peace of mind
Having quietude
In peace
Peaceful
Quiet
Relaxed
Reposed
Requiescent
Rested
Resting
Secure (free of worry)
Sensible
Serene
Tranquil

Group 4: Competence
(6)
Able
Bright (intelligent)
Capable
Competent
Talented
Worthy

Group 5: Health
(3)
Fit
Healthy
Wholesome

Group 6: Engagement
(15)
Confident
En route
Engaged
Full of drive
Having a sense of direction
In flight
In flow
Independent
Inspired
Motivated
On a path
Poised

Secure (confident)
Self-actualized
Self-confident

Group 7: Cheerful Disposition
(29)
Airy
Blithe
Blithesome
Bonny
Bright (sunny)
Cheerful
Delighted
Full of good feeling
Genial
Good sentiments
Good spirits
Good vibes
Happy camper
Heartsome
In good humor
In good spirits
In high spirits
In spirits
Light
Light in spirit
Lighthearted
Of good cheer
Pleased
Smiling
Sparkling
Sunny
Unsoulclogged
Warm
Winsome

Group 8: Jollity
(33)
Cheery
Frolicsome
Full of gaiety
Full of good cheer
Full of hilarity
Full of laughter
Gamesome

Gay (or happy) as a lark
Gleesome
Good humor
Hilarious
Jaunty
Jocose
Jocular
Jocund
Jolly
Jolly as a sand boy
Jolly as a thrush
Jovial
Laughing
Merry
Merry as a cricket
Merry as a marriage
Mirthful
Mirth-loving
Playful
Playsome
Ready to burst with laughter
Ready to die with laughter
Ready to split with laughter
Rollicking
Waggish

Group 9: Passion
(5)
Ardent
Fervent
Having zeal
Passionate
Zealous

Group 10: Cared About
(5)
Aided
Loved
Nurtured
Secure (cared for)
Succored

Group 11: Caring About Others
(9)
Affectionate
Aiding
Empathetic
Loving
Nurturing
Responsive
Sensitive
Succoring
Sympathetic

Group 12: Mature Relationship
(3)
In love
Interdependent
Experiencing affection

Group 13: Pride
(2)
Proud
Triumphant

Group 14: Optimism
(6)
Blessed
Free and easy
Having good fortune
Lacking difficulty
Lucky
Optimistic

Group 15: Feeling Other Worldly
(11)
Beatific
Bed of roses
Bliss
Experiencing rapture
Heavenly
In heaven
In paradise
In seventh heaven
In, or near, Nirvana
Sanctified
Spiritual

Group 16: Material Comfort
(17)
Abundance
Affluent
Among opulence
Comfortable
Content
Cozy
Having creature comforts
Having enough
Having plenty
Having sufficient
In luxury
Leisured
Leisureful
Prosperous
Satisfied
Secure (without material need)
Snug

Group 17: Titillation of the Senses
(8)
Thrill-seeking
Enjoying
Hedonistic
Excitement-seeking
Experiencing pleasure
Sensation-seeking
Having sensory delight
Having sensory pleasure

Group 18: Generally Positive Mood
(5)
Experiencing subjective well-being
Flourishing
Good hedonic tone
Happy
Having a sense of well-being

325

Appendix B

Happiness Quotes Across Three Millennia

A. A. Milne	"Well," said Pooh, "what I like best," and then he had to stop and think. Because although Eating Honey was a very good thing to do, there was a moment just before you began to eat it which was better than when you were, but he didn't know what it was called.
Abd Er-Rahman III of Spain	I have now reigned about 50 years in victory or peace, beloved by my subjects, dreaded by my enemies, and respected by my allies. Riches and honors, power and pleasure, have waited on my call, nor does any earthly blessing appear to have been wanting to my felicity. In this situation, I have diligently numbered the days of pure and genuine happiness which have fallen to my lot. They amount to fourteen. *(960 C.E.)*
Abdul-Baha	If we are not happy and joyous at this season, for what other season shall we wait and for what other time shall we look?
Abraham Lincoln	People are just as happy as they make up their minds to be.
Agnes Repplier	It is not easy to find happiness in ourselves, and it is not possible to find it elsewhere.
Albert Camus	All men have a sweetness in their life. That is what helps them go on. It is towards that they turn when they feel too worn out.
Albert Camus	But what is happiness except the simple harmony between a man and the life he leads?
Albert Camus	When you have once seen the glow of happiness on the face of a beloved person, you know that a man can have no vocation but to awaken that light on the faces surrounding him; and you are torn by the thought of the unhappiness and night you cast, by the mere fact of living, in the hearts you encounter.
Albert Camus	But what is happiness except the simple harmony between a man and the life he leads?
Albert Camus	You will never be happy if you continue to search for what happiness consists of. You will never live if you are looking for the meaning of life.
Albert Camus	To be happy, we must not be too concerned with others.

Albert Einstein	A table, a chair, a bowl of fruit and a violin; what else does a man need to be happy?
Albert Schweitzer	Success is not the key to happiness. Happiness is the key to success. If you love what you are doing, you will be successful.
Albert Schweitzer	I don't know what your destiny will be, but one thing I do know: the only ones among you who will be really happy are those who have sought and found how to serve.
Albert Schweitzer	Happiness is nothing more than good health and a bad memory.
Aleksandr Solzhenitsyn	One should never direct people towards happiness, because happiness too is an idol of the market-place. One should direct them towards mutual affection. A beast gnawing at its prey can be happy too, but only human beings can feel affection for each other, and this is the highest achievement they can aspire to.
Alexandre Dumas	There is neither happiness nor misery in the world; there is only the comparison of one state to another, nothing more. He who has felt the deepest grief is best able to experience supreme happiness. We must have felt what it is to die, that we may appreciate the enjoyments of life.
Algernon Black	Why not let people differ about their answers to the great mysteries of the Universe? Let each seek one's own way to the highest, to one's own sense of supreme loyalty in life, one's ideal of life. Let each philosophy, each world-view bring forth its truth and beauty to a larger perspective, that people may grow in vision, stature and dedication.
Allan K. Chalmers	The Grand essentials of happiness are: something to do, something to love, and something to hope for.
Alma Guillermoprieto	There is no point to samba if it doesn't make you smile.
Ambrose Bierce	Happiness: an agreeable sensation arising from contemplating the misery of another.
Amy Lowell	Happiness: We rarely feel it. I would buy it, beg it, steal it, Pay in coins of dripping blood For this one transcendent good.
Andrew Carnegie	If you want to be happy, set a goal that commands your thoughts, liberates your energy, and inspires your hopes.
Andrew Delbanco	As people spin faster and faster in the pursuit of merely personal happiness, they become exhausted in the futile effort of chasing themselves.
Andrew Matthews	The happiest people don't worry too much about whether life is fair or not, they just get on with it.

Andy Rooney	For most of life, nothing wonderful happens. If you don't enjoy getting up and working and finishing your work and sitting down to a meal with family or friends, then the chances are that you're not going to be very happy. If someone bases his happiness or unhappiness on major events like a great new job, huge amounts of money, a flawlessly happy marriage or a trip to Paris, that person isn't going to be happy much of the time. If, on the other hand, happiness depends on a good breakfast, flowers in the yard, a drink or a nap, then we are more likely to live with quite a bit of happiness.
Anne Frank	We all live with the objective of being happy; our lives are all different and yet the same.
Anne Frank	The best remedy for those who are afraid, lonely or unhappy is to go outside, somewhere where they can be quiet, alone with the heavens, nature and God. Because only then does one feel that all is as it should be and that God wishes to see people happy, amidst the simple beauty of nature.
Anthony Robbins	Only those who have learned the power of sincere and selfless contribution experience life's deepest joy: true fulfillment.
Antoine de Saint-Exupéry	If someone loves a flower of which just one example exists among all the millions and millions of stars, that's enough to make him happy when he looks at the stars.
Antoine de Saint-Exupéry	All of us have had the experience of a sudden joy that came when nothing in the world had forewarned us of its coming - a joy so thrilling that if it was born of misery we remembered even the misery with tenderness.
Anton Chekhov	People don't notice whether it's winter or summer when they're happy.
Arab proverb	Look to the neighbor before the house. Look to the companion before the road.
Aristotle	Happiness belongs to the self-sufficient.
Author Unknown	Happiness will never come to those who fail to appreciate what they already have.
Author Unknown	Happiness is in the heart, not in the circumstances.
Author Unknown	It doesn't get any better than this.
Author Unknown	A truly happy person is one who can enjoy the scenery while on a detour.
Author Unknown	Happiness held is the seed; happiness shared is the flower.
Author Unknown	The best vitamin to be a happy person is B1.
Author Unknown	Happiness is the feeling you're feeling when you want to keep feeling it.

Author Unknown	Joy is a flower that blooms when you do.
Author Unknown	Jumping for joy is good exercise.
Author Unknown	You cannot always have happiness, but you can always give happiness.
Author Unknown	Some pursue happiness, others create it.
Author Unknown	The really happy person is one who can enjoy the scenery when on a detour.
Author Unknown	Happiness is not having what you want. It is wanting what you have.
Author Unknown	Gather the crumbs of happiness and they will make you a loaf of contentment.
Author Unknown	For every minute you are angry, you lose sixty seconds of happiness.
Author Unknown	The best way for a person to have happy thoughts is to count his blessings and not his cash.
Barbara de Angelis	No one is in control of your happiness but you; therefore, you have the power to change anything about yourself or your life that you want to change.
Barbara De Angelis	You don't develop courage by being happy in your relationships every day. You develop it by surviving difficult times and challenging adversity.
Baruch Spinoza	What everyone wants from life is continuous and genuine happiness.
Benjamin Disraeli	Action may not always bring happiness, but there is no happiness without action.
Benjamin Franklin	The Constitution only gives people the right to pursue happiness. You have to catch it yourself.
Berke Breathed	It's never too late to have a happy childhood.
Bernard de Fontenelle	A great obstacle to happiness is to expect too much happiness.
Bertrand Russell	The happiness that is genuinely satisfying is accompanied by the fullest exercise of our faculties and the fullest realization of the world in which we live.
Bertrand Russell	If there were in the world today any large number of people who desired their own happiness more than they desired the unhappiness of others, we could have a paradise in a few years.
Bertrand Russell	To be without some of the things you want is an indispensable part of happiness.

Booker T. Washington	I think I began learning long ago that those who are happiest are those who do the most for others.
Booth Tarkington	So long as we can lose any happiness, we possess some.
Buddha	Thousands of candles can be lighted from a single candle, and the life of the candle will not be shortened. Happiness never decreases by being shared.
Buddha	Happiness comes when your work and words are of benefit to yourself and others.
Burton Hills	Happiness is not a destination. It is a method of life.
C. P. Snow	The pursuit of happiness is a most ridiculous phrase, if you pursue happiness you'll never find it.
C. S. Lewis	When we are such as He can love without impediment, we shall in fact be happy.
C. S. Lewis	Affection is responsible for nine-tenths of whatever solid and durable happiness there is in our lives.
C. S. Lewis	There is a kind of happiness and wonder that makes you serious. It is too good to waste on jokes.
Carl Jung	Even a happy life cannot be without a measure of darkness, and the word happy would lose its meaning if it were not balanced by sadness. It is far better take things as they come along with patience and equanimity.
Carl Jung	There are as many nights as days, and the one is just as long as the other in the year's course. Even a happy life cannot be without a measure of darkness, and the word 'happy' would lose its meaning if it were not balanced by sadness.
Carlos Castaneda	We either make ourselves happy or miserable. The amount of work is the same.
Catherine Marshall	Whence comes this idea that if what we are doing is fun, it can't be God's will? The God who made giraffes, a baby's fingernails, a puppy's tail, a crooknecked squash, the bobwhite's call, and a young girl's giggle, has a sense of humor. Make no mistake about that.
Channing Pollock	Happiness is a way station between too little and too much.
Charles Caleb Colton	To be obliged to beg our daily happiness from others bespeaks a more lamentable poverty than that of him who begs his daily bread.
Charles Gow	Many people are extremely happy, but are absolutely worthless to society.

Charles Kingsley	We act as though comfort and luxury were the chief requirements in life, when all we need to make us really happy is something to be enthusiastic about.
Charles Langbridge Morgan	The art of living does not consist in preserving and clinging to a particular mood of happiness, but in allowing happiness to change its form without being disappointed by the change; for happiness, like a child, must be allowed to grow up.
Charles Schulz	My life has no purpose, no direction, no aim, no meaning, and yet I'm happy. I can't figure it out. What am I doing right?
Charlie Brown	This is my "depressed stance." When you're depressed, it makes a lot of difference how you stand. The worst thing you can do is straighten up and hold your head high because then you'll start to feel better. If you're going to get any joy out of being depressed, you've got to stand like this.
Chinese Proverb	One joy scatters a hundred griefs.
Christian N. Bovee	Tranquil pleasures last the longest; we are not fitted to bear the burden of great joys.
Claude Monet	The richness I achieve comes from Nature, the source of my inspiration.
Colette	What a wonderful life I've had! I only wish I'd realized it sooner.
Colette	Be happy. It's one way of being wise.
Colley Cibber	The happy have whole days, and those they choose. The unhappy have but hours, and those they lose.
Cynthia Nelms	Nobody really cares if you're miserable, so you might as well be happy.
Dale Carnegie	Did you ever see an unhappy horse? Did you ever see a bird that had the blues? One reason why birds and horses are not unhappy is because they are not trying to impress other birds and horses.
Dale Carnegie	Many people think that if they were only in some other place, or had some other job, they would be happy. Well, that is doubtful. So get as much happiness out of what you are doing as you can and don't put off being happy until some future date.
David Steindl-Rast	Gratefulness is the key to a happy life that we hold in our hands, because if we are not grateful, then no matter how much we have we will not be happy -- because we will always want to have something else or something more.

Denis Waitley	Happiness cannot be traveled to, owned, earned, worn or consumed. Happiness is the spiritual experience of living every minute with love, grace and gratitude.
Diogenes Laertius	One ought to seek out virtue for its own sake, without being influenced by fear or hope, or by any external influence. Moreover, that in that does happiness consist.
Don Herold	Unhappiness is not knowing what we want and killing ourselves to get it.
Don Marquis	Happiness is the interval between periods of unhappiness.
Doug Larson	Real elation is when you feel you could touch a star without standing on tiptoe.
Doug Larson	The world is full of people looking for spectacular happiness while they snub contentment.
Douglas Jerrold	Happiness grows at our own firesides, and is not to be picked in strangers' gardens.
Joyce Brothers	Those who have easy, cheerful attitudes tend to be happier than those with less pleasant temperaments, regardless of money, 'making it', or success.
E. L. Konigsburg	Happiness is excitement that has found a settling down place. But there is always a little corner that keeps flapping around.
Ecclesiastes 3:1-8	For everything there is a season, And a time for every matter under heaven: A time to be born, and a time to die; A time to plant, and a time to pluck up what is planted; A time to kill, and a time to heal; A time to break down, and a time to build up; A time to weep, and a time to laugh; A time to mourn, and a time to dance; A time to throw away stones, and a time to gather stones together; A time to embrace, And a time to refrain from embracing; A time to seek, and a time to lose; A time to keep, and a time to throw away; A time to tear, and a time to sew; A time to keep silence, and a time to speak; A time to love, and a time to hate, A time for war, and a time for peace.
Edith Wharton	If only we'd stop trying to be happy we could have a pretty good time.
Edward de Bono	Unhappiness is best defined as the difference between our talents and our expectations.

Eleanor Roosevelt	Since you get more joy out of giving joy to others, you should put a good deal of thought into the happiness that you are able to give.
Eleanor Roosevelt	Happiness is not a goal; it is a by-product.
Ella Wheeler Wilcox	The truest greatness lies in being kind, the truest wisdom in a happy mind.
Emily Dickinson	Eden is that old-fashioned house we dwell in every day Without suspecting our abode until we drive away.
Epictetus	The essence of philosophy is that a man should so live that his happiness shall depend as little as possible on external things.
Eric Hoffer	You can never get enough of what you don't need to make you happy.
Eric Hoffer	The search for happiness is one of the chief sources of unhappiness.
Ernest Dimnet	The happiness of most people is not ruined by great catastrophes or fatal errors, but by the repetition of slowly destructive little things.
Eugene O'Neill	One should be either sad or joyful. Contentment is a warm sty for eaters and sleepers.
Faye Wattleton	My satisfaction comes from my commitment to advancing a better world.
Felix Adler	The truth which has made us free will in the end make us glad also.
Fran Leibowitz	Remember that as a teenager you are in the last stage of your life when you will be happy to hear the phone is for you.
Francis Bacon	No pleasure is comparable to the standing upon the vantage-ground of truth.
François Duc de la Rochefoucauld	We are more interested in making others believe we are happy than in trying to be happy ourselves.
François Duc de La Rochefoucauld	Before we set our hearts too much on anything, let us examine how happy are those who already possess it.
Francoise de Motte-ville	The true way to render ourselves happy is to love our work and find in it our pleasure.
Frank McKinney "Kin" Hubbard	It's pretty hard to tell what does bring happiness. Poverty and wealth have both failed.
Frank Tyger	Happiness is more a state of health than of wealth.
Franklin D. Roosevelt	Happiness is not in the mere possession of money; it lies in the joy of achievement, in the thrill of creative effort.

Frederick Koenig	We tend to forget that happiness doesn't come as a result of getting something we don't have, but rather of recognizing and appreciating what we do have.
Freya Stark	There can be no happiness if the things we believe in are different from the things we do.
Friedrich Nietzche	Precisely the least, the softest, lightest, a lizard's rustling, a breath, a flash, a moment - a little makes the way of the best happiness.
Friedrich Nietzsche	There is one thing one has to have: either a soul that is cheerful by nature, or a soul made cheerful by work, love, art, and knowledge.
Friedrich Nietzsche	I love him who does not hold back one drop of spirit for himself, but wants to be entirely the spirit of his virtue: thus he strides over the bridge as spirit. I love him who makes his virtue his addiction and his catastrophe: for his virtue's sake he wants to live on and to live no longer.
Fyodor Dostoevsky	Man is fond of counting his troubles, but he does not count his joys. If he counted them up as he ought to, he would see that every lot has enough happiness provided for it.
George Bernard Shaw	This is the true joy of life, the being used up for a purpose recognized by yourself as a mighty one; being a force of nature instead of a feverish, selfish little clot of ailments and grievances, complaining that the world will not devote itself to making you happy. I am of the opinion that my life belongs to the community, and as long as I live, it is my privilege to do for it what I can.
George Bernard Shaw	The only way to avoid being miserable is not to have enough leisure to wonder whether you are happy or not.
George Bernard Shaw	Give a man health and a course to steer, and he'll never stop to trouble about whether he's happy or not.
George Bernard Shaw	We have no more right to consume happiness without producing it than to consume wealth without producing it.
George Burns	Happiness is having a large, loving, caring, close-knit family in another city.
George Matthew Adams	If you have nothing else to do, look about you and see if there isn't something close at hand that you can improve! It may make you wealthy, thought it is more likely that it will make you happy.
George Sand	There is only one happiness in life, to love and be loved.
George Santayana	Knowledge of what is possible is the beginning of happiness.
Georges Duhamel	It is strange what a contempt men have for the joys that are offered them freely.

Greg Mortenson	"When I die, I want to be used up." [by a board member of Mortenson's Central Asia Institute]
Gretta Brooker Palmer	Happiness is a by-product of an effort to make someone else happy.
Grey Livingston	Happiness is the soundtrack of my life.
Grey Livingston	When you're really happy, the birds chirp and the sun shines even on cold dark winter nights - and flowers will bloom on a barren land.
Groucho Marx	I've had a perfectly wonderful evening but this wasn't it.
Groucho Marx	Each morning when I open my eyes I say to myself: I, not events, have the power to make me happy or unhappy today. I can choose which it shall be. Yesterday is dead, tomorrow hasn't arrived yet. I have just one day, today, and I'm going to be happy in it.
H. Jackson Browne	People take different roads seeking fulfillment and happiness. Just because they're not on your road doesn't mean they've gotten lost.
H. W. Byles	Cheerfulness is what greases the axles of the world. Don't go through life creaking.
Hafiz of Persia	Ever since happiness heard your name, it has been running through the streets trying to find you.
Harrison Ford	Being happy is something you have to learn. I often surprise myself by saying "Wow, this is it. I guess I'm happy. I got a home I love. A career that I love. I'm even feeling more and more at peace with myself." If there's something else to happiness, let me know. I'm ambitious for that, too.
Hazelmarie "Mattie" Elliott	Every now and then, when the world sits just right, a gentle breath of heaven fills my soul with delight...
Hazelmarie "Mattie" Elliott	Happiness and sadness run parallel to each other. When one takes a rest, the other one tends to take up the slack.
Hebrews 1:9	You have loved righteousness and hated wickedness; therefore God, your God, has set you above your companions by anointing you with the oil of joy.
Helen Keller	Happiness cannot come from without. It must come from within. It is not what we see and touch or that which others do for us which makes us happy; it is that which we think and feel and do, first for the other fellow and then for ourselves.

Helen Keller	When one door of happiness closes, another opens; but often we look so long at the closed door that we do not see the one which has been opened for us.
Helen Keller	Many people have a wrong idea of what constitutes true happiness. It is not attained through self-gratification, but through fidelity to a worthy purpose.
Helen Keller	Resolve to keep happy and your joy and you shall form an invincible host against difficulties.
Helen Keller	True happiness is not attained through self-gratification, but through fidelity to a worthy purpose.
Henri Nouwen	Joy does not simply happen to us. We have to choose joy and keep choosing it every day.
Henry David Thoreau	The most I can do for my friend is simply to be his friend. I have no wealth to bestow on him. If he knows that I am happy in loving him, he will want no other reward. Is not friendship divine in this?
Henry David Thoreau	That man is richest whose pleasures are cheapest.
Henry David Thoreau	If the day and night be such that you greet them with joy, and life emits a fragrance like flowers and sweet-scented herbs, is more elastic, more immortal - that is your success. All nature is your congratulation, and you have cause momentarily to bless yourself.
Henry Fielding	Great joy, especially after a sudden change of circumstances, is apt to be silent, and dwells rather in the heart than on the tongue.
Henry Ward Beecher	The art of being happy lies in the power of extracting happiness from common things.
Henry Ward Beecher	He is rich or poor according to what he is, not according to what he has.
Holbrook Jackson	Happiness is a form of courage.
Horace Friess	All seasons are beautiful for the person who carries happiness within.
Hosea Ballou	Real happiness is cheap enough, yet how dearly we pay for its counterfeit.
Hubert H. Humphrey	Here we are the way politics ought to be in America; the politics of happiness, the politics of purpose and the politics of joy.
Immanuel Kant	Happiness is not an ideal of reason, but of imagination.
Iris Murdoch	Happiness is a matter of one's most ordinary and everyday mode of consciousness being busy and lively and unconcerned with self.
J. Robert Oppenheimer	The foolish man seeks happiness in the distance, the wise grows it under his feet.

J.D. Salinger	The fact is always obvious much too late, but the most singular difference between happiness and joy is that happiness is a solid and joy a liquid.
J.D. Salinger	I am a kind of paranoiac in reverse. I suspect people of plotting to make me happy.
J .M. Reinoso	Happiness is distraction from the human tragedy.
Jack C. Yewell	Giving of yourself, learning to be tolerant, giving recognition and approval to others, remaining flexible enough to mature and learn – yields happiness, harmony, contentment and productivity. These are the qualities of a rich life, the bounteous harvest of getting along with people.
Jacques Prévert	Even if happiness forgets you a little bit, never completely forget about it.
James Freeman Clarke	Seek to do good, and you will find that happiness will run after you.
James M. Barrie	Those who bring sunshine into the lives of others, cannot keep it from themselves.
James Oppenheim	The foolish man seeks happiness in the distance, the wise grows it under his feet.
Jan Karon	"Y'know, Preacher, th' more things you own, the more you're owned by things." [Uncle Billy to Father Tim]
Janet Lane	Of all the things you wear, your expression is the most important.
Jean de La Bruyere	We must laugh before we are happy, for fear of dying without having laughed at all.
Jean Ingelow	It is a comely fashion to be glad; Joy is the grace we say to God.
Jerry Gellis	Prosperity is living easily and happily in the real world, whether you have money or not.
Jesus	These things have I spoken unto you, that my joy might remain in you, and that your joy might be full. This is my commandment, That ye love one another, as I have loved you.
Jim Rohn	Happiness is the art of learning how to get joy from your substance.
Joan Rivers	People say that money is not the key to happiness, but I always figured if you have enough money, you can have a key made.
Johann Pestalozzi	Man must search for what is right, and let happiness come on its own.
Johann Wolfgang von Goethe	Whatever you can do, or dream you can, begin it. Boldness has genius, power and magic in it.

Johann Wolfgang von Goethe	The person born with a talent they are meant to use will find their greatest happiness in using it.
John B. Sheerin	Happiness is not in our circumstances but in ourselves. It is not something we see, like a rainbow, or feel, like the heat of a fire. Happiness is something we are.
John Barrymore	Happiness often sneaks in through a door you didn't know you left open.
John D. Rockefeller	I can think of nothing less pleasurable than a life devoted to pleasure.
John Milton	The mind is its own place, and in itself, can make heaven of Hell, and a hell of Heaven.
John Stuart Mill	It is better to be a human being dissatisfied than a pig satisfied; better to be Socrates dissatisfied than a fool satisfied.
John Stuart Mill	Unquestionably, it is possible to do without happiness; it is done involuntarily by nineteen-twentieths of mankind.
John Stuart Mill	Ask yourself whether you are happy and you cease to be so.
John Templeton	If we try hard to bring happiness to others, we cannot stop it from coming to us also. To get joy, we must give it, and to keep joy, we must scatter it.
Johnny Carson	Happiness is your dentist telling you it won't hurt and then having him catch his hand in the drill.
Joseph Addison	Three grand essentials to happiness in this life are something to do, something to love and something to hope for.
Joseph Joubert	Misery is almost always the result of thinking.
Joseph Roux	The happiness which is lacking makes one think even the happiness one has unbearable.
Josh Billings	If you ever find happiness by hunting for it, you will find it, as the old woman did her lost spectacles, safe on her own nose all the time.
Julia Child	Moderation. Small helpings. Sample a little bit of everything. These are the secrets of happiness and good health.

Kalidasa	Listen to the Exhortation of the Dawn! Look to this Day! For it is Life, the very Life of Life. In its brief course lie all the Verities and Realities of your Existence. The Bliss of Growth, The Glory of Action, The Splendor of Beauty; For Yesterday is but a Dream, And To-morrow is only a Vision; But To-day well lived makes Every Yesterday a Dream of Happiness, And every Tomorrow a Vision of Hope. Look well therefore to this Day! Such is the Salutation of the Dawn!
Karl Barth	The Spirit bears witness. Ecstasy and enlightenment, inspiration and intuition are not necessary. Happy is the man who is worthy of these; but woe unto us if we wait for such experiences; woe unto us if we do not perceive that these things are of secondary importance.
Kenneth Goode	No matter how much madder it may make you, get out of bed forcing a smile. You may not smile because you are cheerful; but if you will force yourself to smile, you'll end up laughing. You will be cheerful because you smile. Repeated experiments prove that when man assumes the facial expressions of a given mental mood — any given mood — then that mental mood itself will follow.
Kierkegaard	Most men pursue pleasure with such breathless haste, that they hurry past it.
Kin Hubbard	It's pretty hard to tell what does bring happiness. Poverty an' wealth have both failed.
Kitty O'Neill Collins	What I'm looking for is a blessing that's not in disguise.
Lady Blessington	There is no cosmetic for beauty like happiness.
Lavetta Sue Wegman	You need to learn to be happy by nature, because you'll seldom have the chance to be happy by circumstance.
Lawana Blackwell	I've grown to realize the joy that comes from little victories is preferable to the fun that comes from ease and the pursuit of pleasure.
Leo Buscaglia	What we call the secret of happiness is no more a secret than our willingness to choose life.
Leo C. Rosten	I cannot believe that the purpose of life is to be "happy." I think the purpose of life is to be useful, to be responsible, to be compassionate. It is, above all, to matter and to count, to stand for something, to have made some difference that you lived at all.

Leo Tolstoy	Joy can be real only if people look upon their life as a service, and have a definite object in life outside themselves and their personal happiness.
Leo Tolstoy	Happiness does not depend on outward things, but on the way we see them.
Leo Tolstoy	If you want to be happy, be.
Leslie Caron	In order to have great happiness you have to have great pain and unhappiness - otherwise how would you know when you're happy?
Linus Pauling	Satisfaction of one's curiosity is one of the greatest sources of happiness in life.
Logan Pearsall Smith	There are two things to aim at in life: first, to get what you want; and after that, to enjoy it. Only the wisest of mankind achieve the second.
Louise Bogan	I cannot believe that the inscrutable universe turns on an axis of suffering; surely the strange beauty of the world must somewhere rest on pure joy!
Ludwig Wittgenstein	I don't know why we are here, but I'm pretty sure that it is not in order to enjoy ourselves.
Lydia Maria Child	Usefulness is happiness, and...all other things are but incidental.
M. Scott Peck	The truth is that our finest moments are most likely to occur when we are feeling deeply uncomfortable, unhappy, or unfulfilled. For it is only in such moments, propelled by our discomfort, that we are likely to step out of our ruts and start searching for different ways or truer answers.
Madame de Stael	The greatest happiness is to transform one's feelings into action.
Mahatma Gandhi	Happiness is when what you think, what you say, and what you do are in harmony.
Malcolm Gladwell	By embracing the diversity of human beings, we will find our way to true happiness.
Marcel Proust	Let us be grateful to people who make us happy; they are the charming gardeners who make our souls blossom.
Marcus Antoninus	The happiness of your life depends on the quality of your thoughts.
Margaret Bonnano	It is only possible to live happily ever after on a day to day basis.
Margaret Lee Runbeck	Happiness is not a state to arrive at, but a manner of traveling.

Margaret Young	Often people attempt to live their lives backwards; they try to have more things, or more money, in order to do more of what they want, so they will be happier. The way it actually works is the reverse. You must first be who you really are, then do what you need to do, in order to have what you want.
Mark Twain	Optimist: Person who travels on nothing from nowhere to happiness.
Mark Twain	Sanity and happiness are an impossible combination.
Mark Twain	Happiness is a Swedish sunset -- it is there for all, but most of us look the other way and lose it.
Mark Twain	The perfection of wisdom, and the end of true philosophy is to proportion our wants to our possessions, our ambitions to our capacities, we will then be a happy and a virtuous people.
Mark Twain	Whoever is happy will make others happy, too.
Mark Twain	The best way to cheer yourself up is to try to cheer somebody else up.
Martha Washington	The greater part of our happiness or misery depends on our dispositions, and not on our circumstances. We carry the seeds of the one or the other about with us in our minds wherever we go.
Martin Luther	It is pleasing to God whenever thou rejoicest or laughest from the bottom of thy heart.
Matt Biondi	Enjoy the journey, enjoy every moment, and quit worrying about winning and losing.
Maxim Gorky	Happiness always looks small while you hold it in your hands, but let it go, and you learn at once how big and precious it is.
Maya Angelou	Success is liking yourself, liking what you do, and liking how you do it.
Michelangelo	I saw the angel in the marble and carved until I set him free.
Michelangelo	Every block of stone has a statue inside it and it is the task of the sculptor to discover it.
Michelangelo	The greater danger for most of us lies not in setting our aim too high and falling short, but in setting our aim too low, and achieving our mark.
Mignon McLaughlin	We are seldom happy with what we now have, but would go to pieces if we lost any part of it.
Mignon McLaughlin	Happiness is like the penny candy of our youth: we got a lot more for our money back when we had no money.

Mignon McLaughlin	Many things can make you miserable for weeks; few can bring you a whole day of happiness.
Mildred Barthel	Happiness is a conscious choice, not an automatic response.
Miriam Muhammad	A happy thought is like a seed that sows positivity for all to reap.
Mitsugi Saotome	If you were all alone in the universe with no one to talk to, no one with which to share the beauty of the stars, to laugh with, to touch, what would be your purpose in life? It is other life, it is love, which gives your life meaning. This is harmony. We must discover the joy of each other, the joy of challenge, the joy of growth.
Mohandas K. Gandhi	Happiness is when what you think, what you say, and what you do are in harmony.
Montaigne	The pleasantest things in the world are pleasant thoughts: and the great art of life is to have as many of them as possible.
Mortimer Adler	The ultimate end of education is happiness or a good human life, a life enriched by the possession of every kind of good, by the enjoyment of every type of satisfaction.
Mother Teresa	One filled with joy preaches without preaching.
Nathaniel Hawthorne (multiple attributions—Emerson, etc.)	Happiness is as a butterfly which, when pursued, is always beyond our grasp, but which if you will sit down quietly, may alight upon you.
Niccolo Machiavelli	When neither their property nor their honor is touched, the majority of men live content.
Norm Papernick	Those who can laugh without cause have either found the true meaning of happiness or have gone stark raving mad.
Norman Bradburn	Happiness is the resultant of the relative strengths of positive and negative feelings rather than an absolute amount of one or the other.
Norman MacEwan	Happiness is not so much in having as sharing. We make a living by what we get, but we make a life by what we give.
Oliver Wendell Holmes	The world has to learn that the actual pleasure derived from material things is of rather low quality on the whole and less even in quantity than it looks to those who have not tried it.
Oscar Wilde	Some cause happiness wherever they go; others, whenever they go.
Palmer Sondreal	Happiness is never stopping to think if you are.
Pearl S. Buck	Growth itself contains the germ of happiness.

Pema Chodron	Everything is material for the seed of happiness, if you look into it with inquisitiveness and curiosity. The future is completely open, and we are writing it moment to moment. There always is the potential to create an environment of blame -- or one that is conducive to loving-kindness.
Peyton Conway March	There is a wonderful mythical law of nature that the three things we crave most in life -- happiness, freedom, and peace of mind -- are always attained by giving them to someone else.
Phillips Brooks	Happiness is the natural flower of duty.
Popular saying (source uncertain; one cites the comic strip Ziggy)	Today I can cry because roses have thorns, or I can celebrate that thorns have roses.
Ralph Waldo Emerson	Happiness is a perfume you cannot pour on others without getting a few drops on yourself.
Ralph Waldo Emerson	To fill the hour -- that is happiness.
Ralph Waldo Emerson	To get up each morning with the resolve to be happy...is to set our own conditions to the events of each day. To do this is to condition circumstances instead of being conditioned by them
Ralph Waldo Emerson	Can anything be so elegant as to have few wants, and to serve them one's self?
Ramona L. Anderson	People spend a lifetime searching for happiness; looking for peace. They chase idle dreams, addictions, religions, even other people, hoping to fill the emptiness that plagues them. The irony is the only place they ever needed to search was within.
Rebbe Nachman of Breslov	It is a great mitzvah to be happy always.
Richard L. Evans	May we never let the things we can't have, or don't have, or shouldn't have, spoil our enjoyment of the things we do have and can have. As we value our happiness let us not forget it, for one of the greatest lessons in life is learning to be happy without the things we cannot or should not have.
Rob Thomas	She thinks that happiness is a mat that sits on her doorway.
Robert Anthony	Most people would rather be certain they're miserable, than risk being happy.
Robert Brault	The secret to happiness is to put the burden of proof on unhappiness.

Robert Brault	If you search the world for happiness, you may find it in the end, for the world is round and will lead you back to your door.
Robert Brault	The search for happiness is unlike any other search, for we search last in the likeliest places.
Robert Brault	Seeking happiness, I passed many travelers headed in the opposite direction, seeking happiness.
Robert Brault	There is no expert on what happiness is but many on what it might have been.
Robert Brault	Enjoy the little things, for one day you may look back and realize they were the big things.
Robert Brault	Now and then it's good to pause in our pursuit of happiness and just be happy.
Robert Brault	Looking back on a happy life, one realizes that one was not happy all the time.
Robert Brault	It is not happiness until you capture it and store it out of the reach of time.
Robert Frost	Happiness makes up in height for what it lacks in length.
Robert G. Ingersoll	Happiness is the only good. The time to be happy is now. The place to be happy is here. The way to be happy is to make others so.
Robert Heinlein	Love is a condition in which the happiness of another person is essential to your own.
Robert Louis Stevenson	There is no duty we so underrate as the duty of being happy. By being happy we sow anonymous benefits upon the world.
Robert Muller	To forgive is the highest, most beautiful form of love. In return, you will receive untold peace and happiness.
Robert S. Lynd	Most of us believe in trying to make other people happy only if they can be happy in ways which we approve.
Robertson Davies	If you are not happy you had better stop worrying about it and see what treasures you can pluck from your own brand of unhappiness.
Robertson Davies	Happiness is always a by-product. It is probably a matter of temperament, and for anything I know it may be glandular. But it is not something that can be demanded from life, and if you are not happy you had better stop worrying about it and see what treasures you can pluck from your own brand of unhappiness.
Roger L'Estrange	It is not the place, nor the condition, but the mind alone that can make anyone happy or miserable.

Salvador Dali	There are some days when I think I'm going to die from an overdose of satisfaction.
Sam Harris	What would our world be like if we ceased to worry about "right" and "wrong," or "good" and "evil," and simply acted so as to maximize well-being, our own and that of others? Would we lose anything important?
Samuel Butler	Mr Pontifex never lacked anything he much cared about. True, he might have been happier than he was if he had cared about things which he did not care for, but the gist of this lies in the 'if he had cared.'
Samuel Johnson	Hope is itself a species of happiness, and perhaps, the chief happiness which this world affords.
Samuel Johnson	Pleasure is very seldom found where it is sought. Our brightest blazes are commonly kindled by unexpected sparks.
Samuel Taylor	The happiness of life is made up of minute fractions - the little, soon-forgotten charities of a kiss or smile, a kind look, a heart-felt compliment, and the countless infinitesimals of pleasurable and genial feeling.
Seneca	A man's as miserable as he thinks he is.
Shakespeare	The labor we delight in physics pain.
Sharon Salzberg	It doesn't matter how long we may have been stuck in a sense of our limitations. If we go into a darkened room and turn on the light, it doesn't matter if the room has been dark for a day, a week, or ten thousand years -- we turn on the light and it is illuminated. Once we control our capacity for love and happiness, the light has been turned on.
Sharon Salzberg	By engaging in a delusive quest for happiness, we bring only suffering upon ourselves. In our frantic search for something to quench our thirst, we overlook the water all around us and drive ourselves into exile from our own lives.
Sharon Stone	Real happiness comes from inside. Nobody can give it to you.
Sigmund Freud	Just as a cautious businessman avoids investing all his capital in one concern, so wisdom would probably admonish us also not to anticipate all our happiness from one quarter alone.
Sophocles	Wisdom is the supreme part of happiness.
Sophocles	When a man has lost all happiness, he's not alive. Call him a breathing corpse.

St. Augustine	Indeed, man wishes to be happy even when he so lives as to make happiness impossible.
Starbucks slogan	Happiness is in your choices.
Susan B. Anthony	Independence is happiness.
Susan Faludi	The modern fairy tale ending is the reverse of the traditional one: A woman does not wait for Prince Charming to bring her happiness; she lives happily ever after only by refusing to wait for him -- or by actually rejecting him. It is those who persist in hoping for a Prince Charming who are setting themselves up for disillusionment and unhappiness.
Sydney J. Harris	Happiness is a direction, not a place.
Sydney Smith	Life is to be fortified by many friendships. To love and to be loved is the greatest happiness of existence.
Taisen Deshimaru	If you are not happy here and now, you never will be.
Tenzin Gyatso, 14th Dalai Lama	The basic thing is that everyone wants happiness, no one wants suffering. And happiness mainly comes from our own attitude, rather than from external factors. If your own mental attitude is correct, even if you remain in a hostile atmosphere, you feel happy.
Tenzin Gyatso, 14th Dalai Lama	If you want others to be happy, practice compassion. If you want to be happy, practice compassion.
Tenzin Gyatso, 14th Dalai Lama	When we feel love and kindness toward others, it not only makes others feel loved and cared for, but it helps us also to develop inner happiness and peace.
Tenzin Gyatso, 14th Dalai Lama	Consider the following. We humans are social beings. We come into the world as the result of others' actions. We survive here in dependence on others. Whether we like it or not, there is hardly a moment of our lives when we do not benefit from others' activities. For this reason it is hardly surprising that most of our happiness arises in the context of our relationships with others.
Tenzin Gyatso, 14th Dalai Lamat	The greatest degree of inner tranquility comes from the development of love and compassion. The more we care for the happiness of others, the greater is our own sense of well-being.
Tenzin Gyatso, 14th Dalai Lamat	Genuine happiness consists in those spiritual qualities of love, compassion, patience, tolerance and forgiveness and so on. For it is these which provide both for our happiness and others' happiness.

Theodor Fontane	Happiness, it seems to me, consists of two things: first, in being where you belong, and second -- and best -- in comfortably going through everyday life, that is, having had a good night's sleep and not being hurt by new shoes.
Thich Nhat Hanh	The amount of happiness that you have depends on the amount of freedom you have in your heart.
Thich Nhat Hanh	Sometimes your joy is the source of your smile, but sometimes your smile can be the source of your joy.
Thomas Jefferson	I look to the diffusion of light and education as the resource most to be relied on for ameliorating the condition, promoting the virtue, and advancing the happiness of man.
Thomas Jefferson	The happiest moments of my life have been the few which I have passed at home in the bosom of my family.
Thomas Jefferson	But friendship is precious, not only in the shade, but in the sunshine of life; and thanks to a benevolent arrangement of things, the greater part of life is sunshine.
Thomas Jefferson	Happiness is not being pained in body or troubled in mind.
Thomas Szasz	Happiness is... usually attributed by adults to children, and by children to adults.
Thornton Wilder	My advice to you is not to inquire why or whither, but just enjoy your ice cream while it's on your plate.
V. S. Pritchett	The secret of happiness is to find a congenial monotony.
Vernon Howard	You have succeeded in life when all you really want is only what you really need.
W. Beran Wolfe	If you observe a really happy man you will find him building a boat, writing a symphony, educating his son, growing double dahlias in his garden, or looking for dinosaur eggs in the Gobi desert. He will not be searching for happiness as if it were a collar button that has rolled under the radiator. He will not be striving for it as a goal in itself. He will have become aware that he is happy in the course of living life twenty-four crowded hours of the day.
W. Somerset Maugham	It is an illusion that youth is happy, an illusion of those who have lost it.
Walter Savage Landor	We are no longer happy so soon as we wish to be happier.
Werner Erhard	Happiness is a function of accepting what is.

Willa Cather	That is happiness; to be dissolved into something completely great.
William Blake	He who binds to himself a joy Does the winged life destroy; But he who kisses the joy as it flies Lives in eternity's sun rise.
William Ellery Channing	[Peace] is the highest and most strenuous act of the soul, but an entirely harmonious act, in which all our powers and affections are blending in a beautiful proportion, and sustain and perfect one another. It is more than the silence after storms. It is as the concord of all melodious sounds... an alliance of love with all beings, a sympathy with all that is pure and happy, a surrender of every separate will and interest, a participation of the spirit and life of the universe.... This is peace, and the true happiness of [humanity]
William Feather	Plenty of people miss their share of happiness, not because they never found it, but because they didn't stop to enjoy it.
William James	How pleasant is the day when we give up striving to be young—or slender.
William James	Action may not bring happiness but there is no happiness without action.
William R. Inge	On the whole, the happiest people seem to be those who have no particular cause for being happy except that they are so.
William Saroyan	The greatest happiness you can have is knowing that you do not necessarily require happiness.
William Wordsworth	Pleasure is spread through the earth/In stray gifts to be claimed by whoever shall find.
Woody Allen	There are two types of people in this world, good and bad. The good sleep better, but the bad seem to enjoy the waking hours much more.
Yevgeny Zamyatin	Is it not clear, however, that bliss and envy are the numerator and denominator of the fraction called happiness?

Appendix C

Using Other Tests for N and E Scores

In Chapter 3, we provided a brief questionnaire for the purpose of your computing your levels of Need for Stability (N) and Extraversion (E). Lower scores on N (written as N-) are associated with the relative absence of negative emotions, while higher scores on E (written as E+) are associated with the relative abundance of positive emotions. Persons with the combination of N- and E+ by definition are what we call happy by birth—they are born happy. This occurs to about one person out of every nine.

Perhaps you have taken one of many personality assessments in your lifetime. By using the table below, you can estimate your levels of N and E by knowing your scores on these instruments. If you've taken a test that is not listed below, simply look for scales that measure anxiety, sadness, anger, neuroticism, or resilience and determine your level of N from these scales. Then, look for scales that measure extraversion, surgency, gregariousness, sociability, warmth, or enthusiasm (i.e., the positive emotions) and determine your level of E from these scales. If you are in the lower third of N scores, then you are N-. If you are in the upper third of E scores, then you are E+. If you are both, then you are naturally, temperamentally happy.

Name of Test:	You are N- if...	You are E+ if...	Comments:
WorkPlace Big Five Profile	Your N score is below 45	Your E score is above 55	
SchoolPlace Big Five Profile	Your N score is below 45	Your E score is above 55	
16PF	Look for higher scores on L: Vigilance, O: Apprehension, and Q4: Tension; and lower score on C: Emotional Stability; or, look for lower score on the "Anxiety" global factor.	Look for higher scores on A: Warmth, F: Liveliness, and H: Social Boldness; and lower scores on N: Privateness and Q2: Self-Reliance; or, look for higher score on the "Extraversion" global factor.	
California Personality Inventory (CPI)	Look for higher score on Well-Being (Wb).	Look for higher scores on Sociability (Sy) and Social Presence (Sp).	

Name of Test:	You are N- if...	You are E+ if...	Comments:
DISC	Look for higher score on S, associated with patience and relaxation.	Look for higher score on I, associated with sociability and enthusiasm.	The DISC does not measure N in a pure manner, so high scores here are at best a rough estimate of N-.
Hogan	Look for higher scores on Adjustment, associated with calmness, patience, and nondefensiveness.	Look for higher scores on Sociability, associated with gregariousness and approachability, and also (but less importantly) Ambition, associated with leadership.	The Hogan does not have a pure measure of E, as it is divided into Sociability and Ambition.
Myers-Briggs Type Indicator (MBTI)	(Maybe look for stronger preference for Thinking—but see comments to the right.)	You score clearly into the Extravert zone, and not close to the midpoint.	The MBTI does not directly measure Need for Stability; studies show that a preference for Thinking correlates with N-.
NEO PI-R	Your N score is below 45	Your E score is above 55	
OPQ	Look for higher score on Coping with Pressures & Setbacks.	Look for higher scores on Leading & Supervising, Working with People, Relating & Networking, and Persuading & Influencing.	The OPQ has a rather narrow measure of N (only one subtrait) and a somewhat broader measure of E.
Predictive Index (aka AVA, Activity Vector Analysis)	On the third factor, lower scores are associated with calmness and patience.	On the second factor, lower scores are associated with extraversion.	The Predictive Index and the AVA are clones of one another and are ipsative, thus it is hard to get a good measure of how extreme you score on either scale; also the measure of N is weak.

Appendix D

Action Items

"How small, of all that human hearts endure,
that part which laws or kings can cause or cure."
   --Samuel Johnson

Samuel Johnson poignantly phrases the dilemma facing decision makers: How can leaders make a difference, when so much of happiness and well-being arise from within the individual? Derek Bok attempted to answer that question in his 2010 book *The Politics of Happiness: What Government Can Learn from the New Research on Well-being*. Bok reiterates Johnson's somewhat pessimistic verse in citing Benjamin Constant, an early 19th century Swiss political philosopher: "Let [government officials] confine themselves to being just. We shall assume the responsibility of being happy for ourselves." (Bok, 2010; loc. 793) Bok nonetheless proceeds to review the happiness research with an eye towards actions that governments can take that are likely to create circumstances and choices that foster well-being. Here I list many of his suggestions, along with recommendations of my own and of other happiness researchers. As the emphasis here is on good ideas and not on authorship, I do not identify the author of the individual action items.

If you are a leader—politician, coach, journalist, administrator, teacher, manager, social activist, civic club officer or member, philanthropist, community or neighborhood organizer, religious spokesperson—in short, someone who takes responsibility for effecting necessary change, consider one or more of these action items to implement for the well-being of your people. I have listed them in alphabetical order to avoid placing unintended emphasis on the items at the beginning of the list:

- Aid for those let go who want to go back to school.
- Create independent bodies (i.e., comprised of non-politicians) for evaluating ethics charges against public officials, for evaluating compliance of campaign finance rules, and for overseeing redistricting (that is all too often gerrymandering). In general, institute measures that minimize the practice of politicians putting their re-election above the public's welfare.
- Design sleep evaluation centers with tiered assistance: level one eliminates lifestyle influences, with level two a more expensive sleep study to diagnose systemic problems.
- Educate early teens on the realities of children born out of marriage.
- Eliminate earmarks.
- Eliminate loopholes that permit lobbyists to provide favors to lawmakers.

- Eliminate plastic beverage and food containers made with phthalates and bisphenol A (BPA) —they are especially bad when heated, e.g., in a microwave, sitting in the sun). Look for plastic containers without phthalates or BPA, including containers made from polylactide (PLA, made from corn). Eliminate premature and low birth weight deliveries.
- Encourage the development of programs that serve to make stronger families, marriages, and relationships.
- Establish programs to support individuals who have been affected by crime and violence.
- Include person-job fit in all vocational counseling, so that individuals can pursue jobs that build on their strengths and learn how to compensate when they end up in jobs that do not build on their strengths.
- Increase the extent and effectiveness of educating citizens in the democratic process (e.g., interactive Internet-based simulations, classroom simulation games), including the court system, checks and balances, the role of debate, and so forth.
- Increase opportunities for political involvement of citizens.
- Increase safeguards for the security of retirement funds
- Insure equality of economic opportunity.
- Level the playing field for financing political/electoral campaigns.
- Make pre-kindergarten programs for the poor universal (based on findings from the Perry Pre-School Project, a program influential in getting Head Start established).
- Modify the regulation of pharmaceuticals that address chronic pain and serious depression so that sufferers have appropriate access and guidance/monitoring.
- The news media, broadly defined, needs to balance reporting. Investigative reporting should expose corruption, incompetence, malfeasance, moral turpitude, and other behavior that is against the public's interests. Other reporting should show the hard work of political and government workers, and give the public a sense that perhaps too much is expected of officials, that their shortcomings are often blown out of proportion, and that their many successful achievements often go unrecognized.
- Prepare an annual report on the state of the country's well-being that emphasizes the factors known to foster well-being and downplays simplistic data on economic growth and educational testing that are misleading indicators of the public's health.
- Provide social programming that emphasizes active participation rather than passive (e.g., dancing rather than watching a dance).
- Reduce income inequality.
- Reduce/eliminate environmental neurotoxins such as lead, nitrogen dioxide, coal ash, phthalates.
- Require congressional review and endorsement before committing to any military action.

- Require contact sports at all ages to have qualified concussion-resource persons at every game and practice for all contact sports. They should not be under the authority of the coaches and should have independent authority to keep a concussed player out of play for an appropriate time.
- Require unwed mothers receiving government funds to take appropriate employment.
- Resist diagnosing ADHD in active boys; insist that all five DSM-IV criteria are met; if meds are required, start with weaker ones; do not allow use of meds without behavior therapy.
- Rethink sentencing for perpetrators of victimless crimes.
- Schools and parents need to delay boys' reading instruction and permit more play and exploration; encourage single-sex schools and classrooms, promoted by Leonard Sax (2007) (see www.singlesexschols.org); have adjustable-height tables so boys can stand or kneel, even lie down, while doing schoolwork; follow the German model of Waldkindergarten (www.waldkindergarteninc.com).
- Severely limit video gaming and provide exciting, fun alternatives such as RaceLegal (www.sandiego.gov/qualcomm/event/tenants/racelegal.shtml) and Wii competitions with parents and kids.
- Simplify and expedite the administration of procedures, guidelines, laws, and so forth.
- Stop using GNP as the sole determinant of a nation's health; institute other metrics that assess the subjective quality of life of its citizens.
- Subject young people to positive, demanding role models, whether through Scouting, sports, or other community programs and organizations.
- Toughen the enforcement of child-support requirements.
- Train both younger and older people in skills for leisure, not just skills for work. Broaden school curriculum beyond the liberal arts and sciences and vocational skills to include the skills that make leisure more satisfying.
- Unemployment insurance for those in the workforce who are not now covered.

Perhaps you might present this list to your leadership team and determine which items could build on your special interests and resources. Perhaps you could use this list to evaluate the state of well-being of your community or region.

Appendix E

Worksheet for Evaluating Balance of Goals

(Note: See example of this worksheet filled out with author's goals as sample in Table 7.0.)

Continuum #1: Areas of Endeavor

Area 1-----------Area 2--------------Area 3-----------------Area 4------------------Area 5------------------Area 6--------------------Area 7----------etc.

Continuum #2: Origin

Intrinsic--Partially Internal/Partially External--External

Continuum #3: Survival

Nice but not Necessary---------------------------------Nice and Somewhat Necessary--Necessary for Survival

Continuum #4: Generativity

Impacts Me---Impacts Me and Future Generations--------------------------------Impacts Future Generations

Continuum #5: Stretch

Assured of Success--------------------------------------Moderately Challenging--Extremely Challenging

Continuum #6: Time to Completion

A Day or Less-------------------------Days or Weeks----------------------------Months--------------------------Years----------------------------Decades

Continuum #7: Complexity

Simple--Moderately Complex---Highly Complex

Continuum #8: Balance

Most Clustered in One Extreme/Area-----------------------Moderate Balance---------------------------All Six Continua & Area Set Show Balance

Appendix F

How to Compose Your Life Story

All the world's a stage,
And all the men and women merely players:
They have their exits and their entrances;
And one man in his time plays many parts,
His acts being seven ages. At first the infant,
Mewling and puking in the nurse's arms.
And then the whining school-boy, with his satchel
And shining morning face, creeping like snail
Unwillingly to school. And then the lover,
Sighing like furnace, with a woeful ballad
Made to his mistress' eyebrow. Then a soldier,
Full of strange oaths and bearded like the pard,
Jealous in honour, sudden and quick in quarrel,
Seeking the bubble reputation
Even in the cannon's mouth. And then the justice,
In fair round belly with good capon lined,
With eyes severe and beard of formal cut,
Full of wise saws and modern instances;
And so he plays his part. The sixth age shifts
Into the lean and slipper'd pantaloon,
With spectacles on nose and pouch on side,
His youthful hose, well saved, a world too wide
For his shrunk shank; and his big manly voice,
Turning again toward childish treble, pipes
And whistles in his sound. Last scene of all,
That ends this strange eventful history,
Is second childishness and mere oblivion,
Sans teeth, sans eyes, sans taste, sans everything.
   --William Shakespeare, *As You Like It*

Dan McAdams (1993) proposes autobiography as the most effective path to both understanding oneself and plotting future priorities. I have built on the essence of his process and developed a workshop whose purpose is to emerge with an outline of one's past, present, and future by using the tools of drama and psychology. Here is the process in its barest outline form. Should you take wing with it and leap from here to the writing of your full autobiography and planning the rest of your life, so be it. Or, for some of you who would prefer having a facilitator guide you through the process, please get in touch with me at http://www.centacs.com/contact/ for names of workshop leaders and dates for their programs.

1. Introduction. We begin at the beginning—with our infancy. After getting a fix on our past, we will take a picture of our present. Then taking stock of it all, we will project our future. In this manner, our life is like a book. It is a book—a biography.

2. Past

    a. Think of a play or novel or biography in which the author has listed the characters at the beginning—"dramatis personae." In order to tell your story, you will need to list the characters in your life's drama, and describe the role(s) that each has played. Here's how:

        i. List all of the roles that you have played in your life up to this point— parent, builder, and so forth. For each role, indicate how you feel at this point in your life about that role—whether you'd like to resume, stop, start, modify, increase, decrease, never-again/over-and-done-with, or continue as is (BAU—business as usual).

        ii. List the names of persons who got you started in each role, or who developed you in that role in a memorable way. These folks are your role models, the heroes and heroines of your story.

        iii. Circle or star no more than 10 of the most important role models' names. These are the true heroes of your story. These roles/actors form the core of your life story. You can easily see them in your mind's eye, day in and day out.

    b. The story of your life is the dialog among these roles over time as they compete for resources, etc. See if you can phrase your main roles as mythic "imagoes"—the Good Father, the Loyal Friend, the Untiring Caregiver, etc.

    c. Now, think of your life as a book. Do a mind map for identifying potential chapters. At this point, you can play with different ways of grouping the elements of your past: schools, events, new people, crises, achievements, deaths, births, marriages, challenges, religious events or experiences, physical developments, travel, military experience. By combining, splitting, and so forth, find a scheme that makes sense to you as a way of organizing your life up to this point into chapters. The organizing may be chronological or thematic (role development, achievements, crises, etc.). Identify these chapter groups on the mind map, and then sequence them 1, 2, 3....

    d. Now create the Table of Contents for your life as a book/drama/novel. For each chapter, and beginning with chapter one:

        i. Think of a title for the chapter.

        ii. Enter some notes about the essential contents of the chapter.

        iii. Identify how you transition from one chapter to the next.

e. "Book Review." We now are going to take your life story as though it were a literary work presented for review. And, you will serve as your own reviewer, with perhaps a friend or partner as a sounding board, clarifier, and pattern identifier.

     i. Identify 10 critical events, or nuclear episodes, in your life story. Each should be based on a specific time and place, like "Dubonnet on the Champs Elysees on Bastille Day 1976," not spread out over time, like a "trip to Europe." For each, jot down details of where, when, who with, what happened, what feeling/thinking/doing, and assess its impact on your life story—what it says about who you are or have been or might be. Did it change you? How? Be specific.

    ii. Identify the one or two role models/actors whom you regard as your top heroes/heroines (as in Best Actor/Actress, versus Supporting).

   iii. Evaluate the totality of your life to date, as well as specific periods of your life, according to the balance of agency and communion. Agency is the degree to which you placed priority on achievement and doing things, while communion is the degree to which you placed priority on nurturing relationships. Consider how your role models influenced the agency/communion balance at different points.

   iv. In balance, have you been mostly an optimist, a pessimist, or a realist? Which was dominant at different periods? How did role models influence?

    v. What type of drama has your life been—tragedy, comedy, melodrama, adventure, romance?

   vi. Create the iconography of your life story—the images with strong emotional associations (e.g., the red tricycle/wagon in Citizen Kane). What do they mean, and how do they play today and possibly in your future?

   vii. What is your "ideology"—the ideals or values that have formed the core of your self?

  viii. Identify two areas of your life in which you are currently, or recently, experiencing stress, conflict, or problems that need to be solved. For each, describe its nature, cause/source, history of development, and plan (if any) for dealing with it. Major sources of stress include: Unsupportive personal qualities (traits, abilities, physical characteristics), inappropriate autonomy, comparison to others, rival opportunities, inadequate resources, nature/"acts of God," goal conflict, competition, blockers, threats, scripts, illness, doubt, loss.

    ix. Up to this point in your life, how would you describe the three or so major sources of satisfaction for you, the states/activities/persons/etc. that create the most lasting and satisfying positive mood states.

    x. Just as novels have themes, such as "man's cruelty to man," or "pride goeth before the fall," or "love conquers all," how would you word the theme of your life as lived to this point?

3. Present
   a. The process for exploring the present tense of "you" is essentially that outlined in Chapter 6 of this book, whereby you identify the aspects of "Howardian Person" that define who you are at this juncture of your life history: traits, mental abilities, values, physical characteristics, and memories/experiences.
   b. For each part of you, identify the role that you would like it to play in your future, based on your current feelings about these parts of you (e.g., sociability, spontaneity, worrying, skepticism, mathematical ability, and so forth). Remember the various types of actions:
      i. Do more of it.
      ii. Do less of it.
      iii. Modify how you do it, through training, difficulty level, etc.
      iv. Find synergies—combine activities so you're doing two or more at the same time.
      v. Find new narrative material—travel, behavior experiments, changing work, etc., contexts by moving etc...)
   c. Review your Statement of Personal Priorities from Chapter 10.

4. Future
   a. Use a process similar to the one you used earlier to outline your past. Create a mind map of major events, opportunities, milestones, achievements and other personal and professional goals that you would like to compose your future.
   b. Organize them into a sequence, and create chapters, each with main actors and notes about specific eventualities.

5. Review and Action Items
   a. Review the material in steps 1 to 4.

b. Prepare Action Plan—what are the steps you need to take now to move towards accomplishing your future?

c. Share your autobiography notes with a friend or partner. Ask for their reaction, suggestions, what pitfalls they see, and so forth.

d. Incorporate suggestions you like into your plan.

e. Where to go from here:

    i. Select items from this book's Resources for your reading list.

    ii. Visit web sites recommended throughout this book, and do Internet searches on the names of thinkers whose work intrigues you (Seligman, Lyubomirsky, Bok, etc.).

    iii. Review your notes and action items with persons close to you: partner, children, friend, and so forth.

    iv. Encourage persons close to you to go through the same experience.

    v. Consider using your notes to actually write your autobiography.

    vi. Suggest to one or more of your children that they use your notes, plus further interviews with you or others, to write your biography, perhaps as a school project (history, psychology, English, career exploration, etc.).

    vii. Consider using the process as a focal activity for a family reunion.

    viii. Use the process, either abbreviated or expanded, as a team-building activity, or as a classroom experience, e.g., for leaders in development, or as a part of career exploration.

    ix. Break up the process into smaller units, and use them spread out over time as a part of coaching or counseling relationships. Consider using the process for premarital counseling, marriage enrichment experiences, and midlife counseling.

Definitions

Accelerators. Factors that promote, speed up, solidify, or otherwise support the development of something; in this book, said of "clicking."

Booster. A personal choice or life circumstance that tends to increase happiness, for either shorter or longer periods.

Choice. A causal effect on well-being that is largely within one's personal control. Contrasted with Circumstance.

Circumstance. A causal effect on well-being that is largely out of one's personal control. Contrasted with Choice.

Deafferentation. Another word for "flow"; refers to the shutting down of afferent and efferent nerves and the resulting total absorption in the moment.

Downer. A personal choice or life circumstance that tends to decrease happiness, for either shorter or longer periods.

Eudaimonia. From Aristotle, literally *eu-* "good, well" + *daimon* "genius" meaning one's natural strengths (i.e., genius) are flourishing (i.e. in good shape, well-expressed). Today, it is typically translated as happiness. Aristotle's original meaning is more like my sense of person/environment fit, or flow, in which one's salient characteristics are engaged productively. Aristotle talked of expressing one's "virtue" the way some today would talk of realizing one's "potential," much like the acorn becoming the oak, or the argumentative sort becoming the lawyer.

Flow. Defined by Mihalyi Czikszentmihalyi as a mental state characterized by total absorption in the task at hand, such that temperature, hunger, time, and other possible distractions are of no effect.

Forty percent solution. Sonya Lyubomirsky's explanation of the sources of happiness: 50% from one's genetic set point, 10% from one's circumstances, and 40% from one's daily choices.

Happiness. The same as Subjective Well-Being, or the dominance of positive emotional events in one's life and the relative scarcity of negative emotional events. See PEE:NEE ratio.

Hedonic treadmill. When a personal choice or circumstance provides a momentary increase in happiness, but then returns to one's prior set point, without permanently changing one's set point, and then must be frequently repeated in order to re-experience the increase in happiness, it is said to exhibit the characteristics of a hedonic treadmill.

Myth. A personal choice or life circumstance that is thought to increase or decrease happiness, but that doesn't, or, that is thought to increase happiness for the longer term yet only increases for the short term.

Objective Well-Being (OWB). Contrasted with Subjective Well-Being, OWB is associated with the sense that all of one's accomplishments have added up to an acceptable level.

OWB. (See Objective Well-Being.)

PEE:NEE Ratio. The ratio of positive emotional events (PEEs) to negative emotional events (NEEs) in a person's life. Ratios between roughly 3 and 13 PEE to 1 NEE are associated with Subject Well-Being/flourishing, while ratios lower than 3:1 and greater than 13:1 are associated with languishing.

Self-deception. Occurs when you affirm something about you that is untrue, such as being invincible.

Self-esteem. According to Nathaniel Branden (1992), the way one evaluates oneself on two dimensions—the degree to which we feel capable of taking on life's tasks and successfully dealing with them (self-efficacy or self-confidence) and the degree to which we feel deserving of respect from both self and others (self-respect).

Set Point. The level of a particular trait that is stable over time but that is subject to temporary increases or decreases called states.

Social comparison. The tendency to compare something about me with others, in order to determine whether they have more or less of it than I do, with the typical consequence of being more satisfied with things that I have more of than others around me, and desiring more of things that others have more of than I do at present.

State. A temporary level of a trait due to the effect of extraordinary circumstances, such as winning the lottery or loss of a loved one; a temporary departure, either up or down, from one's set point for a particular trait. See hedonic treadmill and set point.

Subjective well-being. The internal feeling that the positive emotions dominate negative emotions; a synonym for happiness.

SWB. (See Subjective well-being.)

Temperament. An inherited pattern of behavior, such as activity level or level of anxiety. Also called a disposition.

Trait. A temperament or disposition that has been shaped by environmental factors, or, the effect of time and personal history on one's native temperaments.

Warehousing effect. Said of the fact that schools and other institutions keep potential undesirable behavior off the street, with that being a valued consequence of such "warehousing" regardless of whether, e.g., learning takes place.

Well-being. The broadest category of positive mood. It includes two major subcategories: emotional and cognitive well-being. Emotional well-being is often called Subjective Well-Being (SWB), and cognitive well-being is often called Objective Well-Being (OWB). The former tends to be more emotional (e.g., happiness) and resistant to accurate measurement, while the latter tends to be more quantitative (e.g., income) and easier to measure. Happiness is the most talked about kind of SWB.

Zeigarnik effect. Named after Bluma Zeigarnik (a student of Kurt Lewin), states that unfinished (interrupted, ongoing) tasks (goals, activities, promises, etc.) are remembered better, longer, stronger, than finished ones.

Resources

Print Resources

Achor, S. (2010). *The Happiness Advantage: The seven principles of positive psychology that fuel success and performance at work.* New York, NY: Crown Business.

Ames, C. (1992). Classroom goals, structures, and student motivation. *Journal of Educational Psychology, 84*(3), 261-271.

Attwood, J. B., & Attwood, C. (2006). *The passion test: The effortless path to discovering your destiny.* Fairfield, IA: 1st World Publishing.

Baumeister, R. F. & Tierney, J. (2011). *Willpower: Rediscovering the greatest human strength.* New York, NY: The Penguin Press (Kindle version).

Belenky, M. F., Clinchy, B. M., Goldberger, N. R., & Tarule, J. M. (1997). *Women's ways of knowing: The development of self, voice, and mind (10th anniversary edition).* New York, NY: Basic Books.

Benard, B. (2004). *Resiliency: What we have learned.* San Francisco, CA: WestEd.

Ben-Shahar, T. (2007). *Happier: Learn the secrets to daily joy and lasting fulfillment.* New York, NY: McGraw-Hill.

Bjork, R. (1994). Memory and metamemory considerations in the training of human beings. In J. Metcalfe and A. P. Shimamura (Eds.), *Metacognition: Knowing about knowing* (pp. 185B-206). Cambridge Mass.: The MIT Press.

Block, P. (2008). *Community: The structure of belonging.* San Francisco, CA: Berrett-Koehler Publishers.

Bok, D. C. (2010). *The politics of happiness: What government can learn from the new research on well-being.* Princeton University Press (Kindle version).

Bradbury, R. (2000). *Fahrenheit 451.* New York, NY: Del Rey Books. (Original work published 1950).

Brafman, O., & Brafman, R. (2010). *Click: The magic of instant connections.* New York, NY: Broadway Books.

Branden, N. (1992). *The power of self-esteem.* Deerfield Beach, FL: Health Communications.

Branden, N. (1994). *The six pillars of self-esteem.* New York, NY: Bantam Books.

Brickman, P., & Campbell, D. T. (1971). Hedonic relativism and planning the good society. In M. H. Appley (Ed.), *Adaptation level theory: A symposium* (pp. 287-302). New York, NY: Academic Press.

Brickman, P., Coates, D., & Janoff-Bulman, R. (1978). Lottery winners and accident victims: Is happiness relative? *Journal of Personality and Social Psychology, 36*(8), 917-927.

Brooks, D. (2011). *The social animal: The hidden sources of love, character, and achievement.* New York, NY: Random House (Kindle version).

Brown, J., & Fenske, M. (2010). *The winner's brain: 8 strategies great minds use to achieve success.* Cambridge, MA: DaCapo Press.

Brunstein, J. C., Schultheiss, O. C., & Grässman, R. (1998). Personal goals and emotional well-being: The moderating role of motive dispositions. *Journal of Personality and Social Psychology, 75*, 494-508.

Buckingham, M. (2009). *Find your strongest life: What the happiest and most successful women do differently.* Nashville, TN: Thomas Nelson.

Buckingham, M., & Coffman, C. (1999). *First, break all the rules: What the world's greatest managers do differently.* New York, NY: Simon & Schuster.

Butler, S. (2003). *The Way of All Flesh.* (Kindle version; Original work published 1903)

Campbell, J. (with Moyers, B). (1991). *The power of myth.* New York, NY: Anchor Books/Doubleday.

Caspi, A., Sugdenl, K., Moffitt, T. E., Taylor, A., Harrington, H., McClayl, J. . . . Poulton, R. (2003). Influence of life stress on depression: Moderation by a polymorphism in the 5-HTT gene. *Science, 301*, 386-389.

Cattaneo, L. B., & Chapman, A. R. (2010). The process of empowerment: A model for use in research and practice. *American Psychologist, 65*(7), 646-659.

Christakis, N. A., & Fowler, J. H. (2009). *Connected: The surprising power of our social networks and how they shape our lives.* New York, NY: Little, Brown.

Clark, A. E., & Lelkes, O. (2009, January). Let us pray: Religious interactions in life satisfaction. *Paris School of Economics Working Papers,* Number 2009-01.

Cloninger, C. R. (2004). *Feeling good: The science of well-being.* New York, NY: Oxford University Press.

Cohen, G. D. (2005). *The mature mind: The positive power of the aging brain.* New York, NY: Basic Books.

Cooperrider, D. L., & Whitney, D. (2005). *Appreciative inquiry: A positive revolution in change.* San Francisco, CA: Berrett-Koehler.

Costa P. T., Jr., & McCrae R. R. (1992) *Revised NEO Personality Inventory (NEO PI-R) and the NEO Five-Factor Inventory (NEO-FFI) professional manual.* Odessa, FL: Psychological Assessment Resources.

Coyne, J. C., Stefanek, M., & Palmer, S. C. (2007). Psychotherapy and survival in cancer: The conflict between hope and evidence. *Psychological Bulletin, 133*(3), 367-394.

Crawford, M. B. (2009). *Shopcraft as soulcraft: An inquiry into the value of work.* New York, NY: The Penguin Press.

Csikszentmihalyi, M. (1990). *Flow: The psychology of optimal experience.* New York, NY: HarperCollins.

Csikszentmihalyi, M. (1993). *The evolving self: A psychology for the third millennium.* New York, NY: HarperCollins.

Csikszentmihalyi, M. (1996). *Creativity: Flow and the psychology of discovery and invention.* New York, NY: HarperCollins.

Csikszentmihalyi, M. (1999). If we are so rich, why aren't we happy? *American Psychologist, 54*(10), 821–827.

Damasio, A. R. (1994). *Descartes' error: Emotion, reason and the human brain.* New York, NY: Grosset & Dunlap.

Danziger, S., Leva, J., & Avnaim-Pesso, L. (2011). Extraneous factors in judicial decisions. *Proceedings of the National Academy of Sciences.* doi:10.1073/pnas.1018033108

Deci, E. L., & Ryan, R. M. (1985). *Intrinsic motivation and self-determination in human behavior.* New York, NY: Plenum Press.

DeLeire, T., & Kalil, A. (2010). Does consumption buy happiness? Evidence from the United States. *International Review of Economics, 57*, 163-176. doi:10.1007/s12232-010-0093-6

Dennett, D. C. (2006). *Breaking the spell: Religion as a natural phenomenon.* New York, NY: Viking.

DeYoung, C. G., Hirsh, J. B., Shane, M. S., Papademetris, X., Rajeevan, N., & Gray, J. R. (2010). Testing predictions from personality neuroscience: Brain structure and the Big Five. *Psychological Science, 21*(6), 820-828.

Diener, E., & Biswas-Diener, R. (2008). *Happiness: Unlocking the mysteries of psychological wealth*. Malden, MA: Wiley-Blackwell

Diener, E., Lucas, R. E., & Scollon, C. N. (2006). Beyond the hedonic treadmill: Revising the adaptation theory of well-being. *American Psychologist, (61)*, 4, 305-314.

Diener, E., Ng, W., Harter, J., & Arora, R. (2010). Wealth and happiness across the world: Material prosperity predicts life evaluation, whereas psychosocial prosperity predicts positive feeling. *Journal of Personal and Social Psychology, 99*(1), 52-61.

Diener, E., Tay, L., & Myers, D. G. (2011). If religion makes people happy, why are so many dropping out? *Journal of Personality and Social Psychology, 101*(6), 1278-1290.

Duckworth, A. L., & Quinn, P. D. (2009). Development and validation of the Short Grit Scale (Grit-S). *Journal of Personality Assessment, 91,* 166-174.

Dunn, E. W., Gilbert, D. T., & Wilson, T. D. (2011). If money doesn't make you happy, then you probably aren't spending it right. *Journal of Consumer Psychology, 21*, 115-125.

Dweck, C. S. (2006). *Mindset: The new psychology of success*. New York, NY: Random House.

Easterlin, R. A. (1974). Does economic growth improve the human lot? In P. A. David and M. W. Reder, (Eds.), *Nations and households in economic growth: Essays in honor of Moses Abramovitz*. New York, NY: Academic Press.

Ehrenreich, B. (2009). *Bright-sided: How the relentless promotion of positive thinking has undermined America*. New York, NY: Metropolitan Books/Henry Holt.

Emmons, R. A., & McCullough, M. E. (2003). Counting blessings versus burdens: An experimental investigation of gratitude and subjective well-being in daily life. *Journal of Personality and Social Psychology, 84,* 377-389.

Emmons, R. A., & McCullough, M. E. (2004). *The psychology of gratitude*. Oxford, United Kingdom: Oxford University Press.

Ericsson, K. A., and Charness, N. (1994). Expert performance—its structure and acquisition. *American Psychologist, 49*(8), 725–747.

Fischer, R., & Boer, D. (2011). What is more important for national well-being: Money or autonomy? A meta-analysis of well-being, burnout, and anxiety across 63 societies. *Journal of Personality and Social Psychology, 101*(1), 164-184.

Fiske, S. T., Cuddy, A. J. C., & Glick, P. (2007). Universal dimensions of social perception: Warmth and competence. *Trends in Cognitive Science, 11*, 77-83.

Fletcher, J. L. (1993). *Patterns of high performance: Discovering the ways people work best*. San Francisco, CA: Berrett-Koehler.

Frankl, V. E. (1984). *Man's search for meaning*. (3rd ed.) New York, NY: Simon & Schuster.

Frankl, V. E. (2000). *Man's search for ultimate meaning*. New York, NY: Basic Books.

Fredrickson, B. (2009). *Positivity*. New York, NY: Crown.

Fredrickson, B. L., & Losada, M. F. (2005). Positive affect and the complex dynamics of human flourishing. *American Psychologist, 60*(7), 678-686.

Gardner, C. (2006). *The pursuit of happyness*. New York, NY: Amistad/HarperCollins.

Gardner, H. (1983). *Frames of mind: The theory of multiple intelligences*. New York: Basic Books.

Gilbert, D. (2006). *Stumbling on happiness.* New York, NY: Alfred A. Knopf.

Gilbert, D. (2010, January). *This emotional life* [Television series]. Arlington, VA: Public Broadcasting Service.

Goleman, D. (2006). *Social intelligence: The new science of human relationships.* New York, NY: Bantam.

Gollwitzer, P. M. (1999). Implementation intentions: Strong effects of simple plans. *American Psychologist, 54*(7), 493-503.

Gollwitzer, P. M., Sheeran, P., Michalski, V., & Seifert, A. E. (2009, April 6). When intentions go public: Does social reality widen the intention-behavior gap? *Psychological Science, 20*(5), 612-618.

Gottman, J. M. & Silver, N. (1999). *The seven principles for making marriage work.* New York, NY: Three Rivers Press.

Graham, C. (2010). *Happiness around the world: The paradox of happy peasants and miserable millionaires.* Oxford University Press (Kindle version).

Grandin, T., & Johnson, C. (2005). *Animals in translation: Using the mysteries of autism to decode animal behavior.* New York, NY: Scribner.

Gray, J. A. (1982). On mapping anxiety. *Behavioral and Brain Sciences.* doi:10.1017/S0140525X00013297

Haidt, J. (2006). *The happiness hypothesis.* New York, NY: Basic Books.

Hall, S. S. (2010). *Wisdom: From philosophy to neuroscience.* New York, NY: Borzoi Books/Alfred A. Knopf (Kindle version).

Hamer, D., & Copeland, P. (1998). *Living with our genes: Why they matter more than you think.* New York, NY: Doubleday.

Hamermesh, D. S., & Abrevaya, J. (2011). Beauty is the promise of happiness? IZA Discussion Paper No. 5600. Bonn, Germany.

Harris, J. R. (1998). *The nurture assumption: Why children turn out the way they do.* New York, NY: Free Press.

Hecht, J. M. (2007). *The happiness myth: Why what we think is right is wrong.* San Francisco, CA: HarperSanFrancisco.

Hedges, C. (2009). *Empire of illusion: The end of literacy and the triumph of spectacle.* New York, NY: Nation Books.

Helliwell, J. F., & Barrington-Leigh, C. P. (2010). Measuring and understanding subjective well-being. *Canadian Journal of Economics, 43*(3), 729-753.

Hermans, H. J. M., & Hermans-Jansen, E. (1995). *Self-narratives: The construction of meaning in psychotherapy.* New York, NY: Guilford Press.

Hill, N. (2005). *Think and grow rich.* New York, NY: Jeremy P. Tarcher/Penguin.

Howard, P. J. (2006). *The owner's manual for the brain: Everyday applications from mind-brain research.* Austin, TX: Bard Press.

Howard, P. J., & Howard, J. M. (2010). *The owner's manual for personality at work.* 2nd ed. Charlotte, NC: CentACS.

Howard, P. J., & Howard, J. M. (2011). *The owner's manual for personality from 12 to 22.* Charlotte, NC: CentACS.

Hsieh, T. (2010). *Delivering Happiness.* New York, NY: Business Plus.

Ickes, W. (2009*). Strangers in a strange lab: How personality shapes our initial encounters with others.* Oxford, United Kingdom: Oxford University Press.

Iyengar, S. (2010). *The art of choosing.* New York, NY: Hachette Book Group.

Kahneman, D., & Krueger, A. B. (2006). Developments in the measurement of subjective well-being. *Journal of Economic Perspectives, 20*(1), 3–24.

Kahneman, D., Krueger, A. B., Schkade, D., Schwartz, N., and Stone, A. A. (1996). Would you be happier if you were richer? A focusing illusion. *Science, 312,* 1908-1910.

Kelley, H. H., & Thibaut, J. W. (1978). *Interpersonal relations: A theory of interdependence.* New York, NY: Wiley.

Keltner, D. (2009). *Born to be good: The science of a meaningful life.* New York, NY: W. W. Norton.

Kepner, C. H., & Tregoe, B. B. (1981). *The new rational manager.* Princeton, N.J.: Princeton Research Press.

Killingsworth, M. A., & Gilbert, D. T. (2010, November 12). A wandering mind is an unhappy mind. *Science, 330*(6006), 932.

King, L. A., & Hicks, J. A. (2007). Whatever happened to "What might have been"? Regrets, happiness, and maturity. *American Psychologist, 62*(7), 625-636.

Kolbert, E. (2010, March 22). Everybody have fun. *The New Yorker,* pp. 72-74.

Kotter, J. P. (1985). *Power and influence.* New York, NY: Free Press.

Kruger, J., & Dunning, D. (1999). Unskilled and unaware of it: How difficulties in recognizing one's own incompetence lead to inflated self-assessments. *Journal of Personality and Social Psychology, 77*(6), 1121-1134.

Lama, D., Cutler, H., & Cutler, H. C. (1998). *The art of happiness: A handbook for daily living.* New York, NY: Riverhead Books.

Larsen, J. T., & McKibban, A. R. (2008). Is happiness having what you want, wanting what you have, or both? *Psychological Science, 19*(4), 371-377.

Latham, G. P. (2007). *Work motivation: History, theory, research and practice,* Thousand Oaks, CA: Sage.

Latham, G. P., & Yukl, G. A. (1975). A review of research on the application of goal setting in organizations. *Academy of Management Journal, 18,* 824-845.

LeBon, T. (2001). *Wise therapy: Philosophy for counsellors.* New York, NY: Sage.

Lemay, K., McFerran, B., & Laven, M. (2011). Caution: Fragile! Regulating the interpersonal security of chronically insecure partners. *Journal of Personality and Social Psychology, 100*(4), 681-702.

Lewis, C. S. (1956). *Till we have faces: A myth retold.* Orlando, FL: A Harvest Book/Harcourt Brace.

Lewis, C. S. (1960). *The four loves.* San Diego, CA: A Harvest Book/Harcourt Brace.

Liedloff, J. (1977). *The continuum concept: In search of happiness lost.* Cambridge, MA: Da Capo Press/Perseus Books Group.

Locke, E. A., & Latham, G. P. (1990). *A theory of goal setting and task performance.* Englewood Cliffs, NJ: Prentice Hall.

Loehr, J., & Schwartz, T. (2004). *The power of full engagement: Managing energy, not time, is the key to high performance and personal time.* New York, NY: Free Press.

Losada, M. & Heaphy, E. (2004). The role of positivity and connectivity in the performance of business teams: A nonlinear dynamics model. *American Behavioral Scientist, 47*(6), 740–765.

Lucas, R. E., Clark, A. E., Georgellis, Y., & Diener, E. (2003). Reexamining adaptation and the set point model of happiness: Reactions to changes in marital status. *Journal of Personality and Social Psychology, 84,* 527-539.

Lykken, D., & Tellegen, A. (1996). Happiness is a stochastic phenomenon. *Psychological Science, 7,* 186-189.

Lyubomirsky, S. (2008). *The how of happiness: A scientific approach to getting the life you want.* New York, NY: The Penguin Press.

Lyubomirsky, S., King, L., & Diener, E. (2005). The benefits of frequent positive affect: Does happiness lead to success? *Psychological Bulletin, 131*, 803-855.

Marks, N. (2011). *The happiness manifesto: How nations and people can nurture well-being.* New York, NY: TED Conferences (Kindle version).

Masicampo, E. J., & Baumeister, R. F. (2011, October). Consider it done! Plan making can eliminate the cognitive effects of unfulfilled goals. *Journal of Personality and Social Psychology, 101*(4), 667-683.

Mason, D. (2002). *The Piano Tuner.* New York, NY: Random House.

Mauss, I. B., Shallcross, A. J., Troy, A. S., John, O. P., Ferrer, E., & Wilhelm, F. H. (2011). Don't hide your happiness! Positive emotion dissociation, social connectedness, and psychological functioning. *Journal of Personality and Social Psychology, 100*(4), 738-748.

McAdams, D. P. (1993). *The stories we live by: Personal myths and the making of the self.* New York, NY: Guilford Press.

McConnell, A. R., Brown, C. M., Shoda, T. M., Stayton, L. E., & Martin, C. E. (2011). Friends with benefits: On the positive consequences of pet ownership. *Journal of Personality and Social Psychology, 101*(6), 1239-1252.

McCrae, R. R., Martin, T. A., Hrebícková, M., Urbánek, T., Boomsma, D. I., Willemsen, G., & Costa, P. (2008). Personality trait similarity between spouses in four cultures. *Journal of Personality, 76*(5), 1137-1163.

McMahon, D. M. (2006). *Happiness: A history.* Atlantic Monthly Press

Miller, C. A., & Frisch, M. B. (2009). *Creating your best life: The ultimate life list guide.* New York, NY: Sterling.

Mischel, W., Ebbesen, E. B., & Zeiss, A. R. (1972). Cognitive and attentional mechanisms in delay of gratification. *Journal of Personality and Social Psychology, 21*(2), 204–218.

Moll, J., Krueger, F., Zahn, R., Pardini, M., de Oliveira-Souza, R., & Grafman, J. (2006). Human fronto-meso-limbic networks guide decisions about charitable donation. *Proceedings of the National Academy of Sciences, 103*(42), 15623-15628.

Myers, D. G. (1992). *The pursuit of happiness: Who is happy—and why.* New York, NY: William Morrow.

Nettle, D. (2005). *Happiness: The science behind your smile.* New York, NY: Oxford University Press.

Norris, J. I., & Larsen, J. T. (2010). Wanting more than you have and its consequences for well-being. *Journal of Happiness Studies*, doi10.1007/s10902-010-9232-8

Novotney, A. (2011, July/August). Silence, please. *Monitor on Psychology*, 46-49.

Ochsner, K. (2006). Characterizing the functional architecture of affect regulation: Emerging answers and outstanding questions. In Cacioppo, J., Visser, P., & Pickett, C. (Eds). *Social neuroscience: People thinking about thinking people.* Cambridge, MA: The MIT Press.

Peck, M. S. (1987). *The different drum: Community making and peace.* New York, NY: Simon & Schuster.

Pervin, L. A. (1968). Performance and satisfaction as a function of individual-environment fit. *Psychological Bulletin, 69*, 56-68.

Peterson, C. (2006). *A primer in positive psychology.* New York, NY: Oxford University Press.

Peterson, C., Park, N., & Seligman, M. (2005). Orientations to happiness and life satisfaction: The full life versus the empty life. *Journal of Happiness Studies, 6*, 25-41.

Pierpont, N. (2009). *Wind turbine syndrome: A report on a natural experiment.* Santa Fe, NM: K-Selected Books.

Pink, D. (2009). Drive: *The surprising truth about what motivates us.* New York, NY: Riverhead Books.

Pirsig, R. M. (1974). *Zen and the art of motorcycle maintenance: An inquiry into values.* New York, NY: William Morrow.

Plunkett, L. C., and Hale, G. A. (1982). *The proactive manager: The complete book of problem solving and decision making.* New York, NY: Wiley.

Prager, D. (1998). *Happiness Is a serious problem: A human nature repair manual.* New York, NY: ReganBooks/HarperCollins.

Punset, E. (2007). *The happiness trip: A scientific journey.* White River Junction, VT: Chelsea Green.

Putnam, R.D. (2000). *Bowling Alone: The collapse and revival of American community.* New York, NY: Simon & Schuster.

Redfield, J. (1993). *The Celestine prophecy.* New York, NY: Warner Books.

Ricard, M. (2006). *Happiness: A guide to developing life's most important skill.* New York, NY: Little Brown.

Ridley, M. (2003). *Nature via nurture: Genes, experience, and what makes us human.* New York, NY: HarperCollins.

Rinpoche, Y. M. (2007). *The joy of living: Unlocking the secret and science of happiness.* New York, NY: Harmony Books.

Rothbart, M. K., Ahadi, S. A., & Evans, D. E. (2001). Temperament and personality: Origins and outcomes. *Journal of Personality and Social Psychology, 78*, 122-135.

Ryan, R. M., & Deci, E. L. (2001). On happiness and human potentials: A review of research on hedonic and eudaimonic well-being. *Annual Review of Psychology, 52*, 141-166.

Sackeim, H. A., & Gur, R. C. (1979). Self-deception, other deception and self-reported psychopathology. *Journal of Consulting and Clinical Psychology, 47*, 213-215.

Salzberg, S. (2008). *The kindness handbook: A practical companion.* Boulder CO: Sounds True.

Sapolsky, R. M. (2004). *Why zebras don't get ulcers.* 3rd ed. New York, NY: Henry Holt.

Sax, L. (2007). *Boys adrift: The five factors driving the growing epidemic of unmotivated boys and underachieving young men.* New York, NY: Basic Books.

Schachtel, H. J. (1954). *The real enjoyment of living.* New York, NY: Dutton.

Seligman, M. (2011). *Flourish.* New York, NY: Simon & Schuster. (Kindle version)

Seligman, M. E. P. (1984). *Seligman attributional style questionnaire.* (Available by calling Martin Seligman or Peter Schulman at 215-898-2748).

Seligman, M. E. P. (1991). *Learned optimism.* New York, NY: Knopf.

Seligman, M. E. P. (1994). *What you can change and what you can't.* New York, NY: Knopf.

Seligman, M. E. P. (1996, October). Science as an ally of practice. [Special issue: Outcome Assessment of Psychotherapy]. *American Psychologist, 51*(10), 1072–1079.

Seligman, M. E. P. (2002). *Authentic happiness.* New York, NY: Free Press.

Seligman, M. E. P., Reivich, K., Jaycox, L., & Gillham, J. (1995). *The optimistic child.* Boston, MA: Houghton Mifflin.

Seligman, M. E. P., Steen, T. A., Park, N., & Peterson, C. (2005). Positive psychology progress: Empirical validation of interventions. *American Psychologist, 60*(5), 410–421.

Sheldon, K. M., & Elliot, A. J. (1999). Goal striving, need satisfaction, and longitudinal well-being: The self-concordance model. *Journal of Personality and Social Psychology, 76,* 482-497.

Sheldon, K. M., Abad, N., & Hinsch, C. (2011). A two-process view of Facebook use and relatedness need-satisfaction: Disconnection drives use, and connection rewards it. *Journal of Personality and Social Psychology, 100*(4), 766-775.

Shenk, D. (2010). *The genius in all of us: Why everything you've been told about genetics, talent, and IQ is wrong.* New York, NY: Doubleday. Kindle version.

Solnick, S. J., & Hemenway, D. (1998). Is more always better? A survey on positional concerns. *Journal of Economic Behavior and Organization, 37,* 373-383.

Spiegel, D., Bloom, J. R., & Gottheil, E. (1989). Effects of psychosocial treatment on survival of patients with metastatic breast cancer. *Lancet, 2,* 888-891.

Starek, J. E., & Keating, C. F. (1991). Self-deception and its relationship to success in competition. *Basic and Applied Psychology, 12*(2), 145-155.

Steel, P., & Ones, D. S. (2002). Personality and happiness: A national-level analysis. *Journal of Personality and Social Psychology, 83*(3), 767-781.

Stevenson, B., & Wolfers, J. (2009). The paradox of declining female happiness. *American Economic Journal: Economic Policy, 1*(2), 190–225.

Stewart, J. (2011). *Why Noise Matters.* Oxford, United Kingdom: Earthscan Publications.

Stix, G. (2011). The neuroscience of true grit. *Scientific American, 304*(3), 28-33.

Stutzer, A., & Frey, B. (2008). Stress that doesn't pay: The commuting paradox. *Scandinavian Journal of Economics, 110*(2), 339-366.

Uzzi, B. (1996). The sources and consequences of embeddedness for the economic performance of organizations: The network effect. *American Sociological Review, 61,* 674-698.

Van Boven, L. (2005). Experientialism, materialism, and the pursuit of happiness. *Review of General Psychology, 9,* 132-142.

Van Boven, L., & Gilovich, T. (2003). To do or to have? That is the question. *Journal of Personality and Social Psychology, 85,* 1193-1202.

Van Geel, Rolf. (2000). *Agency and communion in self-narratives: A psychometric study of the self-confrontation method.* Nijmegen, Netherlands: Nijmegen University Press.

Warren, R. (2004). *The purpose-driven life.* Grand Rapids, MI: Inspirio.

Waterman, A. S. (1993). Two conceptions of happiness: Contrasts of personal expressiveness (eudaimonia) and hedonic enjoyment. *Journal of Personality and Social Psychology, 64,* 678-691.

Watts, A. (1978). *The meaning of happiness: The quest for freedom of the spirit in modern psychology and the wisdom of the east.* London: Rider & Co. (Original work published 1940).

Waugh, C. E. & Fredrickson, B. L. (2006). Nice to know you: Positive emotions, self-other overlap, and complex understanding in the formation of a new relationship. *The Journal of Positive Psychology, 1*(2), 93–106.

Weiner, E. (2008). *The geography of bliss.* New York, NY: Twelve.

Wilkinson, R, & Pickett, K. (2009). *The spirit level: Why greater equality makes societies stronger.* New York, NY: Bloomsbury Press.

Williams, R. (1989). The trusting heart: Great news about type a behavior. New York, NY: Times Books.

Williams, R., and Williams, V. (1994). Anger Kills. New York, NY: HarperPerennial.

Wilson, E. G. (2008). *Against happiness: In praise of melancholy.* New York, NY: Sarah Crichton Books/Farrar, Straus and Giroux.

Wilson, T. D., & Schooler, J. W. (1991). Thinking too much: Introspection can reduce the quality of preferences and decisions. *Journal of Personality and Social Psychology, 60*(2), 181-192.

Yoshino, K. (2006). *Covering: The hidden assault on our civil rights.* New York, NY: Random House.

Zak, P. J. (2008). *Moral markets: The critical role of values in the economy.* Princeton University Press.

Web Resources

Action for Happiness:

www.actionforhappiness.org

Declaration of Independence:

www.archives.gov/exhibits/charters/declaration_transcript.html

Five Ways to Well-being:

www.fivewaystowellbeing.org

Happy Planet Index:

www.happyplanetindex.org

MIT mood meter

http://moodmeter.media.mit.edu/

National Accounts of Well-being:

www.nationalaccountsofwellbeing.org

nef (new economics foundation)

www.neweconomics.org

nef consulting on well-being at work:

www.well-beingatwork.net

nef's Centre for Well-being:

www.neweconomics.org/programmes/well-being

New Economics Institute, New York:

neweconomicsinstitute.org

Personal website for Nic Marks (*The Happiness Manifesto, The (un)Happy Planet Index*):

www.nicmarks.org

Ruut Veenhoven's Home Page

http://www2.eur.nl/fsw/research/veenhoven/

Stiglitz Commission on the Measurement of Economic Performance and Social Progress (2009) Final Report:

www.stiglitz-sen-fitoussi.fr/en/index.htm

Universal Declaration of Human Rights:

http://www.un.org/en/documents/udhr/

Index

16PF personality test, 351
40% solution, 34, 365
Abad, N., 219
Abdul-Baha, 327
Abrevaya, J., 60
Accelerators of intimacy, 211-212, 365
Accommodation (A), 19, 149-150, 154, 161, 166, 170, 305
Achor, Shawn, 56, 182, 209
ACORNs (communication)
    description, 214-215
    See PEE:NEE ratio
Activity Vector Analysis (AVA), Predictive Index, 352
Adams, George Matthew, 335
Addison, Joseph, 339
Adjustments, minor
    bidimensional (79 adjustments)
        attentional focus (7 adjustments), 262-264
        entertainment alternatives (7), 264-265
        goal types (7), 265-267
        language (8), 267-269
        maintenance (6), 269-271
        money (4), 271-272
        outlook (8), 272-274
        physical mode/state (11), 274-277
        social/interpersonal (12), 277-281
        work style (9), 281-284
    unidimensional (adjustments)
        achievement areas (8 adjustments), 284-286
        entertainment levels (16), 286-291
        health (1), 291
        past experiences (1), 292
        physical characteristics (1), 292
        social (5), 293-294
        talents (8), 294-297
    types, 260-261
Adler, Felix , 334
Adler, Mortimer, 342
Affection, generous
    chattiness, 236
    friendship, 236
    gratefulness, 237
    love, agape, 237
    love, eros, 237-238
    love, philia, 238
    love, storge, 238-239
Ahadi, S. A., 90
Air, fresh, 61-62, 103
Alcohol, 43, 49, 66-67, 305
Allelonyms for happiness, 22-23, 122-123, 323-325
Allen, David 310
Allen, Woody, 349

Altruism
    allelonyms of happiness for, 122-123
    Charter for Compassion, 244-245
    definition, 231-232
    Human Rights, Universal Declaration of, 241-244
    kinds, *see,* Affection, generous; Communication,
        thoughtful; Giving, helpful; Regard,positive;
        Relief, beneficial
    unselfishness (It's Not About You), 246
    See Statement of Personal Priorities
Amygdala, 58, 89, 90, 193, 196
Anderson, Ramona L., 344
Angelis, Barbara de, 330
Angelou, Maya, 122, 145, 342
Anthony, Robert, 344
Anthony, Susan, B., 346
Antoninus, Marcus, 341
Arab proverb, 328
Aristotle, 12, 329, 365
Armstrong, Karen, 244-245
Athleticism, 92
Attention Deficit Hyperactivity Disorder (ADHD), 355
Attwood, C., 188
Attwood, J. B., 188
Augustine, St., 346
Author unknown, quotations, 329-330
Avnaim-Pesso, L., 304
Babette's Feast, 12, 275
Bacon, Sir Francis, 147, 199, 300, 334
Ballou, Hosea, 337
Barrie, James M., 338
Barrington-Leigh, C. P., 64
Barrymore, John, 339
Barth, Karl, 340
Barthel, Mildred, 342
Batters, 23, 82, 110, 115
Baumeister, R., 224, 302, 304, 305, 306-307, 309
Beecher, Henry Ward, 337
Belenky, Mary, 169
Ben-Shahar, Tal, 174, 181, 187
Bentham, Jeremy, 18
Best Exotic Marigold Hotel, The, 235
Bible, 244, 245
Bierce, Ambrose, 328
Big Five model
    CenTACS, 7-8
    evolution of, 113-115
    SchoolPlace Big Five Profile, 8, 153, 351
    self-control, 304-305

traits, 19-20, 150-154, 161, 166
    WorkPlace Big Five Profile, 8, 82, 153-154
Billings, Josh, 339
Biondi, Matt, 342
Bjork, Robert, 134
Black, Algernon, 328
Blake, William, 166, 348
Blackwell, Lawana, 340
Blanchflower, David, 59
Blessington, Lady, 340
Bogan, Louise, 341
Boer, Diana, 63
Bok, Derek, 26, 32, 35, 36, 38, 41, 44, 49, 50, 52, 53, 54,
    58, 60, 62, 63, 64, 65, 66, 72, 73, 74, 77, 124, 181,
    353, 363
Bonanno, George, 90
Bono, Edward de, 333
Boswell, James, 213
Bovee, Christian N., 332
Bradburn. Norman, 343
Bradbury, Ray, 26, 146, 202, 239
Brafman, O., 211
Brafman, R., 211
Branden, N., 366
Brault, Robert, 344
Breathed, Berke, 330
Brecht, Bertolt, 24
Brickman, P., 37
Brooks, D., 36, 46, 57, 60, 61, 62
Brooks, David, 246
Brooks, Phillips, 343
Brothers, Joyce, 333
Brown, C. M., 52
Brown, Charlie, 332
Browne, H. Jackson, 336
Buck, Pearl S., 343
Bucket list, 44, 189-190, 251-254, 311, 317
Buckingham, Marcus, 71, 115, 143
Buddha, 331
Burns, George, 36, 335
Buscaglia, Leo, 340
Butler, Samuel, 111, 146, 315, 345
Byles, H. W., 336
California Personality Inventory (CPI), 351
Campbell, J., 13-14, 144-145, 217
Camus, Albert, 327
Carnegie, Andrew, 328
Carnegie, Dale, 332
Caron, Leslie, 340
Carson, Johnny, 339
Castaneda, Carlos, 331
Cather, Willa, 348
Cattaneo L. B., 174

Center for Applied Cognitive Studies (CentACS), 7-8, 191,
    365
Chalmers, Allan K., 328
Channing, William Ellery, 348
Chapman A. R., 174
Charness, N., 134, 199
Charter for Compassion, 244-245
Chaucer, Geoffrey, 145
Chekhov, Anton, 329
Child, Julia, 339
Child, Lydia Maria, 341
Chinese Proverb, 332
Chodron, Pema, 343
Choice, definition, 365
Christakis, N., 50, 77, 122, 218, 220
Cibber, Colley, 332
Circumstance, definition, 365
Clark, Andrew, 50, 54
Clarke, James Freeman, 338
Coates, D., 37
Coffman, C., 115, 143
Cognitive-behavioral therapy, 36
Collins, Kitty O'Neill, 340
Communication, thoughtful
    apologies, 233
    conflict managing, 234
    crediting, 233-234
    recognition on-the-spot, 234
    response for constructive feedback, 234
    thank you, saying, 234
Community
    allelonyms of happiness for, 122-123
    consistency
        ACORNs (communication), 214-215
        description, 211-213
        (see PEE:NEE ratio)
    description, 122, 208
    isolation, social, 208
    relationships, large group, 223-228
    relationships, small group
        good groups, 219-221
        roles in, 222-223
        support groups, 221-222
    social capital, 208-210
    See Intimacy building; Statement of Personal
        Priorities
Colette, 332
Colton, Charles Caleb, 331
Consolidation (C), 154, 161, 170, 232, 305
Constant, Benjamin, 353
Cooperrider, D. L., 227
Copeland, P., 90
Costa, Paul T., 19
Coyne, James, 39, 221
Csikszentmihalyi, M., 35, 114, 121, 125-129, 134,
    135-136
Cuddy, A. J. C., 212
Dalai Lama, 14th, 346
Dali, Salvador, 345

Dalton, Katharine, 73
Damasio, A. R., 193
Danziger, S., 304
Davies, Robertson, 345
Deafferentation, 139, 365, *See* Flow
Delbanco, Andrew, 328
DeLeire, Thomas, 57
Deshimaru, Taisen, 346
DeYoung, C. G., 90
Dickinson, Emily, 24, 319, 334
Diener, E., 35, 50, 55
Dimnet, Ernest, 334
DISC personality test, 352
Disraeli, Benjamin, 12, 330
Dostoevsky, Fyodor, 335
Downer, definition, 365
Duckworth, A. L., 198
Duhamel, Georges, 335
Dumas, Alexandre, 328
Dunn, Elizabeth, 56
Dunning, D., 68, 200
Dweck, Carol, 134, 166, 183
Easterlin, Richard, 35
Ecclesiastes 3:1-8, 333
Edelman, Gerald, 135
Ehrenreich, Barbara, 38-39
Einstein, Albert, 328
Elliott, Hazelmarie "Mattie," 336
Emerson, Ralph Waldo, 343
Epictetus, 334
Erhard, Werner, 348
Ericcson, K. A., 134, 199
Er-Rahman III, Abd, 327
Eudaimonia, 12, 22, 365
Evans, D. E., 90
Evans, Richard L., 344
Extraversion (E), 18, 84- 90, 152-154, 161, 304, 351-352
Faludi, Susan, 346
Feather, William, 348
Fielding, Henry, 337
Fischer, Ronald, 63, 249
Fiske, R., 212
Fit
    allelonyms of happiness for, 122-123
    definition, 121
    Howardian Person, 148-163
    nature-nurture interaction, 147-149
    self-control and, 304
    See Person to-environment fit (PE Fit);
        Person to environment fit (P-E Fit)
        obstacles; Statement of Personal Priorities
        (SPP); Subtraits
Five Factor Model, *See* Big Five model
Five Modes for staying in gear
    criteria for selecting, 118-119
    definitions, *See* Altruism; Community; Fit; Flow;
        Goals
    evolution of, 111-117
    importance of using all five, 250

mind, using, 119-120
purpose, 117
questionnaire results, 318-319
Fletcher, J. L., 143
Flow
    allelonyms of happiness for, 122-123
    channel, 128-130
    concept of, Csikszentmihalyi's, 116, 120, 125-130
    definition, 121, 365
    descriptions, 51, 53, 69
    examples, 51, 53, 112, 136-139
    harm from being out of, 136
    neurological basis, 135-136
    staying in, 130-135
    See Statement of Personal Priorities
Focus, keeping
    ambitions, lost, 301
    blahs, 312-313
    bordeom, 312
    caffeine, 311
    eating, 311
    fitness, 311
    frustration, 312
    glucose depletion, 311
    neurotoxins, 312
    sleep, 311
    See self-control
Follett, Ken, 25, 137, 173, 238
Fontane, Theodor, 347
Fontenelle, Bernard de, 330
Ford, Harrison, 81, 336
Fowler, J., 50, 77, 122, 218, 220
Frank, Anne, 329
Frankl, Victor, 128
Franklin, Benjamin, 330
Fredrickson, B., 213
Fredrickson, B. L., 213
Freud, Sigmund, 346
Frey, Bruno, 52, 67
Friedman, Richard, 36
Friess, Horace, 337
Frisch, M. B., 190
Fritjers, Paul, 74
Frost, Robert, 370
Fun, 27, 139, 286, 331, 340

Gandhi , Mahatma, 341
Gandhi, Mohandas K., 342
Gardner, Chris, 143, 159
Gardner, Howard, 157
Gellis, Jerry, 338
Georgellis, Y., 50
Gilbert, Daniel T., 28, 56, 69, 130
Giving, helpful
    charity, 239
    donations, 239
    generativity, 239
    gifts, 240
    pro bono, 240

Gladwell, Malcolm, 145, 341
Glick, P., 212
Goals
    adjustments, 265-267
    allelonyms of happiness for, 122-123
    attributes of effective goals, 174-177
    balance of, 353
    description, 121, 173-174
    extrinsic and intrinsic, 73
    flow, and, 126, 127-128, 133-134
    generation (making goals), 187-193
    implementation planning, 178-179
    kinds of goals, 13, 179-187, 265-267
    lack of, 170, 190, 249
    lost, 69, 304-305
    selecting, 193-194, 207
    Statement of Personal Priorities, 250-251, 254
    timid, 166-167
    See Goals, pursuing
Goals, pursuing
    case studies, 202-204
    focus, keeping, 299--312
    optimism and pessimisim, 194-198
    practice and grit, 198-200
    stress and resilience, 201
    See Goals
Goethe, Johann Wolfgang von, 199, 338
Gollwitzer, Peter, 174, 178-179
Goode, Kenneth, 340
Gorky, Maxim, 342
Gottman, John, 114, 216
Government action items, 352-355
Gow, Charles, 331
Graham, Carol, 22, 33, 35, 43, 49, 53, 54, 60, 63, 64, 65, 67
Graham, Martha, 200
Grandin, Temple, 215
Gray, Jeffrey, 90
Groundhog Day, 246
Guillermoprieto, Alma, 328
Gur, R., 52
Hadas, Moses, 53
Hafiz of Persia, 93, 336
Hagen, Walter, 260
Hale, G. A., 194
Hall, S. S., 26
Hamer, D., 90, 135
Hamermesh, D. S., 60
Hammarskjold, Dag, 210
Hanh, Thich Nhat, 347
Happers, 19-20, 23-26, 29, 44, 54, 81-82, 85-86, 115
Happiness
    against, 24-26, 101, 118
    alternatives to, 12, 23-24
    biology of , 87-93
    booster defined, 365
    boosters and downers checklist, 94-100
    definitions/descriptions, 18-19, 27, 110-111, 118,
        120, 121, 134, 159, 181, 365
    national, 27-29, 207-208

    natural versus acquired, 23-24
    nine levels of set point for natural happiness, 86
    quotations about, 327-349
    quotient, 34, 93-105, 116
    synonyms for, See allelonyms
    test/questionnaire, 112, 318-319
    types of people, See Happers; Batters; Mappers;
        Nappers
Happiness boosters, choices
    affairs, 43
    alcohol moderation, 43
    anticipation of good stuff (experiences), 44
    anticipation of purchases, 43
    attendance at group meetings, 44
    busy, being, 44
    boosters and downers checklist, 94-100
    buying for the thing itself, 45
    charitable acts, 45
    childcare, 45
    college/undergrad degree, 45-46
    conversation, 46
    exercising, 47
    experiences, 47
    extrinsic rewards for algorithmic tasks, 48
    gardening, 48
    generativity, 48
    gratitude, 48
    health (perceived), 48-49
    intrinsic motives, 49
    marriage, 50
    meals with family/friends, 50
    meditating/praying, 50-51
    music listening, 51
    optimism, 51
    pets, 52
    playing with children, 52
    political involvement, 52
    pro-market attitude, 53
    reading, 53
    recreational sports, 53
    relationships, 53
    religion/faith, 54-55
    Republican, being, 44
    self-employment, 55
    sex, 55
    shopping, 55
    socializing, 56
    spending for experiences, 56-58
    spending on equipment for experiences, 58
    spending on others, 58
    touch, 58-59
    transcranial magnetic stimulation (TMS), 59
    volunteering, 59
    walking, 58
    See Happiness, boosters and downers checklist
Happiness boosters, circumstances
    aging (approaching seniority), 59-60
    beauty, 60
    boosters and downers checklist, 94-100

democracy, 60
employment, 61
environmental conditions, 61-62
feeling safe, 62
financial freedom, 62
government efficiency, 62
government responsiveness, 62
government trustworthiness, 62-63
law-abiding/law enforcement, 63
minimal corruption/violence, 63
personal freedom, 63-64
retirement, 64
status increase, 64-65
temperate climate. 65
tolerance of minorities. 65
trust. 65
trust in management, 66
trust in public officials, 66
Happiness downers, choices
alcohol abstinence, 67
alcohol excess, 67
boosters and downers checklist, 94-100
commuting, 67-68
deep thinking, 68
envy, 68
graduate educational level, 69
holding onto lost goals, 69
isolation, 69
mind-wandering, 69
personal grooming, 70
Happiness downers, circumstances
aging (approaching middle age), 70-71
anticipation of bad stuff, 71
being female, 71
betrayal of trust, 71-72
boosters and downers checklist, 94-100
chronic pain, 72
disaster, 72
divorce/separation, 72-73
extrinsic rewards for non-algorithmic tasks, 73
hormone fluctuation, 73
job loss, 73
lack of control, 74
loss of a loved one, 74
mental illness, 74
neurotoxins, 75
noise, 75-76
poverty, 76
sleep disorders, 76-77
stressors, 77
working, 77
Happiness myths
crippling accidents, 34
definition, 32-33, 365
eating out, 34
education level, 35
income, 35
insight, 36
kids, 36-37

lotteries, 37
movies, 37
moving, 37-38
new things (buying), 38
positive thinking, 38-40
specator, being a, 40
television, 40
vacation home, 40-41
variety, 41
Harris, Sam, 345
Harris, Sydney J., 346
Hawthorne, Nathaniel, 343
Heaphy, E., 213
Hebrews 1:9, 336
Hedonic treadmill, 32-33, 35, 40, 365
Heinlein, Robert, 345
Hellwell, J. F., 64
Hepburn, Katharine, 70, 249
Herold, Don, 259, 333
Hicks, Joshua, 68, 198
Hill, Napoleon, 204
Hills, Burton, 331
Hinsch, C., 219
Hoffer, Eric, 11, 12, 334
Hogan personality test, 352
Holmes, Oliver Wendell, 343
Hosard, Vernon, 348
Hosseini, Khaled, 146
Howard, Jane Mitchell, *See* Howard, Pierce
Howard, Pierce
7-step values interview, 139
about, 6-7
Big Five model, 19
happiness quotient, 116
mental tools, 154-155
neurotoxins, 75
Owner's Manual for the Brain, The, 174n1, 195n1
SchoolPlace Big Five Profile, 153, 351
WorkPlace Big Five Profile, 82, 153-154, 351
Howardian Person
memories, 159-160
mental talents, 157-158
mental tools, 154-158
overview, 148-150
Person-Environment Fit (PE-Fit), checklist for
assessing, 160-164
physical characteristics, 158-159
subtraits checklist, 154
talents, self-assessment, 157-158
values, 159, 165
See Fit; Person-Environment Fit (PE-Fit), Subtraits
Hubbard, Frank McKinney "Kin," 334
Human Rights, The Universal Declaration of, 241-244
Humphrey, Hubert H., 337
Ickes, W., 165-166
In gear, description, 11-14, 23, 112
Inge, William R., 348
Ingelow, Jean, 338
Ingersoll, Robert G., 345

Insight therapy, problems, 36
Intimacy building
    experience, intense, 212-213
    experiencing, 218
    liking someone, 210-211
    proximity, 211
    resonance, 211-212
    similarity, 212
    sincerity, 217-218
    trust, 218
    vulnerability, 211
    See Community
Irving, John, 203
Iyengar, S., 74
Jackson, Holbrook, 337
James, William, 15, 60, 148, 168, 175, 189, 231, 348
Janoff-Bulman, R., 37
Jefferson,Thomas, 347
Jerrold, Douglas, 333
Jesus, 146, 232, 237, 244-245, 338
Johnson, Catharine, 215
Johnson, Samuel, 345
Joubert, Joseph, 339
Jung, Carl 331
Kahneman, Daniel, 76
Kalidasa, 339
Kalil, Ariel, 57
Kant, Immanuel, 337
Karon, Jan, 337
Keller, Helen, 336-337
Keltner, Dacher, 58-59, 93, 213, 214
Kepner, C. H., 194
Kierkegaard, 340
Killingsworth, Matthew, 69, 130
King, Laura, 68, 198
Kingsley, Charles, 331
Koenig, Frederick, 335
Kolbert, Elizabeth, 25
Konigsburg, E. L., 333
Kruger, J., 68, 200
Kundera, Milan, 118
La Bruyere, Jean de, 338
Laertius, Diogenes, 333
Landor, Walter Savage, 348
Lane, Janet, 338
Larsen, J. I., 110, 111
Larson, Doug, 333
Latham, G. P., 114, 174
Laven, M., 217
Leary, Timothy, 120
LeBon, Tim, 118
Leibowitz, Fran, 334
Lelkes, Orsolya, 54
Lemay, K., 217
L' Estrange, Roger, 345
Leva, J., 304
Lewis, C. S., 221, 237, 331
Lewis, Sinclair, 13, 144
Life is Beautiful, 18

Life story, composing, 361-363
Lincoln, Abraham, 18, 328
Livingston, Grey, 336
Locke, E. A., 174
Losada, M. F., 213
Lowell, Amy, 328
Lucas R. E., 50
Luther, Martin, 342
Lykken, David, 88
Lynd, Robert, 345
Lyubomirsky, S., 34, 50, 59, 89, 114, 115, 216, 232
Machiavelli, Niccolo, 190, 211, 343
MacEwan, Norman, 343
Mappers, 24, 81-82, 110, 112, 115
March, Peyton Conway, 343
Marquis, Don, 333
Marriage, 21, 36, 50, 165-166, 209, 213, 214-217
Marshall, Catherine, 331
Martin, , C. E., 52
Marx, Groucho, 336
Mason, Daniel, 125
Masugham, W. Somerset, 348
Matthews, Andrew, 328
MBTI (Myers-Briggs Type Indicator), 352
McAdams, Dan, 359
McConnell, A. R., 52
McCrae, R. R., 19, 166
McFerran, B., 217
McKibban, A. R., 110
McLaughlin, Mignon, 342
Michelangelo, 109, 183, 342
Mill, John Stuart, 26, 339
Miller, C. A., 190
Milne, A. A., 327
Milton, John, 339
Mitchell, Joni, 24
Mohammed, 232
Moll, Jorge, 232
Monet, Claude, 332
Montaigne, 342
Morgan, Charles Langbridge, 332
Mortenson, Greg, 336
Motteville, Francoise de, 334
Moyers, Bill, 145, 217
Muhammad, Miriam, 342
Muller, Robert, 345
Murdoch, Iris, 338
Myers, D. G., 55
Nachman, Rebbe, 81-82, 344
Nappers, 24, 110, 112, 115
Nash, William P., 90
Nature and nurture, 147-149
NEO PI-R personality tests, 352
Nelms, Cynthia, 332
Need for Stability (N), 19, 84-90, 116, 154, 161, 304,
    351-352
Nettle, Daniel, 18, 19, 93
Nietzsche, Friedrich, 128, 145, 307, 335

Norris, J. T., 110
Nouwen, Henri, 337
Novotney A., 75
Obama, Barack, 200
Objective well-being (OWB), 35, 111, 365
Ochsner, K., 119
O'Neill, Eugene, 334
Ones, Deniz. 19
Oppenheim, James, 338
Oppenheimer, J. Robert, 337
OPQ personality test, 352
Optimism, 198-205
Originality (O), 19, 154, 161, 166, 170, 232, 304
Oswald, Andrew, 59
Owner's Manual for the Brain, The, 6, 174n1, 195n1
Palmer, Gretta Brooker, 336
Papernick, Norm, 343
Pauling, Linus, 340
Peck, M. Scott, 117-118, 341
PERMA concept, 115-116
Person-to-environment fit (PE-Fit)
    checklist for assessing, 160-164
    PERMA model, comparison to, 115-116
    quotations, 144-146
    self-assessment, 160-164
    See Fit, Person-to-environment fit (PE-Fit), obstacles;
        Subtraits
Person-to-environment fit (PE-Fit), obstacles
    context, wrong, 170
    culture, 169-170
    experience, 167
    goal setting, timid, 166-167
    partners 165-166
    self, false, ("covering"), 167-168
    self-esteem, low, 168, *see* Self-esteem
    necessity, 168-169
    traits, self-defeating, 170-171
Personality tests for N and E, 351-352
Pessimism, 195-198
Pestalozzi, Johann, 338
Peterson, Christopher, 197
Piano Tuner, The, 125
Pickles, 27
Pickett, Kate, 76
Pierpoint, N., 75
Pink, D., 48, 49, 73, 117, 136
Pirsig, Robert, 137-138
Plunkett, L. C., 194
Pollock, Channing, 331
Popular saying, 343
Practice, 10,000 hours of, 148, 199-200
Prager, Dennis, 27, 123, 189, 200
Prévert, Jacques, 338
Pritchett, V. S., 347
Prize Winner of Defiance, Ohio, The, 18
Proust, Marcel, 341
Punset, Eduardo, 49, 78, 103-104, 121, 215
Putnam, Robert, 45, 66, 116, 208-209, 220, 223-225, 227
PEE:NEE ratio

defintion, 213, 366
    example, 228
    group, 223
    optimum, 215-218
Priorities, Personal Statement of, *See* Statement of
    Personal Priorities (SPP)
Quinn, P. D., 198
Qur'an, 146
Regard, positive
    compassion, 235
    environment, respect for, 238-239
    optimism, 235
    positive energy, nonverbal, 235
    prayer, 235
    smiling and casual touching, 235-236
    visualization, 236
    zaniness, 236
Reinoso, J .M., 338
Relief, beneficial
    connecting people, 240
    Good Samaritan, 240
    neighborliness, 240
    random acts of kindness, 241
    respite care, 241
    service, 240-241
    volunteering, 241
Repplier, Agnes, 327
Ridley, M., 90
Rivers, Joan, 338
Robbins, Anthony, 329
Rochefoucauld, François Duc de la, 334
Rockefeller, John D., 339
Rohn, Jim, 338
Rooney, Andy, 329
Roosevelt, Eleanor, 334
Roosevelt, Franklin D., 334
Rosten, Leo C., 340
Rothbart, M. K., 90
Roux, Joseph, 339
Runbeck, Margaret Lee 341
Russell, Bertrand, 134, 330
Sackeim, H. A., 52
Saint-Exupéry, Antoine de, 329
Salinger, J.D., 338
Salzberg, Sharon, 346
Sand, George, 335
Santayana, George, 335
Saotome, Mitsugi , 342
Sapolsky, Robert, 20
Saroyan, William, 348
Schachtel, Hyman, 110
Schooler , Jonathan, 36
SchoolPlace Big Five Profile, 153, 351
Schweitzer, Albert, 49, 328
Schulz, Charles, 81
Self-control
    benefits of, 305-306
    compensation strategies
    breaks and snacks, 308

distractions of the good, 308
    environment, modification, 308-309
development of
    competition, entering, 307
    high-mindedness, 307
    interruptions, management, 307
    practice with external distractions, 306
    practice with internal distractions, 306-11
    synergies creation, 307
distractions, 301-304, 309
mechansim of, 301-304
support strategies
    announcement of details, 309
    group, 310
    intentions declared publicly, 309
    partner, 310
    plan, 309-310
    self-reward, 310
religion and, 226-227
who has self-control, 304-305
Self-deception, 52, 366
Self-determination theory, 117
Self-esteem,
    defintion, 366
    increasing, 64
    low, 71, 172, 179
Seligman, Martin, 47, 51-52, 90, 102, 114, 115-116, 139,
    195-197, 214, 223
Selye, Hans, 44, 100, 165
Seneca, 345
Set point for happiness
    changing, 31, 33, 35, 37, 101-105
    definition, 20, 366
    forty percent solution, 34, 365
    happiness quotient, 34, 93-105, 116
    hedonic treadmill, 32, 35, 40, 365
    nine levels, 85-86, 100-101
    state, definition, 366
    survey, 82-86
Shakespeare, William, 11, 201, 294, 359
Shaw, George Bernard, 335
Sheerin, John B., 339
Sheldon, K. M., 219
Shelley, Percy, 299
Shenk, David, 91-93, 134, 148, 166, 184, 199-200,
    202-203, 307
Shoda, , T. M., 52
Siddharta, Gautama, 195
Silver, Nan, 114, 216
Smith, Logan Pearsall, 340
Smith, Sydney, 346
Snow, C. P., 331
Social comparison, descriptions, 56-57, 77-78, 366
Solzhenitsyn, Aleksandr , 328
Sondheim, Stephen, 138
Sophocles, 346
Sondreal, Palmer, 343
Sound of Music, The, 18, 112
Spiegel, David, 39, 221-222

Spinoza, Baruch, 330
Stael, Madame de, 341
Stair, Nadine, 259
Starbucks slogan, 42
State, 20-23, 88, 366
Statement of Personal Priorities (SPP)
    bucket list, 44, 189-190, 251-254, 311
    creating, 250-254
    Five Modes, importance of balancing all, 250
    Personal Optimization Plan (POP), 251
    revision, 300, 316-318
Stayton, L. E., 52
Steel, Piers, 19
Steindl-Rast, David, 332
Stephens, Wallace, 119
Stevenson, Betsy, 71
Stevenson, Robert Louis, 345
Stewart, J., 75
Stix, G., 90, 102
Stone, Sharon, 346
Stutzer, Alois, 52, 67
Subtraits
    Characteristics, physical, 158-159
    Howardian Person, 148-163; *see* Fit
    Memories, 159
    Talents, eight, 157-158
    Tools, mental, 154-157
    Values, 159
    Workplace Big Five Profile, 153-154, 351
    See PE-Fit
Supertraits, *See* Accomodation (A); Consolidation (C);
    Extraversion (E); Need for stability (N); Originality (O)
Subjective well-being (SWB), 35, 111, 366
Synonyms for happiness, *See* allelonyms
Szasz, Thomas, 347
Tarkington, Booth, 331
Tay, L., 55
Taylor, Samuel, 345
Tellegen, Auke, 88
Temperament, 366
Templeton, John, 339
Teresa, Mother, 343
Thomas, Rob, 344
Thoreau, Henry David, 337
Tolstoy, Leo, 146, 250, 340
Traits, 20-22, 153, 165, 170-171, 366, *See* Subtraits
Tregoe, B. B., 194
Twain, Mark, 341
Tyger, Frank, 334
Unbearable Lightness of Being, The, 118
Ura, Karma, 70, 207-208
Van Boven, Leaf, 56
Veenhoven, Ruut, 27
Waiting for Superman, 18
Waitley, Denis, 333
Warehousing effect, 228, 231, 366
Washington, Booker T., 232, 331
Washington, Martha, 342
Watson, John, 146

Wattleton, Faye, 334
Waugh, C. E., 213
Wegman, Lavetta Sue, 340
Weiner, Eric, 27, 70, 74, 104, 118, 120, 123, 169, 207-208,
    220, 225
Well-being, two types defined, 366
Wharton, Edith, 333
Whitney, D., 227
Wilcox, Ella Wheeler, 334
Wilde, Oscar, 343
Wilder, Thornton, 347
Wilkinson, Robert, 76
Williams, Redford, 102
Williams, Ted. 202-203
Wilson, Eric G., 24-25, 26, 38, 74, 101-102, 118, 139
Wilson, Timothy, 36, 56
Wittgenstein, Ludwig, 341
Wolfe, W. Beran, 348
Wolfers, Justin, 71
Wood, Charles Lindley, 231
Wordsworth, William, 349
WorkPlace Big Five Profile, 82, 153-154, 351
Yewell, Jack C., 338
Yoshino, Kenji, 26, 134, 146, 167
Young, Margaret, 341
Yukl, Gary A., 174
Zamyatin, Yevgeny, 349
Zeigarnik effect, 310, 366

How to Order Additional Copies of this Book

To order additional copies of:

The Owner's Manual for Happiness: Essential Elements of a Meaningful Life

Paperback: $15.95
VISA / MASTERCARD / DISCOVER / AMERICAN EXPRESS Accepted

Quantity Discounts Are Available

To order, visit www.amazon.com, or contact us as listed below:

Contact:	Customer Relationship Representative
Publisher:	The Center for Applied Cognitive Studies 4701 Hedgemore Drive, Suite 210 Charlotte, NC 28209-2200 / USA
Telephone:	+1.704.331.0926
US Toll Free:	+1.800.244.5555 (800-BIG-5555)
Fax:	+1.704.331.9408
E-mail:	info@centacs.com
Website:	www.centacs.com

CENTER FOR
APPLIED COGNITIVE STUDIES

CPSIA information can be obtained at www.ICGtesting.com
Printed in the USA
LVOW11s2231121213

365131LV00008B/236/P